GENDERED LIVES

Global Issues

Edited by

Nadine T. Fernandez and
Katie Nelson

The authors gratefully acknowledge the generosity of SUNY OER Services for the financial support they lent to this project.

Published by State University of New York Press, Albany

The OER version of this book is endorsed by GAD (General Anthropology Division) of the American Anthropological Association. The American Anthropological Association also provides support by hosting the OER book's website https://genderedlives.americananthro.org.

For information, contact State University of New York Press, Albany, NY
www.sunypress.edu

Library of Congress Cataloging-in-Publication Data

Names: Fernandez, Nadine T., 1964– editor. ǀ Nelson, Katie, 1980– editor.
Title: Gendered lives : global issues / edited by Nadine T. Fernandez and Katie Nelson.
Description: Albany : State University of New York Press, [2021] ǀ Includes bibliographical references and index.
Identifiers: LCCN 2021040871 (print) ǀ LCCN 2021040872 (ebook) ǀ ISBN 9781438486956 (pbk. : alk. paper) ǀ ISBN 9781438486963 (ebook)
Subjects: LCSH: Sex role—Cross-cultural studies. ǀ Women—Cross-cultural studies.
Classification: LCC GN479.65 .G494 2021 (print) ǀ LCC GN479.65 (ebook) ǀ DDC 305.3—dc23
LC record available at https://lccn.loc.gov/2021040871
LC ebook record available at https://lccn.loc.gov/2021040872

10 9 8 7 6 5 4 3 2 1

CONTENTS

Preface   vi
    Textbook Learning Objectives   vi
    Note to Instructors   viii

Acknowledgments   ix

PART I: INTRODUCTION

Chapter 1: Key Concepts   2
Katie Nelson and Nadine T. Fernandez

    PROFILE: Save the Girl Child Movement   22
    Nolwazi Ncube

Chapter 2: Key Perspectives   35
Nadine T. Fernandez and Katie Nelson

PART II: SOUTH ASIA

Chapter 3: South Asia: Introducing the Region   52
Ina Goel

    PROFILE: Blank Noise: Street Actions and Digital
    Interventions against Street Sexual Harassment in India   69
    Hemangini Gupta

    PROFILE: Vietnam Women's Shelter: Contradictions and
    Complexities   72
    Lynn Kwiatkowski

Chapter 4: Controlling National Borders by Controlling Reproduction:
Gender, Nationalism, and Nepal's Citizenship Laws   79
Dannah Dennis and Abha Lal

Chapter 5: Understanding Caste and Kinship within Hijras,
a "Third" Gender Community in India   98
Ina Goel

Chapter 6: The "City" and "The Easy Life": Work and Gender
among Sherpa in Nepal   116
Alba Castellsagué and Silvia Carrasco

PART III: LATIN AMERICA

Chapter 7: Latin America: Introducing the Region   134
Serena Cosgrove and Ana Marina Tzul Tzul

PROFILE: The Guatemalan Women's Group: Supporting
Survivors of Gender-Based Violence   150
Serena Cosgrove and Ana Marina Tzul Tzul

Chapter 8: Being a Good Mexican Man by Embracing
"Erectile Dysfunction"   156
Emily Wentzell

Chapter 9: Intersectionality and Normative Masculinity in
Northeast Brazil   170
Melanie A. Medeiros

Chapter 10: Mexico's Antipoverty Program Oportunidades and
the Shifting Dynamics of Citizenship for Ñuu Savi (Mixtec)
Village Women   190
Holly Dygert

Chapter 11: Q'eqchi'-Maya Women: Memory, Markets, and
Multilevel Marketing in Guatemala   210
S. Ashley Kistler

PART IV: THE CARIBBEAN

Chapter 12: The Caribbean: Introducing the Region   235
Nadine T. Fernandez

Chapter 13: Quinceañeras: Girls' Coming-of-Age Parties in
Contemporary Havana, Cuba   250
Heidi Härkönen

Chapter 14: Jamaican Realities of Masculinities and Sexualities:
Where Have We Come Since Michel Foucault?   267
Natasha Kay Mortley and Keino T. Senior

PART V: THE GLOBAL NORTH (NORTH AMERICA AND EUROPE)

Chapter 15: The Global North: Introducing the Region   289
Lara Braff and Katie Nelson

   PROFILE: Indian Rights for Indian Women:
   Kathleen Steinhauer, an Indigenous Activist in Canada   304
   Sarah L. Quick

Chapter 16: Mothers Acting Up Online   308
Susan W. Tratner

Chapter 17: Male Sex Work in Canada: Intersections of Gender
and Sexuality   326
Nathan Dawthorne

Chapter 18: Intersectionality and Muslim Women in Belgium   355
Elsa Mescoli

Chapter 19: Fatherhood and Family Relations in Transnational
Migration from Mezcala, Mexico   374
Elizabeth Perez Marquez

Contributors   390

Index   397

PREFACE

TEXTBOOK LEARNING OBJECTIVES

- Apply a feminist intersectional lens to analyze gendered practices.

- Assess how local gendered lives are shaped by global processes.

- Evaluate how gendered practices are culturally constructed and influenced by key regional, economic, historical, and political factors.

- Analyze key gender issues anthropologists study.

Gendered Lives: Global Issues was born from two deeply rooted experiences teaching undergraduates. First, with more than thirty years (cumulative) experience teaching anthropology of sex and gender, we acknowledge the ongoing challenge of imparting to students an understanding that ideologies and practices of gender and sexuality are culturally shaped, historically changing, and globally situated. The comparative study of sex and gender globally helps us understand the diversity of the human experience. By reflecting on this diversity, we can ultimately expand our perspectives on gender and sexuality beyond our own cultural backgrounds. We have consistently seen our students realize that by studying the "other," we learn more about ourselves. In a world that is sometimes violently structured by gender inequalities, these remain key issues for everyone to grasp.

Second, we recognize that many students struggle with the ever-increasing costs of textbooks and that without access to quality educational materials students cannot succeed in their classes (Perry 2014; Senack 2014). Data shows that open educational resources (OERs) help *all* students succeed (Colvard et al. 2018). Creating open resources is one way to demonstrate our commitment to fostering equity and access in higher education. *Gendered Lives: Global Issues* seeks to address these two issues through a peer-reviewed, edited textbook covering key topics related to the cultural construction of gender in locations around the world.

This textbook is organized around two central perspectives: global connections across a regional framework and an intersectional lens.

First, to better understand the gendered lives of men and women, students need to see how their experiences are embedded in a nation's and region's particular histories and cultures. Understanding the broader cultural, historical, political, and economic contexts that shape the social constructions of gender is essential. To this end, the book is organized into sections based on geographic region and the global forces that have linked regions together, often in unequal relationships. Each section begins with an "Introducing the Region" chapter that provides an overview of key historical, cultural, and political factors, as well as outlines central gender-related issues facing that region today.

It is within these broader regional contexts and global linkages that we ask students to situate the gendered lives they are reading about in the individual chapters, each of which present the findings of one ethnographic study. The topics covered range from women and work to parenting and transnational families, masculinity, and gender-based violence. Included in the "Introducing the Region" sections are "Profiles," each of which present the work of an activist or organization fighting for gender equality and justice in their communities.

While cognizant of the earlier critiques of area-studies approaches, more recent research has recognized the value of tracing the global in the local (Alvarez et al. 2011). It is through local analyses that we can best understand the impact of global dynamics. Thus, our geographical approach does not imply the existence of bounded cultural areas or self-contained regions. Rather, the chapters are both deeply place oriented, while solidly linking the local to relevant global processes and histories.

In soliciting chapters for this book we cast a broad net and hoped for contributions that would span all regions of the world. This first edition of the textbook presents the responses to our call for contributors and includes research based in the following regions: Latin America, the Caribbean, South Asia, and the Global North (Europe and North America). In future editions, we hope to expand the coverage to include other areas such as Africa, East Asia, and the Middle East.

The second central perspective in the book is an intersectional lens. In taking an intersectional approach in each chapter, we see how gender is shaped not only by culture but also, for example, by one's particular class, ethnic, or religious identity within that culture. The two threads of intersectional positioning and global linkages connect the chapters across the regions. An intersectional analysis reminds us that power is unequally distributed both within and across cultures. Those ethnic, gender, racial, religious (and other) inequalities shape lives both at home and abroad. The gendered lives readers encounter in the chapters are rooted in particular histories and cultures that are deeply entwined with the Global

North through histories of colonialism and global capitalism. In the connected and inherently comparative perspective of anthropology, we hope readers will examine their own "naturalized and gendered" practices with a critical lens and come to see how their own lives are intersectionally and globally shaped.

NOTE TO INSTRUCTORS

We recognize that in this first edition of the textbook some geographic regions are not represented. If you are interested in contributing to the next edition and helping us expand the geographic and topical coverage of the book—or have a profile of an activist or organization you'd like to add—we would love to hear from you. We also welcome your feedback, suggestions, and corrections so we can improve this OER resource for you and your students. You will find additional resources and our contact information on our book's website: https://genderedlives.americananthro. org/.

ACKNOWLEDGMENTS

This book would not have been possible without the generous support of many people and institutions. SUNY OER Services provided the financial support for this project with funds from New York State's 2018–2019 budget allocation for Open Educational Resources. Our SUNY OER creation grant was supplemented by sabbaticals we both received from our home institutions, Inver Hills Community College and SUNY Empire State College. Without time and money this textbook would never have come about. During Nadine's sabbatical, the Gender Studies Department at Lund University in Sweden provided a welcoming home in the final stages of preparing this book. We deeply appreciate the invaluable assistance of Allison Brown, digital publishing services manager at SUNY Geneseo. Allison helped keep the project on track, and her close eye for detail and expertise in digital publishing created a polished and professional product. We thank Kate Scacchetti (SUNY Empire State College) for expertly administering our budget and resources. The American Anthropological Association welcomed this open access publishing project under their auspices, and we truly appreciate the endorsement from the General Anthropology Division (GAD). SUNY Press skillfully aided us through the copyediting process. We would like to express our gratitude to Professor Deborah Amory (SUNY Empire State College), who contributed both inspiration and guidance from the project's inception to its realization. Finally, a big thank you to all of the authors and reviewers for contributing their expertise and enthusiasm to this project.

Part I

Introduction

1

Key Concepts

Katie Nelson and Nadine T. Fernandez

LEARNING OBJECTIVES

- Distinguish among the concepts of sex, gender, and sexuality.
- Articulate how gender is shaped by culture.
- Identify examples of nonbinary gender expressions.
- Discuss how gender is relational and the importance of understanding masculinity in relation to other gender expressions.

In this textbook we will explore the meanings and experiences of sex and gender from a global perspective. Let's start by posing a basic question: why learn about sex and gender globally? Don't we all know what it means to be a man or a woman? While the answer to that question may seem obvious, in fact, when we learn about gender and sexuality cross-culturally, it becomes clear that these are extremely complicated concepts. Ideas about gender and sexuality differ tremendously across different cultures. To make sense of this complexity, this chapter will introduce some key ideas, such as **sex**, **gender**, sexual orientation, **gender ideologies**, and **masculinity**.

WHAT IS CULTURE AND WHY ANTHROPOLOGY?

Given the fact that we want to learn more about sex and gender from a global perspective, the next question we might ask ourselves is: how will we learn more? We could learn more by reading the literature of different peoples, in different languages, to better understand how they tell stories about their lives and the ways in which people become men, women, or something more in their own cultures. Alternatively, we could take a legal approach and search historical records to learn how laws determined proper gender and sexual behaviors and how people were punished for particular crimes relating to sex and gender. For example, in the United States there have been laws against cross-dressing (men wearing women's clothing, and vice versa), or miscegenation (interracial marriage, or interracial sex). Another option, and the one that we have chosen for this book, is to employ the discipline of cultural anthropology to help us learn about sex and gender from a global perspective.

For anthropologists, culture is defined as "a set of beliefs, practices, and symbols that are learned and shared. Together, they form an all encompassing, integrated whole that binds people together and shapes their worldview and lifeways" (Nelson 2020). These beliefs, traditions, and customs, transmitted through learning, guide the behavior of a people as well as how they think about the world and perceive others. Anthropologists seek to understand the internal logic of a culture and why things that may seem "strange" or "exotic" to us make sense to the people of another culture. As such, anthropology is fundamentally comparative. That is, anthropologists seek to describe, analyze, interpret, and explain social and cultural differences and similarities. In doing so, we often turn a critical eye on our own practices and beliefs to understand them in a different way. We often learn and become more conscious of our own culture when we experience or study other cultures. Thus, North Americans traveling in China or in Europe often become more aware of their own "Americanness"—they become aware of aspects of their own culture and lifestyle that they often took for granted. These cultural characteristics stand out in sharp relief against their experiences in a foreign country.

What is Anthropology?

In the most general terms, anthropology refers to the study of humans. It is a **holistic** field of study that focuses on the wide breadth of what makes us human: from human societies and cultures to past human lifeways, human language and evolution, and even nonhuman primates. In the United States, anthropology is divided into four subfields: cultural anthropology, archaeology, biological anthropology, and linguistic anthropology. Applied anthropology uses the methods and knowledge of these subfields to solve real-world problems faced by different societies and cultures.

Anthropologists are not the only scholars to focus on the human condition. Biologists, sociologists, psychologists, and others also examine human nature and societies. However, anthropologists uniquely draw on four key approaches to their research: holism, comparison, dynamism, and fieldwork. For a more detailed introduction to anthropology, see chapter 1, "Introduction to Anthropology" in *Perspectives: An Open Invitation to Cultural Anthropology*: http://perspectives.americananthro.org/.

holistic/holism
the idea that the parts of a system interconnect and interact to make up the whole.

What Is Culture?

Culture is a set of beliefs, practices, and symbols that are learned and shared. Together, they form an all-encompassing, integrated whole that binds groups of people together and shapes their worldview and lifeways. Additionally:

1. Humans are born with the capacity to learn the culture of any social group. We learn culture both directly and indirectly.

2. Culture changes in response to both internal and external factors.

3. Humans are not bound by culture; they have the capacity to conform to it or not and sometimes change it.

4. Culture is symbolic; individuals create and share the meanings of symbols within their group or society.

5. The degree to which humans rely on culture distinguishes us from other animals and shapes our evolution.

6. Human culture and biology are interrelated: our biology, growth, and development are impacted by culture.

ethnography
the in-depth study of the everyday practices and lives of a people.

We will be reading chapters created by cultural anthropologists who have conducted extensive fieldwork or **ethnography** in the country and culture they are writing about. The term *ethnography* refers both to the books written by anthropologists and to their research processes or fieldwork. So cultural anthropologists gather information through long-term fieldwork by participating in a particular culture over time. Fieldwork is primarily a qualitative research method and involves living among the people you are studying. Over time anthropologists collect information or data about a particular group of people through formal and informal interviews and observations they record in field notes.

Participant observation is the term for the characteristic methodology of ethnographic research. It literally means being simultaneously a participant in and an observer of the culture you are studying. That is why anthropologists usually live with the people they are studying for at least a year and often longer. Originally, anthropologists studied small-scale societies in remote parts of the world, such as hunter-gatherer groups in Africa or Indigenous groups in Latin America. Now anthropologists study all types of cultures: Western and non-Western, urban and rural, industrialized and agricultural. Even the cultures of corporations are now within the domain of anthropology. While early anthropologists attempted to describe and understand the entire culture they studied, now most ethnographies (the books that cultural anthropologists write) focus on a specific aspect of culture such as economics, politics, or religion—or in the case of our readings, gender and sexuality.

Throughout this book we will be exploring a lot of practices that some of us may find "strange" or "unnatural." It is essential that we try to approach these subjects as anthropologists would. That is, to understand these practices from what the famous anthropologist Bronislaw Malinowski called, "the native's point of view." In other words, our goal is to try to learn about and understand the perspective of the people who engage in these particular practices and beliefs. Anthropologists call this type of approach **cultural relativism**. Cultural relativism is the position that the values and standards of cultures differ and deserve respect, and it is a core value of anthropology. Cultural relativism is a particularly useful perspective in anthropology because without understanding a culture from an insider's perspective, we can never fully understand how and why people do what they do. In essence, without cultural relativism, an accurate study of humanity is not possible.

In contrast to cultural relativism, **ethnocentrism** refers to the tendency to view one's own culture as the best and to judge the behavior and beliefs of culturally different people by one's own standards. All cultures tend to be ethnocentric, so it is not only Western, industrialized cultures that think their way of living is the best. In this course, we will all have to work hard to try to put aside our ethnocentrism as we explore meanings and practices of sex and gender across other cultures.

> Check out the video titled "Anthropology Syllabus," by the anthropologist Michael Wesch from Kansas State University. In the video, Dr. Wesch introduces the syllabus he has created for an Introduction to Anthropology course. In it, he describes the nine big ideas of anthropology; they make up the outline of the syllabus he has created. It's a great introduction to anthropology, to the ideas of cultural construction, and to the assumptions we all carry within us that create ethnocentrism. The video is a testament to how important it is for us to understand how we—humans—make the world we live in.

WHAT IS SEX?

In general in the United States today, people often use the terms **sex** and **gender** interchangeably. This is incorrect and leads to a lot of confusion. So first we will define these concepts (and other related ones) so that the terms used in this text are clear.

cultural relativism
the idea that we should seek to understand another person's beliefs and behaviors from the perspective of their own culture and not our own.

ethnocentric/ ethnocentrism
the tendency to view one's own culture as most important and correct and as the yardstick by which to measure all other cultures.

sex
refers to male and female identity based on internal and external sex organs and chromosomes. While male and female are the most common biologic sexes, a percentage of the human population is intersex with ambiguous or mixed biological sex characteristics.

gender
the set of culturally and historically invented beliefs and expectations about gender that one learns and performs. Gender is an "identity" one can choose in some societies, but there is pressure in all societies to conform to expected gender roles and identities.

In the United States, as in other parts of the world, sex is generally understood to be the biological component that marks people as either male or female. Many believe that sex is a fixed characteristic that is determined at birth and can always be easily defined and determined. One way people define sex is by examining the genitalia of a person. For instance, expectant parents often use ultrasounds to get an educated guess of the sex of their baby before it is born (see figure 1.1). Chromosomes provide more definitive evidence, as fetuses or infants typically exhibit an XX or XY chromosomal combination. However, it is important to understand that there are more genetic combinations possible than simply XX or XY, and sometimes genitals are not clearly defined at birth. Intersex people (once referred to by the derogatory term *hermaphrodites*) may display ambiguous genitalia or possess a different chromosomal combination, such as XXY. Intersex people have been born in all societies throughout time. It is estimated that approximately 1.7 percent of the world population is intersex (Fausto-Sterling 2000).

In some societies, intersex people are revered as sacred and take on special roles in the community. In others, such as the United States, they have historically been seen as "deviant" and are often surgically "assigned" a sex shortly after birth. However, starting in the 1990s in the United States this practice has been increasingly challenged. Many parents now refrain from assigning a sex to intersex children at birth, allowing the child to later determine their own sex and gender identities instead.

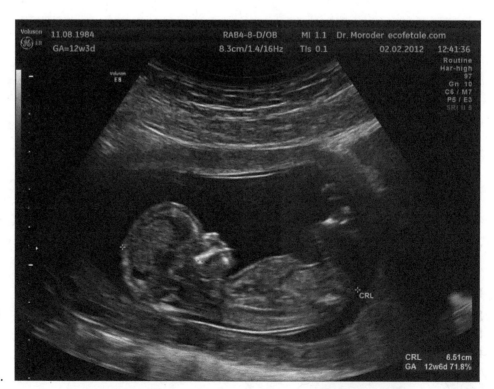

Figure 1.1. Expectant parents often use ultrasounds to get an idea of the sex of their baby before it is born. Dr. Wolfgang Moroder; CC BY-SA.

Another way that people determine sex is by studying hormone levels and traits that develop in puberty. Sex-linked hormones such as testosterone and estrogen are excreted by both men and women and are responsible for the development of secondary sex characteristics such as height, muscle mass, and body fat distribution. However these characteristics are not always clearly defined. For instance, many biologically "normal" women have higher muscle mass than some men and many biologically "normal" men are shorter than some women. And while it is generally understood that men excrete more testosterone than women and women more estrogen, recent research is changing our understanding of human hormone physiology. For instance, some studies have shown that the levels of testosterone can rise in women as a result of wielding power in social situations, regardless of whether it is done in stereotypically masculine or feminine ways (van Anders 2015). Thus it's becoming clear that testosterone and estrogen are not biologically fixed but that gender socialization may affect their excretion by encouraging or discouraging people toward behaviors that can modify their physiology.

There are also conditions in which a person's sex can change throughout their lives. For instance there are documented cases including the *Guevedoce* of the Dominican Republic in which some children (about 1 percent of the population) look like girls at birth, with no testes and what appears to be a vagina. They are subsequently socialized as girls during childhood. However, during puberty, when hormone levels rise, they begin to grow a penis, their testicles descend, they develop a "masculine" physique, and they are frequently then seen as male (Imperato-McGinley 1975). In sum, while sex may refer to biology, it is not easily defined by the binary opposition between "male" and "female." There are actually additional complexities to consider.

> For more information on intersexuality, do some research on the Intersex Society of North America (ISNA) and the Accord Alliance.

WHAT IS SEXUALITY?

As we have discussed, sex refers to the biological basis (male/female/intersex) for gender (man/woman/**trans**/third gender). Just as gender is not inextricably linked to sex, sexuality is experienced independently of both. In short, sexuality refers to "what we find erotic and how we take pleasure in our bodies" (Stryker 2008, 33). Like gender, sexuality and sexual practices vary from culture to culture and across time and so must also be considered socially constructed.

Sexual orientation refers to the ways in which we seek out erotic pleasure or how our sexuality is "oriented" toward particular types of people. Thus, heterosexuality refers to an orientation toward pleasure that takes place between men and women, while homosexuality refers to

transgender
a category for people who transition from one sex to another, either male-to-female or female-to-male.

erotic pleasure between men or between women. Bisexuality refers to an orientation that includes both men and women, while asexuality refers to the absence of a desire or sexual orientation toward other people. However, this is not to say that these are the only ways people experience sexuality. In fact, the concept of humans as either "heterosexual" or "homosexual" is a culturally and historically specific invention that is increasingly being challenged in the United States and elsewhere. Indeed, humans show a great deal of flexibility and variability in their sexual orientations and practices. Rather than being simply natural, human sexuality is one of the most culturally significant, regulated, and symbolic of all human capacities.

WHAT IS GENDER?

While sex refers to one's biology (male, female, intersex), gender refers to a person's internal identity as "masculine," "feminine," or some combination thereof. Gender is also something that is publicly expressed and shaped by culturally acceptable ways of being "male" or "female." People tend to internalize and naturalize these expectations in ways that make gender categories seem "natural" and normal. In fact, the ways that people, things, actions, places, spaces, etc. are gendered sometimes seem invisible to people, even though they are central to the ways that society is organized.

For instance, consider the following thought experiment. Think about the ways that your day is organized by your gender. Consider, first, how you woke up this morning and started your day. What was the pattern of your bedsheets and the color of your toothbrush? Do these reveal something about your gender identity? What do the bottles of shampoo and body soap you used in the shower look like? What does your deodorant smell like? Do these reflect your gender? What style of clothing did you choose to wear today? Did you apply any skin treatments or makeup? Did you apply a perfume/cologne? What does the scent say about your gender? Once you left your home, how did you move your body and walk and talk to others? What was the tone of your voice like, and what were the choices of words you spoke? What do these actions say about your gender? Do they conform with societal expectations, or do they defy them in some ways? Do you think conforming to or defying these expectations make your life easier or more difficult?

As you can see, gender is a pervasive social category that impacts people's lives in multiple and intimate ways. Studies of gender teach us that the categories of "man" and "woman," which we often think of as being "natural" categories, are in fact cultural constructs. That is, they are ways of being, doing, and even performing one's identity that are shaped by a particular culture and often based on the biological labels assigned to us. As children, we begin to learn **gender ideologies** from the moment we are born, and a small blue or pink hat is placed on our head. As babies, our gender label can impact the way our caregivers interact with us. As we grow, we learn the "correct" and "normal" ways to behave based on the category we are assigned to ("boy" or "girl") and then the toys we are given, the advertisements we see, the activities we engage in, and so on (see figure 1.2).

EXPLORE: Watch this video (https://vimeo.com/209451071) by Anne Fausto-Sterling, which elaborates on how gender is formed in childhood and how it can change throughout one's life.

We readily accept that clothing, language, and music are cultural—invented, created, and alterable—but often find it difficult to accept that gender is not natural but deeply embedded in and shaped by culture (see figure 1.3). We struggle with the idea that the division of humans into only two categories, "male" and "female," is not universal, that "male" and "female" are cultural concepts that take different forms and have

gender ideology
a complex set of beliefs about gender and gendered capacities, propensities, roles, identities, and socially expected behaviors and interactions that apply to males, females, and other gender categories. Gender ideology can differ across cultures and is acquired through enculturation.

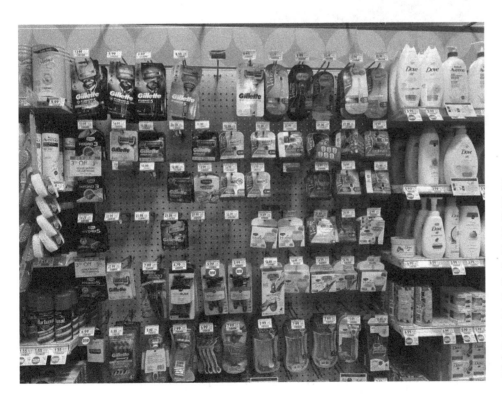

Figure 1.2. Many consumer products are marketed as either masculine or feminine. These include razors, body soap, deodorant, shampoo, and so on. Do you think there are significant differences in the makeup of these products? Why do you think consumers prefer gendered products? Harry Somers, CC-BY.

Figure 1.3a/1.3b. People readily accept that things like clothing are cultural constructions, but many find it more difficult to appreciate the ways that gender is embedded in and shaped by culture. (1.3a) US Marine Corps, Carol Highsmith, (1.3b) Library of Congress, Prints and Photographs Division.

different meanings cross-culturally. For anthropologists, the comparative method—contrasting certain cultural elements cross-culturally—helps us see how categories like "male" and "female" are not universal but are cultural constructions.

Part of the difficulty of seeing gender as a cultural construct is that gender also has a biological component, unlike other types of cultural inventions such as a sewing machine, cell phone, or poem. We do have bodies, and there are some male-female differences, including in reproductive capacities and roles (albeit far fewer than we have been taught). Similarly, sexuality, sexual desires, and responses are partially rooted in natural human capacities. However, in many ways, sexuality and gender are like food. We have a biologically rooted need to eat to survive, and we have the capacity to enjoy eating. What constitutes "food," what is "delicious" or "repulsive," and the contexts and meanings that surround food and human eating—those are cultural. Many potentially edible items are not "food" (for example, rats, bumblebees, and cats in the United States), and the concept of "food" itself is embedded in elaborate conventions about eating: how, when, with whom, where, with "utensils," for what purposes? In short, gender and sexuality, like eating, have biological components. But cultures over time have built complex edifices around them, creating systems of meaning that often barely resemble what is natural and innate. We experience gender and sexuality largely through the prism of the culture or cultures to which we have been exposed and in which we have been raised.

In this book we are asking you to reflect deeply on the ways in which what we have been taught to think of as natural—that is, our sex, gender, and sexuality—is, in fact, deeply embedded in and shaped by our culture. We challenge you to explore exactly which, if any, aspects of our gender and our sexuality are totally natural. One powerful aspect of culture, and one reason cultural norms feel so natural, is that we learn culture the way we learn our native language: without formal instruction, in social contexts, unconsciously picking it up from others around us. Soon, it becomes deeply embedded in our brains. We no longer think consciously about the meaning of the sounds we hear when someone says "hello" unless we do not speak English. Nor is it difficult to "tell the time" on a "clock" even though "time" and "clocks" are complex cultural inventions. These norms seem "natural" to us, and when we go against the norms we are often considered "deviant." These sociocultural norms are continually being reinforced and reinvented as people resist or enforce them. This is what we mean when we refer to *social constructionism*. The same principles apply to gender and sexuality. We learn very early (by at least age three) about the categories of gender in our culture—that individuals are either "male" or "female" and that elaborate beliefs, behaviors, and meanings are associated with each gender. We can think of this complex set of ideas as a gender ideology or a cultural model of gender. Looking at humans and human cultures cross-culturally we can observe incredible variations and diversity that

> EXPLORE: Take a look at Dr. Wesch's video on "The Matrix & the Social Construction of Reality" (https://www.youtube.com/watch?v=rukdvq8v8So). In it, he tries to teach and learn from his young son about social constructionism.

exist in terms of sex and gender. This diversity, along with changing attitudes toward sex and gender, provides evidence to support social constructionist perspectives.

GENDER IDEOLOGIES

Words can reveal cultural beliefs. A good example is the term "sex." In the past, sex referred both to sexuality and to someone's biological sex: male or female. Today, although sex still refers to sexuality, "gender" now means not only the categories of male and female but also other gender possibilities. Why has this occurred? The change in terminology reflects profound alterations in gender ideology in the United States (and elsewhere). Gender ideology refers to the collective set of beliefs about the appropriate roles, rights, and responsibilities of men and women in society. Throughout this book you will read about various historical constructions of gender ideologies in different parts of the world. In particular, you will explore how the systems of colonialism profoundly shaped gender ideologies in places like Latin America and South Asia and how these gender ideologies continue to change.

In the past, influenced by Judeo-Christian religion and nineteenth- and twentieth-century scientific beliefs, biology (and reproductive capacity) was literally considered to be destiny. Males and females—at least "normal" males and females—were thought to be born with different intellectual, physical, and moral capacities, preferences, tastes, personalities, and predispositions for violence and suffering. Ironically, many cultures, including European Christianity in the Middle Ages, viewed women as having a strong, often "insatiable" sexual "drive" and capacity. But by the nineteenth century, women and their sexuality were largely defined in reproductive terms, as in their capacity to "carry a man's child." Even late twentieth-century human sexuality texts often referred only to "reproductive systems," to genitals as "reproductive" organs, and excluded the "clitoris" and other female organs of sexual pleasure that had no reproductive function. For women, the primary (if not sole) legitimate purpose of sexuality was reproduction.

Nineteenth- and mid-twentieth-century European and US gender ideologies linked sexuality and gender in other ways. Sexual preference—the sex to whom one was attracted—was "naturally" heterosexual, at least among "normal" humans, and "normal," according to mid-twentieth-century Freudian-influenced psychology, was defined largely by whether one adhered to conventional gender roles for males and females. So, appropriately, "masculine" men were "naturally" attracted to "feminine" women and vice versa. Homosexuality, too, was depicted not just as a sexual preference but as gender-inappropriate role behavior, including things like gestures, cadence of speech and style of clothing. This is apparent in old stereotypes of gay men as "effeminate" (acting like a female, wearing "female" fabrics such as silk or colors such as pink, and participating in "feminine" professions like ballet) and of lesbian women as "butch" (cropped hair, riding motorcycles, wearing leather—prototypical masculinity). Once again, separate phenomena—sexual preference and gender role performance—were conflated because of beliefs that rooted both in biology. "Abnormality" in one sphere (sexual preference) was linked to "abnormality" in the other sphere (gendered capacities and preferences).

In short, the gender and sexual ideologies were based on **biological determinism**. According to this theory, males and females were supposedly born fundamentally different reproductively and in other major capacities. They were therefore believed to be "naturally" (biologically) capable of different activities and were sexually attracted to each other, although women's sexual "drive" was not very well developed relative to men's and was reproductively oriented.

biological determinism the scientifically unsupported view that biological differences (rather than culture) between males and females lead to fundamentally different capacities, preferences, and gendered behaviors.

REJECTING BIOLOGICAL DETERMINISM

Decades of research on gender and sexuality, including by feminist anthropologists, have challenged these old theories, particularly biological determinism. We now understand that cultures, not nature, create the gender ideologies that go along with being born male, female, or intersex, and the ideologies vary widely, cross-culturally. What is considered "man's work" in some societies, such as carrying heavy loads or farming, can be "woman's work" in others. What is "masculine" and "feminine" varies: pink and blue, for example, are culturally invented gender-color linkages, and skirts and "make-up" can be worn by men, indeed by "warriors" (see figure 1.4).

Margaret Mead was among the first anthropologists to explore the social construction of gender cross-culturally in the 1930s. She traveled to New Guinea and studied among three cultural groups, the Arapesh, the Mundugumor and Tchambuli, documenting gender expressions and personalities, describing her findings in *Sex and Temperament in Three Primitive Societies* (1935). She found that each society had different gender ideologies, and all were significantly distinct from those in the United States at that time. For instance, among the Arapesh both men and women had similar temperaments. They were gentle, cooperative, and sensitive to the needs of others. Men as well as women were intimately

Figure 1.4. Wodaabe men (of the Sahel region of Africa) wear makeup and dance in elaborate dress for an annual courtship ritual competition. Women select the most attractive man to marry. Dan Lundberg; CC BY-SA 2.0.

involved with parenting and childcare, including infant care. Among the Mundugumor, similar to the Araphesh, both men and women had similar characteristics. However the Mundugamor, by contrast, tended to be aggressive, insecure, selfish, individualistic, violent, and lacking in self-control. The Tchambuli differed from these cultural patterns in that both male and female temperaments were distinct from each other. While they were structurally a **patriarchal** society, the women tended to be more dominant, impersonal, efficient, and managerial. They often had the last word in economic decisions and asserted their dominant position frequently and in a variety of ways (Mead 1935, 252). Men were typically less responsible, less forceful, more interested in artistic sensibilities and more emotionally dependent.

Mead's work provided strong evidence against some early twentieth-century anthropology claims positing that specific gender roles and male dominance were part of our evolutionary heritage and fixed characteristics of human biology. This gender ideology argued that males evolved to be food providers—stronger, more aggressive, more effective leaders with cooperative and bonding capacities, planning skills, and technological inventiveness (toolmaking, for example). By contrast, females were never supposed to acquire those capacities because they were burdened by their reproductive roles—pregnancy, giving birth, lactation, and childcare—and thus became dependent on males for food and protection. These gender ideologies were persistent and persuasive; indeed, in many societies today, men are portrayed as active, dominant leaders, and women are viewed as passive, subordinate followers. Similar stories are invoked today for everything from some men's love of hunting to why men dominate "technical" fields, accumulate tools, have extramarital affairs, or commit the vast majority of homicides.

Strength and toughness remain defining characteristics of masculinity in the United States and other countries. However, decades of research have altered our views of human sex and gender and our evolutionary past. As a way to understand the ways humans evolved, many biological anthropologists look to nonhuman primates for insight, as we share a common ancestor that is more recent than other animals. For many years primatologists believed that nonhuman primates live exclusively in male-centered, male-dominated groups and that females are passive. These assumptions were used to claim that this structure in humans is biologically predestined and based on our evolutionary origins. However, more recent research has shown that, in fact, this does not accurately describe our closest primate relatives: gorillas, chimpanzees, and bonobos.

The stereotypes came from 1960s research on ground-dwelling savannah baboons. It suggested they are organized socially by a stable male-dominant hierarchy. The "core" of the group was established through force and regulated sexual access to females, providing internal and external defense of the "troop" in a supposedly hostile savannah environment. Females were thought to lack hierarchies or coalitions, were passive, and were part of dominant male "harems." This understanding changed with more nuanced research. Critics first argued that baboons, as monkeys rather than apes,[1] were too far removed from humans evolutionarily to tell us much about early human social organization. Then, further research on baboons living in other environments by primatologists such as Thelma Rowell discovered that those baboons are neither male focused nor male dominated. Instead, the stable group core is **matrifocal**—a mother and her offspring constituted the central and enduring ties. Her research also illustrated that males do not control females' sexuality. Quite the contrary, in fact: females mate freely and frequently, choosing males of all ages, sometimes establishing special relationships—"friends with favors." Dominance, while infrequent, is not based simply on size or strength; it is learned, situational, and often stress-induced. And like other primates, both male and female baboons use sophisticated strategies, dubbed "primate politics," to predict and manipulate the intricate

matrifocal
groups of related females (e.g., mother, her sisters, their offspring) form the core of the family and constitute the family's most central and enduring social and emotional ties.

---

1. Research indicates that humans are more closely related to African apes than monkeys. The last common ancestor between chimpanzees and humans was alive approximately eight million years ago, whereas Old World monkeys and apes diverged around twenty-five million years ago (Shook et al. 2019).

social networks in which they live. Rowell also restudied the savannah baboons. Even they do not fit the baboon "stereotype," she found that their groups are loosely structured with no specialized stable male-leadership coalitions and are sociable, matrifocal, and infant-centered much like Rhesus monkeys. Females actively initiate sexual encounters with a variety of male partners. When attacked by predators or frightened by some other major threat, males, rather than "defending the troop," typically flee first, leaving the infant-carrying females to follow behind.

Research among primates as well as other lines of research are helping us better understand the complex relationship between behavior and biology among male and female primates, including humans. Ongoing research in a variety of disciplines shows that the biological differences between men and women are less pronounced than we believed previously. For instance, research on human parental care has shown that when caring for infants, men excrete equal amounts of hormones oxytocin and prolactin as women do when they go through childbirth and lactation (Gordon 2010). These hormones play an important role in bonding with infants and encourage positive care behaviors, demonstrating that, biologically, men can be equally sensitive to the needs of infants as women.

Like many other primates, humans show a degree of sexual dimorphism, or differences in stature, musculature, and skeletal robustness between males and females, although much less than other primates (see figure 1.5). Yet there is also a lot of variability among males and females.

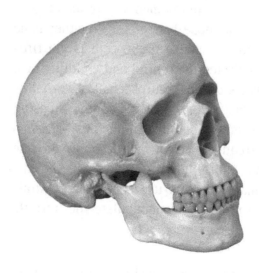
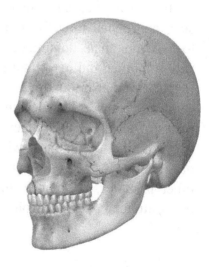

male   female

Figure 1.5a–d. Many non-human primates such as gorillas display much more sexual dimorphism than humans. You can see the differences in size and robustness in the male gorilla compared to the female gorilla. These differences are much less noticeable among humans where the female skull is nearly the same size as the male skull. Henri et George/Shutterstock; Randall Reed/Shutterstock; uzuri/Shutterstock; ivanpavlisko/Shutterstock.

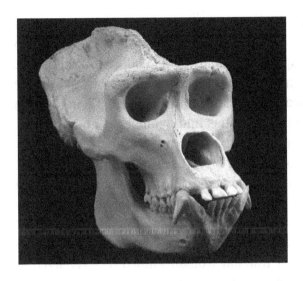

male   female

For instance, some females are taller than some males, and some males have more body fat than some females. Research on cross-cultural gender norms, human biology, primatology among others, demonstrates that these differences do not dictate behaviors nor predict abilities in individuals. The relationship between human biology and behavior is much more complex than we ever knew and strongly influenced by culture. In anthropology, looking at the ways in which our biology influences our culture—and how our culture influences our biology—is called the "biocultural" approach and is an exciting and growing area of research.

BEYOND THE BINARY

As you have seen, anthropologists love to shake up notions of what is "natural" and "normal." One common assumption is that all cultures divide human beings into a binary or dualistic model of gender. However, in some cultures gender is more fluid and flexible, allowing individuals born as one biological sex to assume another gender or creating more than two genders from which individuals can select.

Some examples of nonbinary cultures come from precontact Native America. Anthropologists such as Ruth Benedict long ago identified a fairly widespread phenomenon of so-called **Two-Spirit** people, individuals who did not comfortably conform to the gender roles and gender ideol-

Two-Spirit
A Native American term referring to individuals who combined gendered activities of both men, giving them a unique status. They were considered neither men nor women but were seen as a distinct, alternative third gender.

ogy normally associated with their biological sex. Among the precontact Zuni Pueblo in New Mexico, which was a relatively gender-egalitarian horticultural society, for example, individuals could choose an alternative role of "not-men" or "not-women." A Two-Spirit Zuni man would do the work and wear clothing normally associated with females, having shown a preference for female-identified activities and symbols at an early age. In some cases, he would eventually marry a man (see figure 1.6). Early European ethnocentric reports often described it as a form of homosexuality. Anthropologists suggested more complex motivations, including dreams of selection by spirits, individual psychologies, biological characteristics, and negative aspects of male roles (e.g., warfare). Most significantly, these alternative gender roles were acceptable, publicly recognized, and sometimes venerated. For example, a Kutenai woman known to have lived in 1811 was originally married to a French-Canadian man but then returned to the Kutenai and assumed a male gender role, changing her name to Kauxuma nupika (Gone-to-the-Spirits), becoming a spiritual prophet, and eventually marrying a woman.

Burrnesha, or "sworn virgins" in Albania are another example of a third gender. In traditionally patriarchal parts of Albanian society, gender roles are strict and place substantial limitations on women. Sworn virgins are women who renounce sexual relations completely to become honorary men, taking on the role of the man in their household and community;

Figure 1.6. We Wha (1849–1896), a Zuni Two-Spirit person. Library of Congress, Prints and Photographs Division.

they dress, act, and are treated as men (enjoying the relative freedoms of men as well) (see figure 1.7). Another, more well-known example of a nonbinary gender system is found among the Hijra in India, who are discussed in greater detail in chapter 5 of this book (see figure 1.9). Often referred to as a **third gender**, these individuals are usually biologically male but adopt female clothing, gestures, and names; eschew sexual desire and sexual activity; and go through religious rituals that give them certain divine powers, including blessing or cursing couples' fertility and performing at weddings and births. Hijra may undergo voluntary surgical removal of genitals through a nirvan or rebirth operation. Some hijra are males born with ambiguous external genitals, such as a particularly small penis or testicles that did not fully descend.

third gender
a gender identity that exists in nonbinary gender systems offering one or more gender roles separate from male or female.

Figure 1.7. In Albania, *Burrnesha* or "sworn virgins" are women who become honorary men, taking on the role of men in their community; they dress, act, and are treated like men. © 2011 Jill Peters.

As we have discussed in the section "What Is Sex?," research has shown that individuals with ambiguous genitals, sometimes called "intersex," are surprisingly common, as are those whose internal gender identity does not conform to their socially recognized gender or sex. So what are cultures to do when faced with an infant or child who cannot easily be "sexed"? Some cultures, including in the United States, used to force children into one of the two binary categories, even if it required surgery or hormone therapy. But in other places, such as India and among the Isthmus Zapotec in southern Oaxaca, Mexico, they have instead created a third gender category that has an institutional identity and role to perform in society (Mirande 2015) (see figure 1.8).

Figure 1.8. Muxes are a third gender recognized in indigenous Zapotec Juchitán, Oaxaca, Mexico. Muxes play important social and family roles and are generally respected by the local community. Mario Patinho; CC-SA 4.0 International.

Figure 1.9. In India, many people ask hijras to grant their newborn babies good health, since hijras are believed to have a God-given ability to bestow blessings. Ina Goel.

These cross-cultural examples demonstrate that the traditional rigid binary gender model in the United States is neither universal nor necessary. While all cultures recognize at least two biological sexes, usually based on genitals visible at birth (and have created at least two gender roles), many cultures go beyond the binary model, offering a third or fourth (or more) gender categories. Other cultures allow individuals to adopt, without sanctions, a gender role that is not congruent with their biological sex. In short, biology need not be destiny when it comes to gender roles, as we are increasingly discovering in the United States. Or, as Anne Fausto-Sterling asserts, "Sex and gender are best conceptualized as points in a multidimensional space" (Fausto-Sterling 2000). Indeed, research is increasingly pointing to considerable flexibility in gender and sex throughout human cultures.

Menstrual Equity

Ambivalence and even fear of female sexuality, or negative associations with female bodily fluids, such as menstrual blood, are widespread in the world's major religions. Orthodox Jewish women are not supposed to sleep in the same bed as their husbands when menstruating. In Kypseli, Greece, people believe that menstruating women can cause wine to go bad. In some Catholic Portuguese villages, menstruating women are restricted from preparing fresh pork sausages and from being in the room where the sausages are made as their presence is believed to cause the pork to spoil. Contact with these women also supposedly wilts plants and causes inexplicable movements of objects. Orthodox forms of Hinduism prohibit menstruating women from activities such as cooking and attending temples. These traditions are being challenged. A 2016 British Broadcasting Company (BBC) television program, for example, described "Happy to Bleed," a movement in India to change negative attitudes about menstruation and eliminate the ban on menstruating-age women entering the famous Sabriamala Temple in Kerala. Activists around the world have launched social movements and other projects to make menstruation less taboo and make feminine hygiene products more easily accessible. The film *Period End of Sentence*, which won the 2018 Oscar for Best Documentary, illustrates one example of such an effort in India. The profile that follows describes another important project to further menstrual equity in Zimbabwe.

For more information on the menstrual equity movement, visit The Pad Project: https://thepadproject.org/

PROFILE: SAVE THE GIRL CHILD MOVEMENT

Nolwazi Ncube, University of Cape Town

Save the Girl Child Movement (SGCM; https://www.savethegirlchildmovement.org/) with its flagship program, "Save the Girl-with-a-Vision" (SGV) was founded by Nolwazi Ncube, a Zimbabwean menstrual activist. Girls in Zimbabwe are said to miss as many as 528 days across the full span of their school-going years. SGV is a rural development program in the Umzingwane District of Zimbabwe, which was established to combat this problem and improve educational outcomes for adolescent girls. SGV is a multipronged program providing: (1) sanitary wear relief, (2) mentorship, and (3) financial support. SGV beneficiaries or "Saved Girls" receive free sanitary wear from the time they enter into the program until they have finished school. We have chosen to focus our activities in the Umzingwane district, which lies in the underserved and historically underdeveloped area of Matabeleland South Province; however, SGV also makes donations to other communities in need outside of Umzingwane, since the need for sanitary wear is a nationwide issue. There is an uneven division of the burden of domestic labor that falls more heavily on the shoulders of girls than boys. Cultural practice dictates that disposable sanitary wear is not meant to be disposed of along with household trash. As a result, girls must go into the field or forest and make a fire to burn and dispose of it. SGV focuses mostly on the provision of reusable pads for rural girls

Figure 1.10. The villagers of Mbizingwe after the sanitary wear distribution of April 26, 2019. Josh Webster.

as it is their expressed preference, since disposable sanitary wear comes with its own encumbrances that add to the burden of labor they already participate in.

The high school completion rate for girls in the catchment area is very low, as they are faced with many different challenges that impact their educational outcomes. In order to assist with this, the SGV program

Figure 1.11. Community elder, human rights activist and cofounder of SGV, Joice Dube. Josh Webster.

Figure 1.12. Nolwazi Ncube, founder of SGCM, distributing washable sanitary wear. Josh Webster.

has developed a set of criteria for prioritizing its most needy girls who are at high risk of dropping out of school. It considers factors such as orphanhood, family income, and stability of family structure. SGV also has a "buy-a-bike" initiative whereby sponsors can purchase a bike for a girl and to make the distance to the nearest secondary schools more manageable. Save the Girl Child Movement is supported by a small donor called the Geddes Foundation in Cyprus; donations can also be made on this web link: https://geddesfoundation.com/save-the-girl/.

Each year to raise menstrual education and hygiene awareness and mobilize funds for program activities, Save the Girl Child Movement launches its annual Let's Get Padded Up #LGPU campaign (https://www.gofundme.com/lets-get-padded-up-campaign) with the tagline "Every girl needs pads. PERIOD." Let's Get Padded Up fundraisers are organized in conjunction with strategic partners—with special mention to the Rotaract Club of Harare West, the Rotary Club of Harare West, and the Rotaract Club of Borrowdale Brooke. Rotaract clubs are the youth program for Rotary International for young adults up to age thirty. With the help of these clubs, the 2018 Let's Get Padded Up campaign met its target and was able to obtain a donation of five hundred sanitary hygiene kits from Days for Girls, a nonprofit organization in Australia that sews washable sanitary wear.

Figure 1.13. SGV beneficiaries in the village of Mbizingwe. If you raise up a girl child, you raise a village. Josh Webster.

MASCULINITY

Contributing Author: Melanie Medeiros, SUNY Geneseo

Students in gender studies and anthropology courses on gender are often surprised to find that they will be learning about men as well as women. Early women's studies initially employed what has been called an "add women and stir" approach, which led to examinations of gender as a social construct and of women's issues in contemporary society. In the 1990s women's studies expanded to become gender studies, incorporating the study of other genders, sexuality, and issues of gender and social justice. Gender was recognized as being fundamentally relational: femaleness is linked to maleness, femininity to masculinity. One outgrowth of that work is the field of "masculinity studies." The interdisciplinary study of men and masculinities dates back to the 1970s and consists of a wide field of methodological approaches and thematic foci. As the field has evolved, so have scholars' approaches to defining masculinity. Essentialist definitions of masculinity identify certain characteristics, such as physical strength or a short temper, as intrinsically masculine and argue that masculinity is something physically or psychologically inherent in **cisgender** men (hereafter referred to simply as "men")—that results in these characteristics, irrespective of social or cultural influences. Gender scholars since the 1970s have refuted essentialist notions that there are biological underpinnings to gender norms, roles, and identities that make gender universal (Fausto-Sterling 2013 [2000]). However, studies of masculinity do tend to define masculinity based on the mainstream idea of a gender binary that includes the categories of "men" and "women," which leads to a relational definition of "masculinity" that describes it as being in contrast to "femininity," emphasizing the perceived differences between genders, as well as within gender categories (Connell 2016; Gutmann 1997). Therefore the notion of masculinity and the study of it is more common in societies that emphasize a distinct gender binary, such as in Europe and North America since the nineteenth century (Connell 2016). In the 1990s scholarship shifted from the term *masculinity* (singular) toward the concept of *masculinities* (Connell 2005 [1995]), which acknowledges that there are many forms of masculinity and that there is gender stratification among men—not just between men and women. Conventionally, "masculinity" is an ideal of what society expects men to be and how to act, while the acknowledgment of multiple "masculinities" recognizes that there are men who may or may not aspire to or fulfill local expectations of masculine performance (Connell 2016). Connell (2016)

cisgender
a term used to describe those who identify with the sex and gender they were assigned at birth.

masculinity
the culturally specific traits, behaviors, and discourses expected of men.

hegemonic masculinity theory (HMT)
a theory developed by Connell (1995) arguing that there are certain traits, behaviors, and discourses associated with masculinity that are valued and rewarded by a culture or society's dominant social groups and that the performance of hegemonic masculinity helps to legitimize power and inequality, or more specifically, patriarchy.

hegemony/hegemonic
the dominance of one group over another supported by legitimating norms and ideas that normalize dominance. Using collective consent rather than force, dominant social groups maintain power and social inequalities are naturalized.

argues, "Rather than attempting to define masculinity as an object (a natural character type, a behavioral average, a norm), we need to focus on the processes and relationships through which men and women conduct gendered lives. 'Masculinity,' to the extent the term can be briefly defined at all, is simultaneously a place in gender relations, the practices through which men and women engage that place in gender, and the effects of these practices in bodily experience, personality and culture" (138). In other words, masculinity is not a fixed and tangible object or archetype but a constantly negotiated gender performance that is often part of one's gender identity and gender relations.

Gender scholars have studied masculinity among cisgender men, trans men, and cisgender men and women identifying as gay or queer (Abelson 2016; Connell 2005 [1995], 2001; Gutmann 2007 [1996]); Halberstam 2018 [1998]; Inhorn 2012; Mitchell 2015; Parker 2003; Schilt 2010). These scholars have examined a wide range of topics related to masculinities. For example, some scholars have focused on gender hierarchies and inequality between men and women and among men as well (Wade and Ferree 2019). There is a substantial body of literature on the relationship between men, masculinity, and violence, including examining men as perpetrators and victims of violence (Abelson 2016; Ellis 2016). Another topic of study is representations of men and masculinity in the media (Keith 2017; Zeglin 2016). Scholars have also been interested in understanding masculinities in relationship to kinship and parenting (Edley 2017; Keith 2017). Scholars examine masculinity in conjunction with sexuality, sexual orientation, as well as the relationship between masculinity and homophobia (Bucher 2014; Edley 2017). Ethnographic studies of masculinity highlight cross-cultural and intracultural variation in the construction and performance of masculinity (Conway-Long 1994; Ellis 2016; Gutmann 1997, 2003, 2007 [1996]; Mitchell 2015; Wentzell 2013).

THEORIES OF MASCULINITIES

By far the most frequently utilized theory of masculinities is Connell's (1995) **hegemonic masculinity theory** (HMT). The theoretical concept of **hegemony** (Gramsci 1971) explains how power can function without force when a dominant social group creates collective agreement within a society about such things as behavioral norms, beliefs, and values. This collective consent naturalizes both the power and prestige of the dominant group, as well as social inequality. For example, many people in the United

States believe class inequality is a natural product of human behavior rather than the outcome of our political economic system or the value of individualism. Beliefs or ideals are hegemonic when they are taken for granted and viewed as inevitable realities rather than products of society and culture and when they are supported by the dominant groups who benefit from them and by the marginalized groups who do not benefit. "Hegemony, then, means widespread consent to relations of systematic social disadvantage" (Wage and Ferree 2019, 137) often involving the "willing compliance of the oppressed" (Anderson 2016, 184). Hegemonic masculinity theory in turn argues that there are certain traits, behaviors, and discourses associated with masculinity and the performance of masculinity that are valued and rewarded by a culture or society's dominant social groups. As a result, the performance of and practices associated with hegemonic masculinity help to legitimize power and inequality, or more specifically according to Connell—**patriarchy**. Therefore, hegemonic masculinity is not only a society's ideal of manhood but part of a system of social and gender inequality that preferences certain traits, practices, and discourses over others, oppressing and marginalizing both men and women who do not meet this standard (Wage and Ferree 2019).

According to Connell (2005 [1995]) there are three categories of masculinities subsumed by the term *hegemonic masculinity*: complicit, subordinated, and marginalized. Individuals who exhibit the traits or practices associated with hegemonic masculinity, or who aspire to them, would be "complicit" within this gender system. Connell described men whose other social identities—particularly race and class—place them outside the dominant social groups as having "marginalized" masculinities because their position on the gender hierarchy is beneath that of the dominant group of men who more closely approximate hegemonic masculinity. Interestingly, Connell opted to distinguish sexual orientation from other forms of social identity, arguing that the masculinities of gay men were "subordinated" rather than marginalized. As such, Connell argued that heterosexuality is a key component of hegemonic masculinity, and other scholars have built from this theory to argue that hegemonic masculinity and homophobia are mutually constitutive. As one scholar observed, "Homophobia is not only a tool to enforce masculinity, but is a part of how hegemonic masculinity is constructed. Meaning, just as heterosexuality is part of 'being a man,' so too is denying the masculinity of gay men" (Bucher 2014, 225). Hegemonic masculinity theory opened up awareness that there are many forms of masculinity, that traits and behaviors of men who do not approximate hegemonic masculinity are policed (physically and discursively) and marginalized, and thus not all

patriarchy
a dynamic system of power and inequality that privileges men and boys over women and girls in social interactions and institutions.

men hold an equal position on the gender hierarchy (Anderson 2016; Wage and Ferree 2019). Hegemonic masculinity theory pioneered new directions in gender scholarship and continues to be one of the most widely used theoretical approaches to studying masculinities.

However, no theory is without critique. Anderson (2016) suggests that in using the concept of hegemony, HMT is problematic on the one hand because it does not grant individuals agency to question or challenge hegemonic norms and on the other because it treats hegemonic masculinity as "an archetype of masculinity" rather than "a social process." (Anderson 2016, 183). Revisiting their theory in 2016, Connell does note that the characteristics a society or culture value and associate with ideal masculinity are constantly in flux, and therefore hegemonic masculinity "can be defined as the configuration of gender practice which embodies the currently accepted answer to the problem of the legitimacy of patriarchy which guarantees (or is taken to guarantee) the dominant position of men and the subordination of women" (Connell 2016, 139). Anderson (2016) also points out that while HMT was very useful for examining masculinities in North America in the 1980s and 1990s, it is less applicable in a contemporary North American society. They argue that since heterosexuality and the subjugation of gay or queer men is a key component of HMT, the theory is no longer relevant in a society, or among subgroups (e.g., high school students) for whom **heteronormativity** is no longer a hegemonic ideal. I offer a similar critique, that HMT—with its emphasis on heteronormativity—is inadequate for examining masculinity in societies where sexuality and sexual orientation are more fluid than the gay/straight binary discussed by gender scholars of North America in the late twentieth century. Therefore, valuing the contributions of HMT but recognizing its shortcomings, scholars today employ several alternative concepts, such as "mainstream," "dominant," and most frequently "normative" masculinities to examine the ways that certain traits, behaviors, and practices are idealized by a society, and how those ideals are constantly changing in response to social, cultural, and political economic changes.

Ethnographic studies have contributed a more nuanced approach to the study of masculinities and provide evidence showing that there can be multiple (more than three) masculinities in a given setting and that men are not necessarily aspiring toward one dominant ideal, nor are they limited to one form of masculine performance and identity. Men can aspire to a dominant or normative form of masculinity, challenge norms, or combine aspects of normative gender scripts and performances

heteronormativity
a term coined by French philosopher Michel Foucault to refer to the often-unnoticed system of rights and privileges that accompany normative sexual choices and family formation.

to create a hybrid form of masculinity that is unique or useful to them in a given space and time (Giddings and Hovorka 2010). For example, Gutmann describes how men in Mexico perform a multiplicity of masculinities both in the public sphere and in the home (Gutmann 2007 [1996]). Terms such as variant masculinities (Fonseca 2001; Lindisfarne 1994), emerging masculinities (Inhorn 2012), composite masculinities (Wentzell 2013), and inclusive masculinities (Anderson 2016) challenge the assumption of a fixed or "traditional" masculinity, and show that not all people subscribe to gender norms that reinforce the power of dominant groups while oppressing others.

CONCLUSION

In this chapter we have examined some of the key concepts that will be used throughout this book, including gender, sex, and sexuality as well as nonbinary gender expressions throughout the world. We also addressed how gender is fundamentally shaped by culture and how all gender expressions, including masculinity, must be understood in relation to one another and in the cultural context in which they occur. As you go through the chapters of the book you may wish to refer back to these concepts, using them as a guide and reference to understand the various global perspectives on gender. These key concepts will also form the foundation for the following chapter, which introduces the key perspectives used in this book. These are exciting and perhaps challenging ideas, as they address intimate parts of our own identities and worldviews.

REVIEW QUESTIONS

- Discuss how sex, gender, and sexuality are related but also distinct concepts.

- Discuss two examples of how gender is shaped by culture.

- Identify some cross-cultural examples of nonbinary gender expressions.

- Explain how gender is relational, such as how masculinity is relational to other gender expressions.

KEY TERMS

biological determinism: the scientifically unsupported view that biological differences (rather than culture) between males and females lead to fundamentally different capacities, preferences, and gendered behaviors.

cisgender: a term used to describe those who identify with the sex and gender they were assigned at birth.

cultural relativism: the idea that we should seek to understand another person's beliefs and behaviors from the perspective of their own culture and not our own.

ethnocentric/ethnocentrism: the tendency to view one's own culture as most important and correct and as the yardstick by which to measure all other cultures.

ethnography: the in-depth study of the everyday practices and lives of a people.

gender: the set of culturally and historically invented beliefs and expectations about gender that one learns and performs. Gender is an "identity" one can choose in some societies, but there is pressure in all societies to conform to expected gender roles and identities.

gender ideology: a complex set of beliefs about gender and gendered capacities, propensities, roles, identities, and socially expected behaviors and interactions that apply to males, females, and other gender categories. Gender ideology can differ across cultures and is acquired through enculturation.

hegemony/hegemonic: the dominance of one group over another supported by legitimating norms and ideas that normalize dominance. Using collective consent rather than force, dominant social groups maintain power and social inequalities are naturalized.

holistic/holism: the idea that the parts of a system interconnect and interact to make up the whole.

hegemonic masculinity theory (HMT): a theory developed by Connell (1995) arguing that there are certain traits, behaviors, and discourses associated with masculinity that are valued and rewarded by a culture or society's dominant social groups and that the performance of hegemonic masculinity helps to legitimize power and inequality, or more specifically, patriarchy.

heteronormativity: a term coined by French philosopher Michel Foucault to refer to the often-unnoticed system of rights and privileges that accompany normative sexual choices and family formation.

masculinity: the culturally specific traits, behaviors, and discourses expected of men.

matrifocal: groups of related females (e.g., mother, her sisters, their offspring) form the core of the family and constitute the family's most central and enduring social and emotional ties.

patriarchy: a dynamic system of power and inequality that privileges men and boys over women and girls in social interactions and institutions.

sex: refers to male and female identity based on internal and external sex organs and chromosomes. While male and female are the most common biologic sexes, a percentage of the human population is intersex with ambiguous or mixed biological sex characteristics.

third gender: a gender identity that exists in nonbinary gender systems offering one or more gender roles separate from male or female.

transgender: a category for people who transition from one sex to another, either male-to-female or female-to-male.

Two-Spirit: Traditionally a Native American term referring to individuals who combined gendered activities of both men, giving them a unique status. They were considered neither men nor women but were seen as a distinct, alternative third gender.

RESOURCES FOR FURTHER EXPLORATION

- *Are Men Animals? How Modern Masculinity Sells Men Short* (2019) by Matthew Gutman. Basic Books

- *Masculinities under Neoliberalism.* 2016. Edited by Andrea Cornwall, Frank Karioris, and Nancy Lindisfarne. London: Zed.

- *Toward An Anthropological Understanding of Maleness and Violence.* 2019.

- Fausto-Sterling, Anne. 2012. *Sex/Gender: Biology in a Social World*. New York: Taylor and Francis.

BIBLIOGRAPHY

Abelson, Miriam J. 2016. "Negotiating Vulnerability and Fear: Rethinking the Relationship Between Violence and Contemporary Masculinity." In *Exploring Masculinities: Identity, Inequality, Continuity, and Change*, edited by C. J. Pascoe and T. Bridges, 337–347. New York: Oxford University Press.

Anderson, Eric. 2016. "Inclusive Masculinities." In *Exploring Masculinities: Identity, Inequality, Continuity, and Change*, edited by C. J. Pascoe and T. Bridges, 178–187. New York: Oxford University Press.

Bucher, Jacob. 2014. "But He Can't Be Gay": The Relationship between Masculinity and Homophobia in Father-Son Relationships. *Journal of Men's Studies* 22, no. 3: 222–237.

Connell, Raewyn. 2005 [1995]. *Masculinities*. Cambridge, UK: Polity.

Connell, Raewyn. 2001. *The Men and The Boys*. Berkeley: University of California Press.

Connell, Raewyn. 2016. "The Social Organization of Masculinity." In *Exploring Masculinities: Identity, Inequality, Continuity, and Change*, edited by C. J. Pascoe and T. Bridges, 136–144. New York: Oxford University Press.

Conway-Long, Don. 1994. "Ethnographies and Masculinities." In *Theorizing Masculinities*, edited by H. Brod and M. Kaufman, 61–81. New York: SAGE.

Edley, Nigel. 2017. *Men and Masculinity: The Basics*. New York: Routledge.

Ellis, Anthony. 2016. *Men, Masculinities, and Violence: An Ethnographic Study*. London: Routledge.

Fausto-Sterling, Anne. 2000. "The Five Sexes, Revisited." *The Sciences* 40, no. 4: 18–23.

Fausto-Sterling, Anne. 2013 [2000]. "Dueling Dualisms." In *Sex, Gender and Sexuality: The New Basics*, edited by A. L. Ferber, K. Holcomb and T. Wentling, 6–34. New York: Oxford University Press.

Giddings, Carla, and Alice Hovorka. 2010. "Place, Ideological Mobility and Youth Negotiations of Gender Identities in Urban Botswana." *Gender, Place & Culture* 17, no. 2: 211–229.

Gutmann, Matthew. 1997. "Trafficking in Men: The Anthropology of Masculinity." *Annual Review of Anthropology* 26: 385–409.

———. 2003. *Changing Men and Masculinities in Latin America*. Durham, NC: Duke University Press.

———. 2007 [1996]. *The Meanings of Macho*. Berkeley: University of California Press.

Halberstam, Jack. 2018 [1998]. *Female Masculinity*. Durham, NC: Duke University Press.

Imperato-McGinley, Julianne, Teofilo Gautier Guerrero, and Ralph Peterson. 1974. "Steroid 5α-Reductase Deficiency in Man: An Inherited Form of Male Pseudohermaphroditism." *Science* 186, 4170 (December 1974): 1213–1215.

Inhorn, Marcia C. 2012. *The New Arab Man: Emergent Masculinities, Technologies, and Islam in the Middle East*. Princeton, NJ: Princeton University Press.

Keith, Thomas. 2017. *Masculinities in Contemporary American Culture: An Intersectional Approach to the Complexities and Challenges of Male Identity*. New York: Routledge.

Lindisfarne, N. 1994. "Variant Masculinities and Variant Virginities: Rethinking 'Honor and Shame.'" In *Dislocating Masculinity: Comparative Ethnographies*, edited by A. Cornwall and N. Lindisfarme, 82–96. London: Routledge.

Lorber, Judith. [2005] 2013. "A World without Gender: Making the Revolution." In *Sex, Gender and Sexuality: The New Basics*, edited by A. L. Ferber, K. Holcomb and T. Wentling, 401–409. New York: Oxford University Press.

Mirande, Alfredo. 2015. "Hombres Mujeres: An Indigenous Third Gender." *Men and Masculinities*, 1–27. Los Angeles: SAGE.

Nelson, Katie; Braff, Lara. 2020. *Perspectives: An Open Invitation to Cultural Anthropology*. 2nd ed. Arlington, VA: American Anthropological Association.

Parker, Richard. 2003. "Changing Sexualities: Masculinity and Male Homosexuality in Brazil." In *Changing Men and Masculinities in Latin America*, edited by M. C. Gutmann, 307–332. Durham, NC: Duke University Press.

Petersen, Alan. 2016. "Research on Men and Masculinities: Some Implications of Recent Theory for Future Work." In *Exploring Masculinities: Identity, Inequality, Continuity, and Change*, edited by C. J. Pascoe and T. Bridges, 337–347. New York: Oxford University Press.

Schilt, Kristen. 2010. *Just One of the Guys? Transgender Men and the Persistence of Gender Inequality*. Chicago and London: University of Chicago Press.

Shook, Beth, Katie Nelson, Kelsie Aguilera, and Lara Braff. 2019. *Explorations: An Open Invitation to Biological Anthropology*. Arlington, VA: American Anthropological Association.

van Anders, S. M., J. Steiger, and K. L. Goldey. 2015. Effects of gendered behavior on testosterone in women and men. *Proceedings of the National Academy of Sciences of the United States of America* 112, no. 45, 13805–13810. https://doi.org/10.1073/pnas.1509591112

CREDITS

Some sections of this chapter were adapted from work by Deborah Amory and "Gender and Sexuality," chapter 10 by Carol C. Mukhopadhyay and Tami Blumenfield (with Susan Harper and Abby Gondek) in *Perspectives: An Open Introduction to Cultural Anthropology*, ed. Nina Brown, Thomas McIlwraith, and Laura Tubelle de González, 2nd ed. (Washington, DC: American Anthropological Association, 2020).

2

Key Perspectives

Nadine T. Fernandez and Katie Nelson

LEARNING OBJECTIVES

- Compare and contrast the primary goals of the different waves of feminism.

- Articulate how intersectionality helps explain inequalities.

- Analyze how colonialism and globalization have contributed to global inequalities of wealth and power.

If we want to learn about sex and gender from a global perspective, anthropology is a good place to start. This book examines sex and gender through a few particular perspectives or lenses within anthropology. These "lenses" frame how each chapter approaches the study of gender in a particular place and helps us understand why and how certain gendered practices came to be. This chapter outlines the main perspectives in this book, namely: feminism, **intersectionality**, and globalization. These are all complex terms with long histories, but here we'll try to give just enough background explanation so that you can contextualize the chapters in the book and identify the threads and themes that connect them.

FEMINISM

Anthropology did not escape the gender ideologies of the time and place where the discipline first started. It was shaped by its "founding fathers"—Franz Boas, Bronislaw Malinowski, Alfred Kroeber, among

intersectionality
refers to the interconnected nature of social categories such as race, class, and gender that create overlapping systems of discrimination or disadvantage. The goal of an intersectional analysis is to understand how racism, sexism, and homophobia (for example) interact together to impact our identities and how we live in our society.

first-wave feminism
started in the late 1800s
and early 1900s and was
focused on women's right
to vote.

second-wave feminism
1960s–1980s addressed
issues of equal legal and
social rights for women.
Its emblematic slogan was
"the personal is political."

others—in the late 1800s to early 1900s, about the same time the **first wave** of the feminist movement was fighting for women's right to vote. Despite the early involvement of women in anthropology such as Margaret Mead and Zora Neale Hurston, the contributions of many of its founding "mothers" were dismissed or overlooked. The dominant male perspective shaped much of what early anthropologists studied and how they communicated their findings. In fact, it wasn't until the **second wave** of the feminist movement, namely the women's rights movements of the 1960s and 1970s, that anthropologists started to ask some key questions. And it was feminist anthropologists who were some of the first researchers to ask how social constructions of sex and gender vary cross-culturally. Why were they interested in knowing the answer to this question? These feminist anthropologists reasoned that if gender roles and statuses are different in different places and times, then it means that there is nothing "natural" about the gender inequalities in our own culture: they are culturally constructed.

Since feminism is a concept we will be encountering in some of this book's chapters, let's lay out a working definition before we embark. We take the following definition from Estelle Freedman's book, *No Turning Back: The History of Feminism and the Future of Women*. Freedman defines feminism as follows: "Feminism is a belief that women and men are inherently of equal worth. Because most societies privilege men as a group, social movements are necessary to achieve equality between

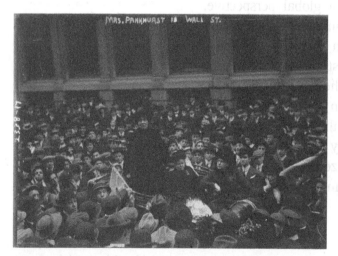

Figure 2.1a. British activist Emmeline Pankhurst traveled constantly, giving speeches throughout Britain and the United States to promote women's suffrage. One of her most famous speeches, "Freedom or Death," was delivered in Connecticut in 1913. Library of Congress, Prints and Photographs Division.

Figure 2.1b. Japanese women engaged in political action to secure women's right to vote (c. 1920). Library of Congress, Prints and Photographs Division.

women and men, with the understanding that gender always intersects with other social hierarchies" (Freedman, 2002).

Freedman continues with some clarifications of the terms in her definition. She uses the term *equal worth* to emphasize that we need to value traditionally female tasks (e.g., child rearing) as highly as the types of work usually done by men. She is not saying men and women are the same, or that they have to be the same, but rather that men's and women's labor should be valued equally. By men being privileged in most societies, she is referring not only to formal legal and political rights but also to cultural preferences and double standards that give men more freedoms and opportunities than women. Finally, by pointing out that gender always "intersects" with other "social hierarchies," she is referring to the ways in which the experience of being a woman is fundamentally influenced by other social structures such as class, race, age, sexuality, etc. Perhaps most importantly, Freedman is not arguing that there is a universal identity as "woman" that in and of itself communicates something about the experiences of *all* women in the world. She recognizes that women experience their lives very differently in different cultural and historical contexts.

Early feminist ideas, like the 1970s concept of a "global sisterhood," were criticized by feminists of color, such as Audre Lorde, for overlooking the multiple forms of oppression faced by women of color and women in the Global South (Schrock 2013). There are other social inequalities that disadvantage both men and women, and feminism cannot ignore those other systems of power and inequality—like poverty, racism, and homophobia. In her definition of feminism Freedman addresses the issues raised in the **third wave** of the feminist movement, namely that second-wave feminism had focused too heavily on the experiences of white, middle-class women and had failed to see how other social inequalities shape people's lives. The concept of feminism has changed over time and has, at times, been given a bad name because it is often oversimplified and misunderstood. However, when presented as Freedman does, it becomes a stance that both men and women can embrace.

As a movement, feminism continues to evolve and grow. We are now in what has been called the **fourth wave** of feminism, which began in about 2008. This wave has focused on sexual harassment, body shaming, and rape culture and, in part, is defined by the use of technology. Fourth-wave feminist activism takes place in the streets, but it is planned and spread online through social media campaigns like the #MeToo movement. Fourth-wave feminism recognizes and celebrates the wide variety of "feminisms" that exist around the world and continues to carry forward ideas of intersectionality. Now, let's take a closer look at intersectionality, which is also central to this book.

third-wave feminism began in the 1990s responding to the shortcomings of the Second Wave, namely that it focused on the experiences of upper-middle-class white women. Third Wave feminism is rooted in the idea of women's lives as intersectional, highlighting how race, ethnicity, class, religion, gender, and nationality are all significant factors when discussing feminism.

fourth-wave feminism began around 2012 to address sexual harassment, body shaming, and rape culture, among other issues. It is characterized by a focus on the global empowerment of women, the greater inclusion of diverse perspectives and voices, and the use of social media in activism.

Table 2.1. Waves of feminism

Waves of Feminism	Characteristics
First wave	Began in late 1800's and focused on the fight for political incorporation of women, primarily the right to vote.
Second wave	1960's-1980's, addressed issues of equal legal and social rights for women. Its emblematic slogan was "the personal is political." Pushed for, but failed to have the ERA (Equal Rights Amendment) added to the US Constitution. Critiqued for primarily focusing on the concerns of white, middle to upper-class women in the Global North.
Third wave	Began in the 1990s responding to the shortcomings of the second wave, namely that it focused on the experiences of upper middle-class white women. This wave is rooted in the idea of women's lives as intersectional, highlighting how race, ethnicity, class, religion, gender, and nationality are all significant factors when discussing feminism.
Fourth wave	Began about 2008 and has focused on sexual harassment, body shaming and rape culture and, in part, is defined by the use of technology. Fourth-wave feminist activism that takes place in the streets, but it is planned and spread online, through social media campaigns like #MeToo movement. Fourth-wave feminism recognizes and celebrates the wide variety of "feminisms" that exist around the world, and continues to carry forward ideas of intersectionality.

Figure 2.3. Second-wave feminists fought for the Equal Rights Amendment (ERA). Here ERA supporters march from the Florida governor's mansion to the capitol building in Tallahassee, Florida (1975). Florida Memory/State Library and Archive of Florida.

INTERSECTIONALITY

A key idea that grew out of the third-wave feminist movement—and out of feminist analyses of how gender and race are socially constructed—is intersectionality. Using an intersectional lens allows us to appreciate the ways different social structures and aspects of our identities intersect in different ways for different people. For example, intersectionality allows us to understand how a person's identity and life experiences are shaped by racism, sexism, class, and homophobia (among other categories of difference). At the "inter-section" of various social forces we experience ways of being and moving about the world that differ from another person whose intersectionality may be distinct from our own. Intersectionality also examines how interlocking systems of power affect the most marginalized people in a society. From an intersectional perspective, multiple forms of discrimination combine and transform the experience of oppression. The purpose of using an intersectional lens is to understand how overlapping categories of identity change in combination with each other and how they impact individuals and institutions. The framework of intersectionality is essential to studying relations of privilege and power in efforts to promote social and political equity.

The theory of intersectionality was first articulated by Kimberlé Crenshaw, a lawyer and critical race theorist who was trying to understand

Figure 2.4. Kimberlé Crenshaw in Berlin, 2019. Mohamed Badarne, CC-BY-SA-4.0.

EXPLORE: Review Crenshaw's TED talk to get a better understanding of exactly what this term, "intersectionality," means, where it came from, and why it is still important today.

EXPLORE: Peter Hopkins, Newcastle University, 2018, April 22. "What Is Intersectionality?" https://vimeo.com/263719865.

how antidiscrimination law could fail to account for the way in which a Black woman might be discriminated against (Crenshaw 1989). She developed the analogy of an "inter-section," where racism and sexism meet, to help us understand and see the ways in which multiple aspects of our identities—and multiple social forces that helped to shape those identities—could impact us. Crenshaw invented the term *intersectionality* in 1989, and it was adopted in the years that followed by feminist and feminist anthropologists. In 2016 Crenshaw delivered a TED talk entitled, "The Urgency of Intersectionality." More than thirty years later, the idea of intersectionality is still an urgent one.

The chapters in this book are grounded in feminist anthropology and as such they examine gendered lives of men and women intersectionally and situate them in their local contexts. The results are culturally contextualized analyses that are often rooted in the concerns of the people who are being studied. Feminist anthropologists like Chandra Mohanty assert that women's experiences across the globe are diverse and argue for studies that are context-specific and historically situated (Schrock 2013). In this book, we embrace this challenge by focusing not only on intersectionality but also on the concept of globalization as a way to understand both the cultural specificity and the historical global connections shaping the gendered experiences explored in each chapter. Let's take a closer look at globalization and the history of colonialism that tied much of the world together centuries ago.

COLONIALISM, GLOBALIZATION, AND GENDER

Inequality among cultural groups, societies, and nations is not a new phenomenon: it has roots in the development of agriculture and a sedentary lifestyle starting ten thousand years ago. Yet the reasons why these inequalities persist have troubled social scientists for decades. In his book *Guns, Germs, and Steel*, Jared Diamond puts forward an excellent argument for why some countries were rich and others were poor prior to 1492 (when Columbus first arrived in the Americas). Europeans, he argues, had many advantages over people in the Americas that allowed them to conquer the Aztec and Incan empires, for example. By the early 1500s the Europeans had domesticated horses, and they possessed guns and steel swords, ocean-going ships, large-scale political organizations, and phonetic writing systems, as well as having resistance to several deadly epidemic diseases. In short, guns, germs, and steel gave them key advantages over the Indigenous groups they encountered (Diamond 1999).

Europeans had these advantages, not because of genetic superiority but rather due to their fortuitous geographic location. The Eurasian land-mass was home to most of the large mammals that could be domesticated and used in the grain harvesting process. This meant that six thousand years ago, the Eurasians were using large draft animals to power their plows, providing more calories and fueling population growth. The large landmass also allowed for ideas to circulate across cultures, like between Europe, North Africa, and China, bringing innovations that fostered the development of more complex and stratified societies. With these advantages, Spain, Great Britain, Portugal, and other European countries set off on an age of exploration to see what they could learn about and acquire from the New World. However, while this history helps explain why Europeans were able to launch an age of exploration to other continents, it does little to help us understand why some countries are rich and others poor after over five hundred years of global trade. The history and legacy of colonialism give us more insight into these persistent inequalities.

As Europeans colonized the world, they transformed societies that were growing food for their own subsistence into exporters of cash crops for European consumption. Europeans used their military might to capture lands and then levied taxes or created large plantations that forced locals to produce export crops like sugar, coffee, cocoa, and tobacco. They also put colonized peoples to work in dangerous mines, extracting precious metals such as gold and silver. Foods, plants, and diseases spread throughout the world, along with ideas, values, technologies, money, and commodities. Over centuries, a global world economic system emerged in which the wealth and profits earned in the **Global North** depended on the cheap labor, raw materials, and lack of development in the **Global South** (see chapter 15, "The Global North—Introducing the Region," for more on sociologist Immanuel Wallerstein's world systems theory).

The slave trade was perhaps the most profound example of this world system in action. Due to the decimation of Indigenous Americans by European diseases, there was ample land for Europeans to settle but not enough labor. Meanwhile, Africans, by virtue of sharing the same continuous landmass with Europeans, had already built up a resistance to European diseases and had a few of their own, like malaria and dengue fever, that made Africa difficult for Europeans to conquer and settle. So instead of settling Africa, Europeans traded with the more powerful

Global North
does not refer to a geographic region in any traditional sense but rather to the relative power and wealth of countries in distinct parts of the world. The Global North encompasses the rich and powerful regions such as North America, Europe, and Australia.

Global South
does not refer to a geographic region in any traditional sense but rather to the relative power and wealth of countries in distinct parts of the world. The Global South encompasses the poor and less powerful countries in areas such as Latin America, Africa, and Asia.

Figure 2.5. Enslaved Africans arriving in the US. Library of Congress, Prints and Photographs Division.

African nations, like the West African Dahomey Kingdom (present-day Benin). The most notable "commodity" they traded was people: enslaved Africans. A total of twelve million enslaved people were brought to the Americas to work in the vast sugar, cotton, and tobacco plantations.

In the plantation system, the colonizers amassed fabulous levels of wealth. The growing wealth set the stage for the Industrial Revolution in Britain, which only elevated the need for raw materials, while also increasing the European's capacity to conquer and rule new lands. Remote regions of Africa and the Amazon that had been impenetrable and difficult for Europeans to settle started to come under European control behind the onslaught of machine guns and armaments shuttled in on a growing network of train tracks.

By the late 1800s, the European powers were engaged in the "scramble for Africa," strategically colonizing every bit of land, laying down train tracks that would slowly drain Africa of its natural resources in rubber, copper, and other precious materials. As had occurred in the Americas and Asia, local subsistence farmers in Africa were forced to transform their production to serve the global market. Northern Ghana shifted production from nutritious yams to cocoa. Liberia produced rubber; Nigeria, palm oil; Tanzania, sisal; and Uganda, cotton. All of them became dependent on global trade for their subsistence. Even after former colonies in Asia, the Americas, and Africa gained independence in the 1960s and 1970s, exploitative economic relationships with the Global North continued. The example in the box below captures this ongoing dynamic of global economic inequality that is the legacy of colonialism.

Structural Power: A Story of Rich and Poor

[Adapted from Michael Wesch, Kansas State University, anth101.com/book]

Let's look at two communities on opposite ends of a world system today. Rüschlikon, a small village in Switzerland, received over 360 million dollars in tax revenue from a single resident, Ivan Glasenberg, in 2011. That amounts to $72,000 for each of the village's five thousand residents. It is one of the richest communities in the world. Glasenberg is the CEO of Glencore, one of the most powerful companies in the world, specializing in mining and commodities. If we follow the commodity chain back to its source, we find copper mines like the Mopani copper mine in Zambia, where 60 percent of people live on less than $1 per day, the residents struggle to find adequate food and health care, education is difficult to attain, and the air and water are frequently polluted by the mines. The Gross Domestic Product (GDP) per capita in Switzerland is the highest in the world at just over $75,000. Zambia is among the lowest at under $2,000. In fact, Glencore's revenues alone are ten times the entire GDP of Zambia.

Over a ten-year period in the early 2000s, $29 billion dollars' worth of copper was extracted from Zambia, yet Zambia only collected $50 million per year in taxes while spending over $150 million a year to provide electricity for the mines. Zambia was actually losing money on their own resources. How did this happen?

During the "scramble for Africa" the region was proclaimed a British Sphere of Influence administered by Cecil Rhodes and named "Rhodesia." When copper was discovered, it became one of the world's largest exporters of copper; but the wealth did little to improve the lives of Africans. By the time Zambia gained independence in 1964, they were rich in resources but lacked the knowledge and capital to mine those resources. Nonetheless, they successfully operated the mines under national control for over a decade, and their economy grew on their copper profits. By the mid-1970s, they were one of the most prosperous countries in sub-Saharan Africa. But their entire economy depended on that single commodity, and in the 1970s, the price of copper dropped dramatically as Russia flooded the market with it. Like many other countries that depend on exports of natural resources, their economy collapsed along with the prices.

The Zambian economy was in crisis and had to look to the International Monetary Fund and World Bank for big loans. But soon they could not keep up with their loan payments. Like other developing countries, the loans that were supposed to save them became crippling. For every $1 they were receiving in aid from rich countries, they were spending $10 on loan interest. By the year 2000, with copper prices falling again, Zambia was in crisis and could not receive any more loans. The copper mines were privatized and sold to companies like Glencore. They were trapped in a system that left them no more options. They wanted to demand a higher price for their copper, but their impoverished neighboring countries would just undersell them.

Over the next decade, the cost of copper soared, and Glencore made massive profits. But the lives of Zambians did not improve because none of that money found its way into Zambia. As a large multinational corporation, Glencore was able to avoid paying taxes in Zambia through a practice called "transfer pricing." Glencore is made up of several smaller subsidiary companies. Their Zambian subsidiaries sell the copper very cheaply to their subsidiaries in Switzerland, which has very low taxes on copper exports. Then the Swiss company marks up the price to its true market value and sells the copper. On paper, Switzerland is the largest importer of Zambian copper (60 percent) and one of the world's largest exporters of copper, yet very little of this copper ever actually arrives in (and then leaves) Switzerland. This little accounting trick is in part why copper accounts for 71 percent of the exports from Zambia, but only contributes 0.2 percent to their GDP.

This is obviously unfair, but Zambia does not have the financial resources to fight Glencore's army of lawyers. This is just one more chapter in a long history that consistently places Zambia on the weaker end of power. At the dawn of colonization, they faced the military might of the British and lacked the power to defend their land. They entered at the bottom of an emerging global economy and have never had the resources to educate their public and prepare them for success. They now find themselves trapped in cycles of poverty. Without a strong tax base, they cannot fund powerful institutions that could raise health and education standards to create jobs that could diversify the economy.

mobilities
the movement of people, things, and ideas, and the social implications of those movements. Mobilities scholars explore topics such as human migration, tourism, and transportation, and the forces that promote or constrain movement.

Colonialism and ongoing globalization have had a gendered impact as well. That is, men and women have been affected differently by colonialism and global capitalism. For example, among the Taureg in Algeria, women had an active role in tribal politics, could own property, and had a respected status as poets in their society. Their position was in stark contrast to many of their Arab neighbors, but the growing influence of Islamo-Arab cultures in the region has diminished women's positions in society (Keenan 2003). Colonialism eroded the status of many Native American women. For example among the matrilineal Cherokee, the Council of Women had significant power including the right to declare war. As a result the British disparagingly referred to them as a "petticoat government" and took measures to undermine their authority (Strickland n.d.). US officials also instituted a "patriarchal colonialism" that destroyed the social foundations and the more egalitarian gender relations of many native peoples (Guerro 2003).

In more recent times, globalization has resulted in the increased flows of people and things across the globe. These **mobilities** can take many forms, from labor migrations, to refugee flows, to travel and tourism, to elite expatriate communities. Here, too, we see how gender, as a fundamental social relation, shapes these phenomena. Scholars have noted a "feminization of migration" as women move around the world to work in domestic service, childcare, large-scale agriculture, and in factories (Hondagneu-Sotelo 2003). Through constructions of femininity, multinational corporations see them as a docile and cheap workforce, well suited for repetitive, detailed tasks required on global assembly lines. Migration can reconfigure gender relations between men and women. Migrant women may gain status through jobs and new social networks, while men may lose power in both the public and domestic spheres if they suffer unemployment and discrimination in the new country (Hondagneu-Sotelo 2003). Ideas of masculinity and fatherhood are also influenced by migration, as we see in chapter 19, as migrant fathers struggle to remake their role by parenting at a distance.

Global movements and migrations are tied to work but also to pleasure. With the tourism industry, a global sex trade has developed involving both men and women. Eroticized and exoticized ideas of men and women in the Global South play into the fantasies of foreign tourists both for pleasure (Cabezas 2009; Frohlick 2012) and as potential spouses (Constable 2003). Many in the Global South who engage in sexual relations with tourists dream of migrating through marriage to a foreigner (Fernandez 2019). However, often these relationships do not provide the hoped-for outcome, and mail-order brides do not always get the marriages they envisioned (Faier 2007). Global mobilities are intertwined for both work and leisure, and the impact these global movements have on individuals are shaped by factors such as gender, class, nationality, and race.

A gendered, intersectional analysis helps us see the uneven impact globalization has had on people around the world. Globalization provides many benefits to societies including the spread of technology, longer life expectancies, and shared cultural innovations. However, it can also be a source of vulnerability. For instance, the COVID-19 crisis is an example of a global phenomenon that has laid bare the intense interdependence of global economies and societies. Starting in December 2019, a novel coronavirus that causes the deadly COVID-19 disease began to spread throughout the world. The resulting pandemic halted global and local economies and disrupted globalized supply chains. The crisis led to hundreds of thousands of deaths and is expected to markedly change local and global societies, cultural norms, and economies in ways that are yet to be fully appreciated.

Early gendered analyses of the crisis in the United States suggest that shifts in gender roles may be one such result. Jobs that tend to be predominantly held by women (grocery retail workers, nurses, childcare workers) were the ones that were deemed as "essential" early on in the crisis. As a result, heterosexual couples experienced swift role reversals with men providing more childcare and domestic work and women laboring outside the home under often stressful and dangerous conditions. However, as the crisis continued women began to lose their jobs in greater numbers than men, underscoring the inherent vulnerability and inequity of women's labor and income (Institute for Women's Policy Research 2020). Furthermore, for many women around the world the home confinement has increased tensions and has led to a surge in domestic violence: with few support resources operating during the crisis, victims have few options for help. The gendered impact of COVID-19 is shaped by the availability of women's resources. Those who usually have adequate or even abundant resources may lack their former access to reproductive health services, while those with the fewest resources may be particularly vulnerable to the virus itself and may be struggling just to keep their families fed.

CONCLUSION

In this chapter we introduced the key perspectives that unite the chapters in this book: feminism(s), intersectionality, and globalization. We explored how feminism has evolved over time and provided anthropology with essential insights into gender diversity and inequality. The following sections, chapters, and profiles will introduce you to the experiences of men, women, and third-gendered people across the globe. The threads that connect them are intersectional analyses and a focus on globalization that links the local to an economic system that spans the globe. We can best understand the practices and cultures we will read about by focusing on how they are connected in the world system and how individual experiences within that culture are shaped by their context-specific position (race, class, gender, age, etc.). From this vantage point, we can see how our own gendered lives, practices, and patterns of consumption are connected to those people we will be reading about.

REVIEW QUESTIONS

1. Compare and contrast the four primary waves of feminism.

2. How does intersectionality help us understand social inequalities?

3. How do colonialism and globalization contribute to the ongoing global inequalities of wealth and power today?

4. Discuss some positive and negative impacts globalization has had on your own life.

KEY TERMS

first-wave feminism: started in the late 1800s and early 1900s and was focused on women's right to vote.

fourth-wave feminism: began around 2012 to address sexual harassment, body shaming, and rape culture, among other issues. It is characterized by a focus on the global empowerment of women, the greater inclusion of diverse perspectives and voices, and the use of social media in activism.

Global North: does not refer to a geographic region in any traditional sense but rather to the relative power and wealth of countries in distinct parts of the world. The Global North encompasses the rich and powerful regions such as North America, Europe, and Australia.

Global South: does not refer to a geographic region in any traditional sense but rather to the relative power and wealth of countries in distinct parts of the world. The Global South encompasses the poor and less powerful countries in areas such as Latin America, Africa, and Asia.

intersectionality: refers to the interconnected nature of social categories such as race, class, and gender that create overlapping systems of discrimination or disadvantage. The goal of an intersectional analysis is to understand how racism, sexism, and homophobia (for example) interact together to impact our identities and how we live in our society.

mobilities: the movement of people, things, and ideas, and the social implications of those movements. Mobilities scholars explore topics such as human migration, tourism, and transportation, and the forces that promote or constrain movement.

second-wave feminism: 1960s–1980s addressed issues of equal legal and social rights for women. Its emblematic slogan was "the personal is political."

third-wave feminism: began in the 1990s responding to the shortcomings of the Second Wave, namely that it focused on the experiences of upper-middle-class white women. Third Wave feminism is rooted in the idea of women's lives as intersectional, highlighting how race, ethnicity, class, religion, gender, and nationality are all significant factors when discussing feminism.

RESOURCES FOR FURTHER EXPLORATION

- *Feminism is for Everybody* (Pluto, 2000) by bell hooks presents a straightforward explanation of key ideas and concepts in feminism.

- *Iron Jawed Angels* (2003) a film on Alice Paul and the women's suffrage movement in the United States.

- National Public Radio (NPR)—Planet Money story that followed the making of a single T-shirt in 2013: https://apps.npr.org/tshirt/#/title

- National Public Radio (NPR)—"Goats and Soda: Stories of Life in a Changing World," a program exploring health and development globally. There's a whole section devoted to stories on women and girls from around the world: https://www.npr.org/sections/goatsandsoda/

- *Sweetness and Power: The Place of Sugar in Modern History* (1986) by anthropologist Sidney Wilfred Mintz (Penguin Press, 1986) presents a fascinating history of how sugar transformed from an elite luxury good to a staple in the working-class diet and what effect that shift had on the world.

- *The Secret History of Wonder Woman* (2015 Vintage) by Jill Lepore recounts the history of the feminist movement in the United States and the evolution of this iconic superhero. There is also a much less inspiring 2017 film based loosely on the book, *Professor Marston and the Wonder Women*.

- The Story of Stuff Project (https://www.storyofstuff.org/about/) has created a number of award-winning short animated documentaries on the detrimental effects of our global consumption-based economy. Check out the movies under the "Learn" tab on their website.

- United Nations 17 Sustainable Development Goals (SDG) to reach by 2030. All countries have agreed to work toward these goals, and you can track their progress at: https://sdg-tracker.org/. For more statistical information across the globe also see: OurWorldinData.org.

- *We Should All Be Feminists* (Fourth Estate, 2014), a powerful short book by Chimamanda Ngozi Adichie. The acclaimed author also presents her ideas on feminism in a TED talk:

https://www.ted.com/talks/chimamanda_ngozi_adichie_we_
should_all_be_feminists?language=en.

- WIDE+ (Women in Development Europe+), a European feminist
  organization, has gathered articles on the gendered impact of the
  COVID-19 pandemic: https://wideplus.org/2020/03/26/covid-
  19-crisis-from-a-feminist-perspective-overview-of-different-
  articles-published/.

BIBLIOGRAPHY

Cabezas, Amalia. 2009. *Economies of Desire: Sex and Tourism in Cuba and the Dominican Republic*. Philadelphia: Temple University Press.

Constable, Nicole. 2003. *Romance on a Global Stage: Pen Pals, Virtual Ethnography, and "Mail-Order" Marriages*. Berkeley: University of California Press.

Covey, R. Alan. 2013. "Inca Gender Relations, from Household to Empire." In *Gender in Cross-Cultural Perspective*, 6th ed., 70–76. Boston: Pearson Education.

Crenshaw, Kimberlé. 1989. "Demarginalizing the Intersection of Race and Sex: A Black Feminist Critique of Antidiscrimination Doctrine, Feminist Theory and Antiracist Politics." *University of Chicago Legal Forum* 1989, no. 8: https://chicagounbound.uchicago.edu/uclf/vol1989/iss1/8.

———. (2016, December 7). The Urgency of Intersectionality (video). https://youtu.be/akOe5-UsQ2o

Diamond, Jared M. 1999. *Guns, Germs and Steel: The Fates of Human Societies*. New York: W.W. Norton.

Ditch, E. 2006. *Reconstructing Gender: A Multicultural Reader*. New York: McGraw-Hill.

Faier, Lieba. 2007. Filipina Migrants in Rural Japan and Their Professions of Love. *American Ethnologist* 34, no. 1: 148–162.

Fernandez, Nadine T. 2019. "Tourist Brides and Migrant Grooms: Cuban–Danish Couples and Family Reunification Policies." *Journal of Ethnic and Migration Studies* 45, no. 16: 3141–56. https://doi.org/10.1080/1369183X.2018.1547025.

Freedman, Estelle. 2002. *No Turning Back: The History of Feminism and the Future of Women*. New York: Ballantine.

Frohlick, Susan. 2012. *Sexuality, Women, and Tourism: Cross-border Desires through Contemporary Travel*. New York: Routledge.

Guerrero, M. A. Jaimes. 2003. " 'Patriarchal Colonialism' and Indigenism: Implications for Native Feminist Spirituality and Native Womanism." *Hypatia* 18, no. 2 (2003): 58–69. http://www.jstor.org/stable/3811011. Accessed May 8, 2020.

Hondagneu-Sotelo, Pierrette, ed. 2003. *Gender and U.S. Immigration: Contemporary Trends*. Berkeley: University of California Press.

Institute for Women's Policy Research. 2020. "Women Lost More Jobs than Men in almost all Sectors of the Economy." Quick Figures, April, 20120. IWRP

#Q080. https://iwpr.org/wp-content/uploads/2020/04/QF-Jobs-Day-April-FINAL.pdf

Keenan, Jeremy. 2003. "The End of the Matriline? The Changing Roles of Women and Descent amongst the Algerian Tuareg." *Journal of North African Studies* 8, nos. 3–4: 121–162. doi:10.1080/13629380308718519.

Schrock, Richelle D. 2013. "The Methodological Imperatives of Feminist Ethnography." *Journal of Feminist Scholarship* 5 (Fall): 48–60. https://youtu.be/NpYlE_EjX9M

Steger, M. 2013. *Globalization: A Very Short Introduction.* Oxford: Oxford University Press.

Strickland, Rennard. n.d. "Cherokee (tribe)." *The Encyclopedia of Oklahoma History and Culture.* https://www.okhistory.org/publications/enc/entry.php?entry=CH014.

CREDITS

Some of the material in this chapter was authored by Deborah Amory and adapted from *The Art of Being Human: A Textbook for Cultural Anthropology* by Michael Wesch, Kansas State University, licensed under a Creative Commons Attribution-Noncommercial-Share Alike 4.0 License. anth101.com/book.

Part II
South Asia

CIA Maps.

3

South Asia

Introducing the Region

Ina Goel

South Asia is a region with unity in diversity, having at least twenty different dominant languages and over two hundred basic dialects. And yet, most of South Asia continues to remain economically poor and "developing" with gender disparity remaining a real concern at the heart of South Asian unity. The 2019 Global Hunger Index ranks all the major South Asian countries in the "serious" category with Sri Lanka coming in 66th, Nepal 73rd, Bangladesh 88th, Pakistan 94th, and India 102nd out of 117 countries. Women suffer the most, as they have to bear the direct burden of gender inequality and, as a consequence, children experience malnutrition. The 2018 Global Nutrition Report states that on average 49 percent of reproductive-age women in South Asia have anemia, and the prevalence of stunting in the population of children under-five is 32.7 percent, which is significantly greater than the global average of 21.9 percent. There is no data available for those who identify as nonbinary, and there is a long way to go before the data gap can be filled despite the official recognition of "third" gender people in Pakistan, Bangladesh, India, and Nepal. Ironically, in spite of the official recognition of a nonheteronormative gender identity, homosexuality has yet to be decriminalized in most of South Asia with the exception of Nepal and India, having decriminalized homosexuality in 2007 and 2018, respectively.

When the British arrived in India, they foisted Victorian sexual mores on Indian culture, criminalized homosexuality, and saw the "third" gender as a threat to morality and political authority (Bhatt, 2018). The precolonial practice of **dowry**, which was then a self-help institution managed by women, became a colonial tool for covering up the economically devastating British agrarian policies leading to a systematic diminishing

dowry
payments made to the groom's family by the bride's family before marriage.

52

of women's entitlements and worsening gender discrimination in India (Oldenburg, 2002). Scholars argue that in the late nineteenth century, Indians were "humiliated by their colonial status" and became "obsessed with the issues of strength and power" (Datta 2006, 2230). Therefore, to explain their defeat and acceptance of the European notion that the "status of women was integral to the strength of the civilisation," Indian customs were concluded to be "degrading to a woman's status" (Datta 2006, 2230). As a result, women became subjects of reformist movements that took up the challenge of modernity, and thereby, problematic notions of middle class femininity were adopted: these were, in turn, based on oppressive cultural practices impacting the future course of gender relations in South Asia.

Although patriarchy and the caste system (explained later) have undergone continuous changes, they retain their salience through a "social silence" around the "inherited [and colonial] legacies of practicing inequality" in South Asia (Chakravarti 2018). On the one hand, data from India shows that there are approximately 10.6 million missing females, as a preference for boys and male births (son preference) leaves India with a skewed sex ratio plunging further from 903 in 2007 to 898 in 2018 (Chao et al. 2019). On the other hand, lessons from Bangladesh on how gender equity can help overcome socioeconomic constraints and significantly improve health outcomes (see Chowdhury et al. 2013) show how South Asia can be a region full of contradictions. This chapter will provide a regional introduction to South Asia, highlighting unique gender issues specific to this region. In doing so, this introduction section will also equip the readers with a sense of the diverse contexts within which ideologies toward gender stem, both locally and globally.

INDEPENDENCE AND PARTITION

The Indian independence movement spanned almost 90 years from 1857 until August 15, 1947, when India got its independence from the British Raj. The following 1947 partition of British India into two countries, India and Pakistan, is the most violent and bloody founding movement defining two nations' existence in recorded history. Millions were uprooted overnight, and it is estimated that about 75,000 women were abducted and raped during this process of redrawing borders (see Butalia 2017). Additionally, Bangladesh's borders were redrawn first as East Bengal in 1905 when it was attached to Assam as a part of India, then as East Pakistan (after the India-Pakistan partition), and finally as the nation-state of Bangladesh in 1971 (see "Resources for Further Exploration" for link to maps showing the partition process).

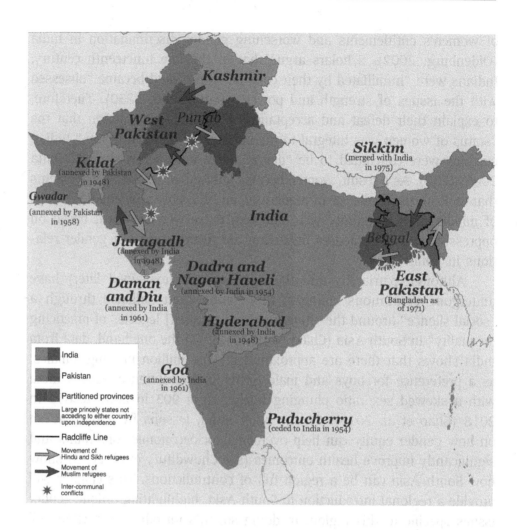

Figure 3.1. Map of the partition of India (1947). Superbenjamin; CC-BY-SA.

During the political partitions, when about twelve million people moved between India and Pakistan in 1947, there was widespread sexual violence. In many instances, women ended up marrying the men who had abducted them, and "because they were now in relationships with men of the 'other' religion, they became 'absences' in their families, absences that also led, in many ways, to an absence of memory" (Butalia 2018, 267). Moreover,

> the idea of women as property—of families, communities, men—underlay the ways in which women's rights were so routinely violated during Partition, under the guise of protection, honour, purity. The violence on women by their own communities . . . was disguised as martyrdom or honour killings and its memories today are almost singularly guarded and recounted by men. (Butalia 2018, 267)

Additionally, practices reinforcing gender inequality in marriage inherited from prepartition times continued for many in India, Pakistan, and

Bangladesh. These practices include Hindu men converting to Islam to take a second wife (without the conversion of the first wife to Islam), nonconsensual polygamy, and divorce customs like **triple talaq** (instant divorce) and **nikah halala**. Other contested practices include mandatory head coverings and seclusion such as **ghoonghat** and **purdah**.

CASTE SYSTEM

The caste system is an obligatory system of graded social stratification based on a person's birth or ancestry morally codified in Manusmriti, "The Laws of Manu," a controversial Hindu scripture. (See "Resources for Further Exploration" for a link to the Laws of Manu.) It was one of the first Sanskrit texts to be translated in 1794 by the British and since then has been used by the colonial government to formulate Hindu law in India. Dividing Hindu society into five groups, called castes, this system laid down the "normative" framework governing and grading all "cultural, economic, religious, spiritual, and political" aspects of social interaction within and between these groups (Simon and Thorat 2020, ii). Furthermore,

> many believe that the groups originated from Brahma, the Hindu God of creation. At the top of the hierarchy were the Brahmins who were mainly teachers and intellectuals and are believed to have come from Brahma's head. Then came the Kshatriyas, or the warriors and rulers, supposedly from his arms. The third slot went to the Vaishyas, or the traders, who were created from his thighs. At the bottom of the heap were the Shudras, who came from Brahma's feet and did all the menial jobs. . . . Outside of this Hindu caste system were the achhoots—the Dalits or the untouchables. (BBC News, 2019)

Since the second century BCE, through the caste system, hierarchies of "quasi-biological groupings" get naturalized by "inherited privilege or stigma," using religion (including Islam and Sikhism) as justification and continue to this day (Simon and Thorat, 2020). Caste discrimination is a chronic human rights violation of Dalits (formerly untouchables) and other persons affected by discrimination, based on their work and descent, found in varying degrees in India, Nepal, Pakistan, Bangladesh, Sri Lanka, and also in diasporic South Asian communities all over the world. According to a compilation report published by the International Dalit Solidarity Network (2019, 6–7):

> The caste system is a strict hierarchical social system based on underlying notions of purity and pollution. Those at the bottom

triple talaq
a form of Islamist divorce used by some Muslims in India that permits a man to legally divorce his wife by simply uttering the word *talaq* (the Arabic word for "divorce") three times orally, in written form or, more recently, in electronic form.

nikah halala
a patriarchal practice whereby women divorced through triple talaq must consummate a second marriage and get divorced again in order to remarry their first husbands.

ghoonghat
a headcovering or headscarf worn by some married Hindu, Jain and Sikh women to cover their heads, and often their faces.

purdah
a practice in certain Muslim and Hindu societies of physical segregation of men and women and the requirement that women cover their bodies in enveloping clothing to conceal their form from men and strangers.

of the system suffer discrimination influencing all spheres of life and violating a cross-section of basic human rights including civil, political, social, economic and cultural rights. Caste discrimination entails social and economic exclusion, segregation in housing, denial and restrictions of access to public and private services, and lack of equal access to education and employment, to mention some effects.

Since its very formation, each caste category aimed to be isolated and socially separated from each other through practicing endogamy (i.e., marrying only within one's caste) (Chakravarti 2018). Despite reformist movements, there is still a stigma associated with intercaste marriages, and love relationships between them are strongly discouraged by families. Even today, many cases of honor killings associated with breaching these social rules continue to arise, particularly targeting women (ANI 2018).

In India, Dalit women often experience violence when attempting to assert their rights to access housing, drinking water, the public distribution system (PDS), education, and basic sanitation services (Irudayam et al. 2015). In Nepal, Dalit rural women are among the most disadvantaged people, scoring at the very bottom for most social indicators, such as literacy (12%), longevity (forty-two years), health, and political participation (Navsarjan Trust et al. 2013). Moreover, there is a rampant problem of caste-based discrimination estimated to affect more than 260 million people, particularly in Asia and Africa (Yokota and Chung 2009).

According to National Family Health Survey (NFHS) data, Dalit women in India die younger than those in the upper-caste category, with the average life expectancy for Dalit women being 14.6 years less than for higher-caste women (Masoodi 2018). Furthermore, disadvantaged groups of women and girls in Bangladesh, including Dalit women, women with disabilities, elderly women, Rohingya refugee women, and women of ethnic minorities face multiple intersecting forms of discrimination due to their gender, health, Indigenous identity, caste, and socioeconomic status (CEDAW 2015).

subaltern
a person from a colonized population who is of low socioeconomic status, displaced to the margins of a society and with little social agency.

CURRENT NATIONALIST STRUGGLES

The relationship between culture and politics often centers on the idea of democracy based on identity and conflict. For instance, ethnic tensions based on the construction of the separate racial identity of ethnic Mongols in Nepal, emerging from differences in cultural practices instead of biological inheritance, shows uses of "race" invoked by those **subaltern** groups who are economically and politically disadvantaged in South Asia (Hangen, 2005). Another example is the denationalization of the people of Nepali origin who claimed to be wrongfully evicted citizens of Bhutan who have been refused the right to return to Bhutan (see Hutt, 2003).

In the politics of belonging in South Asia, there is an overlap between the national, cultural, and ethnic identities of people. For instance, ethno-national conflicts remain, particularly with the history of redrawing Bangladeshi borders. Women are also severely affected in conflict areas, especially in northeast India, with reported cases of mass rapes and sexual violence filed in court by 21 Hmar tribal women in Manipur in 2006; 14 tribal women in the neighboring state of Tripura in 1988; and 37 women of Assam in 1991 with no action taken so far against the perpetrators of violence (WILF 2014).

Efforts for peace and cooperative development are still obstructed by the struggle between India and Pakistan over Kashmir, situating modern South Asia at a decisive crisis in its history (see Bose and Jalal, 2017). On August 5, 2019, the "special status" of the state of Jammu and Kashmir was controversially taken away by the Indian government by dividing it into two union territories and imposing an unprecedented five-month Internet blackout—the longest ever to be imposed in a democracy (Cooper 2020). Scholars predict a possible nuclear war between India and Pakistan fueling further anxieties between the two countries (Toon et al. 2019). Women's voices in the peace processes have largely been absent from the male-dominated Kashmiri nationalist and conflict narratives despite being governed by a female state head for two years (Parashar 2011). Kashmir's marginalized transgender community, mostly working as matchmakers for couples, also struggle with survival for existence and identity under the shadow of curfews and internet blackouts (Bhat 2019).

In August 2019, the Indian government introduced another controversial citizenship policy that required people to prove that they came to the northeast state of Assam by March 24, 1971, the day before Bangladesh declared independence from Pakistan, to obtain citizenship. As a result, 1.9 million people have become "stateless" and stripped of their Indian citizenship because they failed to furnish adequate substantiating documents (BBC 2019). A fact-finding team's research trip to Assam by Women against Sexual Violence and State Repression found that women are the "worst victims" of this process as they are unable to produce "legacy documents" because holding entitlements to land and lineage have historically been guided by patriarchal norms that exclude women from property ownership (Singh 2019). Furthermore, rural women from lower castes and ethnic minority groups face multiple barriers like legal illiteracy and limited knowledge of birth registration procedures, which prevent them from registering births and obtaining birth certificates for their children (CEDAW 2014).

Despite India being created as a secular state during the 1947 partition, the Indian government introduced yet another controversial Citizenship (Amendment) Act in December 2019. This amendment aimed to redefine the category of "illegal immigrant" to include Hindu, Sikh, Parsi, Buddhist, and Christian immigrants from Pakistan, Afghanistan, and Bangladesh who have been living in India for decades without the necessary documentation required to prove their citizenship. Protestors challenging the 2019 Citizenship Amendment in court say that it violates the Indian constitution by discriminating against Muslims, treating them as "second-class citizens" and giving "preferential treatment" to other religious groups (*Economic Times*, 2019). India's increasingly right-wing political climate, which often promotes Hindu nationalism at the expense of other cultures and religions, is also exacerbating fault lines between Hindu and Muslim hijras, a third gender community (Goel, 2019).

To curb the quickly escalating mass protests against the citizenship law all over India, another internet ban was imposed in Assam. It was only when India's first transgender judge, Swati Bidhan Baruah, along with others, filed a petition in court challenging the law that the ban was lifted after nine days of internet blackout in Assam (Agarwala 2019). In other places in India, women led the protests, particularly Muslim women, with a weeks-long sit-in against the citizenship law where some participants have become icons, like eighty-two-year-old toothless Bilkis, endearingly

Figure 3.2. Indians in New Delhi protest against the controversial anti-muslim citizenship amendment (CAA) (2020). Sunil prajapati/Shutterstock.

called "Gangster Granny" (Masih 2020). Thousands of people from the LGBT community who were adversely affected by the citizenship law also marched in protest as many of them were "thrown out of their homes in childhood," and there is an unnecessary burden put on those with name changes and "spelling mistakes" in identity documents (Kuchay 2020). Moreover, gender and sexual minority groups from all across India have been raising their voices in protest, including the All India Network of Sex Workers, Telangana Hijra Intersex Trans Samiti, the Queer Muslim Project, Pink List, TransNow Collective, Birsa Ambedkar Phule Students' Association (BAPSA), National Federation of Indian Women, and many others (Chandra, 2020). Such acts of resistance join forces with global trends in women's movements, like the Aurat March in Pakistan, thereby becoming an intrinsic part of **fourth-wave feminism** (Kurian 2020).

Although isolated, the above examples challenge normative gendered duties toward the process of nation building despite the pressure on women to do the reproductive work of nations—biologically, culturally, and symbolically (see Yuval-Davis 1993). LGBT populations and other gender minority groups who are often forgotten in the process of nation building are also stepping forward to make their voices heard through protests and marches in resistance to a patriarchal and heteronormative process of nation building in South Asia (Saigol 2019). Therefore, the relationship between nationalism, gender, and sexuality is culturally and historically contingent upon each other and is continually evolving and redefining itself in South Asia.

fourth-wave feminism began around 2012 to address sexual harassment, body shaming, and rape culture, among other issues. It is characterized by a focus on the global empowerment of women, the greater inclusion of diverse perspectives and voices, and the use of social media in activism.

Figure 3.3. Pride parade in Mumbai, India 2019. Anna LoFi/Shutterstock.

GENDER-BASED VIOLENCE

Gender inequality is not "one homogeneous phenomenon, but a collection of disparate and inter-linked problems" (Sen 2001, 35). Consequently, gender-based violence is one of the most challenging problems in South Asia. Statistics show that between 2007 and 2016, there were four cases of rape reported every hour in India, making India the most dangerous country for women in the world (Goldsmith and Beresford 2018). After the rape of a twenty-three-year-old student in New Delhi triggered a national uproar, the issue of women's safety in India attracted international media headlines, and social media buzz also declared that India is no place for women (Lakshmi 2012). Since then, many international governments have issued warnings and advised women against solo travel in most countries in South Asia. Feminist observers point out, however, that it is always the women who are issued warnings and who ironically have to be controlled for their own safety and protection instead of the perpetrators of violence.

In the South Asian context, gender-based violence starts at birth or even before. Prenatal sex determination leads to an increasing number of sex-selective abortions and infanticide of girls because of male preference. Therefore, unlike the growing trend in the United States of celebrating parenthood through "gender reveal" parties (King-Miller 2018), after finding out the sex of a child, in India prenatal sex determination has been banned since 1994. Stories of disappointment on the birth of a female child and distribution of sweets on the birth of a male child are so common they have become folklore. There is also a practice of **female genital mutilation/cutting (FGM/C)** among girls who are between six to eight years old in the Bohra communities of India (Lawyers Collective 2017) and Pakistan (Baig 2015), and it is estimated that up to 80 percent of Bohra women have been through this procedure.

In Nepal, intersex children from lower socioeconomic backgrounds suffer from intersex genital mutilation (IGM) practices that are irreversible and harmful (CEDAW 2018). Furthermore, there are known cases of gender-reassignment surgeries being performed on children born with intersex variations in India (Goel 2014; also see Fausto-Sterling 1993). The medical interventions and genetic deselection are based on the presupposition that intersex traits are treated as disorders in South Asia (see Srishti Madurai 2019). Such operations by medical doctors in hospitals are done to prefix a gender that can then be assigned to an intersex child based on their cosmetically "fixed" perceived sex characteristic because there is shame in being a parent to an intersex child in India (Goel 2018a). Parents get away with insisting that the intersex child be surgically rendered a boy

female genital mutilation/cutting (FGM/C) surgeries to alter the external female genitalia. It may include cliterotectomy, removing and/or suturing the labia.

even though it is easier to create functional female organs in cases of sex-selective surgeries in India (Sharma, 2014). However, as an exception, in April 2019, the Indian state of Tamil Nadu became the first in Asia and second globally to ban sex-selective surgeries for intersex children (Daksnamurthy 2019).

On December 5, 2019, a controversial Transgender Person's Bill became Transgender Persons (Protection of Rights) Act in India (see links in "Resources for Further Exploration"). Under this act, intersex births are inaccurately assigned as transgender births. Such confusion exists because often gender identity, gender expression, and sex characteristics are conflated terms. Furthermore, the vague language of the Transgender Persons (Protection of Rights) Act implies that surgery—plus approval from a medical authority and district magistrate—is required for a person to legally change their gender identity. The Transgender Persons (Protection of Rights) Act also defines family as only those related by blood or law despite the National Human Rights Commission survey conveying that only 2 percent of transgender persons in India live with their biological families, failing to accommodate the alternative kinship structures of the remaining 98 percent trans population (Goel, 2018b).

As India is a strongly **patriarchal and patrilocal** society, there is a significant preference for having sons over daughters. In a majority of cases, after marriage, the daughter moves into a joint household with the husband's family with a dowry. Though illegal since 1961, dowries in India are widespread and are given by the bride's family to the groom's: this practice forces women to be seen as a liability by their families. Such a mindset is so ingrained in the cultural fabric that girls as young as seven years old from poverty-stricken families are forced to marry illegally, resulting in underage brides (Strochlic and Khandelwal, 2019). At present, India has the highest number of child brides in the world (Wangchuk, 2018). To tackle this problem, the Indian government came out with innovative "Dear Daughter Schemes" aiming to encourage the birth of female children by gifting one hundred thousand Indian rupees (approx. 1400 USD) to the first and second daughters of a family for their wedding after their eighteenth birthday (*Times of India*, 2019). Similar sentiments have also been echoed by full-page newspaper advertisements on ways a father can save ten million Indian rupees (approx. US$140,000), which can then be invested in his daughter's wedding—in which dowry has been camouflaged as a "gift" for the daughter (Roy 2016).

Subverting the gaze on the daughter as being a "costly" property, other attempts in the form of public information films from India with antidowry themes have centered themselves around the idea that dowry is the amount of money paid by the bride to "buy" the groom and thereby

patriarchal (patriarchy) a dynamic system of power and inequality that privileges men and boys over women and girls in social interactions and institutions.

patrilocal married individuals live with or near the husband's father's family.

insinuate that it is, in fact, the boy who should be treated as property by turning them into "objects" (Dhillon 2016). Reengineering new ideas with such role reversals is equally problematic as this becomes a harbinger of the same patriarchal notions of ownership and control that lead to gender inequality. But desperate attempts like these satirical public service advertisements by the Indian government aim to attack the notions of family prestige—the weight of which is placed on women—by turning the tables on men.

According to the 2019 Global Report published by OECD Development Centre's Social Institutions and Gender Index (SIGI), the lifetime prevalence of domestic violence against women is 25 percent in Nepal, 29 percent in India, 53 percent in Bangladesh, and 85 percent in Pakistan (see link to SIGI in "Resources for Further Exploration"). Within the same report, it has also been found that the proportion of the female population justifying domestic violence is 43 percent in Nepal, 22 percent in India, 28 percent in Bangladesh, and 42 percent in Pakistan. Examples highlighting the rural-urban divide bring to light the ongoing practices of violence against women through "feudal laws" of disinheritance and forced marriages that lead to "blade-cutting," "acid-throwing, stove-burning homicide and nose-cutting" to take revenge from women (Times News Network, 2010; Niaz, 2004, 60). In a majority of South Asian countries, marital rape is not recognized (e.g., Afghanistan, Bangladesh, India, and Pakistan) or the penalties are not severe (e.g., Nepal). Given the rampant practices of gender-based violence in South Asia, it is an underrecognized cause of injury and deaths among women, LGBT communities, and gender-diverse populations.

CONCLUSION

According to the 2019 Global Report published by OECD Development Centre's Social Institutions and Gender Index (SIGI) that measures discrimination against women in social institutions including 180 country notes and ranking 120 countries, there is "very high" gender inequality in Pakistan and Bangladesh and "medium" levels of the same in Nepal and India. Such disparity in terms of gender equality appears paradoxical, when on the one hand there are several countries with examples of female heads of government: Sri Lanka, India, Bangladesh, and Pakistan. This is a feat yet to be achieved even by the United States. And yet, despite allocating for political participation of women, women's agency in the political process is debatable and often seen as a kind of tokenism that does not lead to gender equality (Ban and Rao 2008).

The gender disparity in South Asia demands more local explanations compared to other parts of the world to understand the dichotomous contradiction in attitudes and practices toward gender and sexuality. Inclusion of gender-diverse people, particularly intersex births and the "third" gender population in indices measuring sex ratios and other aspects of gender inequality in South Asia needs to be developed globally. Insufficient data further marginalize the most vulnerable population and widen the gender disparity data gap between different gender and sexual minorities in South Asia.

On the one hand, menstruating Goddess Kamakhya is worshipped in the Indian state of Assam (Das 2008), on the other, in Maharashtra, poor women sugarcane harvesters, some of whom are still in their twenties, are forced to have hysterectomies to stop menstruating (Pandey 2019). Similarly, transphobia and rampant acts of violence against people from the "third" gender contradict the revered attitude toward those who are simultaneously worshipped as cultural demigoddesses in India (Goel 2019). Such ironic regional inequity stretching over the same geographic region becomes a barrier to finding a universal solution to the problem of gender disparity in South Asia. As a consequence, there is a need to strengthen local innovations that aim to bridge the gaps between the rural-urban, class-caste demographic divide of women, nonbinary, and LGBT populations in South Asia.

The chapters in "Part II: South Asia" present anthropological research that showcases some of the ethnic and gender diversity and struggles presented in this introduction to the region. Chapter 4 explores how patriarchy and ethnic and caste hierarchies combine to limit women's access to legal citizenship in Nepal, depriving them of the attendant benefits of such a status. This chapter presents an example of how the ethnic diversity of the region and legacies of the caste system complicate the politics of belonging and disadvantage women's and third-gendered people's access to the rights and privileges of being a legal citizen. Chapter 6 focuses on the Sherpas, an ethnic group in Nepal, and the push to incorporate Sherpa women into wage labor as a way to advance this impoverished country's economic development. However, incorporation into wage labor may not actually benefit the women tasked with implementing this national development strategy. Chapter 5 explores gender diversity, presenting an analysis of the kinship and family structures that operate among the third-gender Hijras in India. Finally, the two profiles at the end of this introduction to the region introduce us to two nonprofit groups addressing the issue of violence against women: one in India and one in the Southeast Asian nation of Vietnam.

KEY TERMS

dowry: payments made to the groom's family by the bride's family before marriage.

female genital mutilation/cutting (FGM/C): surgeries to alter the external female genitalia. It may include cliterotectomy, removing and/or suturing the labia.

fourth-wave feminism: began around 2012 to address sexual harassment, body shaming, and rape culture, among other issues. It is characterized by a focus on the global empowerment of women, the greater inclusion of diverse perspectives and voices, and the use of social media in activism.

ghoonghat: a headcovering or headscarf worn by some married Hindu, Jain and Sikh women to cover their heads, and often their faces.

nikah halala: a patriarchal practice whereby women divorced through triple talaq must consummate a second marriage and get divorced again in order to remarry their first husbands.

patriarchal (patriarchy): a dynamic system of power and inequality that privileges men and boys over women and girls in social interactions and institutions.

patrilocal: married individuals live with or near the husband's father's family.

purdah: a practice in certain Muslim and Hindu societies of physical segregation of men and women and the requirement that women cover their bodies in enveloping clothing to conceal their form from men and strangers.

subaltern: a person from a colonized population who is of low socioeconomic status, displaced to the margins of a society and with little social agency.

triple talaq: a form of Islamist divorce used by some Muslims in India that permits a man to legally divorce his wife by simply uttering the word *talaq* (the Arabic word for "divorce") three times orally, in written form or, more recently, in electronic form.

RESOURCES FOR FURTHER EXPLORATION

- Global Hunger Index (2019) https://www.globalhungerindex.org/results.html.

- Global Nutrition Report (2018) https://globalnutritionreport. org/resources/nutrition-profiles/asia/southern-asia/#profile.

- Maps illustrating the partition process by Pritchett, W. Frances, Columbia University. http://www.columbia.edu/itc/mealac/ pritchett/00maplinks/modern/maps1947/maps1947.html.

- The Laws of Manu. https://www.sacred-texts.com/hin/manu/ (Translator: George Buhler).

- Global Report published by OECD Development Centre's Social Institutions and Gender Index (SIGI) (2019). https://www. oecd.org/development/sigi-2019-global-report-bc56d212-en. htm.

- Transgender Persons (Protection of Rights) Bill (2019) http:// prsindia.org/billtrack/transgender-persons-protection-rights- bill-2019.

- Transgender Persons (Protection of Rights) Act India (2019) http://socialjustice.nic.in/writereaddata/UploadFile/TG%20 bill%20gazette.pdf.

BIBLIOGRAPHY

Agarwala, Tora. 2019. "Taken Offline for Nine Days, Assam Realises Internet Is Much More Than Social Media." *The Indian Express*, December 21, 2019.

ANI. 2018. "Honour Killing: Parents Burn Daughter for Intercaste Marriage." *Business Standard.* December 24. https://www.business-standard.com/ article/news-ani/honour-killing-parents-burn-daughter-for-intercaste-mar- riage-118122400295_1.html.

Avis, Daniel. 2016. "Cannes 'Burkini' Ban: What Do Muslim Women Think?" *BBC News.* August 13. https://www.bbc.com/news/world-europe-37062354

Baig, Saima. 2015. "Female Genital Mutilation: Pakistan's Well-Kept Secret." *Nation.* November 24, 2015.

Ban, R., and V. Rao. 2008. "Tokenism or Agency? The Impact of Women's Res- ervations on Village Democracies in South India." *Economic Development and Cultural Change, 56,* no. 3: 501–530.

BBC News. 2019. "What Is India's Caste System?" June 19. https://www.bbc. com/news/world-asia-india-35650616.

———. 2019. Assam NRC: What Next for 1.9 Million 'Stateless' Indians? August 31.

Bhat, Adnan. 2019. In India, Kashmir's Transgender Community Struggles to Survive under the Shadow of Conflict. *South China Morning Post.* Septem- ber 28, 2019.

Bhatt, Amy. 2018. "India's Sodomy Ban, Now Ruled Illegal, Was a British Colonial Legacy. *Conversation,* September 13.

Bose, Sugata, and Ayesha Jalal. 2017. *Modern South Asia: History, Culture, Political Economy*. London: Routledge.

Butalia, Urvashi. 2017. *The Other Side of Silence: Voices from the Partition of India*. New York: Penguin.

———. 2018. Looking Back on Partition. *Contemporary South Asia*, 26, no. 3: 263–269.

CEDAW (United Nations Committee on the Elimination of Discrimination against Women) (2015). Concluding Observations—Bangladesh 2015 CEDAW/C/BGD/CO/8, CEDAW, New York.

———. 2014. Concluding Observations on the Combined Fourth and Fifth Periodic Reports of India, CEDAW/C/IND/4-5, CEDAW, New York.

———. 2018. Intersex Genital Mutilations Human Rights Violations of Children with Variations of Reproductive Anatomy. NGO Report to the Sixth Report of Nepal CEDAW. http://intersex.shadowreport.org/public/2018-CEDAW-Nepal-NGO-Intersex-IGM.pdf.

Chakravarti, Uma. 2018. *Gendering Caste: Through a Feminist Lens*. New Delhi: SAGE.

Chandra, Jagriti. 2020. Anti-CAA Stir: Queer Groups, Sex Workers Take Centre Stage. *Hindu* January 4, 2020.

Chao, F., P. Gerland, A. R. Cook, and L. Alkema. 2019. Systematic Assessment of the Sex Ratio at Birth for all Countries and Estimation of National Imbalances and Regional Reference Levels. *Proceedings of the National Academy of Sciences* 116, no. 19: 9303–11.

Chowdhury, A. M. R., A. Bhuiya, M. E. Chowdhury, S. Rasheed, Z. Hussain, and L. C. Chen. 2013. "The Bangladesh Paradox: Exceptional Health Achievement Despite Economic Poverty." *Lancet* 382, no. 9906: 1734–45.

Cooper, Havovi. 2020. "Kashmir's 5-Month Internet Blackout is the Longest Ever Imposed in a Democracy—and It's Stifling Local Workers." *Business Insider India*. January 11, 2020.

Daksnamurthy, Aananth. 2019. "1st in India and Asia, and 2nd globally, Tamil Nadu Bans Sex-Selective Surgeries for Infants." *Print*, August 31, 2019.

Dhillon, Amrit. 2016. " 'I Paid the Price, I Own Your Son': Indian Brides Fight Back in Anti-Dowry Films." *Guardian*, February 3, 2016.

Datta, A. B. 2006. "Gendering Oral History of Partition: Interrogating Patriarchy." *Economic and Political Weekly* 41, no. 22: 2229–35.

Das, M. 2008. "Menstruation as Pollution: Taboos in Simlitola, Assam." *Indian Anthropologist* 38, no. 2: 29–42.

Economic Times. 2019. Citizenship (Amendment) Act 2019: What Is It and Why Is It Seen as a Problem. December 31.

Fausto-Sterling, A. 1993. "The Five Sexes: Why Male and Female Are Not Enough." *Sciences* 33, no. 2: 20–24.

Goel, I. 2014. "Beyond the Gender Binary." *Economic & Political Weekly* 49, no. 15: 77–78.

———. 2018a. "What Does It Mean to Be a Hijra Mother?" *Economic & Political Weekly Engage* 53, no. 8.

———. 2018b. "Transgender Identities." *Economic & Political Weekly* 53, no. 36: 4–5.

———. 2019. "India's Third Gender Rises Again." *Sapiens,* September 26.

Goldsmith, B., and M. Beresford. 2018. "Exclusive—India Most Dangerous Country for Women with Sexual Violence Rife—Global Poll." *Thompson Reuters Foundation News*, June 26.

Global Hunger Index. 2019. https://www.globalhungerindex.org/results.html.

Global Nutrition Report. 2018. https://globalnutritionreport.org/resources/nutrition-profiles/asia/southern-asia/#profile.

Hangen, S. 2005. "Race and the Politics of Identity in Nepal." *Ethnology* 44, no. 1: 49–64

Hutt, Michael. 2003. *Unbecoming Citizens: Culture, Nationhood, and the Flight of Refugees from Bhutan*. New Delhi: Oxford University Press.

Irudayam, A., J. P. Mangubhai, and J. G. Lee. 2015. *Dalit Women Speak Out: Caste, Class and Gender Violence in India*. Zubaan: New Delhi.

International Dalit Solidarity Network. 2019. Caste Discrimination and Human Rights. https://idsn.org/wp-content/uploads/2019/12/UNcompilation-March-2019-3.pdf.

King-Miller, Lindsay. 2018. Why Gender Reveal Parties Have Been So Widely Embraced—and Reviled. *Vox*, July 31.

Kuchay, Bilal. 2020. India's LGBTQ Community Joins Citizenship Law Protests. *Al Jazeera*, January 3.

Kurian, Alka. 2020. "Indian Women Protest New Citizenship Laws, Joining a Global 'Fourth Wave' Feminist Movement." *Conversation*, February 25.

Lakshmi, Rama. 2012. "National Uproar over Young Woman's Death Triggers Public Conversation about Rape." *Washington Post,* December 29. https://www.washingtonpost.com/world/asia_pacific/national-uproar-over-young-womans-death-triggers-public-conversation-about-rape/2012/12/29/183f9762-51ab-11e2-835b-02f92c0daa43_story.html

Lawyers Collective. 2017. "Female Genital Mutilation—A Guide to Eliminating the FGM Practice in India." http://www.lawyerscollective.org/wp-content/uploads/2012/07/Female-Genital-Mutilation-A-guide-to-eliminating-the-FGM-practice-in-India.pdf.

Masih, Niha. 2020. India's First-Time Protesters: Mothers and Grandmothers Stage Weeks-Long Sit-In against Citizenship Law. *Washington Post*, January 13.

Masoodi, Ashwaq, and Ajai Sreevatsan. 2018. *Dalit Women in India Die Younger Than Upper Caste Counterparts: Report*. Live Mint (website). https://www.livemint.com/Politics/Dy9bHke2B5vQcWJJWNo6QK/Dalit-women-in-India-die-younger-than-upper-caste-counterpar.html.

Niaz, U. 2004. "Women's Mental Health in Pakistan." *World Psychiatry* 3, no. 1: 60–62.

Oldenburg, T. Veena. 2002. *Dowry Murder: The Imperial Origins of a Cultural Crime*. New York: Oxford University Press.

Pandey, G. 2019. "Why are Menstruating Women in India Removing Their Wombs?" *BBC News*, July 5.

Parashar, S. 2011. "Gender, Jihad, and Jingoism: Women as Perpetrators, Planners, and Patrons of Militancy in Kashmir." *Studies in Conflict & Terrorism* 34, no. 4: 295–317.

Pritchett, W. Frances. Maps Showing the Partition Process. Columbia University. http://www.columbia.edu/itc/mealac/pritchett/00maplinks/modern/maps1947/maps1947.html.

Roy, Vaishna. 2016. "It's Not Dowry, It's a Gift." *Hindu*, February 5.

Saigol, Rubina. 2019. "The Past, Present and Future of Feminist Activism in Pakistan." *Herald*, July 15. https://herald.dawn.com/news/1398878.

Sen, Amartya. 2001. "The Many Faces of Gender Inequality." *New Republic*, September 17.

Sharma, Radha. 2014. "Parents Prefer Male Child in Intersex Operations in Gujrat." *Times of India*, February 5.

SIGI. 2019. Global Report: OECD Development Centre's Social Institutions and Gender Index. https://www.oecd.org/development/sigi-2019-global-report-bc56d212-en.htm.

Simon, L., and S. Thorat. 2020. "Why a Journal on Caste?" *CASTE / A Global Journal on Social Exclusion* 1, no. 1: i–vii.

Singh, Ananya. 2019. "Women 'Worst Victims' of NRC: Gendered and Discriminatory Nature of the Register Revealed." *Citizen*, November 29.

Srishti, Madurai. 2019. http://srishtimadurai.blogspot.com/.

Strochlic, Nina, and Saumya Khandelwal. 2019. "India's Forgotten Child Brides." *National Geographic*, April 19.

The Laws of Manu. https://www.sacred-texts.com/hin/manu/.

Times of India. 2019. " 'Vahli Dikri Yojana' Launched to Save Gujrat's daughters. July 3. https://timesofindia.indiatimes.com/city/ahmedabad/vahli-dikri-yojana-launched-to-save-gujarats-daughters/articleshow/70051134.cms.

Times News Network. 2010. "Man Who Slashed Girls with Blade Nabbed." December 7. https://timesofindia.indiatimes.com/city/delhi/Man-who-slashed-girls-with-blade-nabbed/articleshow/7056915.cms.

Times News Network. 2018. "Take Steps to End Bigamy among Hindus: Law Panel." September 4. https://timesofindia.indiatimes.com/india/take-steps-to-end-bigamy-among-hindus-law-panel/articleshow/65663477.cms.

Toon, O. B., C. G. Bardeen, A. Robock, L. Xia, H. Kristensen, M. McKinzie, R. J. Peterson, C. S. Harrison, N. S. Lovenduski, and R. P. Turco. 2019. "Rapidly Expanding Nuclear Arsenals in Pakistan and India Portend Regional and Global Catastrophe." *Science Advances* 5, no. 10: eaay5478.

Transgender Persons (Protection of Rights) Act India. 2019. http://socialjustice.nic.in/writereaddata/UploadFile/TG%20bill%20gazette.pdf

Transgender Persons (Protection of Rights) Act India. 2019. http://socialjustice.nic.in/writereaddata/UploadFile/TG%20bill%20gazette.pdf

UCA News. 2017. "Report on Hindu Polygamy Draws Mixed Reaction in Bangladesh." August 22. https://www.ucanews.com/news/report-on-hindu-polygamy-draws-mixed-reaction-in-bangladesh/80061.

Wangchuk, N. Rinchen. 2018. "India Has the Highest Number of Child Brides in the World: How Do We Deal With It." *Better India*, April 19.

WILPF (Women's International League for Peace and Freedom). 2014. Caught between Arms: The State of Women's Rights in India. http://wilpf.org/wp-content/uploads/2014/07/CEDAWWILPF-India-shadow-report.pdf.

Wojcik, Nadine. 2017. "Why Do Women Hide Their Hair? *Deutsche Welle*, March 31. https://p.dw.com/p/2aP9K.

Yuval-Davis, N. 1993. "Gender and Nation." *Ethnic and Racial Studies* 16, no. 4: 621–632.

PROFILE: BLANK NOISE: STREET ACTIONS AND DIGITAL INTERVENTIONS AGAINST STREET SEXUAL HARASSMENT IN INDIA

Hemangini Gupta

When Jasmeen Patheja was an undergraduate student in the southern Indian city of Bengaluru (formerly Bangalore) in 2002, she began taking public transport frequently. As she rode buses, took auto-rickshaws, and walked along city streets, she found herself subjected to the range of acts that constitute street sexual harassment and assault: groping, winking, pinching, lewd comments, and men pushing up against her in public. In South Asia, street sexual harassment is often dismissed with the use of the colloquial term "eve teasing" to describe it. As "teasing," it becomes seen as a form of harmless banter, even play, something that can be brushed aside and not taken seriously.

Patheja began asking her friends and classmates if they also experienced such harassment—and they did. The challenge was in bringing people to recognize that what they considered to be routine behavior was in fact harassment; it was so normalized as an aspect of everyday life that women came to expect it every time they stepped out of their homes. She created Blank Noise in 2003 as a community arts project to respond to such harassment through street interventions and public actions. "Blank" references the feeling of numbness and disbelief felt after being harassed; "Noise" indexes the simultaneous eruption of confusion, anger, hurt, and pain—a cacophony of mixed signals.

Since 2003, Blank Noise has invited volunteers to join a range of innovative and hard-hitting public actions and digital interventions.

Figure 3.4. The street intervention "Y R U Looking at Me." Jasmeen Patheja/Blank Noise.

Figure 3.5. Founder/Director of Blank Noise, artist Jasmeen Patheja. Arvind Rajan.

Initially these were oriented toward raising public awareness about street sexual harassment as a criminal offense (punishable by Indian law) and thus a serious infraction. For example, in one street action, volunteers—mostly young women—appeared at a busy intersection when the streetlights turned red. They walked across the zebra crossing to face the sea of commuters waiting for their light to turn; on their T-shirts were pasted one letter of the phrase "Y R U LOOKING AT ME?" In another, volunteers fanned out on the railings of a bustling thoroughfare where many of them had been groped and harassed in the past. During the intervention, however, they occupied the space not as anxious women but as confident members of a joint action. Women leaned back on the railings, looking passersby right in the eye, lounging in public, and enjoying the feeling of occupying public space as watchers rather than as the watched. When small crowds began to gather, other volunteers handed out pamphlets describing street sexual harassment as a serious offense and engaging in conversations around the experience of it.

Volunteers are called "action heroes," "sheroes," or "theyroes"—those who actively subvert the dominant experience of being harassed to question, engage, and subvert expected ways in which gendered bodies occupy public spaces. More recent interventions engender conversations

Figure 3.6. "Talk to Me," action "sheroes." Jasmeen Patheja/Blank Noise.

around public space. In one intervention, "Talk to Me," volunteers ventured into a dark stretch of road that was locally termed "Rapist's Lane." Here they set up tables and invited passersby to stop and chat with them. Participants across socioeconomic class, caste, and gender affiliations were able to move beyond stereotypes of each other to actually converse; each interaction ended with the Blank Noise volunteer offering their guest a rose. The aim was to reshape "Rapist Lane" into "Safest Lane" through respectful conversation and interaction.

Currently Blank Noise is working on "I Never Ask for It," a project ongoing since 2004 in which they invite people to share clothes that they wore while being harassed along with a brief note. All kinds of clothes have been collected over the years toward a final exhibit, intended as a massive material testimony to the widespread prevalence of harassment and evidence that it is not attire that invites unwanted attention. People are invited to bring the clothes they wore when harassed or abused, and these "garment testimonials" represent violations across spaces of home, street, and work. Through "I Never Ask for It" Blank Noise intends to put an end to the consistent use of victim blaming in sexual assault.

Blank Noise is volunteer driven and supported online at blanknoise. org.

Figure 3.7. "I Never Ask For It." Photo by Jasmeen Patheja/Blank Noise.

PROFILE: VIETNAM WOMEN'S SHELTER: CONTRADICTIONS AND COMPLEXITIES

Lynn Kwiatkowski

Domestic violence occurs all over the world. Violence perpetrated by husbands against their wives is a widespread problem in Vietnamese society, despite the approval in 2007 of the first law to overtly make domestic violence illegal. The only survey conducted on a national level in Vietnam, from 2009 to 2010, found that 58 percent of the women interviewed who had ever been married reported experiencing at least one form of domestic violence perpetrated by their husband in their lifetime (including physical, sexual, or emotional violence), and 27 percent had experienced domestic violence during the previous twelve months (GSO, UN-JPGE, and WHO 2010, 21). Anthropologists have been contributing to our understanding of domestic violence cross-culturally through their ethnographic research and their work to develop measures to end violence toward women. This profile explores the contradictions and complexities that can emerge as global values and structures addressing gender violence are translated at the local level into specific societies by examining a Hanoi shelter for women experiencing domestic violence that was originally based on a European model of shelters. (I will refer to this shelter using a pseudonym, "Vietnam Women's Shelter," to protect the identities of the participants in my research study.) As part of contemporary globalization processes involving the circulation of gender ideologies, funding, and professional expertise among diverse societies, Western governments and Western-supported international organizations have introduced to Vietnamese society gender discourses and institutional frameworks that provide a new value regime. These Western ideas include condemning gender violence, novel modes of assistance for women experiencing domestic violence, and innovative approaches to preventing domestic and other forms of gender violence. Some Vietnamese government personnel have reinterpreted elements of Western orientations to gender violence to more closely support cultural and political values of the Vietnamese state and the local sociocultural systems within which abused women's lives are embedded.

In the mid-1980s, the ruling Communist Party implemented a set of economic policy reforms, referred to as "renovation," or *doi moi* policies, which instituted a socialist-oriented market economy. Social reforms also emerged, including the expansion of international and local nongovernmental organizations. These reforms included Vietnam's greater engagement with international organizations, such as the UN, and global social movements to end violence toward women. While the Vietnamese government has promoted gender equality since the 1940s, domestic violence has persisted. Some of the sources of husbands' abuse of their wives are patriarchal ideologies and patrilineal kinship that have been, in part, influenced by Confucianism, which penetrated Vietnamese culture as early as the period of Chinese colonization, beginning in 111 BCE. With recent renovation policies, and an associated renewal of the household economy, traditional family and gender ideologies have been reemphasized by the Vietnamese government and society, while gender equality is simultaneously reinforced through new laws and practices. Western discourses introduced by international organizations, particularly since the 1990s, asserting women's right to be free of gender discrimination and violence (including within the home), conflict with recently revitalized traditional Confucian values that promote, in part through government-sponsored programs, women's responsibilities to ensure their families' happiness, including their duty to meet their husbands' needs. Vietnamese women who are abused by their husbands negotiate these two value systems as they seek assistance in ending their husbands' violence.

Vietnam Women's Shelter is one of only approximately four shelters in the country that have characteristics similar to Western shelters. It began as a project sponsored by the Spanish government's Spanish Agency for International Development Co-operation (AECID) and was implemented in 2007 in conjunction with the Vietnam Women's Union's Center for Women and Development (CWD). The Vietnam Women's Union is a national mass organization largely financially supported by the ruling Communist Party, making the shelter a government-funded institution. This type of shelter constituted a new approach to domestic violence in Vietnam, involving housing abused women and their children for up to three months, or longer if needed. It provides services at no cost to the women, including safe accommodation, employment orientation, vocational training, legal assistance, psychological counseling, health care, education, and other services (Kwiatkowski 2011). Shelter residents can also continue to receive follow-up support for up to two years. The counselors of the Women's Union CWD also work with abusive husbands. Most current and former Vietnam Women's Shelter residents I interviewed found the assistance they received at the shelter to be integral to their emotional, social, and economic survival and their ability to address the domestic violence.

While the services of Vietnam Women's Shelter were highly beneficial to many shelter residents, the shelter personnel and abused women also faced difficulties. Although abused women accessing the shelter's services praised the help they received, many also found contradictory orientations to their situation of violence from state personnel in their local communities, including local leaders of the Women's Union. The center personnel strongly prioritized the safety of the abused women and their children, advocating ideas such as women's potential autonomy from their abusive husbands. Conforming to the strong cultural value placed on women's integration within their families and communities, ensuring protection and support for an abused woman who would like to return to their communities, and carrying out formal government procedures for addressing domestic violence (such as reporting domestic violence to the nearest police station in the women's community, the government commune People's Committee, or the community's leaders), the shelter also contacts local government authorities from an abused woman's community and her family, with the woman's permission, and, in some cases, develops a plan with the woman to reintegrate into her community. This is mandated, according to a counselor working with Vietnam Women's Shelter and the CWD because this shelter "belongs to the [government supported] Central Committee of the Vietnam Women's Union. . . . We have to work with the local authorities." The counselor further stated that "our solution is very different from those of shelters in foreign countries. [This is a shelter that] has to work with the community authorities, other relevant [government] agencies, the [abused woman's] family, and the abuser. Then, this is a good opportunity to communicate with them. In order to solve a case [of domestic violence], we need to change the knowledge and understanding of the whole community, the people around [the abused woman]. It is a circle, starting with the individual [abused woman], then interacting with the family, and then the community. As a result, their awareness of domestic violence will be changed. Communication about domestic violence prevention and the domestic violence law is then based on this case."

Abused women found that the local state personnel's views and practices were, however, often antithetical to Vietnam Women's Shelter's priorities. For example, drawing on traditional gender and family ideologies and state laws, some police officers protected abusive husbands from punishment rather than ensuring the safety of the abused women; some abused women encountered corruption in the judicial system; some Women's Union leaders encouraged its members, during local level meetings of the Women's Union, to meet their husbands' needs; and some government officials, who are only minimally educated about gender violence, blamed women for the violence from their husbands and pressured them to return to their families through government required reconciliation processes. A counselor working with the shelter said, "The commune [level] Women's Union prioritizes reconciliation. . . . It is very common that when the victim returns to her commune [with shelter personnel] to work with relevant [state] agencies, they will judge her behavior rather than focus on handling the husband's violent behavior. . . . And the abuser once again thinks that he has done nothing wrong, that it is her fault. Therefore, they don't change their behavior because they haven't done anything wrong." She continued, "[In one case of a woman who had experienced domestic violence], we had a meeting at the [commune level government] People's Committee. All the related people sat together. There were many people from her husband's family, and they blamed her for having many faults, such as not being clever, being dirty, and having other faults. Then they asked us, 'Why do you support a case like this? The next time, you should learn a lesson from your experience; you shouldn't support such a woman.' . . . Participants [of the meeting] were the [shelter personnel], a woman from the [government] Family Department, the Women's Union, the police. They criticized us for helping her." If abused women were not already situated at Vietnam Women's Shelter, which has limited capacity, there was no (or very little) long-term protection provided by local state personnel to abused women.

The multiple, contradictory Women's Union and other Vietnamese government discourses about domestic violence depict social and cultural change that is occurring as global ideologies of gender violence are introduced into Vietnamese society and as the government shifts its economic orientation. Having been initially introduced and financially supported by the Spanish government's international development agency, AECID, the Vietnam Women's Shelter provides an example of how globalization processes circulate Western professional expertise, new values (including gender, marital, and family values), and innovative social approaches and infrastructures to assist marginalized women. While often helpful to abused women, as Western approaches to gender violence are implemented in Vietnamese society, Vietnamese people interpret them in culturally meaningful ways that sometimes conflict with Western cultural views of gender relations, marriage, and family. Women's Union and other Vietnamese government discourses about domestic violence also demonstrate the multilayered state approaches to domestic violence that are being negotiated by state actors. Demonstrations of the value of shelters of this type through anthropological research and advocacy, specifically the shelter personnel's approach to domestic violence that prioritizes the safety and needs of the women (and of the complexities Vietnam Women's Shelter personnel face) can contribute to making access to support and protection a reality for abused women in need.

Figure 3.8. The proceeds of this Women's Union–sponsored shop directly support women and children survivors of domestic violence and human trafficking who live temporarily in shelters in Vietnam. Lynn Kwiatkowski.

RESOURCES FOR FURTHER EXPLORATION

- Kwiatkowski, Lynn. 2016. "Feminist Anthropology: Approaching Domestic Violence in Northern Việt Nam." In *Mapping Feminist Anthropology in the Twenty-First Century,* edited by Ellen Lewin and Leni M. Silverstein, 234–255. New Brunswick, NJ: Rutgers University Press.

- Kwiatkowski, Lynn. 2011. "Domestic Violence and the 'Happy Family' in Northern Vietnam." *Anthropology Now* 3, no. 3: 20–20.

- Merry, Sally Engle. 2009. *Gender Violence: A Cultural Perspective.* Malden, MA; Oxford: Wiley Blackwell.

- Merry, Sally Engle. 2006. *Human Rights and Gender Violence: Translating International Law into Local Justice.* Chicago: University of Chicago Press.

- Plesset, Sonja. 2006. *Sheltering Women: Negotiating Gender and Violence in Northern Italy.* Stanford, CA: Stanford University Press.

ACKNOWLEDGMENTS

I would like to express my deepest gratitude to the brave women who have experienced domestic violence and the strong individuals I interviewed in Vietnam who provide aid and protection to them. I owe special thanks to Dr. Nguyen Thi Hoai Duc, Dr. Nguyen Van Suu, and Dr. Nguyen Huong for providing me affiliation with their institutions and tremendous help to me in my research. I would also like to thank Le An Ni for her tireless efforts and dedication to assisting me in my research. Members of the Vietnam Women's Union generously offered significant time, information, and insights into shelter and other approaches to assisting abused women for which I am grateful. Without the assistance of all of these individuals, this research would not have been possible. A special thanks to Nadine Fernandez and Katie Nelson for their guidance on this profile and for all their efforts in making this open-access book on gender a reality.

BIBLIOGRAPHY

GSO, UN-JPGE, and WHO (General Statistics Office of Viet Nam, United Nations-Government of Viet Nam Joint Programme on Gender Equality, and World Health

Organization). 2010. *'Keeping Silent Is Dying.' Results from the National Study on Domestic Violence Against Women in Viet Nam*. Hanoi: General Statistics Office of Viet Nam, United Nations-Government of Viet Nam Joint Programme on Gender Equality, and World Health Organization.

Kwiatkowski, Lynn. 2011. "Engaging the Challenges of Alleviating Wife Abuse in Northern Vietnam." *Practicing Anthropology* 33, no. 3: 32–37.

4

Controlling National Borders by Controlling Reproduction

Gender, Nationalism, and Nepal's Citizenship Laws

Dannah Dennis and Abha Lal

In this chapter the authors discuss how Nepal, a small country located between two powerful nations (China and India), struggles to maintain its sovereignty and national identity. The state's politics of belonging exclude certain groups of women from citizenship. Caste, class, national origin, and ethnic markers like language intersect to affect women's access to the rights granted to citizens.

LEARNING OBJECTIVES

- Explain how normative concepts of gender and family have shaped Nepal's most recent citizenship laws, resulting in many people's exclusion from full citizenship rights.

- Articulate the connection between controlling national borders, citizenship, and reproduction in Nepal.

- Contextualize Nepal's citizenship laws within broader global trends.

In many places around the world, states attempt to control the national, racial, ethnic, or other demographic characteristics of their citizen populations by adopting policies that directly or indirectly influence biological reproduction (for examples from Egypt, the United States, and China, see Bier 2010, Collins 1998, and Fong 2004, respectively). In the United States, for example, Donald Trump initially rose to political prominence by casting doubt on the birthplace and family relationships of then-president Barack Obama. This racially motivated strategy of questioning Obama's status as a legitimate US citizen appealed to a wide swath of the US population who implicitly or explicitly link "whiteness" with "Americanness." After being elected president in 2016, Trump continued to appeal to this base of voters by proposing to end birthright citizenship (the legal policy that every person born on US soil is a US citizen, which is guaranteed by the Fourteenth Amendment to the US Constitution) and seeking to severely restrict immigration, particularly from Latin America and Muslim-majority countries. During Trump's presidency, access to abortion and other forms of reproductive health care has been under attack in several US states. These are just a few examples of how, in the words of professor and feminist critic Laura Briggs, "All politics [have become] reproductive politics" in the contemporary United States (2017).

In this chapter, we will provide a case study that illustrates the dynamics of gender, reproduction, citizenship, and nationalism in contemporary Nepal, focusing on the years immediately before and after Nepal's adoption of a new constitution in September 2015. We will demonstrate that the Nepali state's efforts to influence reproduction can have serious impacts on the lives of cisgender women, who are held primarily responsible for the task of reproducing the kind of citizens that the state desires. We will also show how gender politics intersects with geopolitics in Nepal, a small country that borders two larger and more powerful countries (India and China), and explain how this intersection has affected Nepal's citizenship laws. Even though Nepal's border with India is technically an open border, with thousands of people moving back and forth between the two countries every day, many of Nepal's political leaders are concerned about maintaining the distinction between the two countries in order to preserve Nepal's sovereignty. One of the ways they have sought to maintain this distinction is by passing citizenship laws that are discriminatory both toward cisgender women and toward the people who live along the Nepal-India border. The questions of "what does it mean to be Nepali?" and "who counts as fully Nepali?" lie at the heart of public debates around the issue of citizenship. In the final section of this chapter, we will focus on how women who are doubly marginalized by virtue of their gender and ethnicity are seeking to answer these questions in their own words.

Broadly speaking, citizenship laws around the world tend to fall into two major categories: *jus soli* and *jus sanguinis*. In addition to

jus sanguinis
the legal principle of granting citizenship through blood (family relationships).

jus soli
the legal principle of granting citizenship through soil (place of birth).

these major categories, many countries provide other routes to obtaining naturalized citizenship, such as military service, visa lotteries, or sponsorship by citizen relatives. In countries that follow *jus soli* (right of soil), people are entitled to citizenship if they were born within the geographic territory of the country. In countries that follow *jus sanguinis* (right of blood), people are entitled to citizenship if their parents are citizens of the country in question; thus, parentage is more important than place of birth. Nepal's citizenship laws follow the *jus sanguinis* principle. The most prominent public debates over citizenship and gender in contemporary Nepal are focused on the question of whether women, as mothers, are legally capable of passing on their citizenship to their children. In effect, the citizenship clauses of the constitution of 2015 say that a man's right to pass on citizenship to his children is absolute; a woman's right to pass on citizenship to her children is conditional. As we will show, this discriminatory statute is rooted not only in the fact that over the course of Nepal's recent legal history, the Nepali state has linked women's identity and legal status to that of their male kin—a pattern that Seira Tamang has described as "state patriarchy" (2000)—but also in social and geopolitical tensions with India, particularly with regard to nationalistic fears about Indian encroachment into Nepali territory and politics (Grossman-Thompson and Dennis 2017).

While we are focusing in this chapter on the debate about cisgender women's rights to pass on citizenship to the children who are born to them, we recognize that this is only one facet of the complex relationship between gender and citizenship in Nepal. For example, although Nepal officially recognized "third gender" as a legal category in 2007, many people still struggle to get citizenship papers and other legal documents that properly reflect their gender identity. As a result, trans men and women who would prefer to have their documents reflect their identities as "male" or "female" may be inaccurately lumped into the "third gender" category, which is used as a catchall category for anyone who is not cisgender and heterosexual. Having documents that do not match one's gender identity can lead to many forms of harassment and marginalization.

Currently, citizenship laws in Nepal and most of the public debates about those laws are based on the assumption that families are composed of cisgender heterosexual couples who reproduce through intercourse leading to pregnancy and childbirth. This assumption leaves out a wide array of people of diverse gender identities and sexual orientations. It also overlooks the fact that there are many ways for families to have children, such as assisted reproductive technologies, surrogacy, and adoption. Therefore, activists who represent Nepal's gender and sexual minorities are fighting a difficult battle against a legal system and a broader social milieu rooted in patriarchal, cisnormative, and heteronormative ideas about gender and family (please refer to the book's introduction to review definitions of these terms). In this chapter, we will sometimes use the term "women" to refer to people who are perceived to have the capacity to bear children, as this reflects the language that is used by the majority of our interlocutors; however, we want to highlight that cisgender women and their children are not the only people who are directly affected by the gendered framing of Nepal's citizenship laws.

The stakes of acquiring citizenship documents are high. Without documentation of citizenship, Nepali people are denied not only their political rights, such as the right to vote or hold elected office, but also are unable to register marriages or births, pursue higher education, have bank accounts, own land, get driver's licenses, or get passports. According to the most recent estimates, 5.4 million people in Nepal do not have citizenship; this constitutes 24 percent of the population over the age of sixteen (US Department of State 2019, 17).

CITIZENSHIP IN NEPAL'S HISTORICAL CONTEXT

In order to understand citizenship debates in Nepal as they have played out in recent years, it is necessary to understand the dynamics that have shaped Nepali citizenship in the past. Nepal was a monarchy led by a Hindu king since the foundation of the modern nation-state in the eighteenth century. Caste, the system of hereditary class that follows Hindu principles of purity and pollution, was an important structuring principle of the law, including laws that regulated marriage, family structure, and inheritance (Höfer 1979). Ethnocentrism was central to the Nepali nation-building project, and notions of what it meant to be a "Nepali citizen" were shaped by policies of exclusion against women, ethnic minorities, and people on the lower end of the Hindu caste hierarchy. Even though Nepal is a country of more than a hundred distinct ethnic and linguistic groups, the perspectives of high-caste Hindu men from the hills have historically been legally and socially dominant.

The Hindu monarch Mahendra Shah came into power in 1956, and in 1960, he consolidated his hold over Nepali politics and society by installing the *Panchayat* system. Under the *Panchayat* system, Nepal was declared "an independent, indivisible and sovereign monarchical Hindu State" with Nepali as its national language, and all executive, legislative, and judicial power was ultimately derived from the king. There was great state investment in creating a homogenized populace, and the slogan of the government was "one king, one country, one language, one culture." Although Hinduism had been an important source of royal authority in Nepal since at least the 1700s, Mahendra was the first to declare Nepal a constitutionally Hindu nation in the 1960s. Nepal remained a constitutionally Hindu nation until after the Maoist civil war ended in 2006, when secularism was officially adopted and the last king, Gyanendra, was forced to abdicate. Thus, the relationship between Hinduism and the Nepali state has been a significant factor in shaping concepts of Nepali national identity.

By 1967 "partyless democracy" was added to the preamble of the constitution, and all forms of oppositional politics were effectively declared illegal. The policy of enforced homogeneity discriminated against people belonging to different ethnic groups who did not speak the language or share the cultural characteristics of those deemed "authentically Nepali" by Mahendra; namely, upper-caste Hindu Nepali-speaking people from the hilly regions of Nepal. Simultaneously, high-caste people from the hills were privileged because of their knowledge of the Nepali language and practice of norms and customs that the state deemed authentically Nepali. While these upper-caste Hill groups comprise only around 30 percent of Nepal's population, over the course of generations, discriminatory state policies have helped upper-caste people from the hills accrue wealth, economic opportunities, education, and political power that is vastly disproportionate to the size of their population. The capitalized term "Hill" is a translation of the Nepali-language term "Pahadi" (pahad = hill). Like the term "Madhesi," it denotes a broad cultural category as well as a geographic region. Hill culture was also patriarchal, which was reflected in state policies, including those pertaining to citizenship. These laws assumed that women's identities derived from their male relatives—first from fathers, then from husbands—even though this kinship system was not shared among all of Nepal's ethnic groups.

A Citizenship Act was passed in 1964, during the *Panchayat* period, which distinguished between **naturalized citizens** and **citizens by descent**. To acquire citizenship by descent, one's father needed to be a Nepali citizen. To become a naturalized citizen, one needed to speak Nepali. In line with the monocultural patriarchal ethos of the Panchayat state, these provisions discriminated against women, who could not pass on citizenship to their children, and Madhesis, people belonging to the southern plains of Nepal.

Madhesis are people who originate from a broad swath of the southern plains of Nepal, bordering the Indian states of Uttar Pradesh and Bihar. Although people of different religions and caste groups reside in

naturalized citizens
In the current Nepali context, naturalized citizenship is the limited category of citizenship. It is available to people who cannot prove that their fathers were Nepali citizens but have some other family relationship with a Nepali citizen (e.g., their mothers or husbands are Nepali citizens).

citizens by descent
in the current Nepali context, citizenship by descent is the full/first-class category of citizenship. It is available to people who can prove that their fathers are Nepali citizens.

Madhes
the southern part of
Nepal, bordering India.
It is linguistically and
culturally distinct in
many ways from the hilly
regions of Nepal. The
Madhes is also called the
Terai or Tarai.

the **Madhes**, they share strong cultural ties across the border in India. They speak Maithili, Bhojpuri, Awadhi, and Hindi, and many do not speak Nepali. The Nepali language requirement for citizenship in the 1964 Act meant that many Madhesis were effectively denied access to citizenship regardless of factors such as place of birth, place of residence, or family ties in Nepal.

Advocates for a more democratic system organized a movement against the tyranny of the Panchayat system in 1990. This "People's Movement" resulted in protests by thousands of people in the streets of Kathmandu. After the protests of 1990 a new constitution was promulgated. The 1990 constitution retained the legal distinction between **naturalized citizenship** and **citizenship by descent**; however, it also introduced an important change by allowing that one could now speak any "national language" in order to obtain Nepali citizenship, rather than the Nepali language only. This meant that many Madhesi people who did not speak Nepali were now eligible for citizenship, although bureaucratic obstacles to acquiring citizenship remained. For example, a large majority of government officials overseeing the citizenship certification process were from the hills, and many were hesitant to give Nepali citizenship to Madhesis, whom they deemed to be potentially Indian citizens (because of cultural or linguistic factors, family ties, place of birth, and so forth). Since dual citizenship is illegal in Nepal, the actual or potential possession of Indian citizenship renders applicants ineligible for Nepali citizenship. There is also a widespread negative stereotype among Hill Nepalis that Madhesis are liars and cheats, which played into bureaucrats' anxieties about granting them citizenship.

The 1990 People's Movement did not lead to the democratic transformations that many hoped for. Due to this disillusionment, a Nepali Maoist insurgency began in rural areas of the midwestern hills in 1996. The Maoists' list of demands included: the end of the monarchy, state secularism, federalism, land reform, a robust welfare state, and gender equality, particularly as it related to women's ability to inherit property. The Maoist insurgency was long and bloody, with seventeen thousand people killed by state security forces and the rebels from 1996 to 2005. It culminated in the second People's Movement of 2006, where the Maoists and a coalition of seven parliamentary parties reached a compromise in which the Maoists agreed to support a multiparty democracy. This agreement unified the political opposition against the monarchy. Nineteen days of continuous protests in Kathmandu and beyond forced the king, Gyanendra, to yield executive authority to a prime minister in April 2006; Gyandendra was forced to fully abdicate the monarchy in 2008. "His Majesty's Government" now became the "Government of Nepal," and the country was declared secular. The political parties, including the Maoists, set out to restructure the country by writing an interim constitution.

During the writing of this interim constitution in 2006, Madhesis, as well as other historically marginalized groups including Dalits ("lower caste" people) and Janajatis (indigenous peoples) demanded decentralization and ethnicity-based federalism as a system of governance that would change the hill-centered political and cultural system that had been a remnant of the Panchayat era. After the Maoists joined the political mainstream, a mass movement took place in Madhes in early 2007. Although Madhesis had been involved in political organizing against hill domination at least from the 1950s, the scale of the 2007 movement was far larger than movements from the past. The Madhesis were angered by the fact that their needs had been sacrificed by politicians who used them as a support base but did not advocate for them. These protests were motivated by the fact that since the 1950s a combination of state negligence and exploitation had left Madhesis disproportionately poor, jobless, uneducated, and are denied cultural membership in the Nepali nation.

The 2007 Madhes uprisings came as an unexpected shock to the establishment but did lead then Prime Minister G. P. Koirala of the Nepali Congress to declare that principles of inclusion would be enshrined in the constitution. The Interim Constitution was amended to include a provision that guaranteed a "democratic, federal system." As a result of the progressive wave that came with the protests of 2006 and 2007, the citizenship clauses were also notably altered in the constitution. It now specified that one could obtain citizenship by descent through one's mother *or* father. There was also a one-time distribution of citizenship by birth for permanent residents, through which many Madhesis acquired citizenship documents. While there were still some legal and bureaucratic barriers to obtaining citizenship, the changes in the 2007 interim constitution were more ostensibly egalitarian than citizenship provisions had ever been.

CAMPAIGNING FOR CITIZENSHIP, 2014–2015

In September 2014, newspapers reported that the lawmakers who were drafting the constitutional provisions on citizenship had included language that would require applicants to prove the citizenship of both father *and* mother. This was a clear step back from the provisions of the Interim Constitution of 2007, which had technically allowed for citizenship to be granted through father *or* mother. Galvanized by this threat to citizenship rights, activists began an escalating series of protests and demonstrations in fall 2014 that continued into 2015. These activists included a wide array of people and groups, such as the Chaukath feminist network, the Forum for Women, Law, and Development, and the community organized through a Facebook page titled "Citizenship in the Name of the Mother."

The citizenship debate played out openly in the form of frequent street protests, speeches by politicians and public figures, discussion programs organized by civil society groups, and a flood of impassioned editorials in both Nepali and English language newspapers. Activists, policymakers, and intellectuals extensively used social media platforms such as Facebook, Twitter, and Change.org to inform the general public and to organize protest actions targeting those directly involved in the constitution-writing process. Events were organized in Kathmandu, in other districts throughout the country, and even internationally: in January 2015, nonresident Nepalis delivered petitions to Nepali embassies in Ottawa; New York; Washington, DC; and Delhi. However, this section focuses specifically on discourses circulating in Kathmandu, as this is where Dannah Dennis was conducting fieldwork at the time.

At the heart of the citizenship debate is the question of who is fully Nepali. Are women fully Nepali? Are Madhesi people and those from other marginalized ethnic groups and geographic regions fully Nepali? In the 2014–2015 movement to demand citizenship through mothers, activists in Kathmandu framed the issue as an issue of women's rights and gender equality. In effect, they chose to argue primarily that women are fully Nepali and to downplay the claim that Madeshis are fully Nepali. The iconography of protest reflected this focus on women's rights. For example, a cartoon by the artist Diwakar Chettri was the featured image of the Facebook group "Citizenship in the Name of the Mother" and was often printed on signs carried at protests and circulated widely on social

Figure 4.1. Protesters carry a banner during a Human Rights Day march. The slogans on the banner say "Children are born from their mothers' wombs. Why can't they get identity from their names? Give citizenship in the name of the mother, make citizenship rights secure," and "Our children, our identity, we are also Nepali citizens." Bhrikuti Mandap, Kathmandu, December 10, 2014. Dannah Dennis; CC BY.

media (see figure 4.1). The cartoon depicts a human figure without facial features but with many other markers that signal femininity, such as jewelry, long hair with a flower, and wide hips. Moreover, the red sari, red bangles, and beaded necklace suggest the attire of a respectable, married, high-caste Hindu woman. The featureless face seems to invite viewers to imagine their own mothers, or other mothers whom they know, and the large tear emerging from the face makes a moral and affective appeal to the suffering of mothers. Activists also used the iconography of protest to emphasize the uncertain futures of children who would be unable to gain citizenship through their mothers (see figure 4.2).

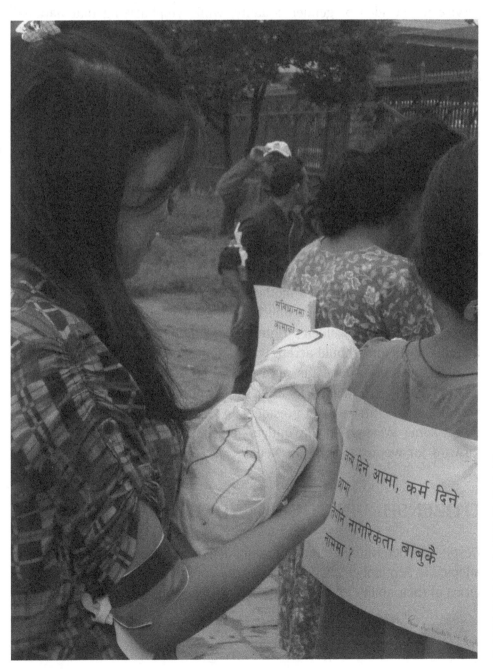

Figure 4.2. A young woman carries an effigy of a baby covered with question marks. The sign pinned to the back of the protester in front of her reads "Birth and karma are given by mothers. Why does citizenship have to be in the father's name?" Tundikhel, Kathmandu, September 20, 2014. Dannah Dennis; CC BY.

Because the debate over a single conjunction, "and" versus "or," could have appeared to be a minor detail of the intractable debates plaguing the Nepali constitution-writing process, activists worked hard to convince their audiences of the enormous impact of this provision. By framing the citizenship debate as a fundamental issue of women's rights, supporters of citizenship through maternal descent attempted to pressure political parties that had made public commitments to the principle of gender equality. Activists sometimes attempted to shame politicians with the argument that the politicians were failing to respect their own mothers if they didn't support the cause of citizenship through mothers.

In response to this public outcry, many political leaders paid lip service to the idea of gender equality, while emphasizing that national security interests were of paramount concern. For example, Jhalanath Khanal a leader of the United Marxist-Leninist Party—at that time, the party with the second-highest number of elected representatives in Nepal's Constituent Assembly—was quoted as saying, "We are always in favor of gender-equality. Issuing citizenship in the name of father and mother, if both are Nepalis, is not a problem for us. But we have to be cautious while issuing citizenship for children born in districts bordering India in Tarai (Madhes) as well as Tibet in the mountains through mothers" (Pun 2015). This type of nationalist rhetoric casts women, and particularly women who live along Nepal's borders, as a potential threat to both the sovereignty and the cultural makeup of the Nepali state because of their ability to have children with non-Nepali men.

Some politicians went even further and denounced the entire movement for citizenship through mothers. For example, in July 2015, Bidhya Devi Bhandari (UML) stated publicly that activists on the citizenship issue and other issues of women's rights were unduly influenced by Western feminist ideas and should accept what she deemed to be an appropriately "Eastern" perspective on the necessary subordination of women to men (Basnet 2015). A few months after these antifeminist remarks, Bhandari became Nepal's first female president in October 2015. With unintended irony, some Western media outlets hailed this development as a step forward for women's rights in Nepal.

CITIZENSHIP IN THE CONSTITUTION OF 2015

Despite the determined efforts of many activists, the constitution that was adopted in September 2015 made a distinction between men and women in terms of their ability to pass on citizenship. Harking back to the Citizenship

Act of 1964, this distinction was couched in terms of two categories of citizenship: citizenship by descent and naturalized citizenship. Citizenship by descent is available to people who have Nepali citizen fathers, whether or not their mothers are Nepali citizens. Naturalized citizenship, on the other hand, is available to people who have Nepali citizen mothers and foreign fathers, and it is subject to some limitations. For instance, people who apply for naturalized citizenship must be permanent residents of Nepal and must be able to prove that they do not hold citizenship in any other country. Naturalized citizens are also barred from holding the highest government offices, such as president, prime minister, and chief justice (Article 289). Furthermore, Nepali citizen men married to foreign women may bestow naturalized citizenship on their wives, but Nepali citizen women are not able to bestow naturalized citizenship on their foreign husbands. The differences between citizenship by descent and naturalized citizenship are outlined in table 4.1. It is also important to note that as in previous iterations of Nepali citizenship law, people who hold Nepali citizenship are not allowed to hold citizenship in any other country; thus, dual citizenship is not an option.

In effect, these constitutional provisions convey the message that a Nepali man's citizenship can be passed on to his children unconditionally or to his wife, if he marries a non-Nepali citizen. A Nepali woman's citizenship, on the other hand, can be passed on to her children only if certain conditions are met and cannot be passed on to her husband. Children of foreign fathers can only receive naturalized Nepali citizenship,

Table 4.1. Summary of Citizenship Provisions in Nepal's 2015 Constitution

Citizenship by descent	Naturalized citizenship
• Available to people who have Nepali father + Nepali mother OR Nepali father + foreign mother • Can hold high office • The right to determine one's gender identity is guaranteed (Article 12)	• Available to people who have Nepali mother + foreign father • Available to foreign wives of Nepali men, but not to foreign husbands of Nepali women • Cannot hold high office • Conditional (must reside in Nepal, must not hold citizenship elsewhere) • The right to determine one's gender identity is not guaranteed

which means that they can never be regarded as full Nepali citizens. On Twitter, public intellectuals Kedar Sharma and Manjushree Thapa dubbed this principle "sperm nationalism" (shukrakit rastriyata).

MADHESI WOMEN AND CITIZENSHIP

As is apparent from Jhalanath Khanal's comments about needing to be "cautious while issuing citizenship for children born in districts bordering India in Tarai (Madhes) as well as Tibet in the mountains through mothers," the controversial citizenship clauses in the 2015 constitution were not just about gender but also ethnicity and national borders. Because the Madhes is proximate to India, both geographically and culturally, and cross-border marriages are the norm, Madhesi women are especially unlikely to be able to pass on their citizenship to their children. In addition to legal discrimination, Madhesi women's frequently binational attachments mean that their citizenship is called into question both legally and socially because they are not understood to be as "authentically Nepali" as women from the hills are. Abha Lal conducted her fieldwork in two towns in the Madhes, Birgunj and Janakpur in 2017 and 2018, where she interviewed women about how they assert themselves as Nepali citizens when the Nepali state refuses to see them as such. All names in this section are pseudonyms.

When asked about whether she saw herself as Nepali and how she understood what that meant, this is what Bibha, a woman who was born in India and married to a Madhesi Nepali man had to say:

> Before I got married I was pure Indian, there is no doubt about that. But as soon as this became my *sasuraal* (marital home), I had to *tyaag* (sacrifice) my Indian citizenship, I became Nepali. It is Madhesi custom that you forget your natal home and become part of your husband's family as soon as you get married. I understand that, but the Nepali state does not. I get naturalized citizenship and have less rights than other citizens. (Bibha, interviewed by Abha Lal)

Bibha's understanding of citizenship being derived from male relatives—first, one's father, then one's husband—was not uncommon. A common refrain heard across the Madhes is that there is *"beti-roti ke sambandha"* between Nepal and India, which roughly translates to a "relationship of daughters and bread." What this is referring to is the fact that India and Nepal share a way of life (bread), and the shared culture means that Indian "daughters" come to Nepal and become Nepali and vice versa.

Bibha did not take issue with the idea that a cross-border marriage meant that a woman's national identity automatically changed. For her, the source of discontent was the fact that the Nepali state treated her, a naturalized citizen, differently than it would a citizen by descent. If citizenship based on kinship, "*beti-roti sambandha*," was to hold true, would need to mean that a "daughter" of India was entitled to all the rights and privileges of Nepali citizenship after becoming a "daughter-in-law."

The "daughter-in-law" versus "daughters" issue was a division that became evident in the fissure between women's rights activists and Madhesi activists in the aftermath of the 2015 constitution (Pudasaini 2017). Because women's rights activists had made the strategic choice to focus on citizenship in the name of the mother, they did not emphasize the fact that the naturalization clause gave fewer rights to women who had become citizens after marrying Nepali men. The fact that the women's rights activists who were most vocal about the citizenship issue were from the hills—and therefore likely shared some of the same anti-Madhesi prejudices as their male counterparts—also played a part in this sidelining of the naturalization issue. Madhesi rights activists, on the other hand, were predominantly men and did not have much to say about women being able to pass on citizenship by descent. Rather, they were concerned with the fact that their "daughters-in-law" did not get immediate and full citizenship that honored the practice of cross-border marriages. The differing priorities held by women's rights activists and Madhesi rights activists meant that the movement against the constitutional citizenship provisions was fragmented, and thus a broad alliance was not able to form.

While activists talking about the "daughters-in-law" in the national political scene were largely men, many Madhesi women, like Bibha, were primarily concerned with the naturalization clause and did not fundamentally question the patriarchal logic of deriving citizenship through kinship. This was most apparent in how they talked about national affiliation changing after marriage but also in the way children were invoked in a manner very different from how the women's rights activists talked about children being entitled to citizenship through the mother. When asked about what she wanted from the Nepali state, here is what a young woman named Bhagyalata in Birgunj had to say:

In India, kids get bicycles to go to school, they get good lunches. Our kids, *ghanta*! (nothing). This *harami sarkar* (bastard government) gives us nothing at all. In India they have fuel, food, rations, why won't this government give us anything? Our kids deserve to have bicycles and food and an education, to have better lives than we do. If Indians can have that, why can't we? (Bhagyalata, interviewed by Abha Lal)

While Bhagyalata's use of the Indian government as an example of what a good government should look like is interesting in itself, her emphasis on what the Nepali state needed to do *for the children* is a common way of asserting citizenship that many Madhesi women used. Regardless of their age or maternal status, many women talked about their children, or "our children" in the abstract, while expressing their political grievances. The logic for this appeared to be whether a Madhesi woman is Nepal-born or India-born, a naturalized citizen, a citizen by descent, or whether or not she holds a citizenship certificate at all; as a mother of a child with a Nepali father, she is the mother of a Nepali child. Therefore, basing claims on children is a mode of legitimating Madhesi demands in the eyes of the Nepali state.

The inversion of the logic of motherhood here is interesting: while campaigners for "citizenship in the name of mother" talked of the uncertain futures of children who would be unable to gain citizenship, Madhesi women based their claims to citizenship on the fact that they are mothers of Nepali children. It is important to note here that while the logic of motherhood to Nepali children made sense to Madhesi women who were talking about their belonging in Nepal in these terms, for elite political forces, Madhesi women's children were not necessarily Nepali. Many politicians dismissed the demands for equitable citizenship laws by claiming that children born to Nepali women married to foreigners were "bhanja-bhanjis" (nieces and nephews by maternal descent) and thus not truly Nepali. So, for them, many Madhesi women were the mothers of "bhanja-bhanjis," rather than "sons and daughters" of Nepal, and thus they and their children were not entitled to full Nepali citizenship. This perspective was reflected in the constitution.

Madhesi women draw on patriarchal notions of citizenship—being entitled to political belonging in the nation as a daughter, a wife, a daughter-in-law and a wife—because they have few other options for staking their claim to belonging in Nepal. The impact of the state patriarchy combined with a deep and abiding legacy of ethnic discrimination means that Madhesi women have been discouraged from seeing themselves as autonomous citizens in their own right, independent of their family attachments. However, Madhesi women's views on this subject are not necessarily monolithic, as evidenced by the following dialogue between Mamata, who was born in India, and Sangeeta, who was born in Nepal:

Mamata: (Smiling) I am Indian. I believe in Modi-*Sarkar* (government). Nepal *sarkar* is completely useless.

Sangeeta: Hey, what a liar!

Mamata: How am I lying? I was born in India, obviously I am Indian.

Sangeeta: Well, what if you were born in India? Women have no *jaat* (caste). As soon as you got married to a Nepali man, you became Nepali. Your household is here, you work here, your children were born here, you are not Indian, you are Nepali. (Mamata and Sangita, interviewed by Abha Lal)

Like Sangeeta, many women rely on patriarchal notions of family membership to make their claims to belonging in Nepal, but these claims are tenuous and only available to those in certain familial and marital arrangements. Madhesi women who do not know the identity of the fathers of their children, are in same-sex relationships, have chosen to end their marriages, or have been abandoned by Nepali men may not be able to obtain citizenship documents for themselves or their children.

CONCLUSION: GENDER AND CITIZENSHIP IN NEPAL AND BEYOND

The constitution of 2015 leaves many details to be resolved through legislation. As of this writing in January 2020, a citizenship bill that will expand on the guidelines in the constitution has been under discussion in the Nepali Parliament for months. In this ongoing process, many lawmakers continue to display patriarchal attitudes. For example, lawmakers have suggested that women who claim that the identity of their children's fathers is unknown must "provide proof" or "provide an explanation," citing a concern that women might lie about the identity of their children's fathers and "indulg[e] in immoral acts" (Gurung 2019). If such provisions are passed into law, women seeking citizenship for their children may be required to recount their complete sexual histories to local bureaucrats, who would still retain the authority to deny the citizenship application if they deem that sufficient "proof" has not been provided. Similarly, lawmakers have also discussed the idea that third-gender or trans people should have to submit a doctor's recommendation in order to get citizenship documents that reflect their correct gender; in turn, activists have pointed out that this medicalization of gender identity is unnecessarily burdensome and invasive, arguing that self-declaration of gender identity should be sufficient (Panday 2019). Both of these discussions highlight the fact that applicants who do not conform to hegemonic norms of gender and family relationships may be expected to provide additional evidence to substantiate their claims to citizenship. Although the citizenship bill remains to be passed, it seems likely that access to citizenship will continue to be restricted along the lines of gender, family structure, ethnicity, and region.

In conclusion, the case study presented in this chapter illustrates three main points that are true not only in Nepal but elsewhere in the world as well. First, many states base their citizenship laws on a set of normative assumptions about gender and family; consequently, people who do not conform to these normative assumptions may not be able to gain access to their full citizenship rights. Second, nationalist anxieties about being overrun by noncitizen "others" are often used by politicians as an effective rationalization for passing laws that are blatantly discriminatory. And finally, people who experience multiple and intersecting forms of marginalization (such as Madhesi women in Nepal) are likely to have particular difficulties in obtaining citizenship, both in the legal sense and in the broader social sense of perceived belonging. Moreover, even though multiply marginalized people are likely to be most deeply impacted by discriminatory laws, their voices are often missing from public debates about the issues that affect them directly; as we have shown, Madhesi women's perspectives and experiences of citizenship were not well represented by either the women's activist movement or the Madhesi activist movement.

REVIEW QUESTIONS

1. Why do governments around the world seek to regulate family relationships and reproduction? What does this have to do with citizenship?

2. What are some of the arguments that Nepali politicians have used to justify their refusal to grant full citizenship through mothers?

3. Why are Madhesi women's perspectives and experiences particularly important for understanding the ongoing debate about Nepal's citizenship laws?

4. Beyond the question of whether citizenship can be inherited through mothers, what are some of the other gender-related issues that shape Nepal's citizenship laws?

5. Choose a country and read about its citizenship laws. What do these laws reveal about how the state sees gender and family relationships? Who are the laws designed to include? Who are they designed to exclude?

KEY TERMS

citizens by descent: in the current Nepali context, citizenship by descent is the full/first-class category of citizenship. It is available to people who can prove that their fathers are Nepali citizens.

jus sanguinis: the legal principle of granting citizenship through blood (family relationships).

jus soli: the legal principle of granting citizenship through soil (place of birth).

Madhes: the southern part of Nepal, bordering India. It is linguistically and culturally distinct in many ways from the hilly regions of Nepal. The Madhes is also called the Terai or Tarai.

naturalized citizens: In the current Nepali context, naturalized citizenship is the limited category of citizenship. It is available to people who cannot prove that their fathers were Nepali citizens but have some other family relationship with a Nepali citizen (e.g., their mothers or husbands are Nepali citizens).

RESOURCES FOR FURTHER EXPLORATION

-   Adhikari, Aditya. 2015. *The Bullet and the Ballot Box: The Story of Nepal's Maoist Revolution*. London: Verso.

-   "Birthstory" podcast from Radiolab—a story about transnational surrogacy, changing laws, and the 2015 earthquake in Nepal: https://www.wnycstudios.org/story/birthstory2018.

-   Facebook page of the Queer Rights Collective of Nepal: www.facebook.com/QRC.np/.

- Forum for Women, Law, and Development. This is a Nepali NGO that works on citizenship advocacy and other issues: www.fwld.org.

- Jha, Kalpana. 2017. *The Madhesi Upsurge and the Contested Idea of Nepal.* Singapore: Springer.

- Pant, Suman. 2019. "The Long and Arduous Journey to Winning a Supreme Court Case as a Same-Sex Married Couple." *Record.* https://www.recordnepal.com/perspective/opinions/the-arduous-journey-to-winning-a-supreme-court-case-as-a-same-sex-married-couple/.

- Tamang, Seira. 2002. "Dis-embedding the Sexual/Social Contract: Citizenship and Gender in Nepal." *Citizenship Studies* 6, no. 3: 309–324.

- Tamang, Seira. 2009. "The Politics of Conflict and Difference or the Difference of Conflict in Politics: The Women's Movement in Nepal." *Feminist Review* 91: 61–80.

ACKNOWLEDGMENTS

The authors would like to thank all of the people who agreed to be interviewed over the course of this research. Rukshana Kapali and Niranjan Kunwar provided valuable insight into how current citizenship laws affect Nepal's gender and sexual minorities. Dannah Dennis's research was carried out with funding from the Wenner-Gren Foundation and the University of Virginia. Abha Lal's research was carried out with funding from Swarthmore College.

BIBLIOGRAPHY

Basnet, Basanta. 2015. "Paschimi Samskarko Prabhavma Mahila Adhikarkarmi: Bidhya Bhandari." *Kantipur*, 2015. https://www.kantipurdaily.com/news/2015-07-14/412678.html.

Bier, Laura. 2010. "The Family Is a Factory: Gender, Citizenship, and the Regulation of Reproduction in Postwar Egypt." *Feminist Studies* 36, no. 2: 404–32.

Briggs, Laura. 2017. *How All Politics Became Reproductive Politics: From Welfare Reform to Foreclosure to Trump.* Berkeley: University of California Press.

Collins, Patricia Hill. 1998. "It's All in the Family: Intersections of Gender, Race, and Nation." *Hypatia* 13, no. 3: 62–82.

Fong, Vanessa. 2004. *Only Hope: Coming of Age under China's One-Child Policy*. Stanford, CA: Stanford University Press.

Grossman-Thompson, Barbara, and Dannah Dennis. 2017. "Citizenship in the Name of the Mother: Nationalism, Social Exclusion, and Gender in Contemporary Nepal." *Positions: Asia Critique* 25, no. 4: 795–820.

Gurung, Tsering. 2019. "Debate over Nepali Women's Right to Pass on Citizenship to Children Reignites as House Committee Holds Discussions on Controversial Provisions." *Kathmandu Post*, March 7, 2019. https://kathmandupost.com/national/2019/03/07/debate-over-nepali-womens-right-to-pass-on-citizenship-to-children-reignites-as-house-committee-holds-discussions-on-controversial-provisions.

Höfer, Andras. 1979. *The Caste Hierarchy and the State in Nepal: A Study of the Muluki Ain of 1854*. Innsbruck: Universitatsverlag Wagner.

Panday, Jagdishor. 2019. "Doc's Recommendation Must for 'Other Gender' to Obtain Citizenship." *Himalayan Times*, March 19, 2019. https://thehimalayantimes.com/nepal/docs-recommendation-must-for-other-gender-to-obtain-citizenship/.

Pudasaini, Surabhi. 2017. "Writing Citizenship: Gender, Race and Tactical Alliances in Nepal's Constitution Drafting." *Studies in Nepali History and Society* 22, no. 1: 85–117.

Pun, Weena. 2015. "UML Blocks Proposal to Issue Citizenship Through Mothers." *Kathmandu Post*, January 14, 2015. https://kathmandupost.com/valley/2015/01/13/uml-blocks-proposal-to-issue-citizenship-through-mothers.

US Department of State. 2019. "Nepal 2018 Human Rights Report." Country Reports on Human Rights Practices for 2018. Bureau of Democracy, Human Rights, and Labor. https://www.state.gov/wp-content/uploads/2019/03/NEPAL-2018.pdf.

5

Understanding Caste and Kinship within Hijras, a "Third" Gender Community in India

Ina Goel

In this chapter, the author looks at the organization and functions of a third-gender group in India: the hijras. Here we see how hierarchy and caste also shape third-gender hijra communities. These communities create and operate through discipleship-kinship systems that both regulate their activities and create a power structure among the hijras. These kinship systems are not recognized and legitimized by the Indian state but by the internal hijra governance councils.

LEARNING OBJECTIVES

By the end of this chapter students should be able to

- Define the hijras, a "third" gender community in India.
- Describe the pattern and complexity of hijra kinship.
- Explain the hijra prestige economy system.

hijras
also known as "third" gender in India; can be understood as subaltern forms of trans-queer identities existing within a prestige economy system of kinship networks.

Dalit
formerly "untouchable" community in India.

Sharmili, a twenty-four-year-old **hijra** from the Dakshinpuri area in New Delhi confided in me that she belongs to the Valmiki community. In north India, the Valmikis are classified as a subcategory of caste belonging to the **Dalit** community. Indian kinship is always grouped around a system of social stratification based on birth status known as the **caste system**, and the Dalits are a historically oppressed caste, formerly known as "untouchables" in India. Most people in Sharmili's natal family work as *safai karamcharis*, or sanitation workers, a job that is socially bound to those in the lowest castes in India. Sharmili's maternal grandmother worked as a *safai karamchari* at Jawaharlal Nehru University in New Delhi, where I completed my MPhil studies in social medicine and community health. Sharmili inherited this job from one of her dying relatives, her maternal uncle, and worked at a national bank in New Delhi as a *safai karamchari*. The passing down of sanitation work from one generation to another within the Valmiki community is made possible because of a government policy that enables *safai karamcharis* to nominate a member of their family to take up the same line of work after their death (Salve et al. 2017).

When Sharmili started her job at a local branch of one of the world's biggest banking corporations (in which even I have an account), Sharmili was still using her deadname. Arriving at work every day on a motorcycle, Sharmili used to wear a black leather jacket and had an outwardly masculine appearance. Based on the belief that people's gender is fixed for life, Sharmili's colleagues at the bank assumed that her then "alpha-male" persona was set in stone. So much so that when Sharmili started showing visible signs of becoming herself by growing her hair and wearing light makeup to work, other colleagues at the bank did not like it. They did not even consider that Sharmili was inwardly always feminine, and when they saw her displaying those traits outwardly, the colleagues at work started making fun of her new effeminate look.

The ongoing teasing at work made Sharmili believe that at least she was being recognized for who she really is, even if that came at a cost. In those taunts, Sharmili found recognition of a gender identity she always thought she belonged to. Mustering courage, Sharmili showed up at work in a *salwar-kameez*, a traditional style of clothing typically worn by women in north India, coordinating her outfit with a dark color shade of lipstick and a long scarf called a *dupatta*. It was on this day, as she clearly remembers, that one of her colleagues pulled at her *dupatta* to shame her for "acting" like a female. Since then, pulling at Sharmili's *dupatta* became an office joke that was quickly shared and spread among some of her male colleagues. Sharmili felt violated. Even though they were colleagues, Sharmili felt "lower" than them in social status, not only because of caste but also because of her transgender identity. Sharmili's colleagues continued to bully her.

Sharmili underestimated just how much a change in her attire would provoke reactions from her colleagues. They were now more open and outwardly bullying Sharmili by calling her derogatory names like *chakka* and *gandu* (asshole or giving ass) (Bhaskaran 2004, 95). The environment

caste system
Indian kinship is always grouped around a system of social stratification based on birth status known as the caste system.

joint-family
a household system
in which members
of more than one
generation of a
unilineal descent group
live together.

grew so hostile that Sharmili would end up crying in the bathroom at her place of work most of the time. Despite the harassment at her job, Sharmili continued to come to work because at that point this was the only means of income available to her natal **joint-family**.

One day, the bank manager and some senior colleagues gave Sharmili an ultimatum that if she wanted to continue her job as a *safai karamchari*, she must not dress as a woman and must return to her "male" disguise. Irrespective of Sharmili being the only breadwinner in her family, a fact known by the bank management, they considered it their duty to provide a "family-friendly environment," which they thought was put at risk by Sharmili's presence. Not only that, Sharmili was considered a "threat" by the bank management, especially to the women colleagues working there, and more so for the "female" customers and their accompanying children visiting the bank. The perceived threat to the bank's image was based on the stereotype that "hijras" kidnap young boys and castrate them to increase the membership of their own community. Therefore, Sharmili's presence in itself was considered a "bad influence" that was perceived as threatening to women working and visiting in the bank.

Not being in a position to negotiate her working relations with the bank management, Sharmili eventually decided to quit her job as a *safai karamchari*. During this distressing time, she came in contact with the hijra community living in her area. She was introduced to a hijra *guru* by her friend who was also her neighbor and the same person who loaned her the *salwar-kameez*.

The hijras are a third-gender group in India and can be understood as subaltern trans-queer identities existing within a prestige economy system of kinship networks. The hijra guru initiated Sharmili into the hijra community through a *reet*, or a ritualistic ceremony. In this ceremony, Sharmili was adopted by the guru to the hijra house or *gharana* to which the guru herself belonged; in this way, she became a new member of the house. It was during this process that the name Sharmili became the only name she wanted to identify with: she did not want to use her natal family surname, which also revealed her caste origins. Her hijra guru accepted Sharmili just as she wanted to be.

In her coming days of apprenticeship with the hijra guru, Sharmili learned the hijra ways of being. She learned how to dress, wear makeup, sing hijra traditional songs, and dance the steps that accompany those songs. Sharmili wanted to earn money through the "traditional" way of hijras, typically by collecting ritual blessings or *toli-badhai* where the hijras shower their blessings on newborns and newlyweds in exchange for gifts both in cash and kind. However, Sharmili's hijra guru had other plans for her.

Despite Sharmili's dancing skills and musical flair, her hijra guru did not allow her to be in the group for *toli badhai*. Instead, Sharmili was encouraged to work as a beggar and assist in begging at traffic signals, or *lal-batti mangna*. If Sharmili wanted to boost her income and earn extra, then she was also given the option for sex work, or *khanjara*, by her hijra contemporaries. Sharmili felt that it was because of her lower-caste status that her hijra guru did not allow her to be a part of the auspicious dances associated with collecting ritual blessings. Historically those coming from the Valmiki community have been denied priestly jobs and even barred by the upper castes from entering temples for the fear that lower castes will "pollute" the sacredness of those spaces.

Sharmili felt fortunate to be accepted by her hijra guru for her chosen gender identity but also felt discriminated against due to her caste identity. Eventually, Sharmili made contacts in another hijra group, in the Trilokpuri area of New Delhi that let her accompany them in their group for *toli badhai*. Sharmili now commutes four hours' round trip on a public bus whenever she can from Dakshinpuri to Trilokpuri just to be able to earn respect and money in traditional hijra performances.

UNDERSTANDING HIJRAS

Distinct from transgender and intersex identities in other countries, hijras occupy a unique and contradictory place in Indian society. Many have understood "third gender" to mean only the hijras; however, numerous other gender nonconforming identities fall under this umbrella term—and yet, some argue against the use of the term "third" gender for all gender nonconforming people.

One of the main differences between trans and hijra identities is that trans people have the freedom to self-identify as trans. To identify as hijra, a person must be initiated through a ritual adoption by a hijra guru into the hijra community (see Nanda 1990 and Reddy 2006). The general trans population in India does not adhere to such an internal social system but subsequently has a less tight-knit community than hijras. Also, conventionally, trans men are not a part of the hijra community.

Legally recognized as the "third" gender in April 2014 by the Supreme Court of India, the hijras are a highly stigmatized minority group with an estimated population of half a million according to the Census of India 2011 (Census of India 2011). However, this figure is widely disputed as the census counted trans people, the hijras, and intersex births under the third-gender category. Therefore, the population counted by the census is not a true representation of hijra demographics in India. In 2018

India also decriminalized homosexual sex, overturning a 160-year-old law instituted by the British.

One explanation for this confusion over the differences between other third-gender identities, transgender persons, and those born intersex could be that the Hindi word *hijra* has been used as a catchall term for all these identities. Moreover, the interchangeability of the term *hijra* with the terms such as *transgender* and *intersex* neglects the historicity of all these three terms that came about in different contexts and sociopolitical settings, and conflating them is problematic.

There is also an inherent public confusion persisting in understanding who hijras are and who they are not. Addressing this confusion are classifications made by the hijra communities themselves on who "real" hijras are and how they are differentiated from those who are "fake." One such way to demarcate the difference between the two is by affiliation to a hijra "house." "Real" hijras have a house affiliation whereas "fake" hijras do not have this affiliation. "Fake" hijras are men who are "cross-dressed beggars" and not "legitimate hijras but are often mistaken as having a hijra identity by the "mainstream public" (Dutta 2012, 838). In India, an authentic hijra identity is based on its affiliation to a **hijra *gharana* (house society)** (see Goel 2016). The hijra *gharanas* are symbolic units of lineage, called a *house*, guiding the overall schematic outlining of the social organization of the hijra community in India.

In this chapter, I will focus on two areas to help understand the ties between gender and kinship in the hijra community in India. I have been working with the hijras for over ten years, first as a social worker and then as an anthropologist witnessing their struggles and successes. I learned to speak Hijra Farsi and was ritually adopted into the community by a guru. The first section of this chapter will highlight the historical roots of the formation of a kinship system within the hijra community and its connection to the contemporary forms of kinship. The second section will focus on the prestige economy system of the hijra community and the various ranks within it. The overall aim is to enable readers to understand the complex multilayered hierarchies and intersectionality between gender and kinship within the hijra community in India.

HIJRA KINSHIP

THE HISTORICAL LENS

In the seventeenth century, eunuchs became trusted servants in the **Mughal** courts. The term *eunuch* in reference to hijras in India is now considered

---

hijra *gharanas*
symbolic units of lineage guiding the overall schematic outlining of the social organization of hijra community in India.

Mughal
early modern empire in South Asia founded in 1526 that spanned two centuries.

pejorative; however, historical research finds the terms *eunuch* and *hijra* used interchangeably. Through their gender "uniqueness," the eunuchs were allowed to travel freely between the *mardana* (men's side) and the *zenana* (women's side), guard the women of the harems, and care for their children (Jaffrey 1996, 53). Travelogues document that the eunuchs were also "intimate servants" and "beloved mistresses" of kings and princes (Jaffrey 1996, 54). The eunuch slaves had many different roles to play, and different tasks were assigned to them in royal courts (Taparia 2011). Eunuch slaves were not only in charge of administrative tasks but also served as confidantes, warriors, and advisors at the helm of diplomatic and military affairs. And in some rare instances they held literary posts in the imperial courts in New Delhi (Chatterjee 2000). However, because of their enslaved status, eunuchs could not establish a life elsewhere and were not allowed to leave the royal territories.

Historical evidence reveals that there were internal relationships among the court eunuchs themselves, like that of a master (guru) and disciple (*chela*) (Hinchy 2015). During the Mughal period, the court eunuchs in India were known as *Khwaja Seras* (Jaffrey 1996, 29). The word *Khwaja Sera* comes from Persian—"(*Khwaja*: honorific, meaning 'real master'; sera, to decorate)," which reads as "male members of the royal household" decorating the real master (Jaffrey 1996, 29). In the mid-eighteenth century, nonbiological kinship relations were formed between child eunuchs and adult *Khwaja Seras*. Such relatedness was formed by a system of discipleship-lineage of the guru-chela relationship. It has been argued by Hinchy (2015, 382) that through this socially recognized kinship, the emotional impact of enslavement was lessened for the enslaved children. Though eunuch slavery has now long been a thing of the past, kinship based on relationships of discipleship among hijras by organizing themselves in households and societies remain central to the hijra community.

DISCIPLESHIP-LINEAGE BOND

Hijra kinship works as a **nonbinary family network**, the continuation of which is based on a nonbiological discipleship-lineage system. Within the hijra community, members use Hindi kinship terms and

> call one another *nani* (grandmother), *dadnani* (great grandmother), *mausi* (mother's sister), *didi* (elder sister), *gurumai* (head of the [house] band), *gurubhai* (disciples of the same guru), *chela* (disciple), *natichela* (disciple of disciple) or *amma* or *ma* (mother). (Saxena 2011, 55)

hijra kinship
androgynous nonbinary family network, the continuation of which is based on a nonbiological discipleship-lineage system, which is based on power relations that are further legitimized by internal hijra councils.

nonbinary family network
kinship pattern for those who identify on the gender spectrum outside the male-female binary.

Though most of the kin relation terms are addressed in the feminine pronoun, *chela* (which is lower in the hierarchy) and *nati-chela* (disciple of a disciple, lowest in the hierarchy) are addressed using male pronouns. Furthermore, all the disciples to the same guru are "brotherly" related to each other as another male pronoun of *bhai* (Hindi term for "brother") is suffixed after *guru* to describe their relationship to each other.

There are some other aspects of kin relatedness that often appear to be contradictory to its gendered status within the hijra community. For instance, those hijras who share a common guru continue to be "brotherly" related to each other, even if they rise higher up in the hijra hierarchy. Therefore, they may be addressed as *ma* (or mother) by their disciples lower in rank but as "brothers" by those who share the same rank. The ambivalence of simultaneously using both male and female gendered pronouns for addressing the kin relatedness to the same person within hijra community creates a unique way to embrace the androgynous nature of hijra kinship.

There are also many descriptive ways and terminologies to identify the same kin relation within hijras. An example of multiple descriptive terms to refer to the bonding between two ranks of hijras—guru and chela—are teacher and student, master and disciple, husband and wife, mother and daughter, and mother-in-law and daughter-in-law, respectively. An example of how the affective bonds between gurus and chelas are formalized by the government of India is through voter ID cards. During fieldwork, I saw that hijras who had valid voter ID cards, listed "TG (transgender) or O (other)" as their gender, had the names of their gurus written in the column that required either their father's or husband's name. Yet, contradictorily, in December 2017, the police did not allow the hijra family of Bhavitha, who was found dead near a dustbin in the city of Warangal, to claim her dead body because their nonbiological kinship networks are not recognized by Indian law (Datta 2017). These examples show the Indian government's ambivalence toward the recognition of hijra kinship in India.

Some scholars also believe that hijras lie "outside" stratification systems of caste in India because hijra kinship contrasts with heteronormative assumptions of family (Hall 2013, 635). Therefore, it is believed that the hijras "are not moderated by the logic of the caste system" (Reddy 2006, 145), and there is no apparent caste-based ritualistic practice to which the hijras collectively subscribe (Belkin 2008). However, Nanda (1990, 40) briefly mentions that hijra "houses" function as divisions between different hijra groups to facilitate intracommunity organization, replicating the patterns of the Indian caste system. When a hijra is adopted by a *guru* through a ritualistic ceremony, along with renouncing the perceived male gender assigned at birth, there is also a renunciation of the caste assigned at birth. As a result, I found that most hijras drop their surnames to hide their caste at birth identity. These dropped surnames are often associated with those caste identities that need hiding in order to protect them from caste-based discrimination in India (see Goel 2018). Other hijras who have higher caste privilege by birth often retain their surnames. In rare instances, newly initiated hijra chelas may also take the surnames of their hijra gurus. Therefore, in the hijra community, the core and the burden of maintaining the guru-chela relationship rests heavily upon the individuals where kin relatedness becomes highly "performative" (see Butler 2006). There are strict rules of kin performativity institutionalized in a **hijra prestige economy system**.

hijra prestige economy system
a system of kin relatedness within the hijra community based on the social standing of hijras to one another.

One of the crucial aspects of the hijra community is its social stratification embedded within a prestige economy system. With the hijra prestige economy system, kin relatedness is rooted in the social standing of hijras to one another. The social standing is based on a number of factors contingent on the power relations between and among different individual hijras and their *gharana* networks. There is no written constitution that the hijra gharanas have to abide by. There is, however, an ideal "expected" hijra behavior and unwritten rules to meet those expectations. This ideal of a "good" hijra, based on behavioral expectations and an unwritten code of conduct, is similar to how gender roles are imposed in any society—though always in the process of transition but often based on unspoken norms. There are three key aspects of performative kin relatedness within the hijra community: respect, livelihoods, and embodiment.

RESPECT

The hierarchical guru-chela relationship is the formative core of the social organization within the hijra community. Working with the hijras of Hyderabad, anthropologist Gayatri Reddy (2001, 96) has highlighted the importance of respect: "If there is no guru . . . in the hijra community, that person [from the community] does not have (honour/respect), and is not recognised as a hijra." Furthermore, Reddy, in another study (2006, 151), argues that the hijra "affective bonds" of guru-disciple are "assigned [by the guru] rather than chosen" and are in contrast with the concept of "chosen families" described by Kath Weston (1991, 1998) in the context of American gay and lesbian relationships.

Based on my fieldwork, one of the many rules within this prestige economy system is the expectation that the chelas always speak in a pitch lower than their gurus and don't interrupt or cross them while the gurus are speaking to others in public. If a chela does not obey this form of kin performativity, then a monetary fine or *dand* is imposed upon the chela by the guru for the infringement of this rule. The chela is not allowed to participate in the hijra activities or earn through their hijra networks until the *dand* is paid in full by the chela to the guru. Despite being in a symbiotic relationship, the gurus have more control over their chelas' appearance and activities, which is consistent with hijra hierarchy. There are internal councils that serve as disciplinary bodies within the hijra community to guide the code of conduct of kin relatedness between the gurus and chelas. There is also a practice of pleasing their gurus as a kin-performative gesture because those who are close to their gurus often inherit the property from them after their death. Some examples include offering unconditional service (seva) like pressing and massaging the guru's feet, which is always instrumental for becoming the guru's "favourite" disciple. A hijra, Saloni in the Seelampur area of east Delhi, reflecting on the relationship with gurus, said that

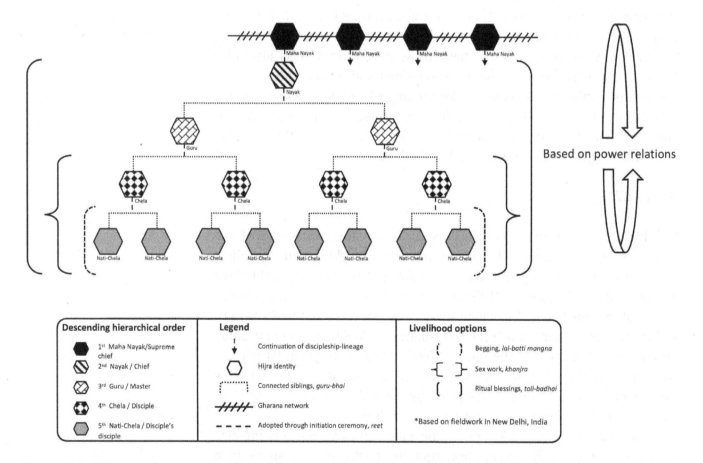

Figure 5.1. Hijra prestige economy. *Note:* I have used hexagons to mark the hijra identity in the kinship diagram as there were no previous formats available to represent nonbinary gender identities on kinship diagrams and charts that I could borrow from. Furthermore, using a hexagon is also my bid to reclaim the six unknown sides for which the hijras are verbally shamed by being called *chakka*.

sometimes the guru–chela relationship is as sweet as a mother-child relationship, but you know how it is these days. A majority is considered similar to that of a mother-in-law–daughter-in-law relationship, which is both sour and sweet at times. (Saloni, interview by author)

Within the prestige economy system, the upward mobility of hijras is also measured by the number of chelas the hijra gurus have under their patronage. Therefore, the more chelas a guru has, the more social status and respect the guru earns in the broader hijra community. This upward mobility then raises a hijra guru to the status of a hijra chief, or *nayak* within the larger community. The nayaks of the hijra community are often those who are financially better off, compared to the rest of the hijra kin under their patronage. Although the nayaks may not be directly involved with the day-to-day life activities of those chelas and *nati-chelas* under them, they often serve as mediators when there are disagreements between gurus and chelas as they serve on the hijra internal councils. Scholars have found that the hijra community is legitimized by these councils, also known as hijra *jamaats* or hijra *panchayats*, which are formed by an internal governing body comprising higher ranked members within the hijra community (Nanda 1990; Reddy 2006; Jaffrey 1996; Goel 2016).

Those hijras who have positive kin relations within the overall community, a large number of people in their *gharana* networks, and superior wealth and rank as compared to the rest of their hijra kin are then voted as greater chiefs, or *maha nayaks* of the community within the internal council of the hijras. These greater chiefs are mostly responsible for maintaining kin relations among different *gharana* networks of hijras within one state or across different states in India.

Those junior in rank have to seek permission from those in higher ranks to engage in activities outside of their hijra ways of life. This may include maintaining kin relations with their natal families or having sexual partners. Hijras' participation in any research- or media-related activities must also be approved by someone higher in rank. The hijras therefore function as a closed social group, tied by their kin relatedness and guided by an internal council that helps to maintain the social order within their prestige economy system.

LIVELIHOODS

Those hijras who are lowest in rank, like nati-chelas, are often assigned to work as beggars at traffic intersections and on public transportation to earn money. Begging is considered to be of the lowest prestige within the hijra community, so those engaged in begging are automatically considered to be lower in rank within the hijra hierarchy. Those in a higher rank have the power to delegate begging to those lower in rank and can choose not to participate in this activity. Those with a slightly higher rank (e.g., chelas) can also work as sex workers to boost their incomes.

However, those in the lower ranks find it challenging to be in sex work because often they do not have the financial resources to sustain their looks. For many lower-rank hijras, it is difficult for them to perform gender the way they would like to, due to the prohibitive costs of makeup, fine clothing, and body transformations. For example, those soliciting sex in cruising areas (often accessed by lower-rank hijras) earn only a pittance since they shave their faces, which leaves "unattractive" chin and jawline stubble. Those hijras (also higher in rank) who earn better money undergo laser hair removal from their faces and bodies, mammo-plasty, and better hormonal injections that enhance their femininity—an aspect that is rewarded by the better-paying sex customers. Moreover, those hijras lower in rank also find it difficult to attract customers in some open cruising areas because of increasing competition from other "effeminate" men (or **kotis**) and female sex workers. Kalyani, a hijra who has not been castrated but has breast implants, said:

> We hijras are well aware today of our health and the consequences that such an atrocious operation (castration ceremony) of removing the most sensitive and important part of our bodies can do. I am still a hijra and I do not want to harm my body permanently for the rest of my life. (Kalyani, interview by author)

kotis
effeminate men who are mostly gay or bisexual and are not affiliated to any hijra *gharana.*

Hijras higher in rank, like gurus, are often those delegating work assignments to the hijra ranks subordinate to them. The gurus have the privilege of choosing who will accompany them for ritual blessings, or *toli badhai.* The guru selects the chelas and nati-chelas based on several factors. These include their mutual cordial relationships, hijras with more money and better methods of "feminine" gender performativity, caste status, and sometimes just circumstantial luck. Ritual work is considered to be of the highest prestige within the hijra community. Therefore, those engaged in toli badhai are automatically considered to be higher in rank within the hijra hierarchy. However, it must be noted that collecting voluntary donations through ritual work is also an institutionalized form of begging—a traditional way of earning a livelihood within the hijra community.

Conventionally, the senior gurus do not engage in sex work openly or visit cruising areas to solicit prostitution. Within the hijra prestige economy system, it is considered disrespectful for gurus to take part in such activities. However, in some cases, the gurus might themselves be involved in sex work but only with a select client base. The chelas have to show respect to the guru by not acknowledging this aspect of their lives in public, despite it being a public secret.

However, before rising to the rank of a guru, the hijras almost always have to work as sex workers and beggars. Therefore, rising in rank within the hijra hierarchy of social systems also entitles the hijras higher in rank to have more bargaining power in choosing their livelihoods. Consequently, if one is higher in rank, the workload for them is less. The money earned through these three income-generating activities is then placed in a central pool and distributed and shared among members of the house based on the power structures within the hijra prestige economy system. Champa, a chela hijra says the following for a senior guru in the Laxmi Nagar area:

> What is it that we have except our gurus? Our gurus are our saviors. They have rescued us from the harsh and brutal world. We have no one that we can trust, even our families, the one to which we were biologically born, have disowned us. Life is not perfect! In such a situation, even when we have to face some difficulties, it is only something that we have earned in return of our ill-doings and we deserve it. There is no other way of skipping it. It is all a part of life. (Champa, interview by author)

The maha nayaks, who are at the uppermost level in the hierarchy, do not have to go out and earn because they receive a portion of the earnings of those in the ranks below them. In exchange, they maintain social relations, order, and harmony within the hijra community by serving on the internal governing councils, known as *panchayats* or *jamaats*.

The hijra financial chain is a structure of systematic payments whereby those at the bottom of the structure pay those above them. Those higher in rank have a duty to care for their subordinates in the hijra prestige economy system. They also look after those who have been victims of sexual harassment, rape, and police violence. Those lower in rank often have multiple jobs. The nati-chelas may work as beggars in the morning and as sex workers in the evening; the chelas might works as ritual workers in the morning and sex workers in the evening. Irrespective of their workload, payments need to be given to their gurus. The gurus then pass a share from their collection to those higher up in rank and so on until it reaches the maha nayaks at the topmost tier.

EMBODIMENT

Within the prestige economy system of the hijra community, those hijras who are castrated gain more respect than those who are not (see Reddy

2006). There is pressure on those lower in rank to be castrated, despite the fact that castration is not a prerequisite for becoming a hijra. Currently, there are both *Nirwana* (castrated) and *Akwa* (noncastrated) hijras in India. Pikoo, a castrated migrant hijra from Bangladesh at the Shashtri Park Theka area in New Delhi said:

> This is a matter of confidence and trust alone. How can we give our lives to untrained and unprofessional hands with no experience at all? This is a question of life and death to us and we would rather go to our community's trusted hands and healers who have been performing this ritual since generations. (Pikoo, interview by author)

This insistence of the religiosity of a castrated hijra body is rooted in three key factors. First, hijras are associated within Hindu mythology to many androgynous avatars of gods and goddesses (Pande 2004; Pattnaik 2015). In the Indian cultural context, hijras are accepted as androgynous avatars of those gods because of their socioreligious status in society. Acknowledging their age-old socioreligious approval, the hijras reappropriate their bargaining power within society by asking for voluntary donations in exchange for their blessings. In this process, there is an implicit understanding of an asexual and castrated hijra body. Kapila, another castrated migrant hijra from Bangladesh at the Shashtri Park Theka area in New Delhi said:

> This is why we Hijras are considered to be god-like as we undergo such pain that ordinary men and women cannot even think of bearing. We are the closest to The Almighty and as folklore has it, in the Mahabharata, the greatest Indian epic of all times, we are called 'Ardhanarishwar,' i.e. half-(wo)man half-god. (Kapila, interview by author)

Within a Hindu cosmological frame of reference, desire is seen as the root of all evil, and renouncing desire through asexuality and castration is seen as a way of being associated with rising above the material pleasures and becoming spiritual. Scholars argue that castration then does not embrace sexual ambiguity since the pressure is on renouncing it (Jaffrey 1996, 56). However, in the context of Muslim hijras, Hossain (2012, 498) argues that despite having Hindu practices, those hijras born Muslim can situate themselves into a Hindu cosmological frame of reference because Islam as a religion is open to this transcendence.

This spiritual status of the hijras is publicly acknowledged and accepted as part of their gender role, which entitles them to rise to the spiritual level of "others" who are nonhijras. Consequently, the hijras are elevated to the status of demigoddesses with spiritual abilities to confer fertility and good luck on those seeking their blessings. It is also considered a sin to refuse hijras money, as their curses are considered highly potent and dangerous. Most dangerous of all is the point in the negotiation when a hijra threatens to shame those who refuse to pay by lifting their skirts and exposing whatever lies beneath the hijra's petticoat.

Second, the British colonialists criminalized hijras by banning them from public areas under the Criminal Tribes Act (CTA) of 1871. This act forced the hijra community underground as they were considered "eunuchs" responsible for sodomy, kidnapping, and castrating male children (see Hinchy 2019). Although the CTA was rescinded in 1952, a collective memory still paints hijras as historical gender deviants with a criminalized sexual variance. Testimony to this fact is that the first colonial antisodomy law introduced by the British in 1861 through Section 377 of the Indian Penal Code (IPC) considered homosexuality an unnatural act and a public offense until 2018 in the postcolonial Indian nation-state. As a result of this colonial baggage, the mainstream society conflates hijras with homosexuals despite hijras being a gender identity and not a sexual identity.

Third, if not associated with castration, then the popular understanding of the hijra body is of those born with intersex variations. In fact, in colloquial Hindi, the term *intersex* is culturally synonymous with the term *hijra*. Within hijra communities, those born intersex are considered "natural" hijras who are "born that way." There are also many Indian folktales about intersex children being donated by the birth parents to hijras who adopt those children with pride and increase the membership of their community. However, no person with an intersex variation can become a hijra without the patronage of a hijra guru.

Therefore, one of the crucial elements of rising in rank is achieving an ideal castrated hijra body—an element central to hijra performativity of gender. Consequently, often the hijra gurus pay for the castration of their chelas, in exchange for which the chelas pay the guru a portion of their income. This way the chelas also compensate their gurus financially for learning the hijra ways of gender performativity. However, the initial sum paid for castration is compounded with interest, and eventually the sum grows to a point where chelas are typically never actually able to repay this debt in full over a lifetime. As an outcome, kin relatedness within the hijra prestige economy system then also forms a kind of economic bond based on financial debt.

Some scholars have also viewed the guru-disciple lineage as a form of disguised "bonded labor," especially if the hijra guru pays for the castration of their hijra disciple, in return for which the disciple is not only expected to remain in bonded servitude to their guru for a lifetime but also because there exists a hijra custom of "leti," which is the amount payable by a hijra disciple to the guru if they leave their hijra guru for another (Saxena 2011, 159). The hijra disciple is also expected to repay the "loan" by turning in a share of their earnings and doing household chores in the hijra commune, which is "invariably greater than the original sum of money borrowed" from their hijra gurus (Mazumdar 2016, 46; see Goel 2019). Such internal rules also bound Sharmili to her hijra guru in Dakshinpuri who discriminated against her because of her lower-caste status, and Sharmili could not afford to pay the "leti" and take patronage under another guru in Trilokpuri.

CONCLUSION

Kinship has been a significant and essential area of study in anthropology, reflecting on the complicated and often contradictory nature of negotiating gender roles and sexuality. In the context of the hijras or "third" gender in India, androgynous nonbinary kinship becomes a critical site of examination for studying the hijra prestige economy system. Decisive aspects of maintaining hijra kin through performative aspects of respect, livelihoods, and embodiment are central to the hijra social system. Hijra kin relatedness is based on a system of informality not recognized by Indian law but, contradictorily and unknowingly, recognized in some aspect by the Indian government through issuing voter ID cards for hijras that carry the names of their gurus either as fathers or husbands. Therefore, hijra kinship functions as an androgynous institutionalized system of discipleship-lineage based on power relations and further legitimized by internal hijra councils.

Caste is an ever-evolving process of engagement between individual hijras within the hijra community, and the negotiation of the hijra caste identity is contingent upon several factors. Many aspects depend on the relationship hijras have with their gurus. As a collective unit, it is difficult to understand the intersection of caste with hijra kinship, and little is known about the intersection of the Indian caste hierarchies with the social stratification in the hijra community. Nonetheless, caste is an important, often hidden factor in determining kin relatedness within the hijra community, particularly through Sharmili's narrative in the opening vignette of this chapter.

Hijra kinship, therefore, is a mutually coordinated support system maintained by a historically oppressed community by making it a hierarchically organized enclave that is mostly hidden from the outside world (Goel 2016). Through kinship, hijras sustain their ordered rankings within their cultural enclaves by justifying their logic according to the rules made by the internal governing councils of the hijra community, and this renders their community a "closed" social group.

REVIEW QUESTIONS

1. Why is kinship so important to the hijra community?

2. How do Indian social hierarchies intersect with hijra kinship?

3. How do power dynamics shape the relationship between hijra guru and chela?

KEY TERMS

caste system: Indian kinship is always grouped around a system of social stratification based on birth status known as the caste system.

Dalit: formerly "untouchable" community in India.

hijras: also known as "third" gender in India; can be understood as subaltern forms of trans-queer identities existing within a prestige economy system of kinship networks.

hijra *gharanas*: symbolic units of lineage guiding the overall schematic outlining of the social organization of hijra community in India.

hijra kinship: androgynous nonbinary family network, the continuation of which is based on a nonbiological discipleship-lineage system, which is based on power relations that are further legitimized by internal hijra councils.

hijra prestige economy system: a system of kin relatedness within the hijra community based on the social standing of hijras to one another.

joint-family: a household system in which members of more than one generation of a unilineal descent group live together.

kotis: effeminate men who are mostly gay or bisexual and are not affiliated to any hijra *gharana*.

Mughal: early modern empire in South Asia founded in 1526 that spanned two centuries.

nonbinary family network: kinship pattern for those who identify on the gender spectrum outside the male-female binary.

RESOURCES FOR FURTHER EXPLORATION

- Butalia, Urvashi. 2011. *Mona's Story*. GRANTA. https://granta.com/monas-story/

- Revathi, A. 2010. *The Truth About Me: A Hijra Life Story*. New Delhi: Penguin

- Interview with Indian activist Laxmi Narayan Tripathi on the third gender, Women in the World, 8 March 2017. https://www.youtube.com/watch?v=Mzhf29NBWbw.

- Goel, Ina. 2020. Impact of Covid-19 on Hijras, a Third-Gender Community in India, Covid-19, *Fieldsights,* May 4. https://culanth.org/fieldsights/impact-of-covid-19-on-hijras-a-third-gender-community-in-india.

BIBLIOGRAPHY

Belkin, E. C. 2008. *Creating Groups Outside the Caste System: The Devadasis and Hijras of India.* Bachelor's thesis, Wesleyan University.

Bhaskaran, Suparna. 2004. *Made in India-Decolonizations, Queer Sexualities, Trans/national projects*. New York: Palgrave Macmillan.

Butler, J. 2006. "Performative Acts and Gender Constitution: An Essay in Phenomenology and Feminist Theory." In *The Routledge Falmer Reader in Gender & Education*, 73–83. London: Routledge.

Census of India. 2011. https://www.census2011.co.in/transgender.php.

Chatterjee, I. 2002. "Alienation, Intimacy, and Gender: Problems for a History of Love in South Asia." *Queering India: Same-Sex Love and Eroticism in Indian Culture and Society*, edited by Ruth Vanita, 61–76. New York: Routledge.

Datta, S. 2017. We Refuse to Be Subjects of Experiment for Those Who Do Not Understand Us: Transgender Persons Bill. *Economic and Political Weekly* 52, no. 49.

Dutta, A. 2012. An Epistemology of Collusion: Hijras, Kothis and the Historical (Dis) Continuity of Gender/Sexual Identities in Eastern India. *Gender & History*, 24, no. 3: 825–849.

Goel, I. 2016. Hijra Communities of Delhi. *Sexualities* 19, no. 5–6: 535–546.

———. 2018. Caste and Religion Create Barriers Within the Hijra Community. *The Wire.* 18 May. https://thewire.in/lgbtqia/caste-religion-hijra-community

———. 2019. Transing-normativities: Understanding Hijra Communes as Queer Homes in *The Everyday Makings of Heteronormativity: Cross-cultural Explorations of Sex, Gender, and Sexuality*, edited by Sertaç Sehlikoglu and Frank G. Karioris, 139–52. London: Lexington.

Hall, K. 2013." Commentary I: 'It's a Hijra!' Queer Linguistics Revisited." *Discourse & Society* 24, no. 5: 634–642.

Hossain, A. 2012. "Beyond Emasculation: Being Muslim and Becoming Hijra in South Asia." *Asian Studies Review* 36, no. 4: 495–513.

Hinchy, J. 2015. "Enslaved Childhoods in Eighteenth-Century Awadh." *South Asian History and Culture* 6, no. 3: 380–400.

Hinchy, Jessica. 2019. *Governing Gender and Sexuality in Colonial India: The Hijra, c. 1850–1900*. Cambridge: Cambridge University Press.

Jaffrey, Zia. 1996. *The Invisibles: A Tale of the Eunuchs of India*. New York: Pantheon.

Mazumdar, M. 2016. *Hijra Lives: Negotiating Social Exclusion and Identities*. Master's thesis, Tata Institute of Social Sciences, Mumbai.

Nanda, Serena. 1990. *Neither Man nor Woman: The Hijras of India*. Belmont, CA: Wadsworth

Pande, Alka. 2004. *Ardhanarishvara, the Androgyne: Probing the Gender Within*. New Delhi: Rupa.

Pattanaik, Devdutt. 2015. *Shikhandi and Others Tales They Don't Tell You*. New Delhi: Penguin.

Reddy, G. 2001. "Crossing 'Lines' of Subjectivity: The Negotiation of Sexual Identity in Hyderabad, India." *South Asia: Journal of South Asian Studies* 24, no. 1: S91–S101.

———. 2006. *With Respect to Sex: Negotiating Hijra Identity in South India*. New Delhi: Yoda.

Salve, P., D. Bansod, and H. Kadlak. 2017. "Safai Karamcharis in a Vicious Cycle: A Study in the Perspective of Caste." *Economic & Political Weekly* 52, no. 13: 38–41.

Saxena, Piyush. 2011. *Life of a Eunuch*. Mumbai: Shanta.

Taparia, S. 2011. Emasculated Bodies of Hijras: Sites of Imposed, Resisted and Negotiated Identities. *Indian Journal of Gender Studies* 18, no. 2: 167–184.

Weston, K. 1991. *Families We Choose: Lesbians, Gays, Kinship*. New York: Columbia University Press.

———. 1998. *Long Slow Burn: Sexuality and Social Science*. London: Routledge.

6

The "City" and "The Easy Life"

Work and Gender among Sherpa in Nepal

Alba Castellsagué and Silvia Carrasco

In this chapter, the authors examine the ongoing poverty of the region that has been the focus of many international development plans and efforts. The authors explore the impact some of these development projects have had on work patterns among ethnic Sherpa women in Nepal. They question whether or not wage labor and urban lifestyles with Western patterns of consumption (the markers of development) actually contribute to women's emancipation and empowerment.

LEARNING OBJECTIVES

- Analyze the gender dimensions of work inequalities through the case of Sherpa in Nepal.

- Identify the gendered effects of mobility.

- Define key concepts such as gender and mobility regimes, sexual division of labor, and productive and reproductive work.

Waged labor has become a central focus in development issues around the world, particularly as it relates to women's equality and emancipation. For example, if we look at the United Nations' Millennium Development Goals, participation in the labor force and having paid work outside of agriculture are both indicators of achievement for goal number three: "promote gender equality and empower women" (United Nations 2010). Similarly, the Global Gender Gap Report measures variables such as female labor force, wage equality, and earned income (World Economic Forum 2017), with the goal of reducing the gap between male and female economic participation and opportunities. However, as this chapter demonstrates, wage labor is not always the best or only path to women's equality or emancipation.

Multiple studies (Escobar 1998; Hirschman 1980; Sen 1999) have challenged the idea that development should solely be based on material and economic growth, and indeed as our study shows, analyzing development from a gender perspective highlights the problems of such a view. First, economic growth has been based on specific models of material development and the subsequent promotion of women as efficient, wage-earning workers. These ideas of women as ideal workers "are embedded in, rely on, and actively reinforce and extend the existing patriarchal structures and gendered relationships of power" (Wilson 2015, 807). Not only do the global production processes and labor markets reproduce an unequal distribution of power between men and women, but they are increasingly made precarious by the dominant neoliberal economies and policies (Mills 2003; Peterson 2016). Second, economic growth is also "defined and measured in a way that arbitrarily excludes the essential, but invisible 'economic inactivity' that goes into making it happen" (Kabeer 2016, 298). The gendered division of labor is therefore essential to unpack and understand gender inequalities, and it has historically been at the center of feminist research and vindications.

In Nepal, changing modes of production and living under the urban-development paradigm have provoked a rapid transformation of social structures and hierarchies, including gender. In this chapter we specifically explore the constant (re)shaping of the meanings and patterns of work for Sherpa women, drawing on data from a multisited ethnography (Marcus 1995) in Gaun and Kathmandu.

Gaun is a small village located at an altitude of thirty-four hundred meters in the Solu region of the Himalayan mountains in Nepal. The village includes roughly twenty households settled around cultivation terraces, three Buddhist monasteries, and a primary school. Its population is mostly Sherpa, an ethnicity native to the mountainous regions in the north and the east of Nepal. Sherpas are 0.43 percent of the population of Nepal (Nepal Population Report 2016), have Tibeto-Burman origins, and are typically engaged with Buddhist traditions. For their knowledge of high-altitude areas and particularly within the Everest region, they are highly regarded and well known as expert mountain climbers. In fact, the term *Sherpa* is nowadays often misused to refer to any mountain guide or expedition staff member in the Himalayas, regardless of their ethnicity.

Most of our informants often move between Gaun and Kathmandu, due to work or school requirements, to visit relatives, and/or for seasonal or temporary changes of residence. The importance of this mobility led us to the multisited approach to our ethnography, allowing us to consider not only both geographic contexts but also the variety of processes relevant to women's mobility flows. Kathmandu is the largest metropolitan area of the Himalayas and the capital city of Nepal. It has the hustle and bustle typical of big cities: noisy, dusty, and busy streets; markets of all kinds; and also temples from diverse religious traditions—all of these attract not only foreign tourists but also pilgrims from all over Nepal.

Our fieldwork in both locations centered on issues of women's work, specifically (1) the construction of femininity and social relations in Gaun, (2) women's narratives on education and development (Castellsagué and Carrasco, 2020b), and (3) women's expectations and desires for mobility in urban settings, both within Nepal and abroad.

WORK: A DRIVER FOR WOMEN'S DEVELOPMENT IN NEPAL

This chapter focuses on three important labor factors from a gender perspective among Sherpas in Nepal. Firstly, there are the continuing ethnic differentiations of women's participation in wage labor. Second, the dominant development discourses situate "modern" wage labor as desirable, particularly for women, who are usually considered by development organizations as independent or empowered if they participate in the productive economy and bring a monetary income to the household. Finally, government and international organizations promote wage labor over other traditional activities such as subsistence farming, as the Nepal Human Development Report (2014) emphasizes: "The pace of economic growth needs to accelerate, and be accompanied by large-scale employment generation and enhanced productivity" (3). In Nepal, although women represent 53 percent of the employed population, there's a significant gender gap when it comes to wage employment—only 8.3 percent are paid—women are overrepresented in the informal sector (including unpaid family workers, unpaid apprentices, and part-time workers) and low-skilled jobs (Acharya 2014). According to the Gender Gap Report, Nepal ranks high among countries in terms of female workforce participation (16th out of 144) but fares much worse when it comes to wage equality for women where it ranks much lower (98th out of 144) for all workers, and 115th out of 144 for professional and technical workers) (World Economic Forum 2017). If we take a more qualitative approach, we see that the organization of female labor reflects Nepal's ethnic and cultural diversity. Acharya and Bannett (1983) noted two differentiated patterns:

Figure 6.2. Village of Gaun: households, fields, and monasteries. Alba Castellsagué.

while the Hindu communities concentrated female labor within domestic work and subsistence production, Tibeto Burman communities, such as Sherpa, showed a higher degree of female participation in the market economy and a more significant role in household economic decisions. Despite dramatic changes in the modes of production in Nepal and the organization of women's labor organization, we found that the patterns described by Acharya and Bennett (1983) still persist.

Mobility is the second (and intimately related) factor as women's movements are tied to job-seeking opportunities (Hagen-Zanker et al.

Figure 6.2. Street in Kathmandu. Alba Castellsagué.

mobility regime
refers to the specific ways in which movements of people are organized in a hierarchical way, privileging some movements over others.

2014). As we have argued (Castellsagué, forthcoming), a particular **mobility regime** in Nepal, embedded within the hegemonic development paradigms, promotes certain flows to urban centers and abroad, mainly to more developed countries (e.g., the Gulf States, Southeast Asia, and India (Maharjan, Bauer, and Knerr 2012; Government of Nepal and Ministry of Labour and Employment 2016). This chapter examines an often-overlooked aspect of mobility, namely the linkage between internal and external migration from a gender perspective. International migration, which is predominantly masculine, is closely tied to national and internal patterns of wives' mobility to the urban centers (Maharjan 2015). Women are increasingly participating in such mobility dynamics and are no longer seen as mere administrators of remittances. Rather, they have an active role in the economic and labor strategies in Nepal and abroad (Hamal Gurung 2015).

Finally, young women see education as a strategic access door to wage labor and modern lifestyles, which mostly means being *educated*, living in a city or abroad, and participating in the wage labor force. Harber (2014) maintains that the promise of access to the labor market, as well as of better jobs and income, is at the core of schooling discourses and constitutes one of the main drivers in the promotion of education in Nepal.

> The education system is being viewed as being "successful" only when a student graduates and secures the job that will take him or, rarely, her out of the village with its traditional values and into the city with its modern lifestyle. (Wynd 1999, 107)

To continue their education, young people must move to Kathmandu or abroad, adapting to more urban livelihoods and job expectations.

LIFE IN GAUN

sexual division of labor
delegation or assignment of different tasks to males and females within a group, family, or society

"It's hard work, but we're satisfied," stated Amita, a thirty-year-old woman who lives in Gaun with her younger son and daughter. Her eldest son lives with her extended family in a nearby village, and her husband spends weekdays in another village where he is employed as the school principal. The organization of work in Gaun is based on a **sexual division of labor**. As Dolma, fifty-eight, describes it, "Women are always busy with the home, the culture. Men work to make the money, they go to the Himalaya, trekking, ride a car in Europe . . . they want to be rich; after all, daily life is carried on by women." Note that Dolma uses the expression "ride a car in Europe" and links it to the idea of being rich; that is, being able to afford a car in Europe and ride it. Everyday life in Gaun for women includes working in the fields, taking care of the animals (usually cows or goats), fetching water for the kitchen, sharing tea and chatting with other women, exchanging products with other families, and visiting relatives, among other activities. Some women, such as Amita or Mingma, also work as teachers in Gaun's school; while others own small shops with basic goods or host guests at their households as forms of business. For men, everyday life can vary depending on their work: they pray and make *puja* (ceremonies) if they are *lamas* (Buddhist monks), they guide trekking expeditions, or work in the school if they are teachers. They also work in the construction sector and take care of the livestock. In the periods between work assignments, they socialize with other men and work in the crops with their relatives.

We quickly noticed that the masculine and feminine spheres are significantly separated in Gaun. The spaces of socialization, the type of work, and the daily activities are organized according not only to sex but also age. Men and women carry out different activities and spend most of the time with their gender equals, while age is used to assign roles within the family and the crop production. Both factors, age and gender, appear to be intertwined, not only for the organization of daily chores but also for the transference of knowledge and social responsibilities. This makes the case for an intersectional approach in our analysis.

Women never viewed the separate gendered spheres of work and socialization as a disadvantage. Due to the work women perform, they also play a central role in resource management and decision making, both within the family unit and the village (Tamang 2000). Their capacity of work is an essential component of the valuation of femininity in Gaun. They consider a "real Sherpa" to be a woman who is strong, both physically and in character, self-confident, and capable of working hard. While working in the fields, women also create strong networks through which they help each other and develop a sense of community (see figure 6.4).

In their workspaces, including the households, they make decisions about social issues. Whenever something happens in Gaun, whether it is a political, economic, or community issue, women informally gather at some household or in a field, and while sharing tea or working together they evaluate the situation, exchange opinions, and usually come up with an agreement on how to address the issue at hand (see figure 6.5). Work becomes an aspect of women's identities, something for which they are socially valued and respected; their labor is much more than just an economic contribution.

If we think about other intrinsic factors, women nowadays carry the majority of the burden of both household and village work due to long absences of men and young people who are away for work or education. The majority of families in Gaun lack some of their male members, either permanently or temporarily. We learn of them through phone calls, photographs, and the many stories we hear from their wives, children, and relatives. Men pursue paid jobs in the mountain region (trekking, expeditions), Kathmandu (work in an office or restaurant), or abroad (mostly construction). Young boys and girls move for educational purposes, as the possibilities for further study are better in the larger cities of Nepal. Male internal migration has an impact on the way work is organized, experienced, and signified by women in Gaun. Productivity decreases due to the lack of laborers, many fields and houses are left unoccupied, and women, both adult and elderly, take an active role in most of the work in Gaun. Amita describes her daily chores, which are "to carry water from the riverside, look after the babies, feed them, look after the animals, work in the fields, cooking, host guests." A common feeling among women, particularly younger women, is that "life is hard in Gaun, because we have to do a lot of work," as the fifteen-year-old Manju states. Other informants also refer to life as *gharo* (hard or difficult) in Gaun because of the lack of amenities. Amita observes that "there is no access to a market, it is hard to bring basic goods and there's a lack of infrastructure, such as electricity." Therefore, the difficulties among Sherpa women encompass not only the amount of work to be done but also the burdens they face due to poor infrastructure and the absence of men. Age, gender, and men's national and international migration are relevant factors in shaping the design and development of women's

Figure 6.3. Sherpa woman and girl taking a cow to the fields in Gaun. It is one of the daily chores usually done by women or young girls. Alba Castellsagué.

mobility projects and their perceptions of life. As we will see in the next section, the perception of rural life as "hard" is usually based on comparisons with urban life either experienced or only imagined.

LIFE IN THE CITY

The reasons for moving to Kathmandu are diverse, depending on each family's situation and their particular **mobility projects**. However, as men migrate to seek better job opportunities, women may also try to avoid relatively unproductive and hard agricultural labor by moving to urban areas, usually to educate children (Maharjan, 2015). We can identify common themes in the organization of work among the families, as well as the way women experience and perceive city life.

mobility project
the intentional family decisions and plans made regarding mobility, as opposed to involuntary movements forced by particular needs.

> Sherpa women have very good facilities here [in the city], and they don't have to work. Most of [the] Sherpa women that stay in Kathmandu, their husbands are abroad, in Dubai, Malaysia, Qatar . . . you know? And they earn money, and they send them (remittances). And the woman's job is only to look after their kids, and look after herself also. Only this. (Mingma, twenty-three years old)

Figure 6.4. Sherpa women working cooperatively to harvest potato crops in Gaun. Photo by Alba Castellsagué.

Figure 6.5. Women drinking tea during a pause from work in the fields. An opportunity to discuss and address social and political issues in Gaun. Photo by Alba Castellsagué.

productive work
human activities that produce goods or services with an exchange value, usually associated with the public spheres.

reproductive work
human activities that sustain the biological and social (re)production of the workforce. The term encompasses all the tasks needed to guarantee the survival, care, and material and emotional well-being of the members of a group, family, or society.

As we notice through Mingma's statement, daily life is notably different for Sherpa women in Kathmandu. She points out some transformations in the organization of work in urban settings, compared to rural life in Gaun. First, life is perceived as much more *sagilo* (easy) for women in the city due to access to better amenities. Although she recognizes that women, due to the absence of men, are still the ones that do all the work, the fact of being in an urban environment and having money completely changes her interpretation of work and its difficulty. She feels that they "only" have to perform reproductive tasks. Dolma also stresses the importance of money in order to reduce the burden of work in the city by saying that "if you have money in the city you can buy everything, you can order food from home, and in the village you have to do it yourself." Men's internal migration is relevant, as their remittances may seem more useful for women in an urban setting, where money can be put to better use. On the other hand, extra money in Gaun does not necessarily contribute to an easier life for women, at least not as they perceive it. We can also see how while in Gaun concepts of "work" did not differentiate between **productive** and **reproductive labor**, in Kathmandu such distinctions are meaningful. Reproductive work in Kathmandu is not just seen as "easier" work but not even considered work at all.

Working less is perceived as an improvement in women's daily lives. However, if we consider how central work is for their self-worth and identity, we must consider whether such changes have other effects in their social lives and relationships. As we noted, life in the city is much more isolated than in Gaun; in fact it represents a loss of social ties and support networks for women living in Kathmandu. Dolma often expresses a feeling of loneliness, while other women feel that they have "nothing to do." Interestingly, while working less is central to the idea of life as being "easier," the informants also see the feeling of "not working at all," in Dolma's own words, as problematic.

Thus, mobility to access urban centers, often embedded within larger mobility projects and men's international migration, shapes the patterns of Sherpa social organization. Women shift from a heavy combination of productive and reproductive work in Gaun to doing mainly household work in the city. With this change in work patterns, women need to (re)think and (re)orient their position and role within the family and the community.

HIGH EXPECTATIONS VERSUS POOR OPPORTUNITIES

Within mainstream development discourse, the city is imagined and portrayed as full of opportunities for women to engage global economies. When asking the young girls from Gaun about their expectations for the future, the majority of them aimed to live in Kathmandu or abroad. Many hoped to keep studying or to work as teachers, nurses, or social workers. Education is therefore seen as a useful tool to access to better job opportunities and gain sources of income (Castellsagué and Carrasco 2020). We found these common ideas embedded in notions of development such as productivity and the promotion of an urban-centered economy that prevail in Nepal to have particular gendered interpretation among our participants.

> Boys can get any job. In the village they can work as a porter, as a trekking guide, as a cook . . . Even if they are uneducated they can get this kind of job easily. In Kathmandu also, they can be a driver, work in the construction. Even abroad, they can do any work. Girls . . . girls they can't. If you are a girl, you have to get good education to get any job. (Mingma, twenty-three years old)

Mingma talks about how education becomes more meaningful for girls, who need it to compete for a job in the labor market. Since "jobs for boys" are often low skilled and can be accessed without any formal

Figure 6.6. Small shop in Kathmandu where the basic products are readily available for purchase. Photo by Alba Castellsagué.

Figure 6.7. Market in Kathmandu where women usually shop on a daily basis. Photo by Alba Castellsagué.

training, Mingma feels that girls need education to access "girls' jobs," such as teaching, working in a call center, or working as an administrative assistant. From an intersectional approach, we see how education is not only meaningful but is also considered valuable along gendered lines.

Nonetheless, one of the frequently mentioned challenges that young women living in the city face is the difficulty of getting jobs.

The problem is that everyone wants to come to Ktm [Kathmandu] to study further and to do something, but they can't because it is very hard, you know? The person who has a bachelor pass or something like this, they can't find a job. So it is very difficult here. (Mingma, twenty-three years old)

As Mingma explains, even having success in school does not guarantee that women will have access to formal jobs in the city. Therefore, the expectations that link schooling in the urban environment to direct access to productive jobs are not always fulfilled.

NEW PROBLEMS, CREATIVE ALTERNATIVES

We have identified the ways women's lives and expectations have changed and been (re)shaped by mobility and access to urban centers. Within their new circumstances in the cities, women face new positions and roles that they need to (re)negotiate and (re)signify in dialogue with their changing individual and social identities.

Facing the difficulties in pursuing job opportunities within the formal labor market, most of the informants have devised creative solutions. The majority of them have, in fact, a part-time job or run businesses in Kathmandu. "Sherpini [Sherpa women] always are looking for a side job, even in Kathmandu," Dolma explains. She works as a volunteer, translator, and is a social activist. Other women prepare *chang* (homemade alcohol), *momo* (sherpa dumplings) or *ghe* (homemade butter) and sell it in the neighborhood, or they import products from the village and distribute them in Kathmandu. Mingma's mother works in the family restaurant, and Jangmu owns a tea house in Boudhanath, the city's Sherpa neighborhood. Their jobs are usually circumscribed within the informal sector, and they are obtained through the (re)activation of social networks, often built on the basis of a common village origin or kinship. "From home to home. With the phone we call the houses and ask what they need. We buy and sell through our own networks," Dolma explains.

Women might seem somehow caught in a paradox. Despite their opinions highlighting a predilection for the "good" and "easy life" of the city, they have also expressed the need or desire to feel themselves active beyond the household. Dolma summarizes some of her reasons:

Money is important for independence. If you keep money you can have power. But it is also good for mental health and depression. You can see other women suffer from these, but the Sherpa we suffer much less, because we keep our minds busy, active, and we never stop working. You have to hold business. Also through work we can have connections with European people, while if you stay home you never get that. I'm almost 60 and I travel, I make new friends. I feel great! (Dolma, fifty-eight years old)

We see how working beyond the household continues to be meaningful for Sherpa women. While women are attracted to city life for the infrastructure and less work burden, they also do not settle for a role that only encompasses reproductive work and domestic chores.

(RE)QUESTIONING WORK AND THE EMANCIPATION OF WOMEN

This chapter has analyzed the transformations of work culture and organization between rural and urban environments, challenging the dominant development paradigm that links particular kinds of work (productive) and lifestyles (urban) with women's empowerment and emancipation.

Our results confirm classic research that unpacks how a particular ideal of a "good" and "easy" life was, and still is, linked to development, which promotes urban settlement and productive work. By contrast, manual labor and agriculture are seen as "too hard," a fact that we interpret as a way of devaluing these rural modes of production. Moreover, this chapter specifically analyzes this phenomenon from a gender perspective, questioning the pertinence and relevance of the dichotomy between productive and reproductive work. In rural contexts, daily life includes multitasking activities, which according to Aikman are "characteristic of women's work and belies sharp divisions between household tasks and productive tasks" (1999, 71). However, such task differentiation becomes more relevant when women move to Kathmandu and they start to integrate the discriminatory logic of the capitalist sexual division of labor (Rosaldo 1979; Federici 2012): that is, not valuing as work the reproductive activities they do and reducing the variety of participation and socialization spaces to the domestic sphere.

The supposed emancipation that comes through participation in productive wage labor needs to be reconsidered. Although research has shown a clear increase in women's participation in the labor market in terms of quantity, it is not clear what they have gained in terms of quality (Kabeer 2016). It is important to assess whether participation in the labor market, in the cases where participation is successfully achieved, is actually an improvement in women's life conditions, since the workplace has been set as another patriarchal space and is broadly segregated along horizontal and vertical lines (Mills 2003; Kabeer 2015, 2016; Wilson 2015). Gender segregation in employment refers to men and women's unequal distribution of access and performance within a certain occupational structure (a company, an economic sector, a state). *Vertical segregation* refers to the concentration of men at the top of the power hierarchies; while *horizontal segregation* is used when the segregation is based on the tasks both men and women do. Moreover, this push for development relies on a very narrow idea of work, which undervalues and excludes the multiple subsistence activities (e.g., agriculture and livestock, manual labor) that are considered unproductive (Shiva 1989). Feminism has historically challenged the very idea of salaried jobs as liberating (Federici 2004) and reclaimed that reproductive tasks are the foundations of any society, particularly within capitalist economies (Federici 2012). We need, therefore, new paradigms and approaches calling for the inclusion of community and familiar spheres as part of the economies, spaces where women are already active and powerful (Norberg-Hodge 1991). This chapter has highlighted the importance of women's networks as sites for gender analysis and as sources of power (Cornwall and Rivas 2015; Rosaldo 1979). Our ethnographic data show how women (re)activate these networks to challenge urban isolation and keep their economic participation vibrant. Finally, ethnographic insights challenge the dominant macro and quantitative approaches to labor and economics. Not only do they enrich the existing knowledge about the "geographies of gender" (Kabeer 2016), but also they also help us imagine diverse and meaningful paths toward development and gender equality worldwide.

REVIEW QUESTIONS

1. What factors should we consider when analyzing work relations among men and women?

2. How does mobility to urban areas affect the organization of work for the Sherpa?

3. Which are the social aspects to take into account when considering women's well-being?

KEY TERMS

mobility project: the intentional family decisions and plans made regarding mobility, as opposed to involuntary movements forced by particular needs.

mobility regime: refers to the specific ways in which movements of people are organized in a hierarchical way, privileging some movements over others.

productive work: human activities that produce goods or services with an exchange value, usually associated with the public spheres.

reproductive work: human activities that sustain the biological and social (re)production of the workforce. The term encompasses all the tasks needed to guarantee the survival, care, and material and emotional well-being of the members of a group, family, or society.

sexual division of labor: delegation or assignment of different tasks to males and females within a group, family, or society

RESOURCES FOR FURTHER EXPLORATION

- Acharya, Meena, and Lynn Bennett. 1983. "Women and the Subsistence Sector: Economic Participation and Household Decision Making in Nepal." World Bank Staff Working Papers, Washington, DC.

- Hamal Gurung, Shobha. 2015. "Coming to America. Gendered Labor, Women's Agency, and Transnationalism." In *Nepali Migrant Women: Resistance and Survival in America*, 1–83. New York: Syracuse University Press.

- Mills, Mary Beth. 2003. "Gender and Inequality in the Global Labor Force." *Annual Review of Anthropology* 32, no. 1: 41–62. https://doi.org/10.1146/annurev.anthro.32.061002.093107.

BIBLIOGRAPHY

Acharya, Meena, and Lynn Bennett. 1983. "Women and the Subsistence Sector: Economic Participation and Household Decision Making in Nepal." *World Bank Staff Working Papers*. Washington, DC.

Acharya, Sushan. 2014. "Gender, Jobs and Education. Prospects and Realities in Nepal." Kathmandu, Nepal: UNESCO Office Kathmandu.

Aikman, Sheila. 1999. "Schooling and Development: Eroding Amazon Women's Knowledge and Diversity." In *Gender, Education & Development. Beyond Access to Empowerment*, edited by Christine Heward and Sheila Bunwaree, 223. New York: Zed.

Castellsagué, Alba. 2020. "La Retórica Del Retorno: Mingma o Las Contradicciones Del Desarrollo En Nepal." *Disparidades. Revista de Antropología* 75, no. 2: e025. https://doi.org/10.3989/dra.2020.025.

Castellsagué, Alba, and Silvia Carrasco. 2020. "Schooling and Development: Global Discourses and Women's Narratives from Nepal." *Compare: A Journal of Comparative and International Education*. https://doi.org/10.1080/030579 25.2019.1709803.

Cornwall, Andrea, and Althea Maria Rivas. 2015. "From 'Gender Equality and 'Women's Empowerment' to Global Justice: Reclaiming a Transformative Agenda for Gender and Development." *Third World Quarterly* 36, no. 2: 396–415. https://doi.org/10.1080/01436597.2015.1013341.

Escobar, Arturo. 1998. *La Invención Del Tercer Mundo: Construcción y Deconstrucción Del Desarrollo*. Vol. 1. Caracas: Fundación Editorial El perro y la Rana. https://doi.org/10.1017/CBO9781107415324.004.

Federici, Silvia. 2004. *El Calibán y La Bruja*. 2010th ed. Madrid: Traficantes de Sueños.

———. 2012. *Revolución En Punto Cero. Trabajo Doméstico, Reproducción y Luchas Feministas*. Edited by Traficantes de Sueños. Madrid: Creative Commons.

Government of Nepal and Ministry of Labour and Employment. 2016. *Labour Migration for Employment A Status Report for Nepal: 2013 / 2014*.

Hagen-zanker, Jessica, Richard Mallett, Anita Ghimire, Qasim Ali Shah, and Bishnu Upreti. 2014. *Migration from the Margins: Mobility, Vulnerability and Inevitability in Mid-Western Nepal and North-Western Pakistan*. London: Secure Livelihoods Research Consortium.

Hamal Gurung, Shobha. 2015. "Coming to America. Gendered Labor, Women's Agency, and Transnationalism." In *Nepali Migrant Women: Resistance and Survival in America*, 1–83. New York: Syracuse University Press.

Harber, Clive. 2014. *Education and International Development: Theory, Practice and Issues*. Oxford: Symposium.

Hirschman, Albert O. 1980. "Auge y Ocaso de La Teoría Económica Del Desarrollo." *Trimestre Económico 47*, no. 188: 1055–77.

Kabeer, Naila. 2015. "Gender, Poverty, and Inequality: A Brief History of Feminist Contributions in the Field of International Development." *Gender and Development* 23, no. 2: 189–205. https://doi.org/10.1080/13552074.2015.106 2300.

———. 2016. "Gender Equality, Economic Growth, and Women's Agency: The 'Endless Variety' and 'Monotonous Similarity' of Patriarchal Constraints." *Feminist Economics* 22, no. 1: 295–321. https://doi.org/10.1080/1354570 1.2015.1090009.

Maharjan, Amina, Siegfried Bauer, and Beatrice Knerr. 2012. "Do Rural Women Who Stay Behind Benefit from Male Out-Migration? A Case Study in the Hills of Nepal." *Gender, Technology and Development* 16, no. 1: 95–123. https://doi.org/10.1177/097185241101600105.

Maharjan, Mahesh Raj. 2015. "Emigrants' Migrant Wives: Linking International and Internal Migration." *Studies in Nepali History and Society* 20, no. 2: 217–47.

Marcus, George E. 1995. "Ethnography in/of the World System: The Emergence of Multi-Sited Ethnography." *Annual Review of Anthropology* 24, no. 1: 95–117. https://doi.org/10.1146/annurev.anthro.24.1.95.

Mills, Mary Beth. 2003. "Gender and Inequality in the Global Labor Force." *Annual Review of Anthropology* 32, no. 1: 41–62. https://doi.org/10.1146/annurev.anthro.32.061002.093107.

Ministry of Population and Environment and Population Education and Health Research Center. 2016. *Nepal Population Report.*

Norberg-Hodge, Helena. 1991. *Ancient Futures.* San Francisco: Sierra Club.

Peterson, S. Spike. 2016. "Gendering Insecurities, Informalization and 'War Economies.'" In *The Palgrave Handbook of Gender and Development. Critical Engagements in Feminist Theory and Practice*, edited by Wendy Harcourt, 441–62. London: Palgrave Macmillan.

Poertner, Ephraim, Mathias Junginger, and Ulrike Müller-Böker. 2011. "Migration in Far West Nepal Intergenerational Linkages between Internal and International Migration of Rural-to-Urban Migrants." *Critical Asian Studies* 43, no. 1: 23–47. https://doi.org/10.1080/14672715.2011.537850.

Rosaldo, Michelle. 1979. "Mujer, Cultura y Sociedad: Una Visión Teórica." In *Antropología y Feminismo*, edited by Olivia Harris and Kate Young, 153–80. Barcelona: Anagrama.

Sen, Amartya. 1999. *Development as Freedom.* New York: Anchor.

Shiva, Vandana. 1989. "Development, Ecology and Women." In *Staying Alive, Women, Ecology and Development*, 1–13. 6th ed. Trowbridge, UK: Redwood.

Tamang, Seira. 2000. "Legalizing State Patriarchy in Nepal." *Studies in Nepali History and Society* 5, no. 1: 127–56.

United Nations. 2010. "The Millennium Development Goals Report." New York: United Nations.

Wilson, Kalpana. 2015. "Towards a Radical Re-Appropriation: Gender, Development and Neoliberal Feminism." *Development and Change* 46, no. 4: 803–32. https://doi.org/10.1111/dech.12176.

World Economic Forum. 2017. "The Global Gender Gap Report 2017." Geneva: World Economic Forum.

Wynd, Shona. 1999. "Education, Schooling and Fertility in Niger." In *Gender, Education & Development. Beyond Access to Empowerment*, edited by Christine Heward and Sheila Bunwaree, 101–16. New York: Zed.

Part III

Latin America
and the Caribbean

CIA Maps.

7

Latin America

Introducing the Region

Serena Cosgrove and Ana Marina Tzul Tzul

INTRODUCTION

Latin America and the Caribbean comprise a vibrant region in relation to women's activism, leadership, and contributions to society, particularly economically and politically, as well as historically and currently. In fact, the organizing efforts of women and people with nonbinary gender identities, transnational solidarity, and state responses have led to increased access to health, education, and other services over the past decades (Cosgrove 2010). These Latin American activists and leaders are uniquely positioned to meet challenges the region faces while continuing to advance their rights. This is because these activists' culturally ascribed roles as caretakers in the home and the community, as well as their activism and volunteerism during periods of economic and political turmoil—such as conflict, **authoritarianism**, and **neoliberal** cuts to state spending, to mention a few—translate directly into important oppositional knowledges and skills such as networking, organizing, cooperating, and listening across difference.

Though women and people with other nondominant gender identities and sexualities across the region have achieved much over the past fifty years, there still exist gender gaps: in many spaces, men have benefited from gender hierarchies—the regional equivalent of which is *machismo*. Gender is best understood relationally; the struggles and experiences of women and people with nondominant gender identities are tied to those of men. Machismo or public and private "exaggerated masculinity" (Ehlers 1991, 3) is a wily term that evades easy definition given its overuse, which stereotypes *macho* Latin American men who are

authoritarianism
A political doctrine that requires strict obedience to authority at the expense of personal freedom.

134

portrayed as unfaithful and who mistreat the women in their lives. This usage can get deployed to depict men from the Global North as angels compared to their counterparts in the Global South. Obviously this is not the case, as gender-based violence and gender discrimination permeate patriarchal societies around the world, not just Latin America and the Caribbean. Terminology is further complicated by women's participation in the perpetuation of harmful gender roles and expectations. In the region, men don't learn gender relations in a vacuum; rather, men, women, and others participate in the maintenance of these cultural roles, even though men generally hold more power and control over resources in patriarchal societies. Sometimes referred to as *marianismo*—or the trope of the long-suffering mother (e.g., Mary, the mother of Jesus Christ)—is a term that can also reaffirm stereotypes of Latin American women; in this case, the term helps sustain beliefs that women are submissive and should stay in abusive relationships because it's a woman's lot to suffer (Ehlers 1991). The machismo/marianismo dichotomy is problematic for a number of reasons. It implies that men and women have equal power, which is not the case given the gender hierarchies in place across the region. And the terms also stereotype male and female roles in ways that do not reflect the complexity or reality of people's lives and relationships. Due to persistent gender inequalities throughout the region, women and people with nondominant gender identities experience higher levels of poverty and discrimination than men (Craske 2003, 58). There are hidden aspects of the discrimination that women and often those with nonbinary gender identities face as well, such as having to work a double shift—income generation and unpaid care work—or a triple shift, which means income generation, unpaid care work, and community activism. This triple burden (Craske 2003, 67; Cosgrove and Curtis 2017, 131) means women and others from poor communities are often working around the clock to guarantee their families' survival.

Even the category of "woman" is heterogeneous in Latin America given the intersectional identities that many women hold. First, Latin America and the Caribbean generally have high levels of income inequality, which means that many women are in poverty, creating a gendered ripple effect given women's responsibilities for children and members of their extended families, particularly the elderly. Second, Latin America and the Caribbean have significant **Indigenous** and Afro-descendant populations. Often Indigenous and Afro-descendant women face exclusion due to racism throughout the region, which is compounded by sexism. Third, there is quite a lot of population movement throughout the region; often women migrants or refugees as well as those with other nondominant gender identities face challenges their community-of-origin counterparts don't face, such as lack of what Goett calls "female sociality and mutual aid" (2017,

marianismo
a gender ideology in which certain feminine characteristics are valued above others. These include being submissive, chaste, virginal, and morally strong.

Indigenous
refers to people who originated in or are the earliest-known inhabitants of an area. Also known as First Peoples, First Nations, Aboriginal peoples or Native peoples.

161) or solidarity that often emerges from kin relations and community life and may not exist for those who are traveling alone from one place to another without documentation or visas. And finally, women aren't the only people in Latin America who face gender discrimination; women as well as people with nonbinary gender identities and nondominant sexualities have not historically held positions of leadership or control over resources. In fact, people with nondominant gender identities often face worse discrimination and exclusion than **cisgender** women. In the rest of this introductory chapter, we review regional gender indicators across several areas; then we provide a brief survey of the historical events that inform current opportunities and challenges for women and others; the third section summarizes present-day political and economic policies and their gendered ramifications.

GENDER AND REGIONAL INDICATORS

cisgender
refers to people whose gender identity corresponds to their sex at birth.

intersectional/ality
refers to the interconnected nature of social categories such as race, class, and gender that create overlapping systems of discrimination or disadvantage. The goal of an intersectional analysis is to understand how racism, sexism, and homophobia (for example) interact to impact our identities and how we live in our society.

The purpose of this section is to describe some of the opportunities that women in Latin America and the Caribbean face in terms of health, education, employment, political participation, and civil society participation as well as some of the challenges they confront related to sexism and the **intersectional** effects of other forms of social and economic difference. Gender-based violence affects women across the region; we explore this topic in greater detail in this section as it puts at risk achievements in other areas and indicates pernicious gender inequality and serious intersectional impacts for women and people with nondominant gender identities and sexualities from poor, rural, or other marginalized backgrounds and ethnic identities, which exacerbate exclusion (World Bank 2012, 15).

Reproductive health is an important topic for women in Latin America, and yet, women's access in some parts of the region is at risk due to conservative values colliding with women's sexuality, which results in oppressive laws, legal frameworks, and enforcement or lack thereof. Many countries in the region provide access to birth control, and the rate of maternal deaths is decreasing, while live births are rising. However, this still hasn't reached across difference (see figure 7.1). There are large gaps across economic, ethnic, and racial groups (PAHO 2017, 11–12) that affect overall health. This means that poor women, Indigenous women, and others affected by multiple forms of social difference suffer disproportionately; this is further exacerbated by severe antiabortion laws that imprison women who seek abortions as well as doctors who provide them (Guthrie 2019). For example, abortion is prohibited in El Salvador, Nicaragua, Honduras, and the Dominican Republic and very limited in many other countries in the region (Guthrie 2019).

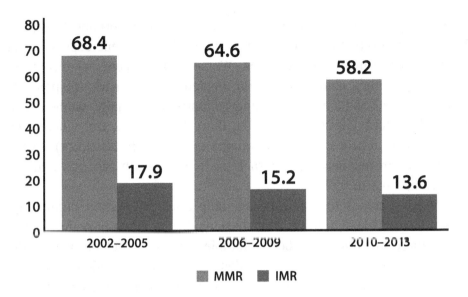

Figure 7.1. Maternal Mortality Rate, Infant Mortality Rate, Pan American Health Organization, 2017.

In terms of education, more girls than boys are attending school—primary through secondary—as well as graduating from college in Latin America and the Caribbean. This has led to the overturn of a historical gender advantage for boys and men (World Bank 2012, 15), but these advances are threatened by the fact that in the face of economic or political crisis, families often encourage girls to drop out of school before boys. This is due to the social expectation that boys will grow up to be providers—therefore they need an education to secure a job—whereas girls will be primarily responsible for homes and unpaid care work and therefore not need an education as much as boys (Cosgrove 2010).

There has been a steady increase in women's participation in the formal economies of Latin America and the Caribbean (World Bank 2012, 20) since the late twentieth century. However, there are a number of factors that continue to impede this participation. At the end of the twentieth century and the beginning of the twenty-first century, new burdens were placed on women. During the crises created by authoritarian military regimes in the 1970s and 1980s, women were often responsible for the survival of their families as men fled the fighting, joined the fighting, or were targeted as subversives. This dire situation saw women working around the clock. Upon the return to democracy across the region in the 1990s, Latin America and the Caribbean were negatively impacted by the structural adjustment policies and neoliberal demands placed on governments by international financial institutions such as the International Monetary Fund and the World Bank. These policies that privatized state enterprises and cut basic food subsidies and welfare programs had gendered impacts on women who were primarily responsible for the survival of their families. When the economic depression of 2008 hit, many men lost their jobs. Women had to generate income in whatever way they could, and again women were primarily responsible for the survival of their families and communities. Finally, women tend to join the informal sector more often than the formal sector where they have fewer legal protections and benefits (World Bank 2012, 21). In the informal sector, women often earn less, have less job security, and are more vulnerable to violence.

When it comes to political leadership and civil society organizing, women have made significant contributions. In the arena of political leadership, there are and have been multiple women presidents across the region over the past couple of decades with multiple women leaders of state in the early twenty-first century. Sixteen out of eighteen countries in Latin America have implemented quotas requiring certain levels of participation of women on electoral lists for political office, and women are drawing close to comprising 30 percent of the parliaments across the region. There are gender inequities across the political sphere (IDEA 2019), such as the fact that in most political party structures men hold higher positions and women congregate at the lower levels, often serving as political organizers at the local level but not holding decision making positions within the parties (IDEA 2019).

Civil society—the wide range of formally registered nongovernmental organizations, community associations, and other organized groups be it at the local or national level—has been led and organized primarily by women for more than a hundred years in Latin America and the Caribbean (Cosgrove 2010). For example, in Argentina, women created a national network of hospitals, schools, and an emergency response system to natural disasters in the late nineteenth century. In El Salvador, women participated in the country-wide protests of the 1930s that led to the *matanza* or slaughter of over thirty-thousand people in 1932; Salvadoran women also comprised a third of the guerrilla forces that fought the government in the 1980–1992 civil war. Similar stories exist across the region.

LGBTQIA rights have expanded in recent decades in Latin America and the Caribbean, which have benefited women and people with nonconforming gender identities and sexualities; interestingly, this is accompanied by the fact there are a number of cultures in the region that allow for more than two genders, such as the *machi* for the Mapuche (Chile) and the *muxes* in southern Mexico, for example. As we've seen in other areas such as health care, changing legal frameworks mean that LGBTQIA individuals have more rights, at least on the books (Corrales

2015, 54). Although there are countries (Argentina, Uruguay, Brazil) as well as cities (Mexico City, Cancún, Bogotá, and Santiago) in the region where the legal framework and implementation of laws have formalized rights (Corrales 2015, 54), there are many places where rights are not guaranteed. In fact, LGBTQIA individuals—like other minority or marginalized groups—face higher levels of vulnerability if their gender identities or sexualities also intersect with other marginalized identities.

A sobering factor that affects women and people with nondominant genders throughout the Americas is violence, in general, and gender-based violence, in particular. We mention violence in general because violence perpetrated by state actors, organized crime, gangs, human trafficking, and violence against displaced and migrant people promotes an atmosphere in which gender-based violence increases (PNUD 2013, 85). In countries with a history of civil war or military dictatorships throughout the region, violence against women can be exacerbated, particularly for Indigenous or Afro-descendant women (Boesten 2010; Cosgrove and Lee 2015; Franco 2007; Hastings 2002), in part due to the failure to hold soldiers accountable for the abuse (Goett 2017, 152).

In the region, **femicide** rates are rising faster than homicide rates; though more men are killed in the region, the rate at which women are killed for being women is rising faster than homicide rates (PNUD 2013,

femicide
refers to the intentional killing of females (women or girls) because of their gender.

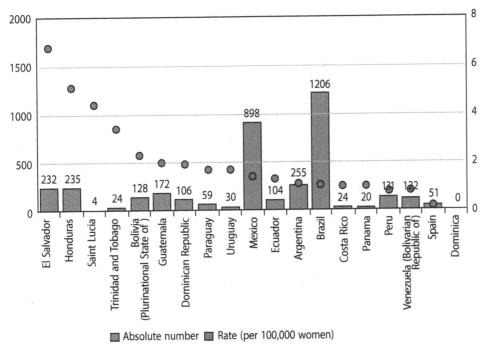

Figure 7.2. Femicide: these are the most recent data available, in absolute numbers and rates per 100,000 women. Gender Equality Observatory, 2019.

85): "Of the 20 countries with the highest rates of homicide in the world, 18 are in Latin America and the Caribbean" (PAHO 2017, 23). Almost one-third of women in Latin America and the Caribbean have been subject to violence in their own homes (PNUD 2013, 23), and two thirds have faced gender-based violence outside of their homes (PNUD 2013, 82). Though domestic and public violence cut across all social classes and other forms of difference, women and people with nondominant gender identities and sexualities often face more obstacles to gain access to justice, which is obviously worse in countries with weak governance and rule of law (PAHO 2017, 13). Though there is agreement that the region is confronting high levels of gender-based violence, it is hard to know the full extent of the problem because sometimes there is underreporting due to the fact that women and others don't feel that their cases will result in any form of justice and/or they are afraid to report violence (PNUD 2013, 83). In some countries, the statistics are increasing, but this isn't necessarily because there is an increase in violence against women but rather because there is an emergent culture in which members of society are more likely to report a crime.

HISTORICAL CONTEXT

The arrival of European conquerors and colonizers to Latin America had disastrous effects on the entire region; the decimation of the region's Indigenous peoples unfolded quickly as people were murdered outright or died from contracting European diseases (Denevan 1992, xvii–xxix). It is argued that in most of the Americas, Indigenous populations had declined by 89 percent by 1650 (Denevan 1992, xvii–xxix; Newson 2005, 143), a mere 150 years after contact with Europeans. In addition to European illnesses, displacement and loss of life due to slavery, war, and genocide, also contributed to the loss of life. Indeed, Indigenous populations did not recover from the conquest, and by the early 1800s Indigenous people "accounted for only 37 percent of Latin America's total population of 21 million" (Newson 2005, 143).

When Christopher Columbus arrived in 1502 to the Caribbean coast of Honduras, Nicaragua, and Costa Rica in Central America, there was a large and thriving population comprising multiple Indigenous cultures—including the Mayas, Aztecs, Pipils, and Lencas, among others—and robust economies, including regional trade from present-day Mexico to Panama (Lovell and Lutz 1990, 127). At that time, it is estimated there was a population of 5.6 million people spread from what is present-day Chiapas in southern Mexico to Panama (Denevan 1992, xvii–xxix).

In South America, there were the Incas in the Andes, the Mapuche in present-day Chile and Argentina, and other Indigenous groups in the Amazon basin. Similar to the Aztecs in Mexico and the Maya in southern Mexico and Central America, European diseases decimated South American Indigenous peoples along with outright genocide and enslavement. It is important to note, however, that the Spanish never conquered the Mapuche, as the Mapuche warriors fought back so hard and ingeniously that they forced the Spanish to sign a treaty respecting their lands south of the Biobio River in south-central Chile. It wasn't until after independence that the Chilean and Argentine armies finally subjugated the Mapuche in the late 1880s.

Whereas the Spanish—and to some extent the British—focused on Central America, and while in South America it was primarily the Spanish and the Portuguese, the Caribbean region had even more colonial powers vying for the region. In the Caribbean, the French, British, Spanish, and others competed for dominance; this, in turn, created obvious problems for local Indigenous populations, as was the case of the Afro-indigenous group, the Garifuna, on the island of St. Vincent. In a treaty in which the French ceded the island to the British, the Garifuna were then exiled to the coast of Honduras by the British, decimating their population: half of the Garifuna died at that time. A big development in the Caribbean—and other places in Latin America—was the introduction of enslaved Africans from the Atlantic slave trade in which twenty-one million Africans were brought to the Americas over the sixteenth, seventeenth, eighteenth, and nineteenth centuries. The colonization of Latin America left an imprint of inequality, elite privilege, racialized and racist institutional practices, gendered legacies, and the dispersal of Indigenous and African descendant peoples across the region. This history has served to naturalize and embed divisions between rich and poor, men and people with nondominant gender identities and sexualities, and mestizos and Indigenous peoples and Afro-descendant peoples in social mores and legal frameworks (Radcliffe 2015, 15).

These processes of enslavement, genocide, and colonization had gendered effects across the region from the beginning. Because initial population flows from Spain and other European colonial powers were primarily male with European female migration unfolding more gradually, Spanish men raped and cohabitated with Indigenous and African women leading to a new generation of *mestizos* or mixed-race people. The foundation of colonies was based on the rape of Indigenous women and then their expected service to this colonial project. This not only normalized violence against women but also affected gender roles between Indigenous men and women. Many historians of Latin America discuss how violence against women today is informed by the rape of women during the Conquest and

mestizos
refers to people of mixed ancestry, including Indigenous and Spanish.

early years of the colonies: this was a "broader acceptance that dated back to the colonial era of using sexual and gender-based violence to uphold patriarchy" (Carey and Torres 2010, 146), in which neither local customs nor community legal frameworks intervened to stop gender-based violence. Though there were differences across the region, colonial culture and law conspired to protect elite interests and subordinate nonelites (Socolow 1980) as well as allow local men to mistreat women as an escape valve for discrimination, poverty, and other indignities (Forster 1999). This, then, continued into the nineteenth century, or the early state-building era under independent countries, in which women were often blamed for the abuse they suffered, called witches, or categorized as sex workers and therefore undeserving of justice. This time also coincides with the neocolonial rise in global power of the United States. From the mid-nineteenth century on, US foreign policy and economic interests played a significant role in the region from supporting the overthrow of leaders critical of the United States, providing military aid to repressive governments aligned with US interests, and promoting US corporations' expansion along the length and breadth of the region (see Chomsky 2021).

During times of dictatorship and authoritarian regimes in the early, mid-, and late twentieth centuries, restrictive gender roles and targeting of so-called **subversive** women furthered gender-based violence to the extent that Drysdale Walsh and Menjívar argue that high present levels of impunity and violence are informed by "deeply intertwined . . . roots in multisided violence—a potent combination of structural, symbolic, political, gender and gendered, and everyday forms of violence" (2016, 586), which moves us past the facile stereotype used to blame gender-based violence on Latin American "macho men" and instead opens up a field of study that posits colonialism, neocolonialism, poverty, state violence, and high levels of impunity as some of the causes of high levels of violence against women in the region today.

ladinos
refers to mestizos and Westernized Indigenous Latin Americans who primarily speak Spanish.

As previously mentioned, the effects of this conquest led to the emergence of a *mestizo* population, or *ladinos* as they are known in Guatemala: the children, and in turn, their descendants, of Europeans and Indigenous or African people. Some members of this hybrid group came to hold power, and upon independence in the early 1800s, an emergent mestizo elite was poised to claim power over poor mestizos, Indigenous peoples, and Afro-descendant groups. European-descendant whites and mestizos hold most of the power today in Latin America. Models of exclusion and repression were thus integrated into the early independent countries of Latin America, which continued to perpetuate exclusion for marginalized groups, including women, with the use of force and "calculated terror . . . an established method of control of the rural population for five centuries" (Woodward 1984, 292), which did spark Indigenous and peasant resistance, revolution, and civil war at different times.

MODERN CONTEXT

The work of historians—often reading between the lines of early colonial diaries and even court proceedings—has uncovered some of the historical and cultural complexities of Indigenous cultures in the Americas and provided insight into the struggles of the marginalized and disenfranchised, substantiating claims of their activism, contributions, and struggles from the sixteenth century onward, especially in the phases of early state building after independence from Spain in the early nineteenth century. This is how a vibrant civil society emerges throughout the region with numerous examples of leadership and activism by women, workers, and Indigenous and Afro-descendant peoples (Cosgrove 2010, 43). Historically, conservative oligarchic interests and dominant Catholic Church teachings had a double standard for women. There were the elite women, bound to uphold social mores and European standards, and there were the peasant, Afro-descendent, and Indigenous women who were expected to do most of the social, economic, and unpaid domestic work during the early years of colonies and independent Latin American states.

Women often chose to participate in struggles as activists and leaders when their livelihoods, families, and customs were threatened. The actions they chose to carry out were obviously shaped by social class, race, and gender. These histories have also affected the amount of solidarity (or lack thereof) that can be found among women activists: the more stratified a society is, the more women are separated by class. Therefore, the less likely it is that cross-cutting movements will form and accomplish social change and transformation (Cosgrove 2010, 44). In Chile and Argentina, for example, it was primarily elite women who were the first to agitate for women's rights due to their access to resources, education, and political ideas from Europe. This consciousness alienated many working-class, poor, and Indigenous women who were doubly or triply oppressed. However, in places like El Salvador, feminism did not emerge until the civil war ended in the early 1990s. Because the war had promoted solidarity among women across difference, the women's movement emerged in the 1990s with a much more integrated and diverse constituency (Cosgrove 2010, 45). In Cuba, by contrast, women played an active role in the 1959 Revolution that overthrew the US-backed dictator Batista and brought the socialist regime of Fidel Castro to power. Socialist Cuba by no means completely eliminated gender or racial inequality, but social reforms in health care, education, and housing greatly lowered health, educational, and income disparities across the population.

Another common theme that emerges for women today across the region is the impact of authoritarian regimes on their respective populations—civil society organizers in general and women activists in particular. Most of the authoritarian regimes of Latin America and the Caribbean—the Dominican Republic, Haiti, Guatemala, El Salvador, Nicaragua, Panama, the civil war in Colombia, Brazil, Chile, Argentina, the civil conflict in Peru with the Shining Path—utilized gendered messages for women and the expectations that they would support the goals of the conservative security forces in charge of each country. Patriotic women were expected to be good mothers but not to take active roles in society or the workplace; women who stepped out of line were sanctioned, often punished, sometimes even more harshly than male subversives. Throughout Latin American history, women have assumed leadership roles in their families, communities, and even countries during periods of economic and political turmoil, which in turn has led to the expansion of opportunities for women to exercise leadership and activist roles.

Latin America and the Caribbean present interesting insights into the ambiguous or contradictory nature of policies meant to address inclusion. Many countries in Central and South America as well as in the Caribbean were forced to adopt neoliberal structural adjustment policies by international financial institutions in the late twentieth and early twenty-first centuries. As many studies have shown, these policies had adverse effects on women and minoritized groups. Nonetheless, out of some of these policies came increased attention for Indigenous groups and their rights. Many countries were "encouraged" to implement land titling policies for Indigenous groups by the very same international agencies that had required them to cut social spending and privatize state-owned banks and electric companies. This created a space in which Indigenous peoples have made gains, but this has also meant they've had to negotiate these gains with state officials and the private sector: these entities had little interest in ceding land when future economic development plans include land for settlers to address the pressure of the urban poor or rural overpopulation and mega-development projects such as dams and hotels, for example. In these negotiations, Indigenous groups have found themselves having to negotiate their rights, making some progress in places and losing ground in others. This is what Hale (2005) calls **neoliberal** multiculturalism. Multiculturalism creates uneven gains for women, Indigenous peoples, and Afro-descendant groups (Radcliffe 2015, 22). "Uneven gains" is the perfect term because it applies to access to land and rights, but it also means doing more with less money, fewer social services, more need for women's unpaid care work.

neoliberal
characterized by free-market trade, deregulation of financial markets, privatization, and limited welfare and social services for populations.

Authoritarian regimes, inequality and poverty, and weak governance and rule of law are factors that contribute to the displacement and migration of people throughout Latin America and the Caribbean today. It is estimated that half the people leaving their places of origin seeking safety or economic opportunities are women or girls (PAHO 2017, 15). Given that gender hierarchies translate as discrimination toward women and people with nondominant gender identities, risks are exacerbated when they do not have official documents for travel. The risks for these undocumented migrants of sexual violence and human trafficking are even higher when they are migrating from Central America to Mexico or the United States or from Paraguay, Bolivia, and Peru to Argentina or from Venezuela to other parts of South America.

CONCLUSIONS

Although women and people with nonbinary gender identities and sexualities in Latin America and the Caribbean have achieved improvements in health, education, and income generation, women still lag behind men in terms of political representation—though the region has higher political participation of women than the United States—equal pay for equal work, and access to formal leadership positions. Throughout the region there are impacts from macro-level policies, such as structural adjustments, and the effects of more generalized violence due to postwar or postconflict realities, weak states with low levels of rule of law, and gang violence, for example, that have even harsher effects on marginalized groups. These effects are exacerbated for Indigenous women, rural women, and people with nondominant gender identities and sexualities. These challenges, though, are balanced by a long history and a multitude of present-day examples of activism and leadership on behalf of rights, the survival of their communities, and commitment to addressing the effects of climate change. A number of international movements across different issues unite people throughout the region: this, in turn, has led to extensive transnational networks, concerted actions, and knowledge sharing throughout the region and with other parts of the world. This includes the Latin American Federation of Associations for Relatives of the Detained-Disappeared (FEDEFAM); the Network of Rural Women in Latin America and the Caribbean (Red LAC), and annual meetings of the Latin American and Caribbean Feminist Association.

The chapters in Part III Latin America present anthropological research that showcases some of the ethnic diversity and ongoing struggles for equality presented in this introduction to the region. Chapter 8 and 9 begin from the standpoint of gender being relational, that is, the experiences of women are tied to the gendered lives of men. In chapter 8 the author explores how older men with erectile dysfunction construct their identities as men in the context of a culture of "machismo" rooted in sexual prowess. The author of chapter 9 in turn, takes an intersectional view of the masculinities of Black working-class men in northeast Brazil. As a marginalized racial group facing widespread unemployment, these men struggle with dominant notions of masculinity that they cannot meet. In chapters 10 and 11, the authors examine the lives of Indigenous women and their efforts to improve the economic conditions of their families. Chapter 10 explores the unintended consequences of an antipoverty project targeting Indigenous rural women in Mexico. Here the program's requirements help adolescent girls but hinder their mothers' efforts to provide for their families. The author in chapter 11 demonstrates how global capitalism dovetails with traditional market practices of Indigenous women in Guatemala, as women engage in a new form of sales as independent distributors for Herbalife, a multinational corporation. Finally, the profile at the end of the introduction to the "region" section presents the work of a nonprofit focused on curbing the high rate of violence against women in Guatemala.

KEY TERMS

authoritarianism: A political doctrine that requires strict obedience to authority at the expense of personal freedom.

cisgender: refers to people whose gender identity corresponds to their sex at birth.

femicide: refers to the intentional killing of females (women or girls) because of their gender.

Indigenous: refers to people who originated in or are the earliest-known inhabitants of an area. Also known as First Peoples, First Nations, Aboriginal peoples or Native peoples.

intersectional/ality: refers to the interconnected nature of social categories such as race, class, and gender that create overlapping systems of discrimination or disadvantage. The goal of an intersectional analysis is to understand how racism, sexism, and homophobia (for example) interact to impact our identities and how we live in our society.

ladinos: refers to mestizos and Westernized Indigenous Latin Americans who primarily speak Spanish.

marianismo: a gender ideology in which certain feminine characteristics are valued above others. These include being submissive, chaste, virginal, and morally strong.

mestizos: refers to people of mixed ancestry, including Indigenous and Spanish.

neoliberal: characterized by free-market trade, deregulation of financial markets, privatization, and limited welfare and social services for populations.

RESOURCES FOR FURTHER EXPLORATION

BOOKS

- Cosgrove, Serena. 2010. *Leadership from the Margins: Women and Civil Society Organizations in Argentina, Chile, and El Salvador.* New Brunswick, NJ: Rutgers University Press.

- Kampwirth, Karen. 2010. *Gender and Populism in Latin America: Passionate Politics.* University Park: Pennsylvania State University Press.

- Marino, Katherine M. 2019. *Feminism for the Americas: The Making of an International Human Rights Movement.* Chapel Hill: University of North Carolina.

- Shayne, Julie. 2004. *The Revolution Question: Feminisms in El Salvador, Chile, and Cuba.* New Brunswick, NJ: Rutgers University Press.

- Stephen, Lynn. 1997. *Women and Social Movements in Latin America Power from Below.* Austin: University of Texas Press.

- Radcliffe, Sarah. 2015. *Dilemmas of Difference: Indigenous Women and the Limits of Postcolonial Development Policy.* Durham, NC: Duke University Press.

ARTICLES

- Burrell, J. L. and E. Moodie. 2021. "Introduction: Generations and Change in Central America." *Journal of Latin American and Caribbean Anthropology* 25, no. 4 (2020): 522–31. https://doi-org.library.esc.edu/10.1111/jlca.12525.

DOCUMENTARIES AND FILMS

- Cabellos, Ernesto, Frigola Torrent, Núria Prieto, Antolín Sánchez, Carlos Giraldo, Jessica Steiner, Hilari Sölle, Miguel Choy-Yin, Martin Ayay, and Nélida Chilón. 2016. *Hija De La Laguna—Daughter of the Lake.* Lima, Peru: Guarango Cine Y Video.

- Guzmán, Patricio, Renate Sachse, Katell Djian, Emmanuelle Joly, José Miguel Miranda, Atacama Productions, Blinker Film-produktion, Westdeutscher Rundfunk, and Cronomedia. 2010. *Nostalgia De La Luz = Nostalgia for the Light.* Brooklyn, NY: Icarus Films Home Video.

- Kinoy, Peter, Pamela Yates, Newton Thomas Sigel, Rigoberta Menchú, Rubén Blades, Susan Sarandon, Skylight Pictures, Production Company, Docurama, and New Video Group. 2004. *When the Mountains Tremble.* 20th Anniversary Special Edition. New York: Docurama.

- Montes-Bradley, E., dir. 2007. *Evita.* Heritage Film Project.

- Portillo, Lourdes, Olivia Crawford, Julie Mackaman, Vivien Hillgrove, Kyle Kibbe, Todd Boekelheide, Xochitl Films, and Zafra Video S.A. 2014. *Señorita Extraviada—Missing Young Woman.* Coyoacán, México: Zafra Video.

- Sickles, Dan, Antonio Santini, and Flavien Berger. 2015. *Mala Mala.* Culver City, CA: Strand Releasing.

- Suffern, R., dir. 2016. *Finding Oscar.* FilmRise.

- Torre, S., and V. Funari, V., dir. 2006. *Maquilapolis: City of Factories.* San Francisco: California Newsreel.

- Wood, Andrés, Gerardo Herrero, Mamoun Hassan et al. 2007. *Machuca.* Venice: Menemsha Films.

ACKNOWLEDGMENTS

We are grateful for the support of our institutions—Seattle University and Universidad Rafael Landívar—and we are inspired daily by the example of all the women activists of Latin America and the Caribbean who are making inclusive social change happen across the region.

BIBLIOGRAPHY

Boesten, Jelke. 2010. "Analyzing Rape Regimes at the Interface of War and Peace in Peru." *International Journal of Transitional Justice* 4, no. 1: 110–29.

Carey, David, and M. Gabriela Torres. 2010. "PRECURSORS TO FEMICIDE: Guatemalan Women in a Vortex of Violence." *Latin American Research Review* 45, no. 3: 142–164.

Chomsky, Aviva. 2021. *Central America's Forgotten History: Revolution, Violence, and the Roots of Migration.* Boston: Beacon.

Corrales, Javier. 2015. "The Politics of LGBT Rights in Latin America and the Caribbean: Research Agendas." *European Review of Latin American and Caribbean Studies* 100: 53–62.

Cosgrove, Serena. 2010. *Leadership from the Margins: Women and Civil Society Organizations in Argentina, Chile, and El Salvador*. New Brunswick, NJ: Rutgers University Press.

Cosgrove, Serena. 2018. "Who Will Use My Loom When I Am Gone? An Intersectional Analysis of Mapuche Women's Progress in Twenty-First Century Chile." In *Bringing Intersectionality to Public Policy*, edited by Julia Jordan-Zachery and Olena Hankivsky, 529–545. New York: Palgrave Macmillan.

Cosgrove, Serena, and Benjamin Curtis. 2017. *Understanding Global Poverty: Causes, Capabilities, and Human Development*. London: Routledge.

Cosgrove, Serena, and Kristi Lee. 2015. "Persistence and Resistance: Women's Leadership and Ending Gender-Based Violence in Guatemala." *Seattle Journal for Social Justice* 14, no. 2: 309–332.

Craske, Nikki. 2003. "Gender, Poverty, and Social Movements." In *Gender in Latin America*, edited by Sylvia Chant with Nikki Craske, 46–70. New Brunswick, NJ: Rutgers University Press.

Denevan, William M., ed. 1992. *The Native Population of the Americas in 1492*. Madison: University of Wisconsin Press.

Drysdale Walsh, Shannon, and Cecilia Menjívar. 2016. "Impunity and Multisided Violence in the Lives of Latin American Women: El Salvador in Comparative Perspective." *Current Sociology Monograph* 64, no. 4: 586–602.

Ehlers, Tracy Bachrach. 1991. "Debunking Marianismo: Economic Vulnerability and Survival Strategies among Guatemalan Wives." *Ethnology* 30, no. 1: 1–16.

Foster, C. 1999. Violent and Violated Women: Justice and Gender in Rural Guatemala, 1936–1956. *Journal of Women's History* 11, no. 3: 55–77.

Franco, Jean. 2007. "Rape: A Weapon of War." *Social Text* 25, no. 2: 23–37.

Goett, Jennifer. 2017. *Black Autonomy: Race, Gender, and Afro-Nicaraguan Activism*. Palo Alto, CA: Stanford University Press.

Guthrie, Amie. 2019. "Explained: Abortion Rights in Mexico and Latin America," *New York NBC News*, September 29. Accessed November 3, 2019. https://www.nbcnewyork.com/news/national-international/Explained-Abortion-Rights-Mexico-Latin-America-561721361.html.

Hale, Charles R. 2005. "Neoliberal Multiculturalism: The Remaking of Cultural Rights and Racial Discrimination in Latin America." *PoLAR: Political and Legal Anthropology Review* 28, no. 1: 10–28.

Hastings, Julie A. 2002. "Silencing State-Sponsored Rape in and beyond a Transnational Guatemalan Community." *Violence against Women* 8, no. 10: 1153–1181.

Lovell, W. George, and Christopher H. Lutz. 1990. "The Historical Demography of Colonial Central America." In *Yearbook (Conference of Latin Americanist Geographers)* (17/18), 127–138. Austin: University of Texas Press.

Newson, Linda A. 2005. "The Demographic Impact of Colonization." In *The Cambridge Economic History of Latin America,* edited by V. Bulmer-Thomas, J. Coatsworth, and R. Cortes-Conde, 143–184. Cambridge: Cambridge University Press.

Pan American Health Organization. 2017. "Health in the Americas+." *Summary: Regional Outlook and Country Profiles.* Washington, DC: PAHO. https://www.paho.org/salud-en-las-americas-2017/wp-content/uploads/2017/09/Print-Version-English.pdf. Accessed November 2, 2019.

PNUD (Programa de las Naciones Unidas para el Desarrollo). 2013. Seguridad Ciudadana con Rostro Humano: Diagnostico y Propuestas para América Latina. New York: Centro Regional de Servicios para América Latina y el Caribe. https://www.undp.org/content/dam/rblac/img/IDH/IDH-AL%20Informe%20completo.pdf. Accessed November 3, 2019.

Radcliffe, Sarah. 2015. *Dilemmas of Difference: Indigenous Women and the Limits of Postcolonial Development Policy.* Durham, NC: Duke University Press.

Socolow, Susan Migden. 1980. "Women and Crime: Buenos Aires, 1757–97." *Journal of Latin American Studies* 12, no. 1: 39–54.

Tello Rozas, Pilar, and Carolina Floru. 2017. *Women's Political Participation in Latin America: Some Progress and Many Challenges.* International IDEA. https://www.idea.int/news-media/news/women%E2%80%99s-political-participation-latin-america-some-progress-and-many-challenges.

Woodward, Ralph Lee. 1984. "The Rise and Decline of Liberalism in Central America: Historical Perspectives on the Contemporary Crisis." *Journal of Interamerican Studies and World Affairs* 26, no. 3: 291–312. doi:10.2307/165672.

World Bank. 2012. "Women's Economic Empowerment in Latin America and the Caribbean Policy Lessons from the World Bank Gender Action Plan." *World Bank Poverty, Inequality, and Gender Group Latin America and the Caribbean Region.* https://openknowledge.worldbank.org/bitstream/handle/10986/16509/761170WP0Women00Box374362B00PUBLIC0.pdf?sequence=1&isAllowed=y. Accessed November 2, 2019.

PROFILE: THE GUATEMALAN WOMEN'S GROUP: SUPPORTING SURVIVORS OF GENDER-BASED VIOLENCE

Serena Cosgrove and Ana Marina Tzul Tzul

INTRODUCTION

Inspired by the work of civil society women leaders in Guatemala, this profile focuses on the achievements and mutual support that connect the women's organizations that belong to the Guatemalan Women's Group (Grupo Guatemalteco de Mujeres, or GGM), an umbrella organization based in the capital Guatemala City. GGM's mission is to support women's organizations across the country, providing much-needed services to women survivors of gender-based violence.

HISTORY

Many argue that there are multiple historical events in Guatemala—Spanish colonization, early statehood consolidation and the emergence of political and economic elites, and the thirty-six-year civil war (1960–1996)—that contribute to today's high levels of gender-based violence (see Carey and Torres 2010, Sanford 2008, and Nolin Hanlon and Shankar 2000). Gender-based violence is defined as "any act that results in, or is likely to result in physical, sexual, or psychological hard or suffering to women [and people with non-dominant gender identities and sexualities], including threats of such acts, coercion or arbitrary deprivation of liberty, whether occurring in public or private life" (Russo and Pirlott 2006, 181). There are also a number of current social factors such as inequality, poverty, and discrimination due to gender and ethnicity as well as high levels of violence due to insecurity, gangs, and drug trafficking—that contribute to the "normalization" of gender-based violence in the private, domestic sphere, as well as in the public sphere.

The countries with the highest femicide rates in Latin America are El Salvador, Honduras, and Guatemala (Gender Equality Observatory 2018). **Femicide** is the killing of a woman because of her gender; it is an extreme example of gender-based violence, which is on the rise according to Musalo and Bookey (2014, 107) and Cosgrove and Lee (2015, 309). From 2000 to 2019, 11,519 women were violently killed in Guatemala (GGM 2019); the rate of violent deaths of women is growing faster than homicide levels (though homicide rates remain higher than femicide rates). In 2018 alone, 661 women were killed violently in Guatemala (GGM 2019). In fact, violence against women is one of the most highly reported crimes in Guatemala, yet impunity rates are also abysmally high: only 3.46 percent of cases presented between 2008 and 2017 were resolved according to the International Commission against Impunity in Guatemala (CICIG, 9).

ORGANIZATIONAL HISTORY AND MISSION

The Guatemalan Women's Group (GGM) was officially founded in 1988, and in 1991, they opened their first Center for Integrated Support for Women (or CAIMUS) in Guatemala City with the goal of providing an integrated package of services to women survivors in the capital. Today, GGM is an umbrella organization that oversees 10 CAIMUS across the country (with four new organizations coming onboard).

In its early years, GGM played a leadership role at the national level convening diverse women's organizations across the country to assure that women's voices were being heard in the peace process and in the early implementation of the peace accords in post–civil war Guatemala. GGM encouraged women to talk to each other from across the country, and this contributed to bridging the class divide between feminists in the capital and women committed to women's issues from across the country. GGM also played an important role in the No Violence against Women Network, which brought together organizations around the country actively working to eradicate gender-based violence locally and to lobby for improved laws and public-sector accountability at the national level.

This activism by women led to the law against gender-based violence being passed in 1996, as well as the 2008 law against femicide and other forms of violence against women. These laws, in turn, pressured the government to form a public sector–civil society commission to promote state accountability and collaboration with women's organizations. However, the government has never fully supported GGM or their goals. In 2018, the government only provided a small percentage of funding it had promised to the CAIMUS for their functioning. In 2019, the CAIMUS weren't even included in the national budget, a sign that the government's commitment to addressing gender-based violence is waning.

Today GGM provides oversight, training, and fundraising for the CAIMUS, which use the GGM model of integrated services for women survivors including social, medical, psychological, and legal services as well as access to women's shelters. In addition to seeking resources for CAIMUS and creating a space for mutual support in a struggle that often feels overwhelming, GGM is also a think tank and advocacy organization gathering and analyzing data about the rates of violence against women and leading public campaigns to change the perceptions of Guatemalans about violence against women. Always in coordination with other organizations and social movements across the country, GGM uses key dates for women's liberation—such as March 8, the International Women's Day, or May 28, International Day of Action for Women's Health, among other dates—to organize national campaigns to raise awareness about women's rights, gender-based violence, and related issues. These campaigns use billboards and other opportunities for public outreach such as radio spots, social media, and events and programming to spread their message. See GGM's website for more information: http://ggm.org.gt/.

LEADERSHIP

The founder and director of GGM is Giovana Lemus. Her story embodies sacrifice and commitment to women's participation and contributions to

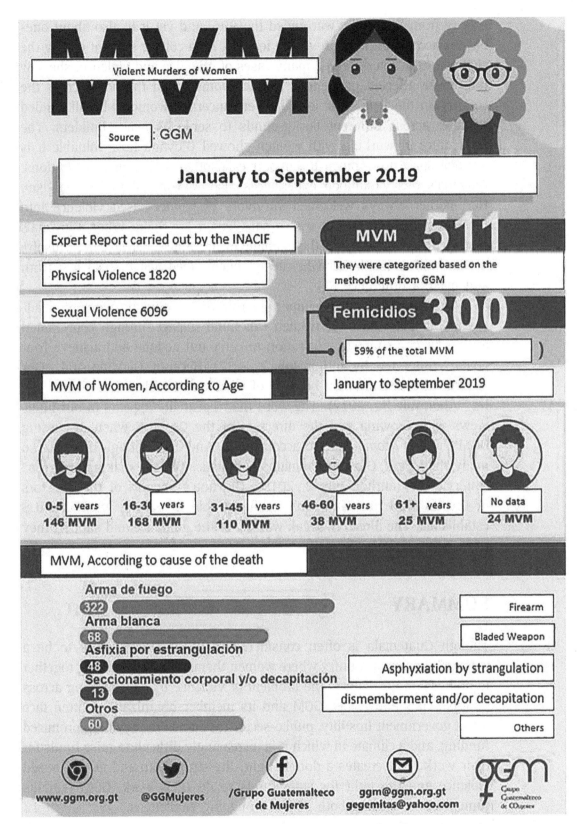

Figure 7.3. Informational flyer about number of women murdered in Guatemala. *Source:* Grupo Guatemalteco de Mujeres (GGM), a feminist organization in Guatemala. Translation by authors.

society from before the war ended in 1996, and yet it is also about one-on-one accompaniment of women leaders. As a college student during the civil war, Giovana observed many cases of injustice and violence; she saw how these affected Indigenous people, women, and the poor across the country. In the 1980s she joined other concerned women who all banded together across different backgrounds to serve as peace builders. The importance of working with women showed Giovana how valuable it is to open space for women to support each other and their contributions. Giovana's own childhood experiences also contributed to her activism. Her mother always welcomed survivors of gender-based violence into the home, making sure it was a safe haven for them. When Giovana's mother died, Giovana had the example of her nine older sisters to inspire her, as well as her father who always encouraged her to speak her truth and make a difference.

Giovana sums up the important role that promoting women's leadership can play and that women can build impact through coordinated action: "It is a concrete inspiration to carry out actions and achieve [our goals]" (Interview by author, July 2, 2013). Recently Giovana said, "Our sisterhood grows stronger because of what we've had to face" (Interview by author, July 30, 2019). The word that repeatedly appears in our interviews with Giovana and the directors of the CAIMUS when discussing GGM's role is *acompañar* (to accompany). And even though there are so many challenges, Giovanna remains optimistic: "We are making progress" (interview by author, July 2, 2013). Giovana's support of the directors of the CAIMUS has played a significant role in getting more CAIMUS established. The directors speak warmly of the guidance and support they have received from Giovana.

SUMMARY

Though Guatemala is often considered to be a difficult place to be a woman, it is also a country where women themselves are working together to address and transform the problem of violence by collaborating across multiple sites and levels. GGM and its member organizations often face direct government hostility, public-sector resistance in providing promised funding, and a climate in which it is increasingly difficult to raise funds for their work. This creates a double fight: the struggle to end gender-based violence and the fight for state funds to do their work. GGM remains committed to tackling both of these ongoing challenges.

ACKNOWLEDGMENTS

We are grateful for the support of our institutions—Seattle University and Universidad Rafael Landívar—and we are inspired daily by the example of all the women activists of Latin America and the Caribbean who are making inclusive, social change happen across the region.

BIBLIOGRAPHY

Carey, David, and M. Gabriela Torres. 2010. "Precursors to Femicide: Guatemalan women in a Vortex of Violence." *Latin American Research Review* 45, no. 3: 142–164.

Comisión Internacional contra la Impunidad en Guatemala (CICIG). 2019. "Diálogos por el fortalecimiento de la justicia y el combate a la impunidad en Guatemala." Report can be found on CICIG website. https://www.cicig.org/comunicados-2019-c/informe-dialogos-por-el-fortalecimiento-de-la-justicia/. Accessed August 12, 2019.

Cosgrove, Serena, and Kristi Lee. 2015. "Persistence and Resistance: Women's Leadership and Ending Gender-Based Violence in Guatemala." *Seattle Journal for Social Justice* 14, no. 2: 309–332.

Gender Equality Observatory for Latin America and the Caribbean. 2018. "Femicide, the Most Extreme Expression of Violence against Women." Oig.cepal (website). https://oig.cepal.org/sites/default/files/nota_27_eng.pdf. Accessed July 20, 2019.

Grupo Guatemalteco de Mujeres (GGM). 2019. "Datos estadísticos: Muertes Violentas de Mujeres-MVM y República de Guatemala ACTUALIZADO (20/05/19)." GGM (website). http://ggm.org.gt/wp-content/uploads/2019/06/Datos-Estad%C3%ADsticos-MVM-ACTUALIZADO-20-DE-MAYO-DE-2019.pdf. Accessed July 20, 2019.

Musalo, Karen, and Blaine Bookey. 2014. "Crimes without Punishment: An Update on Violence against Women and Impunity in Guatemala." *Social Justice* 40, no. 4: 106–117.

Nolin Hanlon, Catherine, and Finola Shankar. 2000. "Gendered Spaces of Terror and Assault: The Testimonio of REMHI and the Commission for Historical Clarification in Guatemala." *Gender, Place & Culture* 7, no. 3: 265–286.

Russo, Nancy Felipe, and Angela Pirlott, A. 2006. "Gender-based Violence: Concepts, Methods, and Findings." *Annals of the New York Academy of Sciences* 1087: 178–205.

Sanford, Victoria. 2008. "From Genocide to Feminicide: Impunity and Human Rights in Twenty-First Century Guatemala." *Journal of Human Rights* 7: 104–122.

8

Being a Good Mexican Man by Embracing "Erectile Dysfunction"

Emily Wentzell

LEARNING OBJECTIVES

- Define key terms including "medicalization," "masculinity," "companionate marriage," "machismo," and "erectile dysfunction."

- Understand that cultural ideas about masculinity determine what kinds of erectile function people define as healthy and normal.

- Explain how cultural ideas about race, gender, and age influenced Mexican men's understandings of decreasing erectile function.

In this chapter, the author discusses the gendered experiences of older, urban, working-class Mexican men as they navigate changes in their bodies, cultural ideals of masculinity, and the available array of sexual medical interventions as they seek to be good men in later life. The author explores how the "macho" stereotype, now widely critiqued in Mexican society, is seen as a form of masculinity that thwarts national modernization. Older men come to accept their erectile dysfunction as a natural part of the aging process and an alternative form of masculinity that counters the macho stereotype.

If you were born in the 1990s or later, throughout your life you've heard ads for pills like Viagra define not being able to get firm enough penile erections as the medical problem "erectile dysfunction" (ED). However, the concept of ED was actually created fairly recently and is only one of many ways to understand men's changing sexual function over the life course. In different times and places, people have understood the inability to get desired erections as variously as a consequence of witchcraft, as a punishment for "bad" sexual behavior earlier in life, and as a psychological issue called "impotence" (McLaren 2007; Wentzell 2008). In the United States in the 1990s, psychotherapists, psychologists, urologists, and other kinds of professionals were debating both the causes of erections that did not meet social ideals and which professionals should treat this issue. Since the then-common term *impotence* had become stigmatized, some of them decided to rename this issue **erectile dysfunction**.

While the goal of this terminology change was to destigmatize this experience by framing it as a medical pathology rather than a personal failing, this renaming also enabled medical professionals to claim expertise over the condition (Tiefer 1995). At the same time, drug companies were developing the first oral pills that could enhance erectile function. The first of these, Viagra, came on the global scene in 1998. These developments enabled a worldwide **medicalization** of less-than-ideal penile erection. Medicalization is a social process in which areas of life previously understood in other ways (for example, as social, religious, or other kinds of issues) come to be seen as medical concerns to be treated by doctors (Tiefer 1994). Examples of medicalization range from reframings of bad breath as halitosis (a shift engineered by the marketers of Listerine mouthwash in the United States), to more recent reconceptualizations of shyness as social anxiety disorder and period-related mood changes as premenstrual dysphoric disorder. The medicalization of erectile difficulty into ED has now become so prevalent that people who grew up after 1998 might not question the idea that this issue could be understood in any other way.

However, understanding ED as a simple biological fact has significant social consequences. The medical definition of ED is "the persistent inability to achieve or maintain an erection sufficient for satisfactory sexual performance" (Lizza and Rosen 1999, 141). Yet what counts as "sufficient erection" and "satisfactory" sex are actually profoundly personal and variable. Failure to acknowledge that variability in ED drug marketing and prescription suggests that there is a single norm for healthy erections and sexual practice.

Since the concept of ED was developed in the United States, that norm comes from the US cultural ideas about sex, sexuality, and **masculinity**. It is the idea that penetrative (penis-in-vagina), heterosexual sex is what counts as "real" sex and is the kind of sex that is healthy

erectile dysfunction (ED)
the idea that penile erections that do not meet cultural ideals are a medical pathology, defined clinically as the persistent inability to achieve or maintain an erection sufficient for satisfactory sexual performance.

medicalization
a social process in which areas of life previously understood in other ways (for example, as social, religious or other kinds of issues) come to be seen as medical concerns to be treated by doctors.

masculinity
the culturally specific traits, behaviors, and discourses expected of men.

and normal (Rubin 1992). This idea also relates to particular cultural ideas about masculinity, which anthropologist Matthew Gutmann (1996, 17, italics in original) defines as "what men say and do *to be men.*" ED drugs thus function as "masculinity pills," enabling men to conform to the idea that healthy and normal men should want (and be physically able to have) penetrative sex whenever possible—despite aging, illness, conflict with their partners, or other life issues (Loe 2004a, 58; Marshall and Katz 2002).

The ability to use ED drugs to attain more firm or frequent erections can ease the emotional pain of men who wish to live out this kind of masculinity. However, casting penetrative sex-oriented manliness as the only healthy or normal way to be a man also creates more suffering. It does so by promoting narrow norms for masculinity and sexuality that exclude those who want anything other than lifelong, penetrative, heterosexual sex as abnormal (Loe 2006; Tiefer 1994; Potts 2000; Mamo and Fishman 2001).

Further, the globalization of this ideology through the worldwide marketing and prescription of ED drugs has pitfalls. Drugs like Viagra are huge sellers, with 2017 global sales reaching almost five billion (Zion Market Research 2018). The worldwide diffusion of the ED concept that those sales reflect has been achieved by promoting specifically Euro–North American cultural ideas about what counts as normal and healthy sex, sexuality, and masculinity as if they were universal, biological facts. Framing such culturally specific ideologies as objective descriptions of the nature of men's health, bodies, and ideal behaviors both promotes the problematic dominance of one culture over others and reduces the set of possibilities men have for understanding themselves and their bodies.

Yet despite the worldwide popularity and marketing of ED drugs, many men and their sexual partners do not accept these norms. Even among heterosexual couples, people often value or prefer nonpenetrative forms of sexual interaction (including the many women who experience greater pleasure from nonpenetrative sex acts) (Potts et al. 2003; Potts et al. 2004; Loe 2004b). In contexts as diverse as rural Ghana and urban Sweden, people often understand focusing on nonsexual forms of intimacy and interaction in later life as more respectable, age-appropriate, and emotionally fulfilling than continuing the kinds of sex they had as youths (van der Geest 2001; Sandberg 2013). Further, even two people married to each other might disagree about what kinds of sex or intimacy are desirable at particular life stages (Moore 2010).

My aim in this chapter is to analyze a specific case—the experiences of older, working-class men in urban central Mexico—to demonstrate how people might draw on cultural ideals different from those made to seem natural in ED marketing to understand men's changing erectile function.

After discussing the study site and methods, I present data from interviews with over 250 older Mexican men receiving medical treatment for urological issues other than ED. Despite the popularity of ED drugs in Mexico, these particular men overwhelmingly rejected the idea that decreasing erectile function was a medical problem. Instead, they understood decreasing erections in later life in relation to changing local cultural ideals of masculinity and marriage, as well as to local understandings of respectable manhood in older age. By analyzing how they came to these understandings, I show that people's ideas about what kinds of sexual function are healthy, manly, and age-appropriate reflected context-specific cultural ideologies rather than a universal biological truth about what constitutes a normal erection. This analysis reveals how medical treatments for gendered ailments both reflect and reproduce gender ideals specific to particular places and times.

CHANGING MASCULINITIES IN MEXICO

Urban central Mexico is a particularly interesting site for studying masculinities because it has been the site of long-standing and heated debate about what it is to be a good man. The notion of **machismo** figures prominently in such discussions. This is the idea that Mexican men are inherently predisposed to "macho" masculinity, which involves emotional closure, violence, womanizing, and dominance over women (McKee Irwin 2003). Mexican public intellectuals popularized the concept of machismo in the 1950s, defining it as an inheritance from coerced reproduction among Spanish Conquistador forefathers and Indigenous foremothers (see Paz 1985). Importantly, this notion is based on elite critics' interpretations of the behaviors attributed to lower-class men, rather than any actual sociological or biological data. It is also based on ideas about race—specifically, the idea that Mexicans form a unique race generated by this Conquistador/Indigena mixing and thus are biologically and culturally susceptible to forms of behavioral backwardness, like machismo, but are also capable of advancing beyond them through "modern" health and social practices (Alonso 2004).

Neither this idea of race nor the concept of machismo it includes are biological truths about Mexican people. It is crucial to note that racial ideologies are not scientifically valid accounts of biology. They are instead cultural ideas that have the social power to influence people's behavior in ways that then influence people's health and well-being (Ackermann et al. 2019). Nevertheless, the idea that machismo exists caught on in Mexican and global popular cultures.

machismo
a widely critiqued form of masculinity characterized by violence and womanizing, often attributed to Latin American men's cultural inheritance from Spanish Conquistadors. The idea of machismo is rooted in unfounded assumptions about the nature of Latin American men; however, these ideas have social consequences that then affect people's bodies and behavior.

However, people in Mexico today generally discuss machismo as both a reality of life and a problematic barrier to desired social change. Amid calls for more equal gender roles, local ideas of marriage have shifted dramatically in recent decades, most visibly in urban areas (Amuchástegui and Szasz 2007). While women and men were once expected to occupy fairly separate spheres, in Mexico, as in many parts of the world, people now value **companionate marriage**. This is a form of marriage based on emotional fulfillment rather than the traditional foci of economic production and social reproduction (Hirsch 2003; Wardlow and Hirsch 2006). While men were once expected to provide economically for their families but also to demonstrate virility through extramarital sexuality, being a good and modern Mexican man now involves being purposefully different from that model, meeting ideals of fidelity and emotional engagement with one's spouse and children (Ramirez 2009; Wentzell 2013a).

Given the rise of companionate marriage, Mexican people as diverse as feminist activists and male gang members now critique machismo as a problematic, regressive form of masculinity (Gutmann 1996; Ramirez 2009; Sverdlin 2017). However, while some people decry machismo as a racist stereotype, critiques more often focus on the need for good men to fight against their inherent macho impulses, thus keeping this idea of Mexican male nature alive even while deploring it (Amuchástegui Herrera 2008). This meant that both the cultural idea of machismo as a natural trait among Mexican men, and the major changes in local ideas about what constitutes good marriage and masculinity, fundamentally influenced experiences and perceptions of the research participants I worked with.

STUDY SITE AND METHODS

These participants were urology patients in the central Mexican city of Cuernavaca, a growing metropolis near the nation's capital with a largely mestizo-identified population that utilizes biomedicine much more frequently than traditional forms of healing. The outpatient urology clinic these participants attended was based in the regional flagship hospital of the federal Instituto Méxicano del Seguro Social (IMSS) system. The IMSS provides care to privately employed workers and their families, or about half of the Mexican population. While the care at the research site was of high quality, waits were long: so IMSS-eligible patients with enough money often sought private treatment. This meant that most men in my study were working class. It also meant that although in some contexts physicians experience economic incentives for diagnosing ED and prescribing ED drugs, the resource-strapped IMSS setting posed a disincentive

companionate marriage
a marriage based on emotional fulfillment rather than the traditional foci of economic production and social reproduction. It has become the ideal type of marriage in many parts of the world.

to medicalizing new conditions. In 2007–2008 I held Spanish-language, semistructured interviews with over 250 of these men, about 50 with their wives who had accompanied them to the clinic. They ranged widely in age, but most were in their fifties and sixties and considered themselves "older" after a lifetime of hard work.

About 96 percent of the men invited to participate in this research did so; despite stereotypes they themselves voiced about Mexican men being unwilling to discuss these issues, they often said they "enjoyed the chance to talk" about intimate issues with an interested stranger. My identity as a white, North American woman researcher facilitated this interaction. Being a foreigner helped, since many men said they felt able to tell me potentially embarrassing information they kept from other men or their social circle (since I didn't know any of their friends or relatives). Being a white woman from the United States helped in that some men admitted being reluctant to talk about sexual issues with a woman but then voiced beliefs that Anglo-American women were more comfortable talking about such things than Mexican women, hence they felt comfortable discussing these topics with me. Finally, my status as a researcher aided our interactions, as many participants voiced respect for education and said they felt grateful to be included in an academic study.

Despite men's willingness to participate, they presented the partial and context-specific narratives of their lives that characterize all interview data. For example, none mentioned same-sex sexuality, which was statistically likely to have happened in such a large group of men but was a stigmatized topic among them (see, for context, Carillo 2002). Further, while they did not appear to shape their statements in relation to preconceived ideas they expected me to have about Mexican men, they often took it upon themselves to provide context for a foreigner, such as explaining who Mexican men are in the abstract. This focus reflects the role my own positionality played in data collection.

MEN'S EXPERIENCES OF DECREASING ERECTILE FUNCTION

Most research participants referred to the concept of machismo when discussing their experiences of being a man. They often described it as a fundamental if negative quality of Mexican men—sometimes including themselves—which would shape those men's understandings of sexual issues. For instance, as one man explained, "Here in Mexico, [infidelity is] something normal. They say the Mexican is passionate. They say the man is polygamous by nature." Others discussed the "hot" constitution of Mexican men as an innate biological impetus to have a lot of sex. Some described machismo as a cultural inheritance that was prevalent but problematic. One man noted, "A lot of machismo exists. . . . They're afraid that if they let their guard down, they'll become whipped. That's the closed psychology of the macho man" (interview by author).

Yet even the men who described some of their own actions as "macho" noted that this form of masculinity was problematic and that men would "have to change" to keep up with the times. For example, one participant noted that he and other men his age had been taught that "the woman needs to be behind" but now needed to realize that "the wife isn't a thing—she's a person, she's a comrade" (interview by author). Thus, men who had always practiced fidelity—as well as those who had conformed to "macho" stereotypes in their youth—described the need for men "today" to be faithful and emotionally engaged with their wives and families. One participant even identified himself as an "ex-machista" who had changed his ways in later life.

This idea that good, modern men should reject macho sexuality fundamentally influenced participants' responses to decreasing erectile function. Despite often identifying themselves or their peer group as pre-disposed to the kind of male sexuality that would be aided by ED drugs, participants overwhelmingly rejected medical ED treatments. Despite the fact that all the men were aware of (and knew how to get) ED drugs, and that 70 percent of participants reported decreased erectile function, only 11 percent of men even considered seeking medical intervention for decreasing erectile function—and very few of those actually did so. This was because they drew on local cultural ideals of change over time in masculinity and marriage to interpret this bodily change in ways other than as a biological problem.

Men understood ED drugs to enable youthful and macho forms of sexuality in later life, which were now age (and societally) inappropriate. They expected to live out a specific form of male life-course change as they aged, which they frequently termed the "second stage" or "other level" of life. One man said that after his retirement he would change focus and "dedicate myself to my wife, the house, gardening, caring for the grandchildren." He described this shift as so common that he considered it "the Mexican classic" (interview by author). This second stage was focused on the kinds of emotional engagement with family that had more recently become ideal for men more generally and study participants saw as particularly key for living out respectable masculinity in later life. One man explained, "Erectile dysfunction isn't important. When I was young, it would have been, but not now." Another laughed while noting, "Here in Mexico, we have a saying: 'After old age, chickenpox' . . . it means that some things become silly when one is older" (interview by author). He saw older men chasing youthful sexuality as silly in this way.

This was the case both for men who had focused on extramarital virility in their youths and those who had always lived out masculinities closer to current ideals of companionate marriage including fidelity. One man who had always been faithful to and emotionally close with his wife described his decreasing erectile capacity as part of "my nature. I never sought a medical solution to this problem—I just thought that my sex life was ending." He continued, "In our married life, we were very happy. When the sex life ended, okay, we knew it would end one day. So, there wasn't treatment—I never tried anything. I really didn't have a problem with it" (interview by author).

A different participant who noted that he was a "womanizer" in his youth said that his changing body had enabled him to alter his behavior and relationship. He explained, "The truth is, now I don't have the same capacity. I'm fifty-five, I know what I am. I don't want problems with my wife. Like I deserve respect from her, she deserves it from me as well" (interview by author). Both men understood decreasing erectile function to be a "normal" and "natural" part of aging; one felt able to incorporate it into his already close marriage, while the other saw it as an aid for relating to his wife in a more respectful way.

Participants often identified decreased erectile function as both a prompt to start acting more maturely and as a way of overcoming bodily urges to now-inappropriately youthful and macho sexuality. One man noted that his generation of Mexican men had confused machismo with manliness, defining the former as seeking to "restrict" one's wife and children and the latter as being "responsible" for them. He understood machismo as an innate biological urge, for example, explaining that in his younger days, "I saw a pretty prostitute, with a really nice body. In such cases, the macho comes out of us. So I slept with her" (interview by author). However, now that his erectile function had diminished, he believed he was free from such overwhelming urges and felt more able to be the kind of husband he now thought he should be.

It often took wives' encouragement to help men embrace this change. Women who accompanied their husbands in our interviews reported defining decreasing erectile function change in later life as "natural," "normal," and acceptable to them as men's sexual partners. In an interview with a couple who had not previously discussed the issue, the husband revealed that he worried his wife was unhappy with their decreased sex life. She reassured him, "It wasn't the same, but it's not serious, it happens with age and health problems" (interview by author). This exchange was mirrored by a less happy couple, with a husband who had pursued frequent affairs and a wife who had not enjoyed their sex life in part because of his behavior. When the man remarked somewhat wistfully that "the machinery of erection has broken down," she shouted the qualifier, "Now we don't want any more!" (interview by author).

As these example demonstrate, men's interactions with a range of other people influenced their understandings of decreased erectile function. For instance, some men's adult children encouraged them to be different kinds of men in older age. In an extreme example, one couple said that their children had saved up to buy their mother a separate residence so that she could leave their father if he did not change his ways. IMSS urologists' attitudes also influenced men's experiences of decreasing erectile function. Importantly, the urologists did not try to medicalize this bodily change, even though they reported that they did treat ED as a medical problem in their private practices with younger and wealthier patients. This was partly because they shared the same views about respectable male aging as the interviewees (who they saw as older than wealthier men of similar ages—including themselves—because the IMSS patients often appeared older after lifetimes of physical labor). It was also partly because the IMSS system did not offer economic incentives for departing from this ideology to promote medical treatment for ED.

For all these reasons, study participants saw ED drugs as so inappropriate for older men that they were likely to do physical harm. Some saw their aging bodies as increasingly vulnerable to the dangerous side effects of pharmaceuticals. One of the few men who initially sought ED treatment decided not to use it for this reason. He explained that "I was prescribed pills, but I haven't used them. As a diabetic, I could have a heart attack" (interview by author). Many others saw the drugs as dangerous for older men because they would induce artificially youthful sexual behavior that would be physically taxing. A participant noted, "I don't like to use things that aren't normal. I don't like to force my body" (interview by author). Participants often voiced concerns that ED drugs would inappropriately "accelerate" their bodies. One explained that they could "accelerate you to your death. Many friends have told me, they will accelerate you a lot, then you'll collapse, that stuff will kill you" (interview by author). The idea that "people are dying of Viagra" was common, illustrating just how normal participants saw the "Mexican classic" form of male life-course change to be and how abnormal and potentially damaging they saw the use of ED drugs to resist this change to be. So, while many men reported that it took time for them to accept their decreased erectile function and come to terms with their older selves, even those who felt unhappy at first still rejected ED drugs, instead often trying gentle interventions like exercise or vitamins to avoid "unbalancing" their bodies.

CONCLUSION

Overall, a range of factors influenced older, working-class Mexican men's rejection of the globally prevalent idea that decreasing erectile function was a medical pathology to be treated with drugs. These included local cultural changes in ideals of masculinity and marriage, specifically the rise of companionate marriage and critiques of machismo, which emerged over the courses of older men's lives and made them want to be different kinds of men as they aged. This goal of change reflected another key cultural factor: the idea that good Mexican men should live out a specific life course, which included shifting one's focus from work (and for some, extramarital sexuality) outside the home as a younger man to a later life emphasis on being present with one's family. Interpersonal interactions, especially with wives and doctors who understood decreasing erectile function in older age to be "natural" and "normal," were crucial for helping men decide that it was time for them to mature in this way.

This case demonstrates that people can understand changing erectile function in varied ways. Thus, it can help readers to understand how cultural ideas about things like gender, race, and aging influence what people define as healthy, normal bodily functions. The example here reveals that the physical attributes people define as fundamentally "natural" and "normal," and those they define as abnormal states to be treated medically, are in fact determined by cultural ideologies rather than reflections of a universal biological truth. As such, they incorporate local ideals and prejudices into seemingly objective medical statements. Readers can keep these takeaways in mind as they seek to make their own decisions about what counts as normal human variation versus medical pathology. This will help them to think critically about the phenomenon of widespread medicalization in which bodily and behavioral difference is increasingly defined as disease rather than diversity. It will also help them to identify the range of ways that people come to view culturally specific ideals of gender, sexuality, and aging as inherently "natural" or universal, and the suffering that this can cause for people who do not conform to those ideals.

REVIEW QUESTIONS

1. How and why did older men's ideas about ideal male sexuality change over their life courses?

2. What is "machismo," and how did ideas about it influence older men's understandings of respectable sexual practice?

3. How did other people, like wives and doctors, influence men's understandings of their changing erectile function?

4. Why did most men in the study reject erectile dysfunction treatment?

5. What are examples from your own society of bodily traits or changes that have been medicalized based on cultural ideas about normal and healthy gender, sexuality, or aging?

KEY TERMS

companionate marriage: a marriage based on emotional fulfillment rather than the traditional foci of economic production and social reproduction. It has become the ideal type of marriage in many parts of the world.

erectile dysfunction (ED): the idea that penile erections that do not meet cultural ideals are a medical pathology, defined clinically as the persistent inability to achieve or maintain an erection sufficient for satisfactory sexual performance.

machismo: a widely critiqued form of masculinity characterized by violence and womanizing, often attributed to Latin American men's cultural inheritance from Spanish Conquistadors. The idea of machismo is rooted in unfounded assumptions about the nature of Latin American men; however, these ideas have social consequences that then affect people's bodies and behavior.

masculinity: the culturally specific traits, behaviors, and discourses expected of men.

medicalization: a social process in which areas of life previously understood in other ways (for example, as social, religious or other kinds of issues) come to be seen as medical concerns to be treated by doctors.

RESOURCES FOR FURTHER EXPLORATION

- AAPA Statement on Race and Racism: http://physanth.org/about/position-statements/aapa-statement-race-and-racism-2019/.

- Amuchástegui, Ana, and Ivonne Szasz, eds. 2007. *Sucede que me canso de ser hombre.* Mexico City: El Colegio de Mexico.

- Gutmann, Matthew C. 1996. *The Meanings of Macho: Being a Man in Mexico City.* Berkeley: University of California Press.

- Loe, Meika. 2004. *The Rise of Viagra: How the Little Blue Pill Changed Sex in America*. New York: New York University Press.

- Tiefer, Leonore. 1995. *Sex is Not a Natural Act and Other Essays*. Boulder, CO: Westview.

- Wentzell, Emily A. 2013. *Maturing Masculinities: Aging, Chronic Illness, and Viagra in Mexico*. Durham, NC: Duke University Press.

ACKNOWLEDGMENTS

I am grateful to the people who so generously participated in this research, as well as the IMSS physicians, nurses, public health researchers, and staff members who made it possible. This research was funded by Fulbright IIE, the Wenner-Gren Foundation for Anthropological Research, and the American Association of University Women.

BIBLIOGRAPHY

Ackermann, Rebecca, Sheela Athreya, Deborah Bolnick, Agustín Fuentes, Tina Lasisi, Sang-Hee Lee, Shay-Akil McLean, and Robin Nelson. 2019. AAPA Statement on Race and Racism. American Association of Physical Anthropologists. http://physanth.org/about/position-statements/aapa-statement-race-and-racism-2019/.

Alonso, Ana María. 2004. "Conforming Disconformity: 'Mestizaje,' Hybridity, and the Aesthetics of Mexican Nationalism." *Cultural Anthropology* 19, no. 4: 459–490.

Amuchástegui, Ana, and Ivonne Szasz, eds. 2007. *Sucede que me canso de ser hombre*. Mexico City: El Colegio de Mexico.

Amuchástegui Herrera, Ana. 2008. "La masculinidad como culpa esencial: subjetivación, género y tecnología de sí en un programa de reeducación para hombres violentos." II Congreso Nacional Los Estudios de Género de los Hombres en México: Caminos Andados y Nuevos Retos en Investigación y Acción, Mexico City, February 14.

Carillo, Héctor. 2002. *The Night is Young: Sexuality in Mexico in the Time of AIDS*. Chicago: University of Chicago Press.

Gutmann, Matthew C. 1996. *The Meanings of Macho: Being a Man in Mexico City*. Berkeley: University of California Press.

Hirsch, Jennifer. 2003. *A Courtship After Marriage: Sexuality and Love in Mexican Transnational Families*. Berkeley: University of California Press.

Linde, Charlotte. 1993. *Life Stories: The Creation of Coherence*. New York: Oxford University Press.

Lizza, E. F., and R. C. Rosen. 1999. "Definition and Classification of Erectile Dysfunction: Report of the Nomenclature Committee of the International Society of Impotence Research." *International Journal of Impotence Research* 11:141–143.

Loe, Meika. 2004a. *The Rise of Viagra: How the Little Blue Pill Changed Sex in America.* New York: New York University Press.

———. 2004b. "Sex and the Senior Woman: Pleasure and Danger in the Viagra Era." *Sexualities* 7, no. 3: 303–326.

———. 2006. "The Viagra Blues: Embracing or Resisting the Viagra Body." In *Medicalized Masculinities*, edited by Dana Rosenfeld and Christopher A. Faircloth, 21–44. Philadelphia: Temple University Press.

Mamo, L., and J. Fishman. 2001. "Potency in All the Right Places: Viagra as a Technology of the Gendered Body." *Body & Society* 7, no. 4: 13–35.

Marshall, Barbara L., and Stephen Katz. 2002. "Forever Functional: Sexual Fitness and the Ageing Male Body." *Body & Society* 8, no. 4: 43–70.

McKee Irwin, Robert. 2003. *Mexican Masculinities.* Minneapolis: University of Minnesota Press.

McLaren, Angus. 2007. *Impotence: A Cultural History.* Chicago: University of Chicago Press.

Moore, Katrina L. 2010. "Sexuality and Sense of Self in Later Life: Japanese Men's and Women's Reflections on Sex and Aging." *Journal of Cross-cultural Gerontology* 25, no. 2: 149–163.

Paz, Octavio. 1985. *The Labyrinth of Solitude and other Writings.* Translated by Lysander Kemp. New York: Grove Weidenfeld.

Potts, Annie. 2000. "The Essence of the Hard On": Hegemonic Masculinity and the Cultural Construction of 'Erectile Dysfunction.' " *Men and Masculinities* 3, no. 1: 85–103.

Potts, Annie, Nicola Gavey, Victoria M Grace, and Tiina Vares. 2003. "The Downside of Viagra: Women's Experiences and Concerns." *Sociology of Health & Illness* 25, no. 7: 697–719.

Potts, Annie, Victoria Grace, Nicola Gavey, and Tiina Vares. 2004. "Viagra Stories: Challenging 'Erectile Dysfunction." *Social Science & Medicine* 59:489–499.

Ramirez, Josué. 2009. *Against Machismo: Young Adult Voices in Mexico City.* New York: Berghahn.

Rubin, Gayle. 1992. "Thinking Sex." In *Pleasure and Danger: Exploring Female Sexuality*, edited by Carole Vance. New York: HarperCollins.

Sandberg, Linn. 2013. "Just Feeling a Naked Body Close to You: Men, Sexuality and Intimacy in Later Life." *Sexualities* 16, no. 3–4: 261–282.

Sverdlin, Adina Radosh. 2017. "Bandas beyond their 'Ethnographic Present': Neoliberalism and the Possibility of Meaning in Mexico City." *Journal of Extreme Anthropology* 1, no. 3: 102–124.

Tiefer, Leonore. 1994. "The Medicalization of Impotence: Normalizing Phallocentrism." *Gender and Society* 8, no. 3: 363–377.

———. 1995. *Sex is Not a Natural Act and Other Essays.* Boulder, CO: Westview.

van der Geest, Sjaak. 2001. " 'No Strength': Sex and Old Age in a Rural Town in Ghana." *Social Science and Medicine* 53:1383–1396.

Wardlow, Holly, and Jennifer S. Hirsch. 2006. "Introduction." In *Modern Loves: The Anthropology of Romantic Courtship and Companionate Marriage*, edited by Jennifer S. Hirsch and Holly Wardlow, 1–31. Ann Arbor: University of Michigan Press.

Wentzell, Emily. 2008. "Imagining Impotence in America: From Men's Deeds to Men's Minds to Viagra." *Michigan Discussions in Anthropology* 25:153–178.

———. 2013a. "I Don't Want to Be Like My Father: Masculinity, Modernity, and Intergenerational Relationships in Mexico." In *Transitions And Transformations: Cultural Perspectives on Aging and the Life Course*, edited by Caitrin Lynch and Jason Danely, 64–78. New York: Berghahn.

———. 2013b. *Maturing Masculinities: Aging, Chronic Illness, and Viagra in Mexico*. Durham, NC: Duke University Press.

Zion Market Research. 2018. "Global Erectile Dysfunction Drugs Market Will Reach USD 7.10 Billion by 2024." https://www.globenewswire.com/news-release/2018/10/05/1617442/0/en/Global-Erectile-Dysfunction-Drugs-Market-Will-Reach-USD-7-10-Billion-by-2024-Zion-Market-Research.html.

9

Intersectionality and Normative Masculinity in Northeast Brazil

Melanie A. Medeiros

LEARNING OBJECTIVES

- To define intersectionality and explain the importance of an intersectional approach to the study of masculinity.

- To describe the concepts of marginalized masculinities, thwarted masculinity, and crisis of masculinity.

- To define the concepts of compensatory masculinity and exculpatory chauvinism and apply these to the Brazilian ethnographic case study presented in this chapter.

- To describe how this case study helps to demonstrate the value of an intersectional approach to understanding masculinities.

In this chapter, the author uses an intersectional lens to examine how gender, race, and class affect the gender roles, gender performance, and lived experiences of working-class, cisgender, Black Brazilian men. The author explores how in a rural Northeast Brazilian community, a decrease in demand for male workers prevented men from maintaining their roles as financial providers for their families, which challenged dominant notions of manhood and authority, creating a "crisis of masculinity" for working-class Black men.

North American media often use stereotypes to portray men in Latin America and the Caribbean as *macho*, a term associated with aggressive masculinity. This portrayal hides the fact that there are many forms of masculinity, and the macho stereotype ignores the historical, sociocultural, political, and economic issues influencing men's performance of masculinity. As you read in chapter 1, normative masculinity is socially constructed and comprises traits and practices that are idealized and upheld by the dominant social groups in a society. For example, in North America, Latin América, and the Caribbean some characteristics associated with normative masculinity are whiteness, heterosexuality, and middle- or upper-class status. Research shows that not all men meet (or aspire to meet) sociocultural standards of normative masculinity, and their ability or willingness to do so affects their position on gender hierarchies (Wade and Ferree 2019). We should not assume, for example, that all cisgender men have the same level of power over all women. Cisgender men (referred to hereafter as "men") who are not able to meet a society's standard of normative masculinity may have a more marginal position on the gender power hierarchy than men who do meet it, and this position is often influenced by men's other social identities. **Intersectionality** is an approach to the study of social inequality that examines how gender, race, ethnicity, class, and sexuality overlap to form an individual's social identity and the ways their social identity influences their position in social hierarchies (Crenshaw 1989). Although an intersectional lens is most often used to examine the experiences and oppression of working-class, cisgender, and trans women of color, it is also a useful framework for understanding the identities and experiences of working-class, cisgender Black, Indigenous, and men of color. Race, class, and sexuality all influence men's ability to perform normative masculinity (Abelson 2016; Brooms and Perry 2016; Grove 2015; hooks 2004; Lawrence 2019; Linke 2011; Mutua 2006; Neal 2013; Slutskaya 2016; Ward 2016; White 2011).

The inability to meet social and personal expectations of normative masculinity can cause some men to view themselves (or be perceived) as inadequate (Wade and Ferree 2019). Wade and Ferree (2019) argue, in fact, that many if not most men find it impossible to perform all of the dominant or idealized characteristics and behaviors associated with normative masculinity and are therefore frequently in a position where they might be viewed as failing at masculinity or at least feel like they are failing. For men whose intersecting social identities distance them from the dominant or normative paradigm, the potential sense of inadequacy can be more pronounced. Furthermore, since dominant ideals of masculinity are continually changing, men are often tasked with adjusting their gender performance to meet transforming expectations (Wade and Ferree 2019). In other words, masculinity is fragile and fleeting. Scholars use a variety of concepts to refer to men who do not meet the normative or dominant standard their society prescribes. Connell (2016) advocates for

intersectionality
Refers to the interconnected nature of social categories such as race, class, and gender that creates overlapping systems of discrimination or disadvantage. The goal of an intersectional analysis is to understand how racism, sexism, and homophobia (for example) interact together to impact our identities and how we live.

the term *marginalized masculinities* to describe men whose intersecting social identities challenge their ability to fulfill what Connell refers to as "hegemonic masculinity." Chant (2000) refers to a *crisis of masculinity* to explain how socioeconomic and political changes and/or challenges can prevent men (even those who met standards previously) from fulfilling dominant social expectations of masculinity. Researchers working in the United States (Moore 1994), Brazil (Hautzinger 2007), and the Congo (Hollander 2014) have used the term *thwarted masculinity*, which I also use in this chapter.

In this chapter, I describe how rural, working-class, Black Brazilian men's efforts to meet standards of normative masculinity are both informed and constrained by socioeconomic marginalization at the intersection of gender, race, and class, as well as by geographic location. Subsequently, the strategies these men employ in their pursuit of normative masculinity pose a direct threat to their marriages, as changing gender norms and marriage expectations call into question some of the practices historically associated with normative masculinity in Brazil. I argue that the study of normative masculinity must consider the historical, sociocultural, and political economic structures that influence both the construction of normative masculinity and men's ability to perform it, as well as the effects of thwarted masculinity on individuals and families.

Figure 9.1. Two boys and a young man in a rural Northeast Brazilian town. Photo by Melanie A. Medeiros.

INTERSECTIONALITY AND NORMATIVE MASCULINITY IN NORTHEAST BRAZIL

I employ an intersectional lens to examine how gender, race, class, and sexuality affect the gender roles, gender performance, and lived experiences of working-class Black Brazilian men living in the rural interior of the Northeast state of Bahia. For several reasons, Northeast Brazil is an important site for examining masculinity among working-class, rural, Black Brazilian men. First, due to historical trends and contemporary policies, the northeast region of Brazil is one of the poorest in the country, with social indicators well below the southern regions. In 2017, 70.6 percent of the households in Northeast Brazil had an income of less than or equal to the Brazilian monthly minimum wage, approximately US$234 per month (IBGE 2017). The political and socioeconomic marginalization of working-class Brazilians, especially those living in the rural Northeast interior, where there are even fewer employment opportunities than in urban areas, constrains men's performance of normative masculinity.

Second, Northeast Brazil's colonial economy centered on the production of sugar cane, for which Brazil imported an estimated four million enslaved Africans—40 percent of all slaves in the Americas (Graden 2006). The legacy of slavery includes not only the socioeconomic marginalization of the descendants of enslaved people and a long history of racial mixing but also racial ideology that informs perceptions of Black men and their self-perceptions, which I will discuss in more depth later in this chapter. Furthermore, the history of slavery has left a demographic footprint on the region, and 70 percent of northeast Brazilians identified as "Black" or "brown/mixed-race" in the 2010 census (IBGE 2011). In fact, Brazilians select from over one hundred terms to self-identify racially or by skin color, although the Brazilian census employs only five: *branca* (white), *parda* (brown/mixed), *preta* (Black), *amarela* (yellow), and *indígena* (Indigenous). Notably, race in Brazil is a complex category that encompasses not only phenotypic traits such as skin color and hair texture but also social class, education level, language and communication style, clothing style, and geographic location. A working-class Brazilian who lives in Northeast Brazil, and has phenotypic traits that indicate they have some African ancestry, will often be socially classified as "Black" or "brown/mixed" irrespective of how they self-identify. This is also the result of the racialization of the entire Northeast region, which in the imaginary of Brazilians in southern and central Brazil, is more "African," "Afro-Brazilian," or "Black" than the rest of Brazil. This image of the Northeast region is so pervasive that southern Brazilians use the word *nordestino* (northeasterner) as a derogatory euphemism for a working-class Black

Brazilian (O'Dougherty 2002). Furthermore, people who are from and/ or continue to live in the rural interior of the Northeast region are also racialized, largely because people from the interior are viewed as uneducated, unsophisticated, and poor—all qualities associated with Blackness rather than whiteness in Brazil. Brazilians also perceive urban, middle- and upper-class Brazilians, especially those from the large southern and central Brazilian cities (e.g., Rio de Janeiro, São Paulo, Brasília) as more educated and cosmopolitan and therefore "whiter" irrespective of their phenotypic traits. Understanding that the category of skin color/race in Brazil encompasses more than just phenotypic traits is central to examining why and how working-class men in rural Northeast Brazil are socially and economically marginalized as a result of them being racialized as Black.

I lived in the rural interior of the Northeast Brazilian state of Bahia for two years and continued to visit every year for ten years while I conducted ethnographic fieldwork on gender roles, marriage, divorce, and distress, which I wrote about in my book *Marriage, Divorce and Distress in Northeast Brazil: Black Women's Perspectives on Love, Respect and Kinship* (2018). The small town I lived in, which I will call Brogodó, was undergoing socioeconomic changes due to the growth of the town's ecotourism industry. I found that these changes affected gender roles and community members' identities in important ways.

Figure 9.2. A group of American students visits the national park at the center of Brogodó's ecotourism industry. Photo by Melanie A. Medeiros.

In Brazil, normative gender roles are associated with marriage, in and of itself a heteronormative institution. Historically in Brazil, heterosexual men and women's gender roles and their identities were grounded in their responsibilities to their spouses and households. Marriage was also a site where patriarchal values were upheld, granting husbands authority and decision-making power over their wives and their families: although it is important to recognize that women also exerted power within the household. Men's authority was tied to their responsibility to financially provide for their families and ensure the respectability of their households, including safeguarding the sexuality and morality of the household's women and girls. Women contributed to the household through their domestic labor and safeguarded their husband's honor by being faithful wives (Sarti 1995). Men's responsibilities to their households afforded them the opportunity of a life in the public sphere, colloquially known as the *rua* (street). Life in the rua consists of work or the search for employment but also includes socializing with friends, consuming alcohol, and flirting with women other than their wives. Life in the rua is also associated with men's ability to have extramarital affairs, which for generations have been considered a gendered behavioral norm for men (but not for women). In short, men's and women's responsibilities to their households and relationships with one another defined gender roles and norms within and outside the household; the gender hierarchy within the patriarchal society was reflected in the household, and vice versa (DaMatta 1985).

However, gender roles and norms are never fixed; over time they continually shift and change within both the private and public spheres. In Brazil, political economic change has challenged men's authority in the patriarchal family and subsequently gender hierarchies outside of the family. And yet gender roles and norms continue to be informed by historically salient ideas about gender and marital relationships. For example, my research demonstrates that by finding employment outside their households, women contested gender roles and norms that confined them to the household. As a result of their employment, women were able to transform their gender roles and subsequently their identities, describing themselves as "independent" and "modern" women. Employment also granted women more authority and decision-making power within the household. And, pertinent to our discussion of masculinities, all over Brazil and in Brogodó changes to women's gender roles and to their identities had domino effects that impacted men's gender roles and their identities as well.

Figure 9.3. Every June, rural northeast Brazilians celebrate the *festa de São João* [St. John's Day] with a weeklong festival honoring the saint and the corn harvest, paying homage to rural life in Northeast Brazil. As part of these celebrations, local groups organize amateur dance troupes to act out a *casamento do caipira* (wedding of a country bumpkin) and perform a *quadrilha* folk dance. The performances portray gender roles and marital relations that are being renegotiated amid sociopolitical economic change. Photo by Mclanie A. Medeiros.

MEN'S UNEMPLOYMENT AND CHALLENGES TO NORMATIVE MASCULINITY

Ethnographic studies demonstrate that in many sites in Latin America and the Caribbean, policies that promote gender equality, combined with increases in women's education and employment, lead to shifts in women's gender roles and their identities. These shifts often challenge men's authority, gender roles, and their identities (Chant 2000; Hautzinger 2007).

Scholars argue that masculinity is "precarious" in this sense (Wade and Ferree 2019, 142) and that male power is limited by social expectations, obligations, and social judgment (Mayblin 2010). In this section, I will describe the socioeconomic factors influencing men's unemployment rates in Brogodó and the effect underemployment had on men's ability to perform normative masculinity. This will ground my later discussion of the ways that men compensated for unemployment and their thwarted masculinity with behaviors that put their marriages in jeopardy. Ultimately, I argue that rather than merely a product of patriarchal norms, men's responses to thwarted masculinity were a result of social inequality and marginalization at the intersection of race, gender, and class.

The growth of the ecotourism industry in Brogodó created more job opportunities in the service sector, but those jobs—housekeepers, cooks, laundresses—were locally viewed as "women's work." Gender ideology also informed local ideas about what constitutes "men's work" in the ecotourism industry, mainly jobs such as hiking and backpacking guides. However, many tour agencies preferentially hired guides from Brazilian cities rather than local men. Elsewhere, Medeiros and Henriksen (2019) describe in detail the ways in which employers justified hiring urban Brazilians, examining the ways they assumed that urban Brazilians were better educated and were more suited to the job of guiding domestic and international tourists. By contrast, employers explained to us that local men were unqualified because of their lack of education and foreign language skills, even though many of them had extensive local knowledge of the park's hiking trails. Discourses surrounding employees' qualifications masked racial ideology that framed urban Brazilians as "whiter" and therefore more capable and rural Brazilians as "Black" and unqualified or unreliable. These discourses also disregarded the fact that the local working-class men's subpar education was a product of structural inequities in the Brazilian education system (Medeiros and Henricksen 2019). Other forms of employment, such as working as day laborers on construction sites or as skilled masons or electricians, were not available or consistent, a situation that contributed to high rates of underemployment among men. In sum, men's underemployment was the result of gender and racial ideologies and structural inequities, and it had significant ramifications for men's gender roles, their identities, and marital relationships.

Men's roles as *chefes da família* (heads of the family) is a central characteristic of normative gender identity in Brazil (Mayblin 2010). For working-class men in Brazil, fatherhood and the ability to protect and financially support their children and spouses is critical to the successful performance of masculinity (Penglase 2010, 2014). Mayblin (2010), for example, found that many men in Northeast Brazil subscribed to a more pragmatic form of intimacy linked to their roles as financial providers. For these men, their inability to be primary breadwinners challenged their ability to demonstrate care for their families.

Men caught up in Brogodó's persistent underemployment were prevented from fulfilling their gender roles as household providers. This jeopardized their ability to perform normative masculinity and challenged their identities. The inability to financially support their households and the subsequent decrease in household authority that came with their reduced financial contribution (and their wives' increased contribution) challenged men's sense of themselves as "men." For some men, their reliance on wives, mothers, and sisters for financial support was humiliating because it suggested that they were "not man enough" to support their families (Scheper-Hughes 1992, 50). Twenty-seven-year-old Lucas explained, "I think a man who doesn't work is not a real man. . . . People look at you differently when you work. You have a little more *moral* (esteem). [When you have a job] they know that you are a stand-up guy. People look at you with different eyes" (Lucas, interview by author). Lucas described social perceptions of employed and unemployed men, demonstrating how the sociocultural link between men's gender roles, paid labor,

Unemployment and Normative Masculinity in a Brazilian Film

In the film *The Middle of the World* (Amorim 2003), the protagonist Romão is a married man and a father of five children. He takes his family on a cross-country journey by bicycle in search of employment opportunities in the metropolitan city of Rio de Janeiro in southeastern Brazil. While the entire film gives us a glimpse into the effect of poverty on families and family relations, there are two scenes in particular that indicate the relationship between employment and normative masculinity in Brazil. In one scene, Romão turns to his adolescent son and says, "A man has to work from an early age. When I was your age I was a man." His son replies, "I am a man." In a mocking tone, Romão rebukes his son and asks, "A man who makes no money, and has no woman?" Later in the film, Romão tells his wife, "I'm not a man if I can't provide for my wife and kids. How can you put up with living with a man who doesn't give you a decent life?" Romão questions the manhood of his son who does not work and is unmarried and then later questions his own manhood due to his inability to provide for his wife and children. This fictional account mirrors the reality of working-class men's insecurities over their roles in their households and in society and depicts normative notions of Brazilian masculinity.

and masculinity influenced those perceptions. Both men and women in Brogodó sometimes shamed unemployed men, labeling them as "lazy," less reliable, and not "real men." This discourse further challenged men's sense of masculinity and self-esteem.

Unemployment is particularly demeaning for working-class Black Brazilian men whose masculinity is marginalized (Connell 2016) because they are less able than white and middle- and upper-class men to perform normative masculinity both in the family and in society (Hautzinger 2007). In Brogodó, the frustration surrounding local men's unemployment was aggravated by the fact that local businesses were almost exclusively owned by white, middle-class men and women. These business owners preferred to hire individuals who were from Brazilian cities, educated and socially classified as white over locals who were racialized as Black (Medeiros and Henriksen 2019). This case exemplifies why masculinity must be examined at the intersection of race and class to understand how men cope with racial hierarchies and masculinity (Hordge-Freeman 2015). For Black Brazilian men in particular, structural inequities and daily microaggressions—such as harassment from the local police, or job discrimination—have historically limited their options in society, threatening their social status in the public sphere and increasingly in the private sphere as well (Hordge-Freeman 2015).

In Brogodó, men's experiences of marginalization and thwarted masculinity were distressing. Thirty-two-year-old Karolina explained the effects of unemployment on two of her former intimate partners:

> Men have that thing to be men. That old taboo that it's a man who provides for the household, that it is the man who speaks loudly, that it is the man who gives the commands. So an unemployed man feels worse [than an unemployed woman]; he feels like garbage. I say this because there are men that I've seen, in some of the relationships I've had. . . . I saw how my ex-husband and my ex-boyfriend both changed when they were unemployed. When my boyfriend was unemployed, he'd become very sad. . . . There were times when he cried, saying, 'I can't believe I'm unemployed.' He felt like less of a man. (Karolina, interview by author)

Karolina also described her interactions with her ex-husband when he was unemployed: "When I would talk to him he would say, 'You are speaking to me in this way because I don't have a job.' One time he got a job and he became all . . . you know . . . feeling like he was the man" (Karolina, interview by author). According to Karolina, her ex-husband believed that his unemployment caused Karolina to question his authority or "speak to him that way," which demonstrates the relationship between employment and perceptions of authority, a key component of masculinity for these men.

In Latin America and the Caribbean, and other parts of the world, the stress of thwarted masculine identities sometimes leads to problematic behaviors such as substance abuse (Maier 2010). When I asked Lucas why he thought it was important for a man to work, he argued that men needed to work for financial and "psychological" reasons. He explained how work prevented men from "losing themselves in life, for example, drinking and other things" (Lucas, interview by author). Women and men in Brogodó perceived a relationship between unemployment and alcohol abuse. Karolina made the connection between her ex-husband's abuse of alcohol and his status as an unemployed man: "My ex-husband, he drank, drank, drank, and couldn't get a job" (Karolina, interview by author). Aggravating the situation, when Brazilian men abuse alcohol, they lose the respect of their families, further perpetuating their loss of authority in the household and challenging their masculinity (Sarti 2011). Women in Brogodó also sometimes attributed the verbal or physical abuse of romantic partners to men's unemployment. Hautzinger (2007) discusses how in Brazil violence serves as a resource for performing masculinity when men's dominance in the gender hierarchy is threatened by changes that increase women's rights and autonomy. Thus rather than assume that male violence is the result of a patriarchal culture, it is necessary to acknowledge the structural circumstances and social discourses shaping their identities within a context of social inequality and marginalization. The masculinity of rural, working-class, Black men in Brogodó was fragile; it was compromised by their marginalized social status as well as the socioeconomic changes occurring locally. Furthermore, their inability to perform normative masculinity resulted in compensatory practices that threatened their marriages.

MEN'S INFIDELITY AS COMPENSATORY MASCULINITY

Brazilian men's participation in the public sphere affords them rights and opportunities that are associated with normative masculinity. In addition to spending time in the rua socializing with their friends, the ability to have extramarital affairs has long been a gender norm for Brazilian men (Gregg 2003). Another component of normative masculinity in Northeast Brazil is *malandragem* (roguishness), which is associated with activities such as flirting, sex (including extramarital sex), drinking,

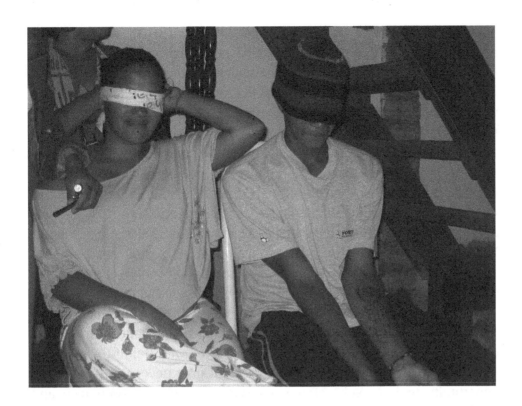

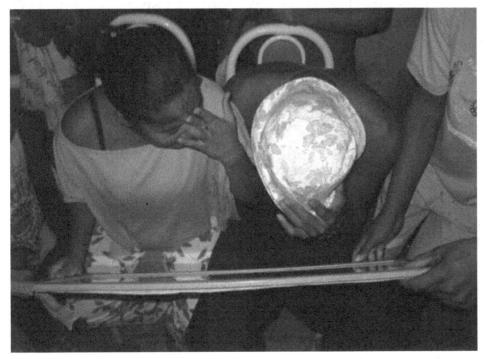

Figures 9.4 and 9.5. One example of how gender roles and norms are changing is the inclusion of fathers in baby shower activities. The pregnant woman
and her partner are blindfolded and asked to guess what each baby shower
gift is by touching it (Figure 9.4). Every time they guess incorrectly, they are
dressed up or made-up by the partygoers. Fathers are usually made to wear
women's clothing and makeup, which they are allowed to see once the game
is over (Figure 9.5). Photo by Melanie A. Medeiros.

exculpatory chauvinism
The tendency to absolve men of responsibility for performances that embody negative male stereotypes, while simultaneously offering social rewards [such as social status] for such behavior (Wade and Ferree 2019, 139).

and the freedom to be out in the street (Mayblin 2010). Married men's infidelity is in part (although of course not completely) a reflection of their desire to perform normative masculinity and affirm their masculine identities. For generations, Northeast Brazilian men's extramarital affairs were considered annoying by their wives but were accepted as long as the husband was financially supporting his household (Rebhun 1999). Essentialist discourses surrounding men's sexuality that justify men's infidelity as "natural" exemplify **exculpatory chauvinism**: "the tendency to absolve men of responsibility for performances that embody negative male stereotypes, while simultaneously offering social rewards [such as social status] for such behavior" (Wade and Ferree 2019, 139). Men in Brogodó reported that "real men" did not refuse sexual opportunities, even when such affairs jeopardized a marriage. Twenty-year-old Tiago explained to me the connection between sex and masculinity: "Men don't cheat on their wives to be men. Having sex with many women makes a man feel like a man. For a married man to do that, he has to cheat on his wife. Men are starting to learn that being *fiel* (faithful) is a good thing, but they can't help themselves. A real man never turns down the opportunity to have sex" (Tiago, interview by author). Both men and women in Brogodó rationalized this behavior by saying that men "can't help themselves" and that having multiple partners "makes a man feel like a man." Men who rejected sex from women other than their wives and who spent more time at home than in the rua risk being mocked as *homens caseiros* (house-bound men; see Hautzinger 2007). So although in Brogodó women expressed a desire for husbands who are homens caseiros, they told me they were difficult to find. This suggests that men in Brogodó did not aspire to be homens caseiros and that there was a stigma associated with being a "house-bound man."

In Brazil, stereotypes of Black male hypersexuality also naturalize and normalize male promiscuity, often through a discourse of Black men's blood as *quente* "hot" (Hordge-Freeman 2015; Mayblin 2010; Mitchell 2015). Discourses surrounding Black male hypersexuality are based in historical constructions of Black men as dangerous and sexually aggressive. These discourses, institutionalized in the legal and medical system, were used to justify the brutal treatment of enslaved men and the post-abolition subjugation of Black men in the late nineteenth century and persist today (Mitchell 2015). In Brogoó, twenty-four-year-old Jacqueline compared Black married men to white married men: "I think at times women think white men are more faithful in relationships. . . . They don't cheat. . . . Bahians are born thinking that they are everything and that they can be with all the women. . . . Many men, principally the Bahians, they look at other women, even in front of their wives, and show that they are desiring them. They [white men] don't do this, sometimes they don't even look. For this I think that they are faithful" (Jacqueline, interview by author). Jacqueline used the label "Bahians" (people from the state of Bahia) as a euphemism for Black men and compared them to white men. The talk of women in Brogodó revealed the continued circulation of such racialized notions of sexuality and fidelity; they sometimes verbally contrasted the infidelity of Black men to the perceived fidelity of white men.

Women's perceptions were often informed by widely circulated media portrayals of relationships, especially in *telenovelas* (Brazilian soap operas). The telenovela is the most popular television genre among Brazilian women. For working-class women who cannot afford satellite television, telenovelas and the news are the main genres of television programming available in the evening. Hour-long episodes of four different telenovelas air daily from six o'clock to ten o'clock in the evening, and repeat episodes are often aired during the daytime. These telenovelas portray storylines that associate romantic love with fidelity and depict these values as characteristics of white, middle- and upper-class couples. As Fernandez (2010) described in her ethnography of interracial romances in Cuba, the notion of white men's fidelity represents a "racialized fantasy," which people in Brogodó contrasted with tropes about Black men's perceived inability to be faithful.

In my research I found that as women's gender roles and their identities changed, they began to desire fidelity in their marriages as part of an aspiration for the ideal of romantic love and marriage qualities associated with romantic love, such as fidelity. Their expectation of fidelity was informed largely by messages in the telenovelas that they consumed and often heeded. While women in Brogodó naturalized men's hypersexuality, they no longer excused men for this behavior. Even men like Lucas who acknowledged that monogamy was becoming a sociocultural ideal argued that men were not capable of controlling their sexuality in the attempt to be faithful. In this community where socioeconomic change threatened men's ability to fulfill the masculine role of breadwinner, behaviors such as extramarital affairs functioned as **compensatory masculinity**—"acts undertaken to reassert one's manliness in the face of a threat" (Wade and Ferree 2019, 142). Hordge-Freeman (2015) notes that young Black Brazilian men in particular struggle with psychological distress as they "try to cope with racial hierarchies and sexual expectations" (Hordge-Freeman 2015, 125). She explains how "Black men with limited options and faced with structural exclusion, superficial cultural inclusion, and the day-to-day microaggressions that reinforce their devalued status" seek ways to "regain their self-esteem and to assert their masculinity" in order to alleviate their distress (Hordge-Freeman 2015, 125–126). In

compensatory masculinity
Acts undertaken to reassert one's manliness in the face of a threat (Wade and Ferree 2019, 142).

Figure 9.6. Children in a rural Northeast Brazilian town. Photo by Melanie A. Medeiros.

Brogodó men were challenged with trying to satisfy both normative views of masculinity, including financial support of their households, as well as contemporary marriage expectations that countered normative expressions of masculinity, including sexual behaviors. The very practices that enabled men in Brogodó to assert normative masculine identities—such as being out in the rua and having extramarital affairs—were criticized by their wives whose marriage expectations led to their disapproval of these behaviors. Therefore, men's efforts to meet standards of normative masculinity were detrimental to their marriages, often resulting in marital conflict and divorce.

CONCLUSION

Normative masculinity is neither a fixed set of traits or behaviors nor is it universally defined. The characteristics, behaviors, and types of interactions associated with an ideal or dominant form of masculinity change and shift over time and space. In Northeast Brazil, for generations men's financial support for their families, freedom to have a robust social life outside of the home, and unabashed sexual pursuits were all components of normative conceptions of masculinity. For working-class Black men in rural

Bahia, their marginalization at the intersection of various social identities often challenges their ability to fulfill some of their own (and society's) expectations for their performance of masculinity. In Brogodó, high rates of male underemployment made it difficult for men to meet the expectation of household providership. Although for decades sexual promiscuity was a common practice associated with normative masculinity, and tropes of Black male hypersexuality further normalized men's extramarital affairs, changes in gender roles and marital expectations in Brogodó affected women's acceptance of infidelity. Therefore, while for some unemployed men a life in the rua and the freedom to have flirtations and sexual relationships with more than one woman was potentially a form of compensatory masculinity, women were increasingly unlikely to *aguentar* (tolerate) this behavior. The junction of transformations in women's gender roles and marriage expectations and men's experiences of thwarted masculinity resulted in marital conflict and instability among couples in Brogodó.

REVIEW QUESTIONS

1. Why is an intersectional approach important for the study of masculinities?

2. What do the concepts of marginalized masculinity, thwarted masculinity, and crisis of masculinity mean? How do these concepts help us to understand the experiences of working-class Black men in rural Northeast Brazil?

3. How is infidelity in northeast Brazil an example of compensatory masculinity?

4. How does the case study in this chapter help to demonstrate the value of an intersectional approach to understanding masculinities?

KEY TERMS

compensatory masculinity: Acts undertaken to reassert one's manliness in the face of a threat (Wade and Ferree 2019, 142).

exculpatory chauvinism: The tendency to absolve men of responsibility for performances that embody negative male stereotypes, while simultaneously offering social rewards [such as social status] for such behavior (Wade and Ferree 2019, 139).

intersectionality: Refers to the interconnected nature of social categories such as race, class, and gender that creates overlapping systems of discrimination or disadvantage. The goal of an intersectional analysis is to understand how racism, sexism, and homophobia (for example) interact together to impact our identities and how we live.

RESOURCES FOR FURTHER EXPLORATION

- Gutmann, Matthew. *Changing Men and Masculinities in Latin America.* 2003. Durham, NC: Duke University Press.

- Gutmann, Matthew. *The Meanings of Macho.* 2007. Berkeley: University of California Press.

- Hordge-Freeman, Elizabeth. *The Color of Love: Racial Features, Stigma, and Socialization in Black Brazilian Families.* 2015. Austin: University of Texas Press.

- hooks, bell. *We Real Cool: Black Men and Masculinity.* 2004. New York: Routledge.

- Keith, Thomas. *Masculinities in Contemporary American Culture: An Intersectional Approach to the Complexities and Challenges of Male Identity.* 2017. New York: Routledge.

- Mayblin, Maya. *Gender, Catholicism, and Morality in Brazil: Virtuous Husbands, Powerful Wives.* 2010. New York: Palgrave Macmillan.

- Medeiros, Melanie A. *Marriage, Divorce and Distress in Northeast Brazil: Black Women's Perspectives on Love, Respect and Kinship.* 2018. New Brunswick, NJ: Rutgers University Press.

- Mutua, Athena D. *Progressive Black Masculinities.* 2006. New York: Routledge.

- Neal, Mark Anthony. *Looking for Leroy: Illegible Black Masculinities.* 2013. New York: New York University Press.

- Mitchell, Gregory. *Tourist Attractions: Performing Race and Masculinity in Brazil's Sexual Economy.* 2015. Chicago: University of Chicago Press.

- Pascoe, C. J., and Tristan Bridges. *Exploring Masculinities: Identity, Inequality, Continuity, and Change.* 2016. New York: Oxford University Press.

ACKNOWLEDGMENTS

Thank you to Rutgers University Press for granting permission for us to use a portion of the original text from *Marriage, Divorce and Distress in Northeast Brazil*. Thank you also to the women and men in Brogodó, Bahia, Brazil who generously opened up their homes and shared their stories with me.

BIBLIOGRAPHY

Abelson, Miriam J. 2016. "Negotiating Vulnerability and Fear: Rethinking the Relationship Between Violence and Contemporary Masculinity." In *Exploring Masculinities: Identity, Inequality, Continuity, and Change*, edited by C. J. Pascoe and T. Bridges, 337–347. New York: Oxford University Press.

Brooms, Derrick R., and Armon R. Perry. 2016. "It's Simply Because We're Black Men": Black Men's Responses to the Killing of Black Men." *Journal of Men's Studies* 24, no. 2: 166–184.

Chant, Sylvia. 2000. "Men in Crisis? Reflections on Masculinities, Work and Family in Northwest Costa Rica." *European Journal of Development Research* 12, no. 2: 199–218.

Connell, Raewyn. 2016. "The Social Organization of Masculinity. In *Exploring Masculinities: Identity, Inequality, Continuity, and Change*, edited by C. J. Pascoe and T. Bridges, 136–144. New York: Oxford University Press.

Crenshaw, Kimberlé Williams. 1989. "Demarginalizing the Intersection of Race and Sex: A Black Feminist Critique of Anti-discrimination Doctrine, Feminist Theory and Antiracist Politics." *University of Chicago Legal Forum* 1989, no. 1: 139–167,

DaMatta, Roberto. 1985. *A Casa e a Rua: Espaço, Cidadania, Mulher e Morte no Brasil*. São Paulo: Brasiliense.

Fernandez, Nadine T. 2010. *Revolutionizing Romance: Interracial Couples in Contemporary Cuba*. New Brunswick, NJ: Rutgers University Press.

Fonseca, Claudia. 2001. "Philanders, Cuckolds, and Wily Women: A Reexamination of Gender Relations in a Brazilian Working-Class Neighborhood." *Men and Masculinities* 3 no. 3: 261–277.

Graden, Dale Torston. 2006. *From Slavery to Freedom in Brazil: Bahia, 1835–1900*. Albuquerque: University of New Mexico Press.

Gregg, Jessica. 2003. *Virtually Virgins: Sexual Strategies and Cervical Cancer in Recife, Brazil*. Palo Alto, CA: Stanford University Press.

Grove, Jonathan K. 2015. "Unmarked and Unheard: "Researching" Working-Class White Men in an Appalachian Borderland—a Narrative." *Journal of Men's Studies* 23, no. 2: 133–146.

Hautzinger, Sarah. 2007. *Violence in the City of Women: Police and Batterers in Bahia, Brazil*. Berkeley: University of California Press.

Hollander, Theo. 2014. "Men, Masculinities, and the Demise of a State: Examining Masculinities in the Context of Economic, Political, and Social Crisis in a Small Town in the Democratic Republic of the Congo." *Men and Masculinities* 17, no. 4: 417–439.

hooks, bell. 2004. *We Real Cool: Black Men and Masculinity*. New York: Routledge.

Hordge-Freeman, Elizabeth. 2015. *The Color of Love: Racial Features, Stigma, and Socialization in Black Brazilian Families*. Austin: University of Texas Press.

IBGE—Instituto Brasileiro de Geografia e Estatística. 2011. "Censo Demográfico 2010—Características da População e dos Domicílios—Resultados do Universo." Rio de Janeiro.

———. 2017. "Arranjos domiciliares residentes em domicílios particulares, total e respectiva distribuição percentual, por classes de rendimento real efetivo domiciliar per capita, com indicação do coeficiente de variação, segundo as Grandes Regiões e as Unidades da Federação—2017." Rio de Janeiro. https://www.ibge.gov.br/estatisticas/multidominio/condicoes-de-vida-desigualdade-e--pobreza/9221-sintese-de-indicadores-sociais.html?=&t=resultados. Accessed November 4, 2019.

Lawrence, Stefan. 2019. "White Heterosexual Men, Athletic Bodies, and the Pleasure of Unruly Racialization." *Men and Masculinities* 23, no. 3–4: 600–617.

Linke, Uli. 2011. "Technologies of Othering: Black Masculinities in the Carceral Zones of European Whiteness." *Europe in Black and White: Interdisciplinary Perspectives on Immigration, Race, and Identity in the "Old Continent,"* edited by Manuela Ribeiro Sanches, Fernando Clara, João Ferreira, Leonor Pires Martins, 125–141. Chicago: Intellect.

Maier, Elizabeth. 2010. "Concluding Reflections: Renegotiating Gender in Latin America and the Caribbean." In *Women's Activism in Latin America and the Caribbean: Engendering Social Justice, Democratizing Citizenship*, edited by Elizabeth Maier and Nathalie Lebon, 337–351. New Brunswick, NJ: Rutgers University Press.

Mayblin, Maya. 2010. *Gender, Catholicism, and Morality in Brazil: Virtuous Husbands, Powerful Wives*. New York: Palgrave Macmillan.

Medeiros, Melanie A. 2018. *Marriage, Divorce and Distress in Northeast Brazil: Black Women's Perspectives on Love, Respect and Kinship*. New Brunswick, NJ: Rutgers University Press.

Medeiros, Melanie A., and Tiffany Henriksen. 2019. "Race and Employment Practices in Northeast Brazil's Ecotourism Industry: An Analysis of Cultural Capital, Symbolic Capital, and Symbolic Power." *Latin American Research Review* 54, no. 2: 1–15.

Mitchell, Gregory. 2015. *Tourist Attractions: Performing Race and Masculinity in Brazil's Sexual Economy*. Chicago: University of Chicago Press.

Moore, Henrietta. 1994. *A Passion for Difference: Essays in Anthropology and Gender*. Bloomington: Indiana University Press.

Mutua, Athena D. 2006. *Progressive Black Masculinities*. New York: Routledge.

Neal, Mark Anthony. 2013. *Looking for Leroy: Illegible Black Masculinities*. New York: New York University Press.

O'Dougherty, Maureen. 2002. *Consumption Intensified: The Politics of Middle-Class Life in Brazil*. Chapel Hill, NC: Duke University Press.

Penglase, Ben. 2010. "The Owner of the Hill: Masculinity and Drug Trafficker Power in Rio de Janeiro, Brazil." *Journal of Latin American and Caribbean Anthropology* 15, no. 2: 317–337.

———. 2014. *Living with Insecurity in a Brazilian Favela: Urban Violence and Daily Life*. New Brunswick, NJ: Rutgers University Press.

Rebhun, Laura Ann. 1999. *The Heart Is Unknown Country: Love in the Changing Economy of Northeast Brazil*. Palo Alto, CA: Stanford University Press.

Sarti, Cynthia. 1995. "O Valor da Família para os Pobres." In *Família em Processos Contemporâneos: Inovações Culturais na Sociedade Brasileira*, edited by I. Ribeiro and A. C. T. Ribeiro, 131–150. São Paulo: Loyola.

———. 2011. *A Família Como Espelho: Um Estudo Sobre a Moral dos Pobres*. 7th ed. São Paulo: Cortez.

Scheper-Hughes, Nancy. 1992. *Death without Weeping: The Violence of Everyday Life in Brazil*. Berkeley: University of California Press.

Slutskaya, Natasha, Ruth Simpson, Jason Hughes, Alexander Simpson and Selçuk Uygur. 2016. "Masculinity and Class in the Context of Dirty Work." *Gender, Work & Organization* 23, no. 2: 165–182.

Wade, Lisa, and Myra Marx Ferree. 2019. "Inequality: Men and Masculinities." In *Gender: Ideas, Interactions, Institutions*, edited by L. Wade and M. M. Ferree, 124–157. New York: Norton.

Ward, Jane. 2016. "Dude-Sex: White Masculinities and 'Authentic' Heterosexual among Dudes Who Have Sex with Dudes." In *Exploring Masculinities: Identity, Inequality, Continuity, and Change*, edited by C. J. Pascoe and T. Bridges, 402–411. New York: Oxford University Press.

10

Mexico's Antipoverty Program Oportunidades and the Shifting Dynamics of Citizenship for Ñuu Savi (Mixtec) Village Women

Holly Dygert

LEARNING OBJECTIVES

- Analyze the role of gender in shaping conceptions and practices of citizenship.

- Examine how gender identities are produced and transformed in association with social programs.

- Define the key characteristics of maternal citizenship.

- Compare different assumptions about the economy and its relationship to maternal citizenship.

This chapter examines how the Mexican antipoverty program, Oportunidades, transformed Indigenous village women's economic status while promoting a type of "maternal citizenship." The author discusses how program officials pressured low socioeconomic status mothers to make their income-generating opportunities secondary to their care-work obligations. Yet these women saw income-generating activities to be central to mothering. They contested the ways the program threatened their precarious economic status and their social bonds.

In the late 1990s, Mexican officials launched Oportunidades, a new kind of social program that has greatly transformed the nature of **citizenship** for economically marginalized Mexican women. The program was originally launched in 1997 by the Ernesto Zedillo administration as Progresa. In 2002 the Vicente Fox administration expanded the program and renamed it Oportunidades. More recently, in 2014, the Enrique Peña Nieto administration renamed the program Prospera. I refer to the program here as Oportunidades because my research focused on the Oportunidades period. Officials launched the program during an extended period of neoliberal reforms. The reforms marked an end to Mexican officials' efforts to spur economic growth through investment in "priority" economic sectors and a shift toward greater reliance on "the market" and, more specifically, investors' desires to generate wealth—to drive economic growth (see chapter 1). In this context, officials designed Oportunidades to improve the health and education status (or "human capital") of youth in economically marginalized families. In doing so, they aimed to equip the next generation to take advantage of the income-generating opportunities that the neoliberal strategy would create. They adopted a multipronged strategy to achieve this goal: first, they designated female household heads as formal Oportunidades beneficiaries, or *titulares*, in recognition of women's key roles in caring for their children. Second, they made titulares eligible for small payments (of about $30 bimonthly in 2004) to help them secure the material resources needed to meet their children's health and education needs. And third, they made access to these funds contingent on the fulfillment of multiple health- and education-related "co-responsibilities," including for members of recipient families to attend annual health consults, for school-aged children to attend school, and for mothers to attend monthly health education sessions. Moreover, officials provided additional payments to families with children in the third grade and beyond in order to combat declines in school attendance among older children. They increased the size of these payments for children in higher grades and among girls in an effort to reduce dropout rates among these populations.

At the same time that Mexican officials launched Oportunidades, they implemented a rigorous program of evaluations to measure the program's effectiveness. Data from these evaluations have consistently demonstrated the success of the "conditional cash transfer" (CCT) approach in achieving key goals, such as improving child nutrition and health outcomes and increasing educational attainment (see Fitzbein and Schady 2009 for an

citizenship
the whole range of political, economic, and social rights and duties attached to membership in a nation or community.

overview). These results have prompted officials to implement versions of the approach in diverse regions across the globe (Peck and Theodore 2010).

With the popularization of CCTs, researchers have begun examining the broader social transformations that these programs engender. In doing so, feminist scholars have directed attention to their role in advancing new conceptions of maternal duty (see, e.g., Molyneux 2006; Cookson 2018). This scholarship builds on a robust body of feminist inquiry on citizenship, which has critically examined the gendered dynamics through which individuals are differentially positioned in relation to the civic, political, and social rights and duties attached to membership in a community. Some of this work has examined the gender biases of Western liberal traditions of citizenship, tracing how the privileges of citizenship were historically bestowed on a "free" (male) public sphere that was premised on the hidden (female) labor and dependency in the private space of the home (Lister 1997; Warby 1994). More recent studies of how CCTs are producing new kinds of **maternal citizens**—citizens whose rights and duties are based on their maternal status—underscore the importance that state initiatives continue to play in reproducing these gendered forms of citizenship.

In this chapter, I build on this work by examining the economic dimensions of the form of maternal citizenship that officials promoted through Oportunidades. To do so, I draw from observations of the program in a rural, Tu'un Savi (Mixtec)–speaking village in southern Mexico, which I call "Ñuquii." (I use pseudonyms for the village and the individuals whose experiences I describe here.) Ñuquii means "Green Village" in the Tu'un Savi language. Ñuquii is a village of about twelve hundred residents located in the Mixteca Alta (Mixtec Highlands) region of the state of Oaxaca. At the time I began working in the village in late 2003, the municipality had an average per capita annual income of $933—a tiny fraction of the national average of $7,495 (INEGI n.d.). Accordingly, a full three-quarters of Ñuquii's households had been designated significantly economically marginalized to receive Oportunidades and so were enrolled in the program.

By emphasizing the economic significance of Oportunidades' positioning of titulares, this chapter captures the important role that gendered assumptions about economic gain played in shaping the program's conceptions of maternal citizenship. It also facilitates an examination of how particular legacies of nation building shaped the economic realities of maternal citizenship for women. As I show below, the processes through which these legacies intersected with Oportunidades' form of maternal citizenship had great significance for the experiences of titulares in Ñuquii.

I collected the data that I draw from here primarily during an eighteen-month period of ethnographic research in 2003 and 2004. I returned

maternal citizenship
a form of citizenship in which women's rights and duties are based on their maternal status.

to Ñuquii in the summer of 2011 to present the findings from the initial period of research and to learn about continuities and changes in the program since my departure. In 2012 I returned again and conducted additional interviews with villagers and health providers and officials. This chapter draws primarily from the 2003 and 2004 data. In doing so, it provides insights into how Oportunidades had transformed the lived dynamics of citizenship for low-income village women in the earliest years of the twenty-first century.

I begin below by tracing how key aspects of twentieth-century Mexican statecraft produced the gendered spaces of marginality that villagers in Ñuquii (and other communities across Mexico's rural south) inhabited. I then turn to an examination of the positioning of titulares as maternal citizens in Oportunidades, giving particular consideration to the economic dimensions of this positioning. In doing so, I describe important divergences between titulares' conceptions of maternal duty and those of village women. Finally, I explore the material consequences of this conception of maternal citizenship for the women who were designated Oportunidades beneficiaries in Ñuquii.

ÑUQUII: BACKGROUND AND CONTEXT

Mexican officials' twentieth-century economic development efforts helped shape the context in which villagers struggled to *seguir adelante* ("get ahead") in Ñuquii in 2003 and 2004. In the early twentieth century, Mexican leaders envisioned a key role for small-scale agricultural producers in the nation's economic development. As they began to devote significant investments in key economic sectors in the 1940s and 1950s, however, they largely neglected the agrarian sector. Instead, they prioritized the development of manufacturing along key urban corridors and the northern border and large-scale, industrialized agricultural production in the north. These and other investments (e.g., the development of Mexico's petroleum industry) produced the so-called Mexican miracle, in which the economy maintained average growth rates of 6 percent per year from the 1940s through the 1960s. This growth was limited to specific regions and sectors of the economy, however, and the south—and especially the rural south—languished.

The legacies of this history were evident in Ñuquii, where a full 91 percent of the villagers that I interviewed indicated that their households carried out some form of *milpa* production (intercropping corn, beans, and squash on small, mainly rainfed plots). Many villagers received payments (e.g., $150) from the government-run PROCAMPO program to support this production, but the small size of agricultural plots (typ-

milpa
a sustainable system of farming where multiple types of crops are planted together. The crops planted are nutritionally and environmentally complementary such as beans, corn, and squash.

ically less than 1 hectare), limited access to irrigation, and poor-quality soils limited the productivity of the milpa. In fact, the harvest usually fell short of meeting even families' own needs for consumption. Thus, villagers carried out a range of additional activities to generate income, such as producing artisan crafts (either weaving palm or threading silk) (84 percent), working intermittently as *mozos* (agricultural day laborers) on fellow villagers' plots (40 percent), planting additional crops for sale in area markets (e.g., a few bundles of cilantro or a basket of tomatoes), and raising a hog or two for sale. In addition, a small but significant population of village women had carved out a place for themselves in the regional economy as full-time market vendors (purchasing goods wholesale and reselling them in area markets).

The returns from most of these activities were meager. For example, in 2004, a man could earn about $5 and a meal for a day's work as a mozo, while a woman could earn about $4 and a meal. Among the two forms of artisan craft production, silk production provided better earnings. Silk buyers paid about US$250 per kilo, which villagers said that they could produce in about three months if they worked consistently. With local income-generating options so limited, villagers had long migrated to take advantage of better opportunities elsewhere, and 38 percent of the villagers that I interviewed in 2004 reported receiving some form of remittance from migrants. Typically, men migrated to destinations such as Mexico City to work in the industrial or construction sectors, or to northern Mexico to work in the agricultural fields. More recently, villagers had also begun migrating to destinations in the United States to work in the agricultural and service sectors. Because of these gendered patterns of migration, women predominated among resident villagers, especially among those of working age. For example, while girls and boys were equally represented among youth aged five to nineteen in the census that I conducted, women were overrepresented among villagers and older. The imbalance was especially pronounced among villagers aged thirty to forty-four, among whom only about half as many men (54) were in residence as women (103).

In Ñuquii, villagers' struggles to generate a livelihood were further shaped by Mexico's twentieth-century nation-building efforts. During the 1920s, Mexican leaders claimed modern Mexico as a distinctly **mestizo** nation, one that would be grounded in the orientations and conventions of the "mixed-blood" descendants of the Spanish colonizers and the Indigenous inhabitants of the land. They launched an ***Indigenista* project** to "incorporate" Indigenous populations into this nation-state by providing the training in the Spanish language and mestizo habits and orientations that they deemed necessary (see, e.g., Dawson 2004). As officials extended initiatives to provide this training, mainly through the

mestizo
literally means "mixed race," and refers to people of Spanish and Indigenous descent. In the early twentieth century, Mexican officials celebrated Mexico as a mestizo nation. In practice, mestizos are usually defined culturally by markers such as the use of Spanish language and Western (non-Indigenous) dress.

Indigenista **project**
the twentieth-century effort by Mexican leaders to promote the Spanish language and Mestizo culture to Indigenous communities in order to facilitate their "integration" into the "modern" nation-state.

educational sector, Indigenous populations increasingly gained familiarity with the skills, styles, and orientations needed to navigate mestizo spaces.

Within Indigenous communities, however, this process was uneven. One source of unevenness was the incremental process through which these opportunities were made available. For example, the first villagers to access formal educational training in Ñuquii received just one or two years of study, but local educational opportunities expanded over the second half of the twentieth century to include both primary and secondary schools. Because of this incremental process, age is closely linked to educational status and, therefore, to a facility with the Spanish language and familiarity with Mestizo social conventions in Ñuquii. Historical gender divergences in relation to these initiatives were another important source of unevenness. When educational opportunities first became available in Ñuquii, most families determined that they would best serve men as they navigated mestizo spaces on behalf of their families and the community. Accordingly, these opportunities were often initially limited to men and boys. Although women's educational status has increased significantly over the second half of the twentieth century, gendered disparities in educational attainment in Ñuquii reflect this legacy. For example, as table 1 shows, while slightly over half of the villagers who were thirty years old or older when I interviewed them in 2004 had no formal educational training, 71 percent (12) were women, while only 29 percent (5) were

Figure 10.1. Ñuquii women taking a break from dancing for the Patron Saint festival in 2004. Holly Dygert.

men. Moreover, all of the men were sixty-four years old or older, while the youngest woman with no formal educational training was twenty-nine years old, and several were in their forties and fifties. Rates of educational attainment were significantly higher among villagers aged fifteen to twenty-nine, but gender divergences remain evident. Most significantly, of the five villagers whose educational training was limited to some degree of primary school training, four were women.

Since economic and political power was (and still remains) concentrated in mestizo spaces, these divergent rates of education had great significance for villagers' efforts to secure a livelihood. The economic advantages that education conferred were especially evident in the experiences of professionals. Since Mexican officials had failed to invest in productive activities in the region, professional positions associated with the Indigenista project itself were among the few well-paid local income-generating opportunities (i.e., in the educational sector). In more recent years, with the launch of Oportunidades, new professional opportunities have emerged in the health sector. Only those with the most extensive formal educational training could compete for these posts. They typically earned between a thousand and fifteen hundred pesos per week, which was equivalent to about US$100 to US$150 at the time. Even those with less extensive educational training benefited from the ability to navigate the Mestizo worlds that existed outside the community in order to access better income-generating opportunities. As a result, in 2003 and 2004, professionals and the most successful migrants comprised the approximately one-quarter of households that had accumulated sufficient wealth to make them ineligible for Oportunidades. They typically invested some of their earnings in local businesses (e.g., variety stores, a corn mill, a pharmacy, a school supplies store), and in doing so further augmented their wealth. They owned the fifty-three cement and brick homes that clinic officials identified in their census of early 2004, nineteen of which comprised five or more rooms. They also owned the few dozen manufactured stoves (41) and refrigerators (42) that the same census located in Ñuquii at the time. And a select few owned automobiles (12), telephones (7), and septic systems (4).

Meanwhile, most households enrolled in Oportunidades in 2004 possessed little material wealth. They lived in one- or two-room residences. Their homes were usually constructed of adobe bricks, but those with the fewest resources lived in residences constructed of drafty wooden planks. Most of these residences had floors made of dirt and roofs made of corrugated tin or asbestos. And while virtually all households possessed a radio, most lacked more expensive manufactured goods such as stoves, televisions, and refrigerators.

Those with minimal or no formal educational training faced formidable barriers to accessing better economic opportunities. In practical terms, lack of familiarity with the Spanish language and mestizo social conventions made navigating the mestizo-dominant social contexts that prevailed outside of the village extremely challenging. Na Martha (Na is an honorific that conveys age and gender status, meaning "Mrs." or "grandmother") a monolingual Mixtec-speaking woman who was in her early seventies in 2004, referred to these challenges on multiple occasions during our conversations, exclaiming that she "couldn't survive" outside of Ñuquii because she "wouldn't know what to eat" (Na Martha, personal communication). Maria Luisa, a forty-two-year-old bilingual woman conveyed similar sentiments, asserting "I can't travel because I can't read and I'm scared to leave!" (Maria Luisa, interview by author)

When villagers did leave the community, those who failed to uphold the conventions of mestizo social engagement were often treated poorly. Indeed, even in the one area where low-income village women had carved out a successful space for themselves in the economy—as merchants in regional markets—they frequently experienced mistreatment while going about their work. For example, villagers complained to me that transport workers often mishandled these women's goods when they traveled to area markets, carelessly tossing their wares, and that bus drivers sometimes tricked them into paying extra for their fares. In addition, in Tlaxiaco, the site of the region's largest market, locals referred disparagingly to these women as "Marias" and treated them disrespectfully when they attempted to make their own purchases. And villagers recounted that district officials had harassed the women for taxes that they couldn't afford and dismantled their stalls when they failed to pay up.

Thus, the gendered dynamics of the twentieth-century Indigenista project left many village women at the bottom of regional social hierarchies. Juana, who was fifty-five years old when I interviewed her in September of 2004, provided a keen reflection on the resulting gendered (and generational) differences in villagers' positions in relation to these broader inequalities:

> Like, the people of my generation, as you see—I say for myself—we still dress dirty. Because I'm always in front of the fire [cooking]. I'm poor, at home . . . It began to change when [people] started to leave . . . They dress differently. They travel, get some money, build a house, get more money, and the homes improve. And in my case I don't go anywhere and—well, things stay the same as before. (Juana, interview by author)

This was the context in which three-quarters of Ñuquii's households received Oportunidades assistance in 2003 and 2004. Below, I examine how the positioning of titulares as maternal citizens in Oportunidades shaped their experiences in the program.

MATERNAL CITIZENSHIP IN OPORTUNIDADES

Since members of households that received Oportunidades assistance were obliged to attend health consults, and titulares were required to attend monthly health education sessions, the public health sector played a primary role in administering the program. In Ñuquii, villagers received health services from a federally run IMSS-Oportunidades health clinic that officials had established in the village in 1996. A physician presided over the clinic's health initiative and was assisted by two local health aides and a local rural health assistant. The mestiza physician who presided over the clinic when I initially arrived in Ñuquii in 2003 was replaced by a new mestiza physician in 2004. Meanwhile, Carmen, a village woman who turned twenty-eight in early 2004, had served as the clinic's full-time health auxiliary since the clinic opened in 1996, while Teresa, who was twenty-seven, served as the part-time health auxiliary. A third village woman, thirty-six-year-old Veronica, held the rural health assistant post. Together, the four shared responsibility for providing the health consults and health education sessions and certifying titulares' compliance with these requirements. Titulares who failed to fulfill these obligations risked receiving a *falta* (or absence), and those who accumulated three faltas could lose their economic assistance.

The health officials and providers that I spoke with in 2003 and 2004 viewed their work as a source of empowerment for women like those I came to know in Ñuquii. They claimed that gender inequalities were especially a hindrance for Indigenous women. For example, in an interview in May 2004, Teresa exclaimed, with great frustration, "There is so much machismo, and machismo doesn't allow women to develop as women!" Shortly thereafter, she elaborated:

> They [women] are very submissive. They wait for everything, everything from their husbands, when really they are very capable of making decisions. Whatever action they want to take, or whatever they want to do [*realizar*], they must decide for themselves! (Teresa, interview by author)

In this context, Teresa and others believed that Oportunidades was empowering village women to overcome this subordinate position so they could determine their futures in line with their own desires and interests.

As I noted above, however, Oportunidades positioned titulares as maternal citizens whose rights and duties were based on their role as mothers (see Molyneux 2006). For example, the creators of the program cited evidence that women invest more of their resources in their children than men do in order to name them beneficiaries (Fitzbein and Schady 2009). By making payments to women, they sought to take advantage of this "maternal altruism" in order to maximize the amount of program funds that were ultimately invested in children. Moreover, the program's creators built on existing patterns in which women were tasked with overseeing the needs of the family in making them responsible for ensuring that their children attended school and that all family members attended health appointments. Finally, the monthly health education sessions, or *pláticas*, that titulares were required to attend were primarily aimed at strengthening and shaping their care work. In the abovementioned interview, Teresa aptly summarized the altruistic, care-oriented form of maternal citizenship that the program was aimed to produce as she explained the logic behind the pláticas:

> Women are the ones who receive the pláticas because it is understood that the woman is the heart (*seno*) of the family and she is the one who cares for the children, and it's her who looks out for the well-being of the family. (Teresa, interview by author)

As Teresa suggests, Oportunidades was not designed to support titulares in foregrounding their own interests but rather to build on their tendency to prioritize the interests of their family members. Thus, in pláticas, providers counseled titulares on the preparation of nutritious meals, strategies for organizing and maintaining the household in order to reduce illness, and personal health management (with a special emphasis on managing their own reproductive capacities in ways that maximize opportunities to "invest" in each child).

In many ways, the emphasis on care work in this conception of maternal duties accorded well with normative accounts of the gendered division of labor in Ñuquii. When I asked villagers about this division of labor, many described a public/private split in which men were responsible for generating wealth outside of the home (including in the milpa) and representing the household in public affairs, while women were responsible for work in the *solar*, or household compound.

Ta Javier and Na Martha, the seventy-something heads of the household where I lived in 2003 and 2004, approximated this ideal as much as anyone else I came to know in the village. As a younger man, Ta Javier's primary contribution to the household economy had been cultivating the family's milpa plot. He had sold any surplus they were lucky enough to produce and traveled intermittently to the coast to sell regional goods, returning with coastal goods to sell in and around Ñuquii. In addition, he had represented the family in the municipal polity by participating in communal work details and taking on leadership positions in the civil hierarchy. In 2003 and 2004, he no longer traveled to the coast but continued to work the milpa, now alongside his son and son-in-law. He also participated in communal work assignments and attended the assemblies through which decisions over how to manage village affairs were made.

Na Martha, for her part, carried out most of her work in the solar, and especially in the center of the solar's social activity: the kitchen. She devoted a significant part of her days to the work of meal preparation. Each evening, she began the process of preparing the next day's tortillas by making *nixtamal* (a mixture of corn boiled with lime to loosen the husks that encase the kernels). Then each morning, she arose early to mold the dough into tortillas and bake them on the *comal* (a special pan used to bake tortillas over an open fire). She also prepared dishes to accompany the tortillas, which always included black beans and salsa; often included eggs, rice, and potatoes or broccoli; and more occasionally included regional specialties like chicken soup with parsley. While carrying out these tasks, she washed dishes, tidied the kitchen, and looked after the chickens that she raised primarily for household consumption. Na Martha took advantage of any time when she was not involved in these tasks to thread silk from the silkworms she raised for sale to a wholesaler.

Villagers' accounts of the gendered division of labor in Ñuquii, and Ta Javier and Na Martha's actual patterns of work, appeared quite compatible with the definition of women's maternal duties within Oportunidades. The two frameworks diverged, however, in their views of mothers' income-generating activities. As Na Martha's example shows, even women who carried out most of their work within the confines of the solar contributed to the household economy. Most produced artisan crafts—either raising silkworms and threading silk, like Na Martha, or weaving palm into straw hats and baskets. Many also sold a few select goods out of the home (e.g., keeping a case of soda or beer on hand to sell individual bottles when opportunities arose). And a few performed domestic chores for the small population of professional households.

Moreover, in practice, few women were as tied to the solar as Na Martha. One force that worked against this ideal was male migration. When male household heads left for work, women often took on their responsibilities in their stead. Women also sought additional income-generating opportunities when remittances from migrant men failed to meet the family's needs. Another force that worked against this ideal was single motherhood. Most of the single mothers with young children that I met in 2003 and 2004 had been abandoned by their partners. In these contexts, and others, women took on a range of activities to generate much-needed income.

In interviews, women characterized these income-generating activities as aspects of their maternal care duties (see Perez 2007). For example, during an interview in September 2004, Maria Luisa, the forty-two-year-old mother of five children whose concerns about managing life beyond Ñuquii I cited previously, said that she became one of the first village women to work as a market vendor while seeking to provide for her son. She recounted that her husband had been working in Mexico City at the time. The money he had sent was insufficient to meet her and her children's needs, so she sought out her own income-generating opportunities in regional centers like Tlaxiaco and Chalcatongo:

> Yes, like I lived with my son, I tell you, and, well, I go to Tlaxiaco, I go to Chalcatongo to search, to sell, even if it is just [to make enough for] a tortilla or [to make] an exchange [barter]. (Maria Luisa, interview by author)

Rosa, a fifty-five-year-old mother of eight, similarly described her work in the market as part of her maternal duties:

> Sometimes I go to sell even though it's just enough [money] for my children, so they can go to school, so they don't suffer like we're suffering. (Rosa, interview by author)

Seen from this perspective, income-generating activities were integral facets of maternal care. This association between income-generating activities and maternal care made sense in Ñuquii, where the exchange of goods was a central part of the processes through which villagers established and maintained social ties (Monaghan 1995). In this context, Gloria, a fifty-one-year-old mother of eleven children who I interviewed in July 2004, asserted that parenthood *produces* a drive to work:

> See now, like people who have more children, they have more money, too, because well, like I say, a person with lots of children (*un montón*) says, I'm going to work hard [to get] what my child needs. (Gloria, interview by author)

Oportunidades health officials and providers, however, viewed income-generating activities as conflicting with women's maternal duties. One occasion on which I noted this economic aspect of providers' conception of maternal duties was during a rabies vaccination campaign that the clinic staff carried out in a neighboring village in March 2004. I traveled to the village with Carmen and Teresa to observe the event, and we were joined by the village's rural health assistant, Elizabeth, upon our arrival. The three women decided to tackle the work of administering the vaccines in teams: I was assigned to assist Elizabeth by recording the name of each titular/dog owner as she stuck the animal with the needle.

After administering the injections in this manner for a few hours, we broke for lunch. As we chatted, Carmen and Elizabeth criticized the villagers, claiming that they "don't do anything for their kids." As a case in point, Carmen asserted that parents of sick children often failed to travel to the capital city of Oaxaca often enough to treat grave illnesses. I interjected that villagers' limited income likely made this quite challenging. On a previous occasion, Carmen had pointed out to me that Yuquijiin's economic situation was particularly dire because the village lacked a local water source for milpa production. Nonetheless, on this occasion, she denied that these circumstances posed a significant barrier. On the contrary, she asserted that parents needed to *echarle ganas*, or apply themselves. Moreover, she claimed that parents needed to learn to prioritize and that they should sell their animals to meet their children's health needs. Elizabeth agreed, asserting that the village was not *that* poor and pointed to some families that owned as many as twenty goats as evidence. Further, she recounted that one mother had indeed sold one of her goats to acquire the funds she needed to provide medical care for her sick child. She viewed this as confirmation that parents who failed to do the same were negligent in the care of their children; as the clinic's physician had lamented on another occasion, they "care[d] more for their animals than for their own children" (Dr. Juana, personal communication).

In this conversation, and others like it, providers construed titulares' economic pursuits as selfish and therefore a violation of their altruistic maternal duties. The clinic's providers and their regional supervisors expressed similar concerns about another aspect of titulares' engagement in the market—their spending. For example, in an informal conversation that I had with Carmen in 2004, she complained that titulares (mis)spent their Oportunidades assistance on beer. A regional supervisor made a similar claim when I sought him out to discuss my observations of the program in summer 2012. I informed him that I had observed providers tack additional conditionalities onto Oportunidades assistance, including a monthly village cleaning (see Dygert 2017). In response, he asked me pointedly whether I supported giving people something for nothing. When I replied that I thought there was great need, he pressed, "But if they spend it on beer?" (Dr. Alejandro, personal communication). The specter of titulares spending Oportunidades funds on beer underscored the potential destructiveness of maternal selfishness and so had become a potent means by which providers asserted the righteousness of pressing titulares to "invest" their limited resources in their children.

These conflicts over titulares' engagement in the market captured how gendered assumptions about economic gain shaped the positioning of titulares as maternal citizens in Oportunidades. While providers expressed expectations that Oportunidades would empower women to act according to their own decisions, their assumption that economic activities conflicted with titulares' duty to uphold ideals of maternal altruism made titulares' participation in the market highly visible, suspect, and subject to critique. Meanwhile, the economic engagements of men and other (nonrecipient) women remained unacknowledged, even when they, too, exploited Oportunidades funds for their own personal gain. In fact, Carmen herself took advantage of the bimonthly bonanza that occurred on Oportunidades paydays: it was by far one of the busiest times for her variety store, as droves of women arrived to buy school supplies, sandwiches, and—indeed—beer, and to square up the debts that they had accumulated in anticipation of the payment. Nonetheless, her exploitation of these opportunities remained unacknowledged by providers.

THE MATERIAL REALITIES OF MATERNAL CITIZENSHIP

When I began working in Ñuquii, I was struck by titulares' willingness to comply with the demands that the clinic's providers made on them, particularly since many were not actual program requirements (see Dygert 2017). Titulares did ultimately complain, and their complaints highlighted how providers' demands pulled them away from their income-generating responsibilities. In underscoring this fact, titulares called attention to the material consequences of these conflicting notions of maternal citizenship, with their divergent assumptions about mothers' economic engagement. Providers' demands were especially consequential for titulares because Oportunidades assistance was not sufficient to ameliorate recipient households' economic marginality. To be sure, in a context in which villagers relied on an average annual income of $993 per capita, the bimonthly base payments of about $30 were a significant source of much-needed income. Nonetheless, the funds were insufficient, in and of themselves, to transform villagers' marginal economic status. This aspect of the program was intentional: in setting the amount of the program's payments, the creators of Oportunidades deliberately limited their size in order to avoid disincentivizing work (Fitzbein and Schady 2009, 117–120). Meanwhile, officials did not take steps to address the gendered ways that twentieth-century Mexican statecraft limited titulares' opportunities: they did not redress the abandonment of the rural south by investing in new economic opportunities, nor did they provide educational training to address the legacies that left village women among the least prepared to compete for the economic opportunities that did exist. As a result, titulares continued to rely on the most poorly paid income-generating activities, such as producing artisan crafts, working as day laborers on fellow villagers' plots, and selling agricultural produce in area markets. This maintained titulares' economic dependence on male partners.

Maria Luisa's recollection of how she struggled to meet her family's needs while her husband was away working in Mexico City—sometimes making just enough for a tortilla—captures the stakes of these gendered dependencies. By 2004 her household's economy was much more secure. Her husband had returned from Mexico City, and they seeded milpa on three small (under 1 hectare) rainfed parcels. In addition, Maria Luisa used a small portion of her sister's land to cultivate some cilantro to sell in area markets. They received PROCAMPO support for their agricultural production. They had purchased a donkey to support this work and were raising six sheep and a pig to sell for income. Maria Luisa also wove palm hats and baskets. She sold some to a wholesale purchaser in the region and others at regional markets. Finally, on Maria Luisa's youngest daughter's most recent visit, she gifted her mother a collection of goods (e.g., sodas, eggs) to sell to other villagers from her home.

With this livelihood strategy, and support from Oportunidades, Maria Luisa and her husband had secured a small wooden home with dirt floors. Wooden plank structures were usually the draftiest (and even dilapidated) residences in Ñuquii; however, their home had been constructed recently, and though small was neat and well put together. They also possessed a couple of small appliances (i.e., a radio and a blender). Although Maria Luisa and her husband had accumulated few possessions, they had been able to send their children to school—an objective that the mothers I came to know in Ñuquii shared with Oportunidades officials. At the time of the interview, they were covering the costs of sending their thirteen-year-old son to middle school in Ñuquii, which included both school supplies and forgone earnings. They had also supported one of their daughters in pursuing more extensive educational training, and she was completing her final year of studies to become a nurse. Moreover, they appeared comfortable in their ability to meet these needs. In fact, the household economy was stable enough that Maria Luisa was able to replace her previous craftwork of threading silk with the more poorly remunerated palm weaving after she decided that harvesting the leaves needed to feed the silkworms was too dangerous for her son. Thus, while Oportunidades payments were not sufficient to transform Maria Luisa's marginal economic status—after all, they still lived in a small home with dirt floors and few possessions—it strengthened their economic security.

While Maria Luisa's experience captures the insecurities that the temporary absence of a male worker could produce, single mothers had among the most precarious economic circumstances that I observed in Ñuquii. One of these was Gudelia, a titular and mother of two daughters who was thirty-six years old when I interviewed her in July 2004. During the interview, she said that she had become pregnant while working in Mexico City, that it had been "a mistake," and that the father of her children had never provided any support. She lived with her eighty-year-old mother and the youngest of her two daughters in a small, drafty wooden home with dirt floors. They did not possess any appliances—not even the ubiquitous radio.

Gudelia and her mother were the only villagers that I met who only grew corn on her mother's small (one-fourth of a hectare) milpa plot—they had decided to invest their scant resources in meeting their consumption needs for the most important staple crop of corn. Even so, Gudelia said that the harvest never outpaced their needs, so she never sold goods in area markets. She generated additional income by working as a mozo in others' fields when opportunities to do so arose and weaving palm. They did not have any animals to augment these earnings, nor did they receive remittances from migrants. During the interview, Gudelia repeatedly emphasized how difficult it was to meet the household's material needs. In fact, she was the only villager among those I spoke with who denied attending celebrations because she was unable to assemble the goods (e.g., a stack of tortillas or a case of soda) that attendees were expected to contribute for such gatherings. Their experience captures the limited potential of Oportunidades to transform villagers' economic status, as well as the gendered relations of dependency that anchored household economies.

With such limited resources, Gudelia had found it difficult to care for her children. The expenses had eased when her fourteen-year-old daughter moved in with a man in the community, and, in doing so, became his common-law wife. This pattern replicated one that several older villagers recounted having experienced in the face of economic adversity: they had to marry "for necessity," in order to reduce the economic burdens on the household. Not long before the interview, Gudelia's daughter had become a mother herself and so was focused on caring for her newborn infant.

CONCLUSIONS

In examining the positioning of low-income village women as maternal citizens in this chapter, I have emphasized the material dimensions of this form of citizenship. Paradoxically, given providers' expectations that

Oportunidades would empower women, they construed maternal citizenship as a form of citizenship that required prioritizing children's needs. Moreover, they viewed titulares' participation in the economy as a violation of this duty. Titulares, by contrast, viewed their income-generating activities as central parts of mothering, and they contested providers' interference in these activities.

Meanwhile, the economic assistance that Oportunidades provided was not sufficient to ameliorate low-income villagers' economic marginality. The program failed to address the gendered legacies of twentieth-century Mexican statecraft that limited income-generating opportunities for women. In this context, the program strengthened the economic security of some households, especially those with a male household head, but failed to do so for the most precarious households. In this regard, the program sustained the gendered relations of dependency that twentieth-century statecraft produced. In order to expand low-income village women's opportunities, future initiatives should also include investment in the regional economy to develop better income-generating opportunities and educational initiatives to ensure that low-income women have the skills they need to access these opportunities.

REVIEW QUESTIONS

1. How did twentieth-century Mexican statecraft shape the struggle of villagers to "*seguir adelante*" (or get ahead) in Ñuquii?

2. What role did gender play in shaping conceptions and practices of citizenship in Ñuquii?

3. What is maternal citizenship? What are the differences in how Oportunidades officials and titulares in Ñuquii understood maternal citizenship?

4. Do you think that Oportunidades transformed gender identities in Ñuquii? Why or why not?

5. Think about other social programs that you are familiar with. How have they influenced the dynamics of citizenship? Have existing gender relations shaped the impact of these programs? If so, how? How have these programs impacted gender relations?

6. If you were the secretary of Mexican development, what kind of social program would you promote to improve Ñuquii women's circumstances?

KEY TERMS

citizenship: the whole range of political, economic, and social rights and duties attached to membership in a nation or community.

Indigenista project: the twentieth-century effort by Mexican leaders to promote the Spanish language and Mestizo culture to Indigenous communities in order to facilitate their "integration" into the "modern" nation-state.

maternal citizenship: a form of citizenship in which women's rights and duties are based on their maternal status.

mestizo: literally means "mixed race," and refers to people of Spanish and Indigenous descent. In the early twentieth century, Mexican officials celebrated Mexico as a mestizo nation. In practice, mestizos are usually defined culturally by markers such as the use of Spanish language and Western (non-Indigenous) dress.

milpa: a sustainable system of farming where multiple types of crops are planted together. The crops planted are nutritionally and environmentally complementary such as beans, corn, and squash.

RESOURCES FOR FURTHER EXPLORATION

- Andrews, Abigail. 2014. "Women's Political Engagement in a Mexican Sending Community: Migration as Crisis and the Struggle to Sustain an Alternative." *Gender and Society* 28, no. 4: 583–608.

- Bronnvik, Josamine. 2018. "Cultural Survival Advocates for Indigenous Women in Mexico." June 19. *Cultural Survival.* https://www.culturalsurvival.org/news/cultural-survival-advocates-indigenous-women-mexico. Accessed July 26, 2021.

- Cookson, Tara Patricia. 2019. "Family Oriented Cash Transfers from a Gender Perspective: Are Conditions Justified?" https://www.unwomen.org/en/digital-library/publications/2019/11/policy-brief-family-oriented-cash-transfers-from-a-gender-perspective. Accessed July 26, 2021.

- Hernandez Castillo, R. Aida. 2016. *Multiple Injustices: Indigenous Women, Law, and Political Struggle in Mexico.* Tucson: University of Arizona Press.

- Poulton, Lindsay, and Jess Gormley. 2021. Interview. "Lupita: The Powerful Voice of One Indigenous Woman Leading a Movement." *The Guardian*, January 5. https://www.theguardian.com/world/2021/jan/05/lupita-powerful-voice-indigenous-woman-leading-movement. Accessed July 26, 2021.

ACKNOWLEDGMENTS

I would like to thank the editors and the anonymous reviewers for their thoughtful comments on the first draft of this chapter. I would also like to extend my deep appreciation to the people of Ñuquii for welcoming me into their community and their homes and teaching me about their daily experiences. I am grateful to IMSS-Oportunidades officials and providers for supporting my work in the village and also to the Wenner-Gren Foundation for Anthropological Research and the Fulbright-IIE/ Garcia Robles program for their generous support for this research. Finally, I would like to thank Dr. Laurie Kroshus Medina for her unwavering support in developing the initial project and her guidance through the initial period of fieldwork and analysis.

BIBLIOGRAPHY

Consejo Nacional de la Evaluacion de la Politica del Desarollo Social (CONEVAL). 2018. Población Indígena con Carencias en Todos sus Derechos Sociales. Electronic document: https://www.coneval.org.mx/SalaPrensa/Comunicadosprensa/Documents/Comunicado-Dia-Pueblos-Indigenas.pdf. Accessed October 27, 2019.

Cookson, Tara Patricia 2018. *Unjust Conditions: Women's Work and the Hidden Costs of Cash Transfer Programs*. Berkeley: University of California Press.

Dawson, Alexander S. 2004. *Indian and Nation in Revolutionary Mexico*. Tucson: University of Arizona Press.

Dygert, Holly. 2017. "The Fight against Poverty and the Gendered Remaking of Community in Mexico: New Patriarchal Collusions and Gender Solidarities." *Political and Legal Anthropology Review (PoLAR)* 40, no. 1: 171–187.

Fiszbein, Ariel, and Norbert Schady. 2009. *Conditional Cash Transfers: Reducing Present and Future Poverty*. Washington, DC: World Bank.

Instituto Nacional de Estadística Geografía e Informática (INEGI) n.d. II Conteo de Población y Vivienda. http://www.inegi.gob.mx. Accessed January 21, 2007.

Instituto Nacional de la Evaluación de la Educación Mexico (INEE) and UNICEF 2018. Panorama Educativa de la Educacion Indígena y Afrodescendiente 2017. Mexico.

Kearney, Michael. 2000. "Transnational Oaxacan Indigenous Identity: The Case of Mixtecs and Zapotecs." *Identities: Global Studies in Culture and Power* 7, no. 2: 173–195.

Lister, Ruth. 1997. *Citizenship: Feminist Perspectives*. Palgrave: London.

Molyneux, Maxine. 2006. Mothers at the Service of the New Poverty Agenda: Progresa/Oportunidades, Mexico's Conditional Transfer Programme. *Social Policy & Administration* 40, no. 4: 425–449.

Monaghan, John. 1995. *The Covenants with Earth and Rain: Exchange, Sacrifice, and Revelation in Mixtec Sociality*. Norman: University of Oklahoma Press.

Perez, Ramona. 2007. Challenges to Motherhood: The Moral Economy of Oaxacan Ceramic Production and the Politics of Reproduction. *Journal of Anthropological Research* 63, no. 3: 305–330.

Peck, Jamie, and Nik Theodore. 2010. "Recombinant Workfare, across the Americas: Transnationalizing 'Fast' Social Policy." *Geoforum* 41:195–208.

Smith-Oka, Vania. 2013. *Shaping the Motherhood of Indigenous Mexico*. Nashville: Vanderbilt University Press.

Walby, Sylvia. 1994. "Is Citizenship Gendered?" *Sociology* 28, no. 2: 379–395.

11

Q'eqchi'-Maya Women

Memory, Markets, and Multilevel Marketing in Guatemala

S. Ashley Kistler

LEARNING OBJECTIVES

- Assess how Indigenous women in Guatemala engage with capitalism to reinforce long-standing Indigenous cultural values.

- Identify the social factors that lead Maya women to get involved with multiple forms of marketing.

- Compare and contrast the motivations for and outcomes of Q'eqchi' women's work in traditional subsistence markets and new forms of capitalist exchange, specifically multilevel marketing.

- Explain how participation in economic exchange can play a role in defining one's social status and gendered identity.

In this chapter, the author explores the intersections between globalization, marketing, kinship, and gender in San Juan Chamelco, Guatemala. The author discusses how Indigenous Q'eqchi'-Maya women use subsistence and multilevel marketing to challenge local gendered norms, reproduce longstanding Q'eqchi' notions of family, and honor the legacies of their female ancestors who were also involved in market sales. The author concludes that Chamelco's Q'eqchi' market women moderate two distinct cultural realities and systems of value: that of their community's Indigenous past and that of their town's ever-increasing incorporation into global capitalism.

During the summer of 2014, an interesting theme emerged on the social media accounts of several of my Q'eqchi'-Maya friends in San Juan Chamelco, Guatemala. They began to post with increasing frequency about Herbalife, a multilevel marketing corporation new to the region. I watched as friends posted photos of themselves drinking Herbalife shakes, shared statements of admiration for Herbalife, and documented their weight-loss journeys. Many of these newly minted Herbalife distributors were the children or relatives of subsistence vendors in Chamelco's municipal marketplace, taking their family histories of marketing in new directions. I set out to learn more about their connection to Herbalife and how their work related to the role of Q'eqchi' women in Chamelco's market.

In this chapter, I explore the intersections between globalization, marketing, and gender in San Juan Chamelco, a Q'eqchi'-Maya community in Guatemala. **Q'eqchi'** is one of twenty-two Indigenous languages spoken in Guatemala and speakers of Q'eqchi' use their language as an identifying ethnic designation. I examine how Q'eqchi' women engage with global capitalism, as defined in the introduction to this text, to challenge local gendered norms and reproduce Indigenous values. Participation in local and global markets empowers Indigenous women by giving them a level of prestige and recognition available to few Indigenous women in Chamelco. Through work in the local subsistence marketplace, Q'eqchi' women in Chamelco become embodiments of local value, recognized as compassionate, hardworking, and intelligent. Community members identify marketing as an ancient and valued occupation, further enhancing market women's status.

In addition, some women elevate their visibility through new forms of market exchange, including selling nutritional supplements produced by **Herbalife**. While involvement with Herbalife represents a new form of marketing outside the bounds of "traditional" market work, women sell Herbalife for many of the same reasons that others engage in subsistence marketing: to challenge local gendered norms and connect the community to long-standing Indigenous values, centered on honoring and remembering Q'eqchi' ancestors. Here, I explore how Q'eqchi'-Maya women use local market sales and **multilevel marketing**, a hierarchical business model in which salespeople earn not only what they sell but also a percentage of the sales made by those at lower levels, to reinforce Q'eqchi' notions of value.

Q'eqchi'
one of twenty-two Indigenous groups in Guatemala that trace descent from the ancient Maya civilization and who speak a Mayan language.

Herbalife
a company that makes and sells nutritional supplements and whose sales model is a multilevel marketing scheme focused on direct sales.

multilevel marketing
a hierarchical business model in which salespeople earn not only what they sell but also a percentage of the sales made by those at levels lower than their own.

GENDER, STATUS, AND CAPITALIST EXCHANGE

Around the world, women accrue capital and develop power through exchange (Buechler 1978, 1985, 1997; Kistler 2014; Seligmann 1989, 1993; Sikkink 2001; Weiner 1976). Although capitalism can widen inequities in gendered status (Amadiume 1987; Chaney and Schmink 1976; Chinchilla 1975; Nash 1993; Stephen 1993), women have long used capitalist exchange to define their social identities (Chiñas 1973, 2002; Clark 1994; Elmendorf 1976; Hendrickson 1995; Marti 2001; Nash 1994; Seligmann 1989, 1993, 2001, 2004; Weismantel 2001). Women who work in market sales earn prestige by accruing capital wealth, forming social networks, and achieving leadership positions (Babb 1985, 1986, 1989, 2001; Little 2004; Mintz 1971; Tax 1953).

Women change their status not only through market sales but through other forms of exchange. Multilevel marketing companies (MLMs) like Avon, Amway, Tupperware, Omnilife, and Herbalife have served as a vehicle for garnering status and elevating the sellers' socioeconomic class (Clarke 1999; Cahn 2008; Moutsatsous 2001). MLMs are "networks of member-distributors whose earnings come both from selling products and recruiting new members" (Sparks and Schenk 2001). Most MLMs engage in **direct sales** methods, meaning that clients purchase goods only in face-to-face interactions with distributors outside of a set storefront (Peterson and Wotruba 1996). While MLMs gained popularity in the United States decades ago, they have recently entered new markets around the world (Biggart 1989; Cahn 2006, 2008; Dolan and Scott 2009; Fadzillah 2005; Gu 2004; Hall-Clifford 2015; Hedwig 2012; Lan 200; Preston-Werner 2007). Cahn (2008) suggests that MLMs expanded in Latin America in the late 1980s as markets were deregulated.

The growing body of literature on MLMs reveals that for many distributors have trouble turning a profit through direct sales. In fact, many distributors lose money but find other benefits, including maintaining or enhancing class identity (Cahn 2008), gaining independence and autonomy (Preston-Werner 2007), expanding social networks (Oliveira 2017), and generating status and prestige (Dolan and Scott 2009; Fadzillah 2005; Hall-Clifford 2015; Moutsatsos 2001). These perceived benefits of MLMs are particularly appealing to women, as direct sales work is open to anyone—regardless of age, gender, or education—and offers flexible hours. MLMs are controversial, as distributors are often encouraged to invest large amounts of cash up front to buy in bulk materials that they may not be able to resell and use high-pressure sales tactics to recruit new clients (Partnoy 2014; Peterson and Albaum 2007, Vander Nat and Keep 2002). Most MLM distributors make little, if any, profit and rarely find the economic or social incentives they seek.

Indigenous women challenge gendered norms and elevate their social positions by embodying and reproducing local values through their involvement in markets and MLM sales. I draw on Gregory's (1997, 13)

direct sales
a marketing strategy in which sales are made in face-to-face interactions with vendors away from a store or formal retail location

definition of values as "invisible chains that link relations between things to relations between people." Value is what underpins social action and motivates people to engage in exchange and other social realms (Graeber 2001; Gregory 1997; Piot 1991). In some societies, more than one system of value shapes local life, as communities move seamlessly between long-standing local values and more recently introduced capitalist ones, such as the pursuit of wealth and resources (Cahn 2006; Fischer 2002; Fischer and Benson 2006; Gregory 1997; Goldín 2009; Kistler 2014; Little 2004; Sahlins 1988; Uzendoski 2005).

LIFE IN COBÁN AND SAN JUAN CHAMELCO, GUATEMALA

My research is based on fifteen years of ethnographic fieldwork in the community of San Juan Chamelco, Guatemala. Nestled in the mountains of highland Alta Verapaz, San Juan Chamelco has a current population of approximately sixty thousand inhabitants (INE 2014) and consists of an urban municipal center and dozens of affiliated rural villages in the surrounding mountains. The majority of the town's population identifies as Q'eqchi', and Spanish and Q'eqchi' are spoken in government businesses, public celebrations, and educational institutions. While most residents of the municipality live in rural communities and make a living through subsistence farming, others pursue nontraditional forms of employment, including office work, sales, and tourism. There is a marked socioeconomic stratification in Chamelco between those living in the urban center who have more access to capital resources, including land and steady income, and those living in rural communities, most of whom make a living through subsistence agriculture. Indigenous Chamelqueños experience discrimination from Ladinos, or non-Indigenous Guatemalans, in many realms of life, including employment, relationships, education, and pursuit of justice, due to government oppression and persecution of the Maya and resulting historical tensions between the two groups (Carmack 1988; Konefal 2010; Little and Smith 2009; Lovell 2010; Way 2012). I have changed the names of interviewees cited here to protect their identities.

In Chamelco, Q'eqchi' strive to honor their Indigenous ancestors by preserving, engaging with, and perpetuating the practices that they attribute to them, including wearing Indigenous dress, speaking the Q'eqchi' language, eating ancestral foods, and participating in ritual ceremonies (Kistler 2010, 2014). Many Q'eqchi' recall that their ancestors were tough, hardworking, and compassionate individuals who persevered through difficult circumstances. They honor this legacy by embodying these valued characteristics and preserving the practices that they believe that their ancestors left behind.

Reflecting on the value of ancestral practice, one activist in Chamelco told me that these practices "remain in our subconscious. People, despite external pressures or internal pressures, cannot forget their identity" (Rafael, interview by author, 2005). Another local activist similarly stated, "As a community, we have to have a relationship with our history. The past helps us to feel more certain" (Mauricio, interview by author, 2004). Chamelco's mayor in 2006, a young Q'eqchi' man, further elaborated on the value of maintaining perceived ancestral practice. He said, "We [our Q'eqchi' community] have always been very important in the history of Guatemala . . . for this reason, we have really valued what our ancestors left behind, in this case, the shrines, the churches, the customs and traditions of the town, and we have to conserve them" (Pablo Rax, interview by author, 2006). Another Chamelqueño similarly shared, "We participate in folkloric [activities] to remember the customs and traditions that our Maya ancestors left us. The town, the municipality, the state that doesn't have its folklore, is a dead community, because having these activities is remembering and living" (Francisco, interview by author, 2005).

Q'eqchi' also seek to generate good public images so that they will be "taken into consideration" [*inpatz' b'alaq*(Q'eqchi')/*tomada en cuenta* (Spanish)] by others for participation in prestigious social domains, including leadership positions in political, religious, and ritual organizations; godparenthood; and receiving invitations to important social and cultural events. To do so, one must show herself to be compassionate, hardworking, caring, dedicated, and moral, all qualities that Q'eqchi' attribute to their Indigenous ancestors (Kistler 2010, 2014). As one market woman explained, "You earn prestige when people say good things about you. There, you leave a good image, good memories behind" (Sara, interview by author, 2005). Another Chamelqueño explained how the Q'eqchi' define prestige and leadership:

One earns prestige through social relations . . . to be a leader, people look at it like they do a plant. And this plant is well developed because it was well fertilized. It has to grow, according to how it was prepared. But, if you plant something, and it grows crooked, even if you want it to straighten out, you can't . . . this same thing happens with leaders, with people. You give them a lot of respect, because they are going to lead us, because you know how they are. Because they are not

going to name you as a [leader], because how are you going
to lead if you are a bad person? You have to be an example
for the next generation (Francisco, interview by author, 2005).

Being taken into consideration, recognized, and remembered are key values
in contemporary Q'eqchi' life, and these are values that Chamelqueños
identify as long-standing ones.

The accumulation of capital and economic wealth plays an increasingly
important role in how Q'eqchi' residents of Alta Verapaz define value.
The region's Indigenous residents have engaged with global economic
forces for centuries. By the late 1800s, German coffee growers arrived
in the region seeking land on which to cultivate sugar, cardamom, and
coffee (Díaz 1996; Henn 1996; King 1974). These European exporters
seized lands from Q'eqchi' and enslaved them to work their fields. This
dark era marked the introduction of the Q'eqchi' community to capitalist
production. While Q'eqchi' residents of Alta Verapaz have been forced
to confront global capitalism since this time, they have seen a rapid
increase in national and international corporations in their communities
over the last several decades. By 2019 international food distributors,
chain restaurants, banks, and supermarkets were prevalent in Q'eqchi'
communities. Local residents' incorporation into global capitalist networks
in nearly all aspects of life has led some Q'eqchi' to expand definitions
of value to include the accumulation of capital.

Q'EQCHI' WOMEN AND GENDERED STATUS

The body of scholarship on Q'eqchi' life, and my interviews with members
of the Q'eqchi' community, suggest that that according to an idealized
perspective, Q'eqchi' society aspires to **gender complementarity**, with
men and women occupying equal status but with different social functions (Hatse and DeCeuster 2001; Estrada 1990; Adams 1999). Nevertheless, this ideal is not representative of gender dynamics in Chamelco,
where most Q'eqchi' women are subjugated by the norms of *machismo*,
as defined previously in this volume. For example, Q'eqchi' women are
excluded from participation in many ritual events, as they are considered *muxuq*, or "profane," and of lower status and importance than men
(Adams and Brady 2005). Wilk (1991, 201) argues that historically, the
Q'eqchi' community has excluded women from agricultural production or
wage labor as well, meaning that they "have no currency, no ability to
motivate production, no power over the ultimate source of all food and

gender complementarity
the ideal that men and
women have equal
status defined by their
participation in separate
but equally valued social
realms (e.g., men earn
status by farming; women
earn status by completing
housework). Gender
complementarity is rarely
achieved but is often
recognized as a social
ideal.

wealth." In other words, a marked division of labor relegates women to perform domestic work in the home, while men have the freedom to work, participate in ritual, and socialize outside of the home (Adams 1999; Ghidinelli 1975, 252).

This gendered stratification begins at an early age, as Q'eqchi' parents assign their children simple gendered tasks, in which young boys help their fathers tend to fields, while young girls help their mothers with household work (Estrada 1990, 263–264). This division means that, traditionally, most Q'eqchi' women have not pursued higher education or employment outside of the home, though this norm has changed as more women continue their education beyond elementary school. In addition, Q'eqchi' women, as all Maya women in Guatemala, are underrepresented in politics and face sexual harassment and elevated risks of gendered-based violence. Many women in Chamelco reported unhappy marriages, and in some cases, even shared that they must ask their spouse's permission even to go out of the house. Those women who are vendors in Chamelco's subsistence market or who serve as distributors for Herbalife, however, rebuke these patriarchal norms by striving to elevate their gendered status and change their social positions through sales.

Q'EQCHI' WOMEN IN CHAMELCO'S MUNICIPAL MARKET

Recognized by Chamelqueños as an ancient institution, Chamelco's market stands just off the town's central park. It is a bustling, vibrant center of social and economic life in Chamelco, marked by a richness of sounds, sights, and smells. The market is alive with constant movement: clients, wholesale distributors, municipal officials, and friends and family members of market vendors flow through the space throughout the day. The market itself is a large, two-story concrete block building with shops around its exterior perimeter and an outward facing balcony on the second floor. The interior market is an open space made up of brightly painted wooden stalls. In 2005 the market housed approximately 130 stalls in its interior space, with another two dozen stalls located along its exterior perimeter. Most stores in the interior market sell daily consumption goods, including rice, dried beans, sugar; juices, dried soups, *kakaw* (cocoa beans), spices, and produce. The market also has nearly a dozen butcher shops. Other vendors sell Indigenous women's clothing, men's dress clothes, children's clothing, and household goods. Since vendors buy their products from the same sources, the prices of the goods they sell are the same. Clients choose where they buy their goods not according to prices but rather according to their relationships to specific vendors (Kistler 2010, 2014). Residents visit the market on a daily basis, where they purchase household items, catch up on local news, and visit with friends. The markets are one of the few places where women can go and socialize without their husbands' oversight.

All of the vendors in Chamelco's municipal market identify ethnically as Q'eqchi', although they have diverse intersectional identities based on age, socioeconomic class, marital status, educational level, and family histories of market participation, among other factors. They range in age from young adults to women in their eighties and nineties. Nearly 80 percent of the interior market vendors have family histories of market participation, tracing their work in the market matrilineally to female ancestors who taught them to market and who bequeathed them their market stalls. These women have a regular presence in fixed stalls in the market or in the shops on the market's exterior perimeter, where they sell daily subsistence goods or work in butcher shops. Although the majority of the women have only limited formal education, some of the younger generation of market women graduated from middle or high school. Those who sell daily subsistence goods in the market are, for the most part, of lower socioeconomic standing than those who sell meat, as butcher women make much more through market sales than those that sell other foodstuffs. The history of each vendor in the market and their experience of rebuking local gendered norms to elevate their own status varies is based on their own intersectional identities. The women who sell in the interior market have vastly different statuses and experiences than those who sell as ambulant vendors in Chamelco's ever-growing open-air market in the street outside of Chamelco's marketplace. These ambulant vendors offer produce, textiles, and other assorted goods on a semiregular basis. In this chapter, my discussion of Chamelco's marketers is limited to those who sell in the interior marketplace and does not include the ambulant street vendors.

MOTIVATIONS FOR MARKET WORK

In February 2004, the first time I visited Chamelco's municipal market, I was greeted immediately by a young girl, Josefina, who was wearing Indigenous dress and a brightly patterned apron. She was selling coffee, tea, and dried goods in her mother's stall by one of the market's main entrances. Josefina had come to the market directly from school, as she did each day, to relieve her mother from sales work during the afternoon hours. Like Josefina, many other young women also worked in the market each afternoon, learning the art of marketing, just as their mothers, grandmothers, sisters, and aunts had done before them. While some adult marketers attended school as young children, many did not, instead training from a very young age to serve their families' market businesses.

This family connection is what motivates many of Chamelco's marketers to continue their market work. The statement of one vendor, Blanca, echoed sentiments I heard many others during my fieldwork in Chamelco's market. Blanca said that she works in the market because "that is what they [my ancestors] taught me to do. . . . This is what they taught me, and so I like it more." She referred to the market stall that she inherited from her mother as "a gift" (Blanca, interview by author, 2005).

During lapses in market sales each afternoon, I observed that many women told tales of their female ancestors to clients and other vendors. As we sat on burlap sacks of flour, beans, or other grains in their wood-framed stalls during the slow afternoon hours in Chamelco's market, many women told me stories of the women from whom they inherited their market stalls. In between sales, they shared tales of confrontations with municipal authorities, marveled at their ancestors' endurance as in walking the winding mountain roads from Chamelco to Cobán daily to buy and sell their goods, and recalled assisting their mothers and grandmothers with sales in what was then an open-air market. They fondly remembered working all night over open fires in their families' small wooden kitchens to make tamales for their mothers to sell. Marketing was not a choice, they said, but rather a necessary and important way to remember and honor these ancestors and ensure that they continue to be remembered as a part of the town's historical legacy.

Women cited financial need and the desire to build social networks as additional reasons for their work. More than half of the women I interviewed cited financial necessity as a motivating factor for their market work. Many of their husbands did not have steady employment, had abandoned them, or, as some women told me, refused to contribute money toward household expenses or children's education. Given that most marketers had little formal education, marketing was one of the only ways that they could earn the money needed to support their families. A clothing vendor stated, "What else can I do? I don't have work, I don't have an education . . . I have to do this" (Emilia, interview by author, 2005), while another reflected, "Since we don't know how to read or write, that is why we must defend ourselves with this, with marketing" (Gloria, interview by author, 2005).

Despite the many claims of financial necessity as a primary factor underpinning women's work, few women made a reliable profit in the market (Kistler 2010, 2014). Most women remained unaware of how much they made, stating that it was difficult to keep track of what they earned given the outflow of cash they experience on an average market day. One vendor explained:

> I don't know any profit. I only know what I invest. So, on a day like today, where I sold 100 *quetzales*, I give Q10 to my son who goes to study in [a high school], I give 2 *quetzales* to [my other son]. Sometimes, we buy tortillas, we take money out of that for dinner, and the rest I save. The next day, it is the same thing. Then, what I save during the week . . . I use it to buy more products. I do the same thing the next week and all year long (Gloria, interview by author, 2005).

While women make enough to support their families' needs most of the time, they reinvest what they can into their businesses and see little profit. Women continue to market, however, because they have few economic alternatives and because money is perhaps only one of the significant factors that motivate their work.

Marketing allows these women to be independent and expand their social networks. They manage their own businesses, control their own resources, and make their own schedules. Many women remarked that serving as their own bosses in the market gave them "freedom" and "independence" that they would not otherwise have. Simply put, as one vendor told me, "It is a satisfaction to have a small business" (Sara, interview by author, 2005).

Market women develop close friendships with other vendors and clients alike. The husband of one vendor told me that market women "maintain strong interpersonal relations with other women. Their clients get to know them, and if they are very amicable people, then, of course, they are sought after and appreciated in the market. And this gives them a social position, right?" (Rafael, interview by author, 2005). Vendors build these relationships by talking with clients and providing them access to the goods that they need to maintain their own families. In discussing her friendships with clients, one vendor said, "We make an effort to find products, to be hardworking, [to have] a variety of products so that customers come to us. We worry about others, you see" (Melinda, interview by author, 2005). Another vendor reiterated that through sales, "You put yourself out there to be known by other people" (Teresa, interview by author, 2005). Vendors' social networks grow as clients recognize them as hardworking and compassionate individuals who work for the good of their community. In 2005, one of Chamelco's municipal officials explained, "In our town, we all know each other, and give importance to them [market women]. If the market didn't exist, where would we buy our products, where would we spend our days? Visiting the women in the market, we make friendships with them, and that is why they have an important place in our society" (José, interview by the author, 2005).

Chamelco's Q'eqchi' market women value large social networks because it means they have more people on whom they can count in times of need and with whom they share personal successes and failures, joys, and sorrows. For example, Valeria is one of Chamelco's most prominent and well-connected marketers, as she runs a butcher shop in the interior market, a store on the market's outer perimeter, and delivers meat to local restaurants. When her son David died suddenly in 2014, she received an outpouring of support from friends and associates from throughout the region. Reportedly, thousands of people attended his wake and funeral and visited Valeria regularly to express their condolences and offer support. The social networks she developed in the market supported her during one of the most difficult times in her life.

MARKETING AND GENDERED STATUS

In addition to developing relationships through marketing, market vendors "enter into the social circle of other vendors," and clients, as one vendor told me. By entering new social circles in this way, they garner status by connecting to valued social domains, like godparenthood, participation in ritual organizations, and community leadership roles, positions for which not everyone is considered. One marketer explained, "[Participation] is prestigious, it is an honor, really. Because not everyone is sought out to participate. It's a recognition of how you treat others" (Sara, interview by author, 2005). Women receive invitations to attend social events hosted by clients and other vendors, including family celebrations like baptisms, weddings, funerals, and birthday parties. That they are invited guests at these events highlights the status that they earn through market interactions. In this sense, as Piot (1999) suggests happens through exchange, Chamelco's marketers do not just "form" relationships through marketing: they become these relationships.

By perpetuating the occupation of their ancestors, showing moral character in interactions with clients, and building extensive social networks, Chamelco's vendors serve as embodiments of Q'eqchi' value. This recognition elevates their gendered status, moving them from lower status social positions to higher status ones, defined by their work to honor ancestral tradition and Q'eqchi' value in the market. They challenge local gendered norms to stand among their community's most powerful and recognized residents.

FROM THE MARKET TO HERBALIFE

Beginning in 2014, some Q'eqchi' women, many of whom are family members of (or who were recruited by) Chamelco's marketers, have become involved in a new form of marketing: selling Herbalife. Herbalife is an MLM that offers nutritional and weight loss supplements, including shakes, vitamins, and teas. Distributors advertise that products help consumers overcome digestive disorders, combat obesity, regulate blood sugar, and improve their overall health. In addition to selling products through direct sales, some distributors run "nutrition clubs," offering prepared protein shakes to customers with daily, weekly, or monthly memberships. Though Herbalife is controversial due to its questionable business practices, it promises distributors the ability to earn money through sales and by recruiting new distributors.

As Herbalife gained notoriety in the United States for its pyramid-like compensation structure and its potential health risks (Anderson 2018; Braun 2016; FTC 2016; Hiltzik 2016; De Noon 2002; Geller 2008; Partnoy 2014), it expanded its hold in Latin America. By 2014, Herbalife had a prominent presence in Alta Verapaz, Guatemala, an extension of the capitalist forces that have shaped the region for centuries. Although a few community members sold Herbalife before two high-level distributors developed an expansion plan for the region, the number of distributors has grown significantly since 2014. Herbalife has a regional headquarters and nutrition clubs in Chamelco and the departmental capital of Cobán.

Q'eqchi' women's involvement with Herbalife began with controversial former governor of Alta Verapaz, Dominga Tecún Canil. Tecún began taking Herbalife after she was in a car accident in the spring of 2014 and immediately signed on as a distributor. While she died a few short months later due to a preexisting illness, she used her influence as a prominent figure within the Q'eqchi' community to recruit others, including her family members and close friends, to sell Herbalife.

MOTIVATIONS FOR SELLING HERBALIFE

Herlinda is a cheerful young mother of two sons and is married to the son of a well-known Q'eqchi' activist. Born in a rural area of San Pedro Carchá, Herlinda completed only a middle school education. After her marriage and the birth of her children, she tended to her mother-in-law's stall in Chamelco's subsistence market before launching her own business as an Herbalife distributor. In the time that Herlinda worked in Chamelco's market, she was quiet, reserved, and I rarely saw her smile. When I met with her in Herbalife nutrition club in Cobán in the summers of 2017 and 2018, however, she seemed like a different person. She was upbeat, talkative, engaging, and outgoing. She talked and joked with the clients that came to her small, brightly decorated storefront near one of Cobán's established marketplaces each morning for tea and protein shakes. She shared that she began to consume Herbalife for its health benefits—she was overweight after the birth of her children and felt generally unhealthy. She quickly became involved with Herbalife for the lifestyle it offered her, as she began to run in local races, attend training sessions, and make connections and friendships with other vendors and clients. After she took over her nutrition club, she began to generate her own money and became her own boss, gaining independence and the chance to help others. Herbalife gave her "opportunities for success" that she would not otherwise have, as a young Indigenous woman who faced discrimination in nearly all other aspects of life.

Like Herlinda, a growing number of Q'eqchi' women sell Herbalife, either through direct sales or in nutrition clubs. Consuming Herbalife helped them to deal with various health problems, including digestive issues and obesity, and they became "enamored" with the products and became distributors because of the financial possibilities Herbalife offers. The reasons they cite for their continued work as distributors generally fall into three categories: helping others, fostering personal development, and achieving independence.

Herlinda told me that selling Herbalife offered a way to help others improve their health. Another stated that she viewed it as her "moral and ethical duty" to help others by introducing them to Herbalife's products. Having discovered how to improve her own health and financial situation, she said it was her responsibility to help others. This duty to "help others" is a core value for Q'eqchi', and one that also underlies women's participation in subsistence marketing, as the husband of one market woman told me. He identified the market as a place where "people sell, buy things, not to take advantage of one another, but rather according to the concept of mutual help" (Rafael, interview by author, 2005). As women do through subsistence marketing, Herbalife distributors use Herbalife to help others not only to become healthier but also because they get personal satisfaction and enjoy the work. One distributor told me that because Herbalife distributors work together as a team for everyone's mutual benefit, the idea of working together, of helping others, both physically, emotionally, and financially, is what motivates their work.

Personal development emerged as another reason women cited for their work as Herbalife distributors. Each month, Herbalife offers training seminars, lectures, film viewings, and book clubs for distributors in Cobán. Every few months, Herbalife sponsors national events in Guatemala City and hosts annual "extravaganzas" abroad. During these events, invited speakers give testimonials, highlight the health benefits of Herbalife projects, and talk about marketing techniques. For some distributors, these events, and the possibility of continued learning, motivates their work. For example, during our conversation in her nutrition club, Herlinda shared that while she never had the chance to go to college, she is studying at what she called the "university of success" by attending Herbalife training sessions. At these events, she makes friends, socializes, and continues her personal enrichment. Another woman shared that involvement with Herbalife helped her through a difficult personal situation after the death of a loved one that left her feeling frustrated and depressed. "I had to put aside my feelings to talk to clients, serve them in my club, and attend training sessions" (Maria, personal communication, 2018). The friendship and support she found in these events helped her to overcome her personal difficulties. Since there are few opportunities for Indigenous women to socialize outside of the home or continue their educations, these personal enrichment opportunities provide an incentive for continued involvement with sales.

By selling Herbalife, Q'eqchi' women (who were not already market women) achieved independence that they did not experience before becoming distributors. Olga, an Indigenous distributor from one of Chamelco's urban neighborhoods, reflected on the fact that Herbalife offered her financial freedom not attainable through other means. Olga had only a sixth-grade education, meaning that her work opportunities were limited. Prior to Herbalife, she told me as we sat in a nutrition club across the street from Chamelco's Catholic church in July 2018, she ran a small food store from her home. She saw limited profit from this venture, as she sold very little and had to support her children's educational expenses. Herbalife, however, provided her with an opportunity to generate new income, allowing her the freedom to start a nutrition club in the place where her store had been. In my conversations with Herlinda, she, like Olga, reflected on her nutrition club in Cobán and the financial independence it offered her. She proudly stated that since becoming a distributor, she has paid for her children's medical and educational expenses without having to ask for her husband's assistance.

Involvement with Herbalife also offers independence to many Indigenous women distributors. Olga shared that she regularly travels to the town's rural areas to market her product and speak with residents about the benefits of Herbalife. Herlinda stated that she found freedom in being her own boss and setting her own working hours. She finds her work empowering and said she never would have had such confidence before becoming a distributor. Herbalife affords women distributors the ability to overcome established gendered social norms, which limit women's freedom to work or socialize outside the home.

Distributors highlighted the inclusive work environment of Herbalife as something that offered them acceptance as well. All of the Indigenous women distributors with whom I spoke remarked that they felt welcomed by Herbalife clients, distributors, and at events, as Herbalife's philosophy is that it is for all people, regardless of race, gender, or education. One distributor shared, "With Herbalife, they don't say, 'You can't come here with your *uuq* (Indigenous skirt)'" (Maria, interview by author, 2018). Instead, Herbalife offers a community that is accepting of Indigenous vendors and their identities. Indigenous women do not often find this acceptance in other workplaces.

One afternoon in 2018, I talked with an older Herbalife distributor, Imelda, who was visiting Chamelco's municipal marketplace in a busy aisle of Chamelco's market. Imelda shared that throughout her life she had dedicated herself to Maya resurgence efforts, working as a land activist, traditional healer with local plants and natural medicine, and serving as a Maya spiritual guide for ritual ceremonies. Since getting involved with Herbalife, Imelda offers clients Herbalife in addition to "natural medicine" when performing healing services. She viewed Herbalife as a compliment to her fight to preserve Q'eqchi' identity and felt that Herbalife supported this view. While Imelda encountered conflicts with Ladinos in other aspects of her life, there had been no tension within Herbalife. She could express her Indigenous identity in Herbalife sales and felt accepted by the community of distributors and clients, without fear of discrimination. The inclusive community Herbalife offers motivates Imelda's (and many other women's) work as Herbalife distributors.

HERBALIFE AND Q'EQCHI' VALUE

I asked Indigenous distributors how Herbalife's capitalist model of sales relates to their Indigenous values. One afternoon, I talked with Maria, an Herbalife distributor and the daughter of a prominent Maya activist, over lunch at her home in Cobán. Medals from races in which Maria and her husband competed hung on the wall and from every piece of furniture in her home. Herbalife protein shake containers were scattered on the kitchen counters and throughout the home. Maria stated that Herbalife reinforced her connection to her Indigenous identity, though she imagined that it could perhaps weaken one's connection with one's sense of her own Indigenousness if she were "undergoing an identity crisis" already. Maria said that if she had been having an identity crisis, she could wind up losing herself due to Herbalife's emphasis on exercise, beauty, and weight loss. Nevertheless, in 2018, Herbalife's regional leader, Suchit de Thiessen, told me that Herbalife does not seek to change the communities it enters but rather "become a part" of them. She explained that Ladino distributors in the region study the Q'eqchi' language, wear Q'eqchi' dress, and eat traditional foods. The son of a prominent Maya activist in Chamelco, who was Chamelco's first Herbalife distributor, affirmed these claims, stating, "Herbalife does not invade one's culture, it becomes a part of it" (Juan, interview author, 2018)

Q'eqchi' women also emphasized their desire to connect clients with ancestral practice and value through Herbalife. Because Herbalife promotes healthy nutrition and respects Indigenous identities, some distributors saw it as a way to reconnect with ancestral dietary practices, especially in the face of globalization. Maria told me that "Herbalife helps people to recognize that organic foods are ideal." She stated that Herbalife helps bring people back to their roots and eat like their ancestors once did. The prevalence of fast foods in the region has caused a health and identity crisis for Q'eqchi', who have strayed from traditional ways of eating in favor of the convenience of these goods. Herbalife training sessions teach that one should make healthy meal choices in addition to consuming Herbalife's products. In this respect, in Maria's view, Herbalife helps people find their way back to ancestral dietary customs. Prior to getting involved with Herbalife, Maria consumed a lot of packaged goods, fast food, and pizza. However, Herbalife inspired her to go to the local market to buy squash, beans, corn, and other plants: foods that served as the staples of the ancestral Q'eqchi' diet. By promoting the consumption of these "foods that come from the earth," distributors reconnect consumers with Indigenous dietary practices.

Many distributors report that they use the Q'eqchi' language in sales meetings and conversations with other Herbalife vendors and prospective clients. Though some words, notably "micronutrients" and "shakes," have no exact equivalent in Q'eqchi', some women reported that they had heard others create neologisms to represent these terms, using the existing tools of the Q'eqchi' language. When I asked them to share these terms, however, they laughed, stating that they could not remember them and that people often made them up on the spot when promoting these products in the Q'eqchi' language. Nevertheless, by using the Q'eqchi' language in this way, they continued to honor their ancestors and help maintain the Q'eqchi' language.

HERBALIFE AND GENDERED STATUS

Just as vendors do in subsistence markets, Herbalife distributors garner recognition through involvement with Herbalife. The sustained interactions they have with Herbalife leaders, distributors, and clients lead them to receive invitations to social events, including Herbalife gatherings, parties, and weddings. Herbalife distributors play leadership roles in their communities, running fitness classes and nonprofit organizations, organizing ritual and athletic celebrations, and serving as godparents to local children.

As individuals working for the good of their community, Herbalife distributors construct themselves as hardworking and compassionate individuals concerned with others' well-being, showing the personal characteristics that ground Q'eqchi' value They portray themselves as knowledgeable and intelligent by demonstrating knowledge of nutrition in conversations with clients. The recognition they achieve for working to improve the health of their communities—and, in the eyes of some, connect with ancestral practice—elevates them to prominent social positions, just as it does for Chamelco's market women, who reveal similar characteristics in their interactions in the market.

CONCLUSION

Market women and Herbalife distributors earn recognition and elevate their status by embodying Q'eqchi' value. In Q'eqchi' society, value centers on honoring ancestral practice and demonstrating intelligence, compassion, and a hardworking nature so that one will be invited by others for participation in prestigious social domains in life and remembered in death. Chamelco's market women work not solely for financial gain but because marketing offers them the chance to highlight these values, build social networks, and honor their ancestors. Herbalife presents new opportunities for Indigenous women to change their social positions through sales. While many women got involved with Herbalife for its alleged health benefits, they stay involved because of the personal development opportunities it offers and the independence they find through their work. It also provides another way for them to reconnect their community with ancestral foods and dietary customs. They, too, embody value through the characteristics they display in interactions with clients and fellow distributors. In these ways, Chamelco's market women and Q'eqchi' Herbalife distributors construct themselves as people to be recognized and remembered.

REVIEW QUESTIONS

1. How is life different for Q'eqchi' women involved in market exchange and the sale of Herbalife products than it is for other Q'eqchi' women? Why is it different?

2. In what ways are the experiences of Indigenous market women and those of Indigenous women distributors of Herbalife the same? In what ways are they different?

3. In what ways do women embody Q'eqchi' value in their work in the local subsistence marketplace and in selling Herbalife? In what ways do they incorporate new and changing definitions of value?

4. How do women transform their gendered status through their involvement in these two distinct forms of capitalist exchange?

5. Is it surprising that women use global capitalism to reinforce long-standing Indigenous values? Why or why not?

KEY TERMS

direct sales: a marketing strategy in which sales are made in face-to-face interactions with vendors away from a store or formal retail location

gender complementarity: the ideal that men and women have equal status defined by their participation in separate but equally valued social realms (e.g., men earn status by farming; women earn status by completing housework). Gender complementarity is rarely achieved but is often recognized as a social ideal.

Herbalife: a company that makes and sells nutritional supplements and whose sales model is a multilevel marketing scheme focused on direct sales.

multilevel marketing: a hierarchical business model in which salespeople earn not only what they sell but also a percentage of the sales made by those at levels lower than their own.

Q'eqchi': one of twenty-two Indigenous groups in Guatemala that trace descent from the ancient Maya civilization and who speak a Mayan language.

ACKNOWLEDGMENTS

My research on Q'eqchi' market women was generously funded by a National Science Foundation Doctoral Dissertation Research Improvement Grant #0613168 and a Florida State University Dissertation Research Grant. My articles "The House in the Market: How Q'eqchi' Market Women Convert Money and Commodities to Persons and Personhood" (*Global South* 2010) and "All in the *Junkab'al*: The House in Q'eqchi' Society (*The Latin Americanist* 2013) as well as my book *Maya Market Women* (2014) offer more extensive analyses of the material on market women I present here. I also thank Rollins College for the Critchfield grant that funded my research on Herbalife in Guatemala. Finally, I am forever indebted to my friends and family in Guatemala who enabled this research and have supported me throughout my fieldwork journey.

RESOURCES FOR FURTHER EXPLORATION

- Kistler, S. Ashley. 2010. "The House in the Market: How Q'eqchi' Market Women Convert Money and Commodities to Persons and Personhood." *Global South* 4, no. 1: 48–70.

- Kistler, S. Ashley. 2014. *Maya Market Women: Power and Tradition in San Juan Chamelco, Guatemala*. Urbana: University of Illinois Press.

- Little, Walter E. 2004. *Mayas in the Marketplace: Tourism, Globalization, and Cultural Identity*. Austin: University of Texas Press.

- Lovell, W. George. 2010. *A Beauty that Hurts: Life and Death in Guatemala*. Austin: University of Texas Press.

BIBLIOGRAPHY

Adams, Abigail E. 1999. *Word, Work, and Worship: Engendering Evangelical Culture Between Highland Guatemala and the United States*. PhD diss., University of Virginia.

Adams, Abigail E., and James E. Brady. 2005. "Ethnographic Notes on Maya Q'eqchi' Cave Rites: Implications for Archaeological Interpretation." In *In the MAW of the Earth Monster*, edited by James E. Brady and Keith M. Prufer, 301–327. Austin: University of Texas Press.

Amadiume, Ifi. 2000. *Daughters of the Goddess, Daughters of Imperialism: African Women Struggle for Culture, Power, and Democracy*. London: Zed.

Anderson, Curt. 2008. "Herbalife Distributors Claim in \$1B Suit Events Were a Sham." *US News and World Report* (website), August 21. https://www.usnews.com/news/business/articles/2018-08-21/herbalife-distributors-claim-in-1b-suit-events-were-a-sham. Accessed July 20, 2019.

Babb, Florence E. 1985. "Middlemen and "Marginal" Women: Marketing and Dependency in Peru's Informal Sector." In *Markets and Marketing, Monographs in Economic Anthropology, No. 4*, edited by Stuart Plattner, 287–308. New York: University Press of America.

———. 1986 "Producers and Reproducers: Andean Marketwomen in the Economy. *In* Women and Change in Latin America," edited by June Nash and Helen Safa, 53–64. South Hadley: Bergin and Garvey.

———. 1989. *Between Field and Cooking Pot: The Political Economy of Market Women in Peru*. Austin: University of Texas Press.

———. 2001. "Market/Places as Gendered Space: Market/Women's Studies over Two Decades." In *Women Traders in Cross-Cultural Perspective: Mediating Identities, Marketing Wares*, edited by Linda J. Seligmann, 229–240. Stanford, CA: Stanford University Press.

Biggart, Nicole Woolsey. 1989. *Charismatic Capitalism: Direct Selling Organizations in America*. Chicago: University of Chicago Press.

Braun, Ted. 2016. *Betting on Zero*. Zipper Brother Films.

Buechler, Judith Maria 1978. "The Dynamics of the Market in La Paz, Bolivia." *Urban Anthropology* 7, no. 4: 343–359.

———. 1985. "Women in Petty Commerce Production in La Paz, Bolivia. In *Women and Change in Latin America*, edited by June Nash and Helen Safa, 165–188. Boston: Bergin and Garvey.

———. 1997. "The Visible and Vocal Politics of Female Traders and Small-Scale Producers in La Paz, Bolivia." In *Women and Economic Change: Andean Perspectives*, edited by Ann Miles and Hans Buechler, 75–88. Arlington, VA: American Anthropological Association.

Cahn, Peter S. 2006. "Building Down and Dreaming Up: Finding Faith in a Mexican Multilevel Marketer." *American Ethnologist* 33, no. 1: 126–142.

———. 2008. "Consuming Class: Multilevel Marketers in Neoliberal Mexico." *Cultural Anthropology* 23, no. 3: 429–452.

Carmack, Robert. 1988. *Harvest of Violence: The Maya Indians and the Guatemalan Crisis*. Norman: University of Oklahoma Press.

Chaney, Elsa M., and Marianne Schmink. 1976. "Women and Modernization: Access to Tools." In *Sex and Class in Latin America: Women's Perspectives on Politics, Economics, and the Family in the Third World*, edited by June Nash and Helen Safa, 160–182. New York: Praeger.

Chinchilla, Norma S. 1977. "Industrialization, Monopoly Capitalism, and Women's Work in Guatemala." *Signs: Journal of Women in Culture and Society* 3, no. 1: 38–56.

Chiñas, Beverly Newbold. 1973. *The Isthmus Zapotecs: Women's Roles in Cultural Context*. New York: Holt, Rinehart, and Winston.

———. 2002. *The Isthmus Zapotecs: A Matrifocal Culture of Mexico*. 2nd ed. Belmont, CA: Wadsworth/Thompson Learning.

Clark, Gracia. 1994. *Onions are My Husband: Survival and Accumulation by West African Market Women*. Chicago: University of Chicago Press.

Clarke, Alison J. 1999. *Tupperware: The Promise of Plastic in 1950s America*. Washington, DC: Smithsonian Institution Press.

DeNoon, Daniel J. 2002. "Herbalife Diet Linked to Brain Ailment: Poor Nutrition to Blame in Single Italian Case." *Web MD* (website), June 10. https://www.webmd.com/diet/news/20020610/herbalife-diet-linked-to-brain-ailment#1. Accessed July 20, 2019.

Dolan, Catherine, and Linda Scott. 2009. "Lipstick Evangelism: Avon Trading Circles and Gender Empowerment in South Africa." *Gender and Development* 17, no. 2: 203–218.

Díaz Romeu, Guillermo. 1996. "Del Régimen de Carlos Herrera a la Elección de Jorge Ubico." In *Historia General de Guatemala, Tomo V: Época Contemporánea 1898–1944*, edited by Jorge Lujan Muñoz and J. Daniel Contreras. Guatemala City: Asociación Amigos del Pais.

Elmendorf, Mary. 1976. *Nine Mayan Women: A Village Faces Change*. New York: Schenkman.

Estrada Monroy, Augustin. 1990. *Vida Esotérica Maya K'ekchi*. Guatemala City: Ministerio de Cultura y Deportes.

Fadzillah, Ida. 2005. "The Amway Connection: How Transnational Ideas of Beauty and Money Affect Northern Thai Girls' Perceptions of Their Future Options." In *Youthscapes: The Popular, the National, the Global*, edited by Sunaina Maira and Elisabeth Soep, 85–102. Philadelphia: University of Pennsylvania Press.

Federal Trade Commission. 2016. "Herbalife Will Restructure Its Multi-Level Marketing Operations and Pay $200 Million For Consumer Redress to Settle FTC Charges." https://www.ftc.gov/news-events/press-releases/2016/07/herbalife-will-restructure-its-multi-level-marketing-operations.

Fischer, Edward F. 2002. *Cultural Logics and Global Economies: Maya Identity in Thought and Practice*. Austin: University of Texas Press.

Fischer, Edward F., and Peter Benson. 2006. *Broccoli and Desire: Global Connections and Power Struggles in Postwar Guatemala*. Stanford, CA: Stanford University Press.

Geller, Martinne. 2008. "Group Says Herbalife Products Have Too Much Lead." *Reuters* (website), May 19. https://www.reuters.com/article/us-this-hold-toni-herbalife/group-says-herbalife-products-have-too-much-lead-idUSN19556 45920080520. Accessed July 20, 2019.

Ghidinelli, Azzo. 1975. La Familia entre los Caribes, Negros, Ladinos, y Kekchies de Livingston. *Guatemala Indígena* 11, no. 3–4.

Goldín, Liliana. 2009. *Global Maya: Work and Ideology in Rural Guatemala.* Tucson: University of Arizona Press.

Graeber, David. 2001. *Toward an Anthropological Theory of Value: The False Coin of Our Own Dreams.* New York: Palgrave.

Gregory, Christopher. 1997. *Savage Money: The Anthropology and Politics of Commodity Exchange.* Amsterdam: Harwood Academic.

Gu, Chien-Ju. 2004. "Disciplined Bodies in Direct Selling: Amway and Alternative Economic Culture in Taiwan." In *The Minor Arts of Daily Life: Popular Culture in Taiwan*, edited by David K. Jordan, Andrew D. Morris, and Marc L. Moskowitz, 150–174. Honolulu: University of Hawai'i Press.

Hall-Clifford, Rachel. 2015. "Capitalizing on Care: Marketplace Quasi-Pharmaceuticals in Guatemala's Health-Seeking Landscape." In *Privatization and the New Medical Pluralism*, edited by Anita Chary and Peter Rohloff, 71–87. Lanham. MD: Lexington.

Hatse, Inge, and Patrick De Ceuster. 2001. *Cosmovisión y Espiritualidad en la Agricultura Q'eqchi'.* Cobán: Ak' Kutan.

Hedwig, Amelia Waters. 2012. "Globalizing Beauty on the Gobi Desert." *Anthropology Now* 4, no. 3: 67–74.

Hendrickson, Carol. 1995. *Weaving Identities: Construction of Dress and Self in a Highland Guatemala Town.* Austin: University of Texas Press.

Henn, Regina. 1996. "Los Alemanes." In *Historia General de Guatemala, Tomo V: Época Contemporánea* 1898–1944, edited by Jorge Lujan Muñoz and J. Daniel Contreras. Guatemala: Asociación de Amigos del País.

Hiltzik, Michael. 2016. "FTC Moves against Herbalife, but Leaves a Question: Why is This Company Still Allowed in Business?" *Los Angeles Times* (website), July 18. https://www.latimes.com/business/hiltzik/la-fi-hiltzik-herbalife-20160718-snap-story.html. Accessed July 24, 2019.

Instituto Nacional de Estadística. 2014. Caracterización departamental Alta Verapaz 2013. Guatemala: Instituto Nacional de Estadística.

King, Arden. 1974. *Cobán and the Verapaz: History and Cultural Process in Northern Guatemala.* New Orleans: Middle American Research Institute Publication.

Kistler, S. Ashley. 2010. "The House in the Market: How Q'eqchi' Market Women Convert Money and Commodities to Persons and Personhood." *Global South* 4, no. 1: 48–70.

———. 2014. *Maya Market Women: Power and Tradition in San Juan Chamelco, Guatemala.* Urbana: University of Illinois Press.

Konefal, Betsy. 2010. *For Every Indio Who Falls: A History of Maya Activism in Guatemala, 1960–1990.* Albuquerque: University of New Mexico Press.

Lan, Pei-Chia. 2001. "The Body as a Contested Terrain for Labor Control: Cosmetics Retailers in Department Stores and Direct Selling." In *The Critical Study of Work: Labor, Technology, and Global* Production, edited by R. Baldoz, C. Koeber, and P. Kraft, 81–105. Philadelphia: Temple University Press.

Little, Walter E. 2004. *Mayas in the Marketplace: Tourism, Globalization, and Cultural Identity.* Austin: University of Texas Press.

Little, Walter E., and Timothy J. Smith. 2009. *Mayas in Postwar Guatemala*. Tuscaloosa: University of Alabama Press.

Lovell, W. George. 2010. *A Beauty That Hurts: Life and Death in Guatemala*. Austin: University of Texas Press.

Martí, Judith E. 2001. "Nineteenth-Century Views of Women's Participation in Mexico's Markets." In *Women Traders in Cross-Cultural Perspective: Mediating Identities, Marketing Wares*, edited by Linda Seligmann, 27–46. Stanford, CA: Stanford University Press.

Mintz, Sidney W. 1971. "Men, Women, and Trade." *Comparative Studies in Society and History* 13, no. 3: 247–269.

Moutsatsos, Chrissy. 2001. "Transnational Beauty Culture and Local Bodies: An Ethnographic Account of Consumption and Identity in Urban Greece." PhD diss., University of California, Irvine.

Nash, June. 1993. "Maya Household Production in the World Market: The Potters of Amatenango del Valle, Chiapas, Mexico." In *Crafts in the World Market: The Impact of Global Exchange on Middle American Artisans*, edited by June Nash, 127–154. Albany: State University of New York Press.

———. 1994. "Global Integration and Subsistence Insecurity." *American Anthropologist* 96, no. 1: 7–30.

Oliveira, Gabrielle. 2017. "Between Mexico and New York City: Mexican Maternal Migration's Influences on Separated Siblings' Social and Educational Lives." *Anthropology and Education Quarterly* 48, no. 2: 159–175.

Partnoy, Frank. 2014. "Is Herbalife a Pyramid Scheme?" *Atlantic* (website). https://www.theatlantic.com/magazine/archive/2014/06/wall-streets-6-billion-mystery/361624/. Accessed July 20, 2019.

Peterson, Robert A., and Gerald Albaum. 2007. "On the Ethicality of Internal Consumption in Multilevel Marketing." *Journal of Personal Selling and Sales Management* 27, no. 4: 317–323.

Peterson, Robert A., and Thomas R. Wotruba. 1996. "What Is Direct Selling?—Definition, Perspectives, and Research Agenda." *Journal of Personal Selling and Sales Management* 16, no. 4: 1–16.

Piot, Charles. 1991. "Of Persons and Things: Some Reflections on African Spheres of Exchange." *Man* 26, no. 3: 405–424.

———. 1999. *Remotely Global: Village Modernity in West Africa*. Chicago: University of Chicago Press.

Preston-Werner, Theresa. 2007. "Valuing the 'Professional' in an International Direct-Selling Organization: The Commodification of Class Identity in Southern Costa Rica." *Anthropology of Work Review* 28, no. 2: 22–27.

Sahlins, Marshall. 1988. "Cosmologies of Capitalism: The Trans-Pacific Sector of the "World System." *Proceedings of the British Academy* 74:1–51.

Seligmann, Linda J. 1989. "To Be in Between: The Cholas as Market Women." *Comparative Studies in Society and History* 31:694–721.

———. 1993. "Between Worlds of Exchange: Ethnicity among Peruvian Market Women." *Cultural Anthropology* 8, no. 2: 187–213.

———. 2001. "Introduction: Mediating Identities and Marketing Wares." In *Women Traders in Cross-Cultural Perspective: Mediating Identities, Marketing Wares*, edited by Linda J. Seligmann, 1–26. Stanford, CA: Stanford University Press.

———. 2004. *Peruvian Street Lives: Culture, Power and Economy among Market Women of Cuzco*. Urbana: University of Illinois Press.

Sikkink, Lynn. 2001. "Traditional Medicines in the Marketplace: Identity and Ethnicity Among Female Vendors." In *Women Traders in Cross-Cultural Perspective: Mediating Identities, Marketing Wares*, edited by Linda J. Seligmann, 209–225. Stanford, CA: Stanford University Press.

Sparks, John R. and Joseph A. Schenk. 2001. "Explaining the Effects of Transformational Leadership: An Investigation of the Effects of Higher Order Motives in Multilevel Marketing Organizations." *Journal of Organizational Behavior* 22, no. 8: 849–869.

Stephen, Lynn. 1993. "Weaving in the Fast Lane: Class, Ethnicity, and Gender in Zapotec Craft Commercialization." In *Crafts in the World Market: The Impact of Global Exchange on Middle American Artisans*, edited by June Nash, 25–58. Albany: State University of New York Press.

Tax, Sol. 1953. *Penny Capitalism: A Guatemalan Indian Economy*. Chicago: University of Chicago Press.

Uzendoski, Michael A. 2005. *The Napo Runa of Amazonian Ecuador*. Urbana: University of Illinois Press.

Vander Nat, Peter J., and William W. Keep. 2002. Marketing Fraud: An Approach for Differentiating Multilevel Marketing from Pyramid Schemes. *Journal of Public Policy & Marketing* 21, no. 1: 139–151.

Way, J. T. 2012. *The Mayan in the Mall: Globalization, Development, and the Making of Modern Guatemala*. Durham, NC: Duke University Press.

Weiner, Annette B. 1976. *Women of Value: Men of Renown, New Perspectives in Trobriand Exchange*. Austin: University of Texas Press.

Weismantel, Mary. 2001. *Cholas and Pishtacos: Stories of Race and Sex in the Andes*. Chicago: University of Chicago Press.

Wilk, Richard R. 1991. *Household Ecology: Economic Change and Domestic Life among the Kekchi Maya in Belize*. Tucson: University of Arizona Press.

Part IV

The Caribbean

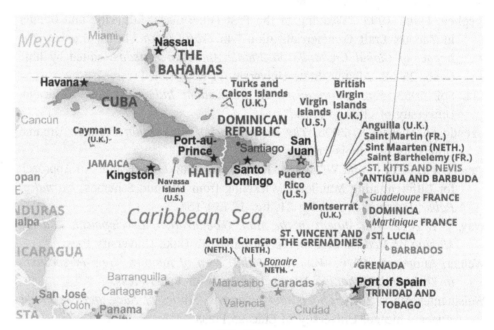

CIA Maps.

12

The Caribbean

Introducing the Region

Nadine T. Fernandez

The region takes its name from the Indigenous ethnic group Christopher Columbus encountered there: the Caribs. The native population of the Caribbean is estimated to have been around 750,000 before European contact. In 1492, Columbus landed with his three ships on the island of Hispaniola, now divided into the countries of Haiti and the Dominican Republic. The Indigenous peoples—such as the Arawak, Tainos, and Caribs—had no immunities to European disease, and through illness, warfare, and enslavement, their populations were virtually wiped out.

It is difficult to know the gender systems of the Indigenous populations of the Caribbean as they were decimated by the colonial conquest of the islands. However, we can glean some knowledge from small-scale hunter-gatherer societies in other parts of the world. In many foraging societies, gender relations tend to be more egalitarian and complementary. Whatever gender ideologies may have been prevalent among the Indigenous Tainos, Arawak, and Carib populations, little to no trace of these remained after conquest.

COLONIAL ERA

Colonialism thrived in the region. The many islands and coastal areas were accessible to European ships, which could easily sail into a cove or bay to make port and claim the island for their home country. After an island or area was claimed, the land was transformed through plantation agriculture. Cash crops—sugarcane, tobacco, cotton, or fruit—were grown for export profits. Most of these crops were not native to the Americas but were imported during colonial times and were planted, tended, and harvested by enslaved Africans.

The resulting trade arrangement is sometimes referred to as the "triangle" trade. Enslaved Africans were shipped to the Americas to produce sugar, cotton, and other raw materials, which were shipped to Europe to produce rum, clothing, and other manufactured goods, which were then shipped back to Africa to trade for more enslaved people who were brought to America to produce more sugar and so on. Europe grew rich not simply on its technological superiority but also on the hard labor of enslaved Africans. Over three centuries, twenty-one million enslaved people were transported from Africa to the Americas.

GATHERING CANE.

Figure 12.1. Gathering sugarcane. NYPL Digital Collections.

Table 12.1. Destination of enslaved Africans (1519–1867)

Destination	Percentage
British mainland North America	3.7%
British Leeward Islands	3.2%
British Windward Islands and Trinidad (British 1797–1867)	3.8%
Jamaica (Spanish 1519–1655, British 1655–1867)	11.2%
Barbados (British)	5.1%
The Guianas (British, Dutch, French)	4.2%
French Windward Islands	3.1%
Saint-Domingue (French)	8.2%
Spanish mainland North and South America	4.4%
Spanish Caribbean islands	8.2%
Dutch Caribbean islands	1.3%
Northeast Brazil (Portuguese)	9.3%
Bahia, Brazil (Portuguese)	10.7%
Southeast Brazil (Portuguese)	21.1%
Elsewhere in the Americas	1.1%
Africa	1.4%

Source: https://en.wikipedia.org/wiki/Slavery_in_the_United_States

Colonialism in the Caribbean was a deeply gendered institution, and its mark still influences contemporary gender relations in the region (Sanabria 2007). The colonial plantation system brought with it a gendered division of labor that assigned particular tasks as appropriate for men and others that were appropriate for women (Sanabria 2007). Europeans also imposed their ideas about women and sexuality at the time. Namely, women were deemed second-class citizens subject to the rule and control of their fathers and husbands. Rooted in a strongly Christian foundation, colonists and **conquistadors** were deeply motivated not only by a desire to conquer the "new world" but also to "civilize" and convert the native and enslaved populations to Christianity. This religious perspective denounced any sexual and gender practices that were non-normative (e.g., premarital sex) or not strictly heterosexual.

The colonial plantation system was particularly concerned with controlling women's sexuality as a way to maintain racial and class hierarchies (Martínez-Alier 1989). White women produced legitimate heirs to continue family lines of inheritance and privilege. Family honor depended on white women's chastity before marriage and their fidelity after marriage. The patriarchal (and legal) family was perceived as the essential foundation of a stable society (Sanabria 2007). Men, by contrast, were not subject to the same sexual control, as any children they fathered out of wedlock

conquistadors
leaders of the Spanish conquest of the Americas during the fifteenth to sixteenth centuries.

were "illegitimate" and thus would have no claim or connection to the family wealth.

Under slavery, the imperative to maintain "racial purity" was also a central part of controlling white women's sexuality. A system of racial subjugation depended on being able to distinguish racial groups. Here we see the intersection of race and class powerfully shaping women's lives. While racial mixing did occur in the colonial period, it was nearly always between white men and women of color (Indigenous or of African descent). Often these were violent rapes or relations of concubinage between white masters and enslaved women. Their mixed-race offspring born into slavery did not threaten the system: they inherited their mother's status (free or slave) and as "illegitimate" offspring could not lay claim to their white father's wealth—although some fathers did recognize and free their mixed-race children (Morrison 2015). On many islands, this type of racial mixing was condoned as it not only increased the population of laborers but also supposedly "improved the race" (adelantar la raza) since the African-descended people were viewed as racially inferior, and "whitening" the population was seen by governments as a way to modernize the nation (Fernandez 2010).

The Spanish were not the only Europeans to take advantage of colonial expansion in the Caribbean. As European powers vied for control of the islands, many of the islands changed hands several times before finally being secured as established colonies (see table 12.2). The cultural traits of each of the European colonizers were injected into the fabric of the islands they colonized; thus, the languages, religions, and

Figure 12.2. African-descended Puerto Ricans, 1898. Library of Congress, Prints and Photographs Division.

economic activities of the colonized islands reflected those of the European colonizers. The four main colonial powers in the Caribbean were the Spanish, English, Dutch, and French. Other countries that held possession of various islands at different times were Portugal, Sweden, and Denmark. The United States became a colonial power when they gained Cuba and Puerto Rico as a result of the Spanish-American War, which ended in 1898. The US Virgin Islands were purchased from Denmark in 1918. Sweden controlled the island of St. Barthélemy from 1784 to 1878 before trading it back to the French, who had been the original colonizer. Portugal originally colonized Barbados before abandoning it to the British (University of Minnesota 2016).

The abolition of slavery in the latter half of the 1800s and the cultural revolutions that occurred challenged the plantation system and brought about land reform. Plantations were transformed into either multiple private plots or large corporate farms. Once slavery became illegal, the colonial powers turned to other sources of cheap labor, including indentured laborers from their Asian colonies and immigrants from China. Cuba was the destination for over one hundred thousand Chinese workers (Havana can claim the first Chinatown in the Western Hemisphere). Laborers from the British colonies of India and other parts of South Asia also arrived in the Caribbean. Currently, about 40 percent of the population of Trinidad can claim South Asian heritage, and many follow the Hindu faith. Colonialism and plantation agriculture resulted in the ethnic, racial, linguistic, and religious diversity that is the hallmark of the Caribbean today. This legacy has meant that the Caribbean has been a global crossroads for centuries.

Table 12.2. Historical Caribbean Colonizers

Colonizer	European colonies
Spain	Cuba, Dominican Republic, Puerto Rico
British	Bahamas, Jamaica, Cayman Islands, Turks and Caicos Islands, Antigua, Dominica, St. Lucia, St. Vincent, Grenada, Barbados, Virgin Islands, Trinidad and Tobago, Montserrat, Anguilla, St. Kitts and Nevis
Dutch	Curaçao, Bonaire, Aruba, St. Eustatius, Saba and Sint Maarten (southern half)
French	Haiti, Guadeloupe, Martinique, St. Martin (northern half), St. Barthélemy
United States	Puerto Rico, Virgin Islands, Cuba

MODERN CONTEXT AND INDEPENDENCE

In the twentieth century, many of the Caribbean islands gained independence, but some remained Crown colonies of their European colonizers with varying degrees of autonomy. For many countries, the road from colony to independent republic has been arduous, at best. Haiti, for example, became the first Black independent republic in the Western Hemisphere after the enslaved population successfully revolted, overthrowing the French in 1804. However, rather than welcoming this new republic, the United States, the French, and other European powers resented Haitians for their uprising and feared it would spark more slave revolts throughout the Caribbean. (Remember, Thomas Jefferson, the US president at the time, was a slave owner.) The United States and other nations refused to recognize Haiti's sovereignty. They refused to trade with the newly independent nation. The French threatened to attack and forced the Haitians to pay $21 billion to compensate French slave owners for their "lost property." It took the Haitians over one hundred years to pay off the debt. So they entered the twentieth century billions of dollars in debt, with no money to fund schools, hospitals, roads, and other essentials of a prosperous nation (Wesch 2018). As a result, even today over 40 percent of the population is illiterate; 25 percent live on less than $2 per day; 30 percent are food insecure. Almost 8 percent of babies will not live to their fifth birthday (http://uis.unesco.org/en/country/ht).

In the aftermath of the Haitian revolution, the United States implemented the Monroe Doctrine in 1823, designed to deter the former European colonial powers from engaging in continued political activity in the Americas and simultaneously giving the United States the right to intervene in the region. In 1898 the United States fought Spain in the Spanish-American War, which was really Cuba's war of independence. At the conclusion of the war, Spain lost its colonies of Cuba, Puerto Rico, and others to the United States. Cuba, instead of gaining independence, was then occupied by the United States for several years. Puerto Rico continues to be under US jurisdiction and is neither an independent country nor a US state, though its residents are US citizens. Over the twentieth century, continued US intervention in the region has supported oppressive dictators such as Trujillo in the Dominican Republic, Papa Doc Duvalier in Haiti, and Batista in Cuba. All of these autocrats stifled democracy and kept most of their populations in poverty while enriching the private coffers of a small elite.

In many Caribbean nations after independence, white or lighter-skinned elites retained power. In many ways, gender roles and the emphasis on male privilege were strengthened as these new nations sought to legitimize themselves in the eyes of the world. Governing elites believed that strong patriarchal families were necessary to build a strong nation-state (Sanabria 2007). Large-scale export agriculture and a strong gendered division of labor continued on many islands after independence, helping to keep women and people of color in subordinate positions. Indeed, we still see the strong patriarchal tendencies as expressed through gender violence in the region. In some countries, such as Haiti, the minority mulatto/mixed-race segment of the population makes up the power base and holds political and economic advantage over the rest of the country; meanwhile, the working poor at the bottom of the pyramid comprise most of the population. Across the Caribbean, the lower economic classes often contain the highest percentage of people of African heritage or those with the darkest skin.

In Cuba, women played an active role in the 1959 revolution that overthrew the US-backed dictator Batista and brought the socialist regime of Fidel Castro to power. Socialist Cuba by no means completely eliminated gender or racial inequality, but social reforms in health care, education, and housing greatly reduced health, educational, and income inequality across the population. After the revolution, the state sought to actively incorporate women into the Communist Party, the workforce, and the state through organizations like the Federation of Cuban Women (FMC). Female revolutionary activity was not incompatible with motherhood, nevertheless the Cuban revolution remained "masculine" (Sanabria 2007).

In the twentieth century, independent Caribbean nations continued to be concerned with controlling women's sexuality, which was tied to morality, "modernity," and national progress. In Puerto Rico (a US protectorate), there were government campaigns to control poor women's fertility, which was seen as a social problem; these campaigns included widespread sterilizations from the 1930s to 1970s (Lopez 2008). The government also sought to promote "proper" childrearing and formal (legal) marriages (Sanabria 2007). Nonetheless, attempts by governments and elites to promote a strong patriarchal family were never fully successful (Safa 1995). According to Dore (1997), depending on the country, region, and class position, 25 percent to 50 percent of households in the nineteenth-century Caribbean were matrifocal: that is, headed by women (Dore 1997). Mothers and their children formed the basis of the family unit, and women relied on female relatives to help care for their families (Blank 2013). Thus the "proper" nuclear family for much of Caribbean history was mostly visible in the middle and upper classes. In some cases, this was partly due to the cost of a legal marriage, which in nineteenth-century Cuba, for example, kept some long-term consensual unions from formal matrimony (Morrison 2015).

Today, female-headed households continue to make up a significant portion of families in many Caribbean nations, especially among the poorer, more marginalized segments of the population. While these households often face significant economic hardships, women do have considerable control over resources and decision-making power. State power is rarely absolute, and dominant gender ideologies are never uniformly espoused by all segments of the population. Indeed, we see that stereotypes of "ideal men and women" and the "ideal family" seldom reflect actual people's gendered, raced, and classed lives.

Despite the strong role of women in the family, Caribbean societies remain predominantly patriarchal. Overall, women hold fewer positions of power and leadership in the highest levels of political, economic, and religious realms (Blank 2013). Women account for over 40 percent of the labor force in many Caribbean nations (Fetterolf 2017). Though often in low-wage jobs, women began replacing men as principal breadwinners in the 1980s (Safa 1995). Women also make up a large percentage of workers in the informal sectors (such as hairdressers, seamstresses, traders, etc.). Some scholars suggest that as a result of this shift, men in the region feel threatened as they can no longer uphold the role of as the financial provider and head of a household (Safa 2001). Some men may be responding to the erosion of their economic power through acts of domestic violence and high rates of substance abuse (Blank 2013).

The economy of the region is no longer based on monocrop export agriculture, which dominated most of the islands from colonial times through the 1970s. Today, the islands vary dramatically in levels of wealth (as measured by GDP per capita). The offshore banking and financial industry has made some countries such as the Cayman Islands, the Bahamas, Turks and Caicos, and the Virgin Islands quite wealthy, but many of the more populous countries (e.g., Cuba, Dominican Republic, Haiti, and Jamaica) are markedly poorer (Faure 2018). The economies of all countries in the region are still deeply shaped by global flows of people. Today two flows in particular play key roles in the islands' economic, social, and political development, namely: tourism and migration.

In most countries across the region, the global tourism industry is now the main economic engine. Technological developments and the rise of air travel birthed this massive international industry capitalizing on the physical beauty of the islands and the tropical weather. The economic benefits of tourism have been mixed for most of the islands. While the mainstay of most island economies, the large cruise ships and pleasure crafts can overtax the environment; and there have been occasions where there were actually more tourists than citizens on an island. An increase in tourist activity brings with it an increase in environmental pollution (University of Minnesota 2016).

Figure 12.3. Cruise ships docked at a Caribbean port. Sgbirch, CC BY 2.0.

Most people in the Caribbean still live below the poverty line, and the investment in tourism infrastructure, such as exclusive hotels and five-star resorts, takes away resources that could be allocated to schools, roads, medical clinics, and housing. However, without the income from tourism, there would be no money for infrastructure. Tourism attracts people who can afford to travel. Most of the jobs in the hotels, ports, and restaurants where wealthy tourists visit employ people from poorer communities at low wages. There is a stark disparity between the rich tourists and the poor workers. Local businesses in the Caribbean do gain income from tourists who spend their money there; however, the big money is in the cruise ship lines and the resort hotels, which are mainly owned by international corporations or the local wealthy elite (University of Minnesota 2016).

Tourism is a powerful force of contemporary globalization, as it greatly accelerates the flow of money, technologies, ideas, and bodies across national borders. International tourists flock to the islands to enjoy the sea and sun but also often to engage in sexual adventures. Here again we see the intersection of race, gender, and class emerge as local populations are eroticized and marketed along with the white sand beaches. Local men and women become involved in sex and romance tourism as a way to better their lives and possibly escape poverty through migration via marriage to a foreigner (Cabezas 2009; Roland 2011; Brennan 2004; Fernandez 2019). Tourism can be seen as a new colonizing force, one that alters both the economic and social relations of the entire region.

While tourism brings millions of foreigners to the islands in the Caribbean as temporary visitors, for decades thousands of islanders

Table 12.3. Caribbean 2017 Statistics

COUNTRY	# Tourist Arrivals*	Tourism as % of GDP**	% of population below poverty line**	Public Debt as % of GDP**	Remittances as % of GDP***
Bahamas	6,136,000	50	9.3	54.6	NA
Cayman Islands	2,147,000	70	1.9	NA	NA
Cuba	4,654,000	10.4	NA	47.7	NA
Dominican Republic	7,296,000	11	30.5	37.2	7
Grenada	468,000	44.6	38	70.4	4
Haiti	1,262,000	7	58.5	31.1	23
Jamaica	4,276,000	20	17.1	101	14
St. Lucia	1,064,000	65	25	70.7	1.67
Trinidad & Tobago	464,000	3.3	20	41.8	.58
Puerto Rico	3,600,000	7	43	51.6	NA

emigration
the act of leaving one's home country to permanently settle in another country.

themselves have been migrating out of their countries to seek prosperity and security abroad. **Emigration** has long affected the Caribbean, and we find well-established Caribbean communities in England, Canada, and the United States, such as the Cubans in Miami and Puerto Ricans and Dominicans in New York City. More than 750,000 people of Caribbean origin live in Canada largely from Jamaica, Guyana, Trinidad and Tobago, and Haiti (Labelle, Larose, and Piché 2010). Most reside in the cities of Toronto and Montreal.

Much of the emigration has followed historical colonial links. As posters in 1970s Britain noted succinctly, "We are here because you were there." That is, communities of African and Asian descent are in England because the British had colonized their homelands and transported enslaved Africans to their colonies in the Caribbean. Often migrants were recruited to address labor shortages in former colonial powers, such as the Windrush Generation (1948–71) who came to Britain after World War II. The Windrush Generation is named after the ship that brought them to Britain, the *Empire Windrush*. In 2018 some of these migrants and their children, largely from Jamaica, Trinidad and Tobago, and Barbados, who have lived and worked for decades in Britain, were wrongly denied rights and benefits and were threatened with deportation in what became known as the "Windrush scandal."

Figure 12.4. Protest march in London in 2018 in support of the Windrush Generation. Steve Eason, CC BY-NC-SA 2.0.

Migrants emigrating from the Caribbean are often the educated and the young workers. As Faure (2018) notes, "Between 1965 and 2000 about 12% of the labour force of the Caribbean region has emigrated to **OECD** countries, which is almost twice the rate for Central America (i.e. 7%), and six times the average rate for developing countries (i.e. 2%)." While this can lead to a damaging **brain drain** depleting the small countries of their most educated and capable workforce, migrants also send money home in the form of **remittances**, which for some countries (like Haiti) are an important component of the national economy. Many migrants circulate, traveling and living transnational lives while bringing skills and capital from abroad to foster trade and business in the Caribbean. Some migrants also return to their home countries to retire. We also see the gendered aspect of migration, as many Caribbean women migrate to the United States and Europe and find work as nurses, nannies, caregivers, and domestic workers. Women are seen as an inexpensive and docile labor force, and the jobs available to them are insecure and low wage.

Some Caribbean migration flows are the result of natural disasters (e.g., 2010 earthquake in Haiti, 2017 Hurricane Maria in Puerto Rico) or political upheavals that have forced millions of people to emigrate to the United States. The Cuban Revolution of 1959, the Mariel boatlift of 1980, and the Cuban rafter crisis of 1994 each brought tens of thousands of Cubans to the United States. People seeking freedom from political

OECD
Organisation for Economic Co-operation and Development is an intergovernmental economic organization with thirty-six member countries. Members are developed countries with thriving economies.

brain drain
the phenomenon of well-educated, skilled workers emigrating from countries in the Global South to countries in the Global North where they have prospects for better pay and living conditions.

remittances
money or goods sent by migrants back to family and friends in their home country.

oppression and dictatorships in Haiti and the Dominican Republic also came to America. In recent years, natural disasters have devastated countries like Haiti and Puerto Rico, which lack the infrastructure and capital to effectively respond to and recover from the destruction. In the wake of Hurricane Maria, thousands of Puerto Ricans (who are US citizens) relocated to the mainland United States to rebuild their lives.

SEXUAL AND GENDER DIVERSITY

From the colonial legacy, the region has strong patriarchal roots that have contributed to cultures that do not always embrace sexual and gender diversity. Popular cultural expressions such as dancehall music can be deeply misogynistic and homophobic (see chapter 14). In general, societal acceptance of LGBTQ people is rare, and LGBTQ issues are taboo in many Caribbean nations (Human Rights Watch 2017). Most of the former British colonies still have laws that criminalize same-sex relations (known as "buggery or gross indecency laws") leftover from British colonial rule. While these laws are vaguely worded and do not explicitly mention gender identity or expression, police and law enforcement often conflate gender identity with sexual orientation and, as a result, these laws can at times be used to criminalize gender identity that does not correspond with the norms associated with the sex assigned at birth. However, in recent years a growing movement for LGBTQ rights activism is spreading across the region. In 2016, for example, Trinidad and Tobago repealed "buggery laws." In other countries including Jamaica, Barbados, and Dominica, activist groups and individuals have launched cases to repeal similar laws in their penal codes (Human Rights Watch 2017).

Cuba has been more progressive in recognizing LGBTQ rights in recent years. While in the early years of the Cuban Revolution gay men (and others deemed socially marginal) were sent to work camps. Military Units to Aid Production (UMAP) were agricultural labor camps operated by the Cuban government from November 1965 to July 1968. People sent to the work camps included homosexuals, conscientious objectors to the mandatory military service, Christians and other religious believers, and antirevolutionaries. In the last ten years the country has made a number of important advances to secure LGBTQ rights. For example, the country guarantees free sex-change operations and forbids discrimination based on sexual orientation.

However, support of LGBTQ rights is far from universal in the Spanish-speaking Caribbean. In 2019 the Cuban government proposed an amendment to the constitution to legalize same-sex marriage, but evangelical churches on the island, a growing force, protested. The amendment did not pass, but the government vowed to address the issue through changes in the country's civil code rather than in the constitution. In 2010 the Dominican Republic banned same-sex marriage in its constitution. LGBTQ people in many parts of the Spanish-speaking Caribbean are subject to violence and discrimination based on their sexual orientation and/or gender identity. Activists across the Caribbean are working to repeal discriminatory laws and end the marginalization of LGBTQ people.

CONCLUSION

As we learn in other chapters of this book, globalization is not a new phenomenon, and the Caribbean region has been "global" since Columbus arrived in 1492. The centuries of European colonial rule and subsequent US interventions, the plantation agriculture system, and most notably the slave trade have had a profound impact on all aspects of life on the islands today, from the economy to family relations. Large-scale incoming (enslaved Africans) and outgoing migrations (contemporary political, climate, and economic migrants) continue to shape the islands with roughly 22 percent of the Caribbean population living abroad (mainly in the United States, United Kingdom, and Canada) (Faure 2018). In the twenty-first century, the island nations continue to struggle with violence against women, gender inequalities, and LBGTQ acceptance with the ongoing dominance of patriarchy.

The chapters in Part IV: The Caribbean present anthropological research that showcases the legacy of the strong patriarchal history of colonialism in the region. Chapter 13 explores the lavish quinceañera (fifteenth) birthday parties for girls in Cuba. These parties, celebrated throughout the Spanish-speaking world, traditionally mark a girl's eligibility for marriage. Today, the parties provide a stage for the girls to display their physical and sexual (heterosexual) attractiveness, while allowing families to demonstrate their socioeconomic status. Emerging class disparities in Cuba are evident in the money and resources families have available to host these festivities for their daughters. Chapter 14 explores the construction of masculinities among Jamaican men. Displays of heterosexual prowess are a key element of male identity, and men assert their power and status through sexual relations with multiple female partners. These sexual behaviors are enshrined in popular culture through dancehall music whose lyrics celebrate male sexual conquests and at times violence toward women.

KEY TERMS

brain drain: the phenomenon of well-educated, skilled workers emigrating from countries in the Global South to countries in the Global North where they have prospects for better pay and living conditions.

conquistadors: leaders of the Spanish conquest of the Americas during the fifteenth to sixteenth centuries.

emigration: the act of leaving one's home country to permanently settle in another country.

OECD: Organisation for Economic Co-operation and Development is an intergovernmental economic organization with thirty-six member countries. Members are developed countries with thriving economies.

remittances: money or goods sent by migrants back to family and friends in their home country.

RESOURCES FOR FURTHER EXPLORATION

- Alvarez, Julia. 2010. *In the Time of the Butterflies*. New York: Algonquin.

- Danticat, Edwidge. 2008. *Brother, I'm Dying*. New York: Vintage.

- Farmer, Paul. 1992. *AIDS and Accusation: Haiti and the Geography of Blame*. Berkeley: University of California Press.

- Kincaid, Jamaica. 2000. *A Small Place*. New York: Farrar, Straus and Giroux.

- Slocum, K., and Thomas, D. A. 2003. Rethinking Global and Area Studies: Insights from Caribbeanist Anthropology. *American Anthropologist*, 105: 553–565. doi:10.1525/aa.2003. 105.3.553.

BIBLIOGRAPHY

Blank, Sharla. 2013. "An Historical and Contemporary Overview of Gendered Caribbean Relations." *Journal of Arts and Humanities* 2, no. 4: 1–10.
Brennan, Denise. 2004. *What's Love Got to Do with It? Transnational Desires and Sex Tourism in the Dominican Republic*. Durham, NC: Duke University Press.

Cabezas, Amalia. 2009. *Economies of Desire: Sex and Tourism in Cuba and the Dominican Republic*. Philadelphia: Temple University Press.

Dore, Elizabeth. 1997. "The Holy Family: Imagined Households in Latin American History." In *Gender Politics in Latin America*, edited by Elizabeth Dore, 101–17. New York: Monthly Review.

Faure, Aymeric. 2018. *Migratory Patterns in the Caribbean: Impacts and Perspectives for Caribbean Countries*. Open Diplomacy. http://www.open-diplomacy.eu/blog/migratory-patterns-in-the-caribbean-impacts-and-perspectives-for-caribbean.

Fernandez, Nadine T. 2010. *Revolutionizing Romance: Interracial Couples in Contemporary Cuba*, 45. New Brunswick, NJ: Rutgers University Press.

———. 2019. "Tourist Brides and Migrant Grooms: Cuban–Danish Couples and Family Reunification Policies." *Journal of Ethnic and Migration Studies* 45, no. 16: 3141–56.

Fetterolf, Janell. 2017. *In Many Countries, at Least Four-in-Ten in the Labor Force Are Women*. Fact Tank: News in the Numbers. https://www.pewresearch.org/fact-tank/2017/03/07/in-many-countries-at-least-four-in-ten-in-the-labor-force-are-women/.

Human Rights Watch. 2017. *"I Have to Leave to Be Me" Discriminatory Laws against LGBT People in the Eastern Caribbean*. New York: Human Rights Watch. https://www.hrw.org/report/2018/03/21/i-have-leave-be-me/discriminatory-laws-against-lgbt-people-eastern-caribbean.

Labelle, M., Serge Larose, and V. Piché. 2010. *Caribbean Canadians*. The Canadian Encyclopedia. https://www.thecanadianencyclopedia.ca/en/article/caribbean-canadians.

Lopez, Iris. 2008. *Matters of Choice: Puerto Rican Women's Struggle for Reproductive Freedom*. New Brunswick, NJ: Rutgers University Press.

Martínez-Alier, Verena. 1989. *Marriage, Class, and Colour in 19th Century Cuba: A Study of Racial Attitudes and Sexual Values in a Slave Society*. Ann Arbor: University of Michigan Press.

Morrison, Karen Yvette. 2015. *Cuba's Racial Crucible: The Sexual Economy of Social Identities, 1750–2000*. Bloomington: Indiana University Press.

Roland, L. Kaifa. 2011. *Cuban Color in Tourism and La Lucha: An Ethnography of Racial Meanings*. New York: Oxford University Press.

Safa, Helen. 1995. *The Myth of the Male Breadwinner: Women and Industrialization in the Caribbean*. Boulder: Westview.

Sanabria, Harry. 2007. *The Anthropology of Latin America and the Caribbean*. Boston: Pearson.

University of Minnesota. 2016. *World Regional Geography: People, Places and Globalization*. https://open.umn.edu/opentextbooks/textbooks/world-regional-geography-people-places-and-globalization.

13

Quinceañeras
Girls' Coming-of-Age Parties in Contemporary Havana, Cuba

Heidi Härkönen

LEARNING OBJECTIVES

- Describe how rituals can reproduce gender as a socially significant category of differentiation.

- Evaluate how global and state-level historical processes and politics shape local gendered ritual practices.

- Articulate how questions of gendered power and agency are embedded in ritual practices.

In this chapter, the author explores the phenomenon of flamboyant girls' fifteenth birthday parties (quinceañeras) as a gender-specific ritual. The author discusses the ways that this life-cycle ritual celebrates the girl's entry into sexual adulthood, portrays her as an object of heterosexual desire, while simultaneously granting the girls ritual and exotic agency. The author concludes that contemporary quinceañera rituals also reflect the island's recent political and economic turn toward a more capitalist society and displays the growing racialized and gendered inequalities on the island.

When *Habanera* (Havana resident) girls turn fifteen, their birthday is usually celebrated with a lavish *fiesta de los quince años* that in its most elaborate form includes a dance party with hundreds of guests and food, drink, and entertainment. The festivities typically include the girl dressing up in puffy dresses imitating eighteenth-century European court fashions and dancing a waltz with a male relative in front of her kin, friends, and neighbors. Boys' fifteenth birthdays are not celebrated in a similarly grandiose way, making the quince a highly gender specific ritual.

A central part of the ritual consists of the photos taken by a professional photographer where the girl poses in diverse outfits ranging from the latest fashion gear to mermaid costumes. Although the photos often portray the **quinceañera** as a sensual seductress, the rituals' meanings are more complex than just presenting the girl as a passive sexual object. In Havana, the **quince** forms a markedly women's ritual, highlighting simultaneously the girl's entry into young adulthood in her kin group and in the process, gaining gendered "**erotic agency**," which Holly Wardlow (2006, 232) defines as "the power and delight of being desired."

Although quinceañeras are celebrated across the Americas, I first encountered the ritual when I was in Havana conducting ethnographic research for my master's thesis in 2003–2004 (Härkönen 2005). My initial focus was to explore the Catholic confirmation ritual, but I had trouble locating Catholic Cubans who would have undergone confirmation. Although Cuba is historically a Catholic country, its many years as a socialist, officially atheist, society have greatly diminished the role of the Catholic Church on the island. However, Habanera women enthusiastically showed me girls' quince photos. And as I began to realize how important the

quinceañera
a girl celebrating her fifteenth birthday; can also refer to the festivities or to the party connected with a girl's fifteenth birthday.

quince
the festivities that mark a girl's fifteenth birthday, including the party, the photoshoot, and other possible events.

erotic agency
the ability to act and gain pleasure and even a position of power due to being considered erotically attractive.

Figure 13.1. The figure of the quinceañera standing proudly alone at the top of a lavish cake. Heidi Härkönen.

ritual was, I shifted my focus to the quince. The quince was a topic that I as a young woman at the time of my initial, relatively brief fieldwork (three months), could easily access. This change of subject exemplifies the unpredictable, frequently improvised character of ethnographic research (Cerwonka and Malkki 2007): instead of strict, preconceived plans, we often need to accommodate our research to locally significant topics. It also shows how our personas—formed by such intersectional (Crenshaw 1989) differences as gender, race, age, and class—shape our research experiences and the information we are able to access (Härkönen 2016b). Our academic selves thus influence the knowledge that we produce, highlighting the importance of **reflexivity** (Gould and Uusihakala 2016) throughout the research process.

Since my first fieldwork period, I have been back to Havana several times—in 2006, 2007, and 2008—to conduct research on gender, kinship, life cycle, and the state (Härkönen 2014, 2016) and in 2017 and 2019 on well-being and social change. Still, I have always kept an eye on the quince. I have continually worked with the same community of low-income, racially mixed people. However, over the years, I have seen multiple quince photos and videos, spoken with many Habanera girls and women, and participated in quince parties, photoshoots, and dance rehearsals, widening my perspective on the ritual beyond my immediate interlocutors.

I approach the quince as a **coming-of-age ritual** that is best understood in the context of my interlocutors' views of kinship and the **life course**. I define the quince as a coming-of-age ritual because it marks a girl's transition from childhood into young adulthood. Quince forms part of the larger group of **life-cycle rituals** that mark important social transitions such as birth, death, and marriage. These rituals have long been of interest to anthropologists (e.g., Richards [1956] 1982; Turner 1969). In a classical study, Arnold van Gennep ([1909] 1960) argues that in these kinds of moments of transition, social categorizations such as gender often become especially visible. Coming-of-age rituals are in many ways similar to **initiation rituals**, which also typically take place during youth. In initiation rituals, a person is initiated into a new group membership or status (La Fontaine 1985). In initiation rituals, the ritual itself *performs* the transformation (see La Fontaine 1985); weddings turn lovers into married couples. However, the coming-of-age ritual only *marks* a change that will occur but may be a more gradual process, such as becoming an adult.

As the quince marks a specific moment in a girl's life cycle, to understand the ritual in its context, it is important to explore the quince in its full temporal and social framework (Barraud et al. 1994). I connect the

reflexivity
critically examining one's own assumptions, motivations, power, conceptualizations, and practices in the research process.

coming-of-age ritual
rituals that mark a transition from youth to adulthood.

life course
the lifetime of an individual person from birth to death.

life-cycle ritual
a ritual that marks or performs life-course transitions such as birth, marriage, and death.

initiation ritual
a ritual that incorporates a person into a certain group or community.

centrality of Habanera girls' quince ritual to women's important position as mothers in my interlocutors' kin relations (Härkönen 2016a). Wider Afro-Caribbean ideas of kinship that highlight women's role as mothers regardless of legal marriage or the (il)legitimacy of children, and the importance of "blood" relations over marital relations, have for long been central in Havana, especially among low-income, racially mixed people like my Cuban interlocutors (Martinez-Alier 1974). These understandings of kinship and gender differentiate Habanera girls' experiences from those of girls in many other parts of the Americas.

Cuba is different from other contexts also because of its historical particularities as a socialist society. In **prerevolutionary** Cuba, racialized inequalities of wealth and status were blatant: a legacy of Spanish colonialism, plantation slavery, and the US-dominated republican period (Martinez-Alier 1974). Material wealth was concentrated in the hands of a white minority, while the Afro-Cuban population suffered multiple forms of discrimination and poverty (de la Fuente 2001). The 1959 Cuban revolution sought to equalize such differences with its policies of social justice, many of which benefited the poorest and darker-skinned segments of the population in particular (Eckstein 1994, 149–157). The revolution's aim was to create a socialist society that would abolish inequalities of gender, race, class, and wealth. The state would nurture individuals from cradle to grave, providing basic services such as food, housing, jobs, commodities, childcare, education, and health care. Everyone would have state-guaranteed access to goods and services and disparities of wealth would cease to exist. Over the years, though never fully achieved, Cuba made significant advances in creating an egalitarian society. However, everything changed in the 1990s, when Cuba's closest political and economic ally, the Soviet Union, disintegrated. Cuba lost 70 percent of its foreign trade and fell into a severe crisis, known as the "Special Period in Peacetime" (Eckstein 1994, 88–91). Cuba was forced to cut its earlier state subsidies and supports to individuals, liberalize its economy, and gradually open the island to global tourism and market influences. Since the 1990s, Cuba has once again become divided by racialized inequalities, in particular between those who have access to foreign remittances (mostly white and lighter-skinned Cubans) and those who have to survive on their devalued, local wages. These changes in Cuba's internal policies, and in its place in the global political and economic order, are reflected in the Habanera girls' quince parties, as they exemplify the contemporary inequalities of wealth and transnational flows of people, goods, ideas, and fashions. This chapter will focus on how ideas of gender, sexuality, and kinship take shape in the quinces and how Habaneros conceptualize the ritual as a part of Cuba's global and local history.

prerevolutionary
the time before the Cuban revolution in 1959.

QUINCE'S HISTORY: A COLONIAL-ERA RITUAL ON A SOCIALIST ISLAND

As quinceañera celebrations are popular across the Americas, many aspects of the ritual are shared across diverse national contexts. However, there are also local particularities. In Havana, the quince is conceptualized as a legacy of Cuba's historical tradition as a Spanish colony. My interlocutors usually emphasized the island as being a rich mixture of Spanish, African, Indigenous Taíno, Chinese, and Arab influences: "In Cuba, there is not a single drop of pure blood, it is all mixed." However, they saw the quince as representing a markedly European aspect of this cultural legacy. Oswaldo (this name is a pseudonym, like all the other Cuban interlocutors' names in this chapter), a Cuban art historian who was also a professional quince party choreographer, described the quince's origins in the European court celebrations when young girls coming into a marriageable age were presented to the high society for the first time:

> During colonialism, many rich families of Spanish origin settled in Havana. Quince comes from the representations of the girl that were made in Spain, and also in the courts in other parts of Europe, when the girl turned into a woman. . . . These dresses that you see now in the quince photos, it's the same cut with a lot of lace, a lot of layers. That's why they dance the waltz, all that is a reflection of those European [practices]. . . . [In colonial Cuba] the Habanero aristocracy was invited to the celebration. [Later, during the first half of the 20th century] in the more modern form of quince parties, social class was still decisive, it was about who had the most money (Oswaldo, interview by author).

Prerevolutionary Cuban newspapers like *El Mundo* display photos and announcements featuring wealthy girls' sophisticated quince parties in Havana. In 2003–2004, one of my interlocutors showed me quince photos taken by her late husband who was a photographer. In the photos, girls can be seen in long, elegant gowns posing with an elaborate cake. However, since the quince (due to its historical roots) was conceptualized as a white, colonialist, and elitist ritual, it was politically incompatible with the 1959 revolution that emphasized an ideology of socialist egalitarianism. The quince also did not mesh well with socialist ideas of gender, which rejected such decorative womanhood as bourgeois, idle vanity (Härkönen 2011). Oswaldo explained to me that during many years in revolutionary Cuba, quince celebrations were toned down:

Figure 13.2. Quinceañeras in prerevolutionary Havana. Heidi Härkönen, courtesy of Mrs. Henrietta Pryce.

> For a while these parties [quinces] were not celebrated due to certain situations . . . What were done were activities at home with the quinceañera: a family fiesta or a meal. Later this tradition of dancing the quince parties came back (Oswaldo, interview by author).

While during the ideologically stricter years of the revolution, quinces were celebrated as smaller fiestas, the grandiose parties were revived in the 1990s as a part of the more general political, economic, and sociocultural changes in Cuba. Due to an economic crisis, the Cuban government was forced to make ideological concessions to capitalism: new global consumerism and more contacts with the capitalist world started to shape life on the island. These changes simultaneously introduced intensified **monetization** and racialized, economic inequalities to Cuba (Eckstein 2004; Fernandez 1999). Foreign **remittances** and new entrepreneurial and professional possibilities in the lucrative tourist industry brought wealth most importantly to white, historically privileged Cubans who had relatives abroad and were favored in tourism work, while others, such as my low-income, racially mixed Habanero friends, had to struggle to make ends meet (Martinez 2013; Hansing and Hoffman 2019). Before the 1990s, the highest-paid Cuban workers, such as doctors and engineers,

monetization
when money enters areas of a society where it has previously played a minor role.

remittances
money or goods sent by migrants back to family and friends in their home country.

earned 4.5 times as much as the lowest-paid workers (Uriarte-Gaston 2004, 109–110). But in 2017, one of my state-employed friends earned only US\$25 per month, while an extremely successful private entrepreneur could earn up to US\$50,000 per month (though that is quite uncommon).

Due to increased cultural interaction with the United States, since the 1990s the quince parties have incorporated influences from the Cuban diaspora in Florida and elsewhere in the Americas. Exemplifying important **transnational** connections, Cuban migrants sometimes return to Cuba for quince celebrations from abroad, and Cubans on the island receive material items, money, and visitors to their parties. Quince photos circulate between Cubans on the island and those elsewhere; they are posted on social media, and fashions are closely followed in terms of the latest styles and poses. This global circulation also comes with a beauty ideal that contradicts Cuba's earlier socialist efforts to reject narrow Western representations. Since the 1990s, the ritual has become more emphatically a part of a globalized Latina (Alvarez 2007) portrayal of gender differences but with some local specificities.

QUINCE AS A SEXUAL RITUAL

Certain aspects distinguish my Habanero interlocutors' quince parties from many other Latin American quinces (Napolitano 1997; Davalos 2003; Alvarez 2007): their portrayal of sexuality, the ritual centrality of the mother, and the lack of Christian religiosity. These features are related to the region's Afro-Caribbean kinship tradition and to Cuba's history as a socialist country. While in the Mexican quinceañera ritual (Napolitano 1997), the girl is represented in a virginlike, Catholic manner, in Havana the quince ritual celebrates positive, heterosexual femininity in a playful way (see also Pertierra 2015 for eastern Cuba).

The quince is considered a girl's "moment of beauty" when the whole world is at her feet. Habanera girls stated that the quince marks a transition "from childhood to adolescence" and that "starting from then, you begin to see life differently." (Yailen, Danaisy, and Odalys, interviews by author). Yadira, a woman who had turned fifteen in the early 1980s, stated: "In my time, before you turned fifteen, you couldn't shave your legs or pluck your eyebrows or use makeup, that day [of your quince] they dyed your hair, fixed it, and gave you a haircut." This embodied change marks a girl's entry into young adulthood, one aspect of which is her becoming a sexual woman. Anaisa, a mother who had recently celebrated her daughter's quince, reflected on the subject:

They feel themselves a little . . . like adults, they look different. A little more responsibility is on her because one already has to start telling her that she has to take care [of herself] and all the things that can happen to her starting from then. You know that everybody starts to see her as a bigger person. Men who did not see her as . . . a woman, start to eye her because she is fifteen, and men start to see her differently. (Anaisa, interview by author)

I interpret Anaisa's insinuation that due to her daughter's quince, men approach her sexually and that she should be wary of them, as she could become pregnant. Even though some girls start their sex lives before turning fifteen, not everybody has sexual relations at that age: after turning fifteen, girls are considered to be sexually (quasi) adults and as such, potentially reproductive. Officially, in Cuba, the age of sexual consent is sixteen years, and eighteen years for marriage, but with the consent of their parents, girls can marry at the age of fourteen and boys when they are sixteen. Understandings of sexuality are thereby ambiguously shaped by gender and age.

Female sexuality is displayed in the most salient way in the quince photos, which my interlocutors considered to be the most important part of the ritual. In these photos, girls can pose in a stripper's outfit, hanging

Figure 13.3. Quince photos displaying the girl as sexual seductress. Heidi Härkönen.

off a dancing pole—or totally nude with just props covering their breasts and genitals. Girls also pose in other outfits, many of which display the ritual's (supposed) historical aspects and feature big, frilly dresses designated as *trajes coloniales* (colonial dresses). Other costumes include playful outfits such as that of a Japanese geisha or more modern movie-star imagery. The photos always depict girls as highly feminine and follow heterosexual notions of attractiveness. This portrayal highlights the gendering of female bodies as different from and complementary to male bodies (Härkönen 2014; see also Lundgren 2011). The photos reproduce and affirm both feminine gender and heterosexuality as socially central categorizations in the community (Härkönen 2014; see also Lundgren 2011).

While the prerevolutionary photos were also highlighting gender difference, contemporary photos differ significantly by their heightened sexual portrayal. The photos reflect changes in attitudes toward sexuality over Cuba's socialist history, especially since the 1970s, when Cuba started to offer sexual education in schools (Hamilton 2012, 36–37). The aim was to reject bourgeois, patriarchal notions of sexuality and to embrace modernist, socialist, egalitarian views (Hamilton 2012: 36). This emphasis on female sexual agency is reflected in the contemporary photos.

As a life-cycle ritual, the quince is in many ways comparable to a wedding, and traditionally, it is conceptualized as a ritual preparing girls for marriage. Juan, a middle-aged man, defined the quince as "a party that is done so that everyone can see that they are ready to get married." However, many other Habaneros told me that quince is more important than a wedding: "You can divorce and remarry but the quince is just once in a lifetime." Among my low-income interlocutors, the quinces certainly were a more popular ritual than weddings.

I connect the quince's importance among my Habanero interlocutors to their kinship relations that conformed in many ways to long-standing Afro-Caribbean ideas that emphasize women's position as mothers over their position as wives, and the significance of biogenetic, "blood" connections over marital relations (Härkönen 2016; see also Safa 2005). As many Habaneros live in **consensual unions**, and legal marriage is not a central institution regulating either sexuality or the birth of children, it is more important to mark a girl becoming a sexual, potentially reproductive adult woman/mother than to prepare her for marriage. As a matter of fact, instead of a husband, some of my young interlocutors tended to have a baby in their arms soon after turning fifteen. Cuba has had high numbers of teenage pregnancies since the late 1970s (Catasus Cervera and Gantt 1996), and this same tendency continues (Fariñas Acosta 2018). In 2007–2008, my friends told me that it was "in fashion to give birth at

consensual union
a couple that cohabitates without being legally married.

a young age." Children are loved and wanted, sometimes already during youth (Härkönen 2014; see also Andaya 2014). This tendency supports local ideas of kinship that emphasize the importance of living **relational** lives surrounded by one's family members (Härkönen 2016a). The quince thus marks a girl's change of position within her kin group.

relational
surrounded by relationships, differing from an individualist emphasis on personal autonomy.

AGENCY, RACE, AND CLASS: THE QUINCE AS A WOMAN'S RITUAL

The quince is a ritual where women hold the most important ritual agency. My interlocutors described the quince primarily as the mother's ritual: "My mum did it all." The quinceañera's mother bears the primary responsibility for organizing her daughter's celebration, as one woman described: "In my daughter's quince party I have full responsibility; the mother is the one who decides." Mothers may save for years for the festivities, and they often described their daughter's quince as "exhausting" (*acabando*). Typically other female kin help in the practical arrangements, and there is an expectation that the girl's father contributes money, but not all fathers fulfill such expectations.

Even though in the fiesta, the girl traditionally dances the waltz with her father who then gives her away to a male dancing partner (sometimes

Figure 13.4. A mother watches over as her daughter is prepared for her quince photoshoot in Havana. Heidi Härkönen.

the girl's boyfriend), the mother is still ritually central both at the party and during the photo session. She is the one congratulated for having raised such a beautiful young woman.

Sometimes the mother is more eager to celebrate her daughter's quince than the girl herself. Cuban sociologist Yanelis remarked: "When I ask her (a quinceañera) why you had the photos taken, the girl says: to please my mother, my grandmother. And that's why they have the party." Fifteen-year-old Youmara told me that her mother had pushed her to have a formal fiesta, when she would have just preferred to have her photos taken and go to the beach with her friends: "I don't want to have a fiesta . . . I want to go out with my friends, it's better." However, she ended up having a party when her aunt visited from Miami and helped pay for the fiesta.

As a coming-of-age ritual, the quince is so strongly normative that nearly all the girls I met found it both important and attractive. I did not meet anyone openly challenging the heterosexual imagery of the ritual. Instead, girls stated that they were "happy" and that the day was "special"—something that "all girls dream about." While the ritual in many ways objectifies girls, this issue has to be explored in the context of wider Habanero understandings of sexuality. My female interlocutors usually saw men's admiring looks or comments on their bodies as a positive affirmation of their sexually attractive womanhood. Beauty grants them erotic agency. At the same time, they rejected women who in their opinion failed to look feminine: "That woman is horrible. . . . She is not feminine like us. . . . She is like a man." This emphasis on beauty creates inequalities among women, as they are expected to conform to narrow, globalized standards of attractiveness.

These changes in post-Soviet Cuba also relate to heightened inequalities of race and class. During my earlier fieldwork periods, in 2003–2004 and 2007–2008 in Havana, all kinds of girls celebrated their quince, so the ritual was not clearly racialized or differentiated by class as such. However, there were some intersectional differences in the magnitude of the celebration. Girls from a low-income background tended to have more modest parties, such as street fiestas, while wealthier girls could have their parties in private salons or hotels in exclusive, glamorous settings. As differences of wealth are significantly racialized in Cuba, white girls often had the most elaborate quince parties. Still, during my fieldwork in 2007–2008, most girls I met had their quince photos taken in a state "wedding palace" (*palacio de los matrimonios* or *palacio de las novias*). By contrast, in contemporary Cuba, the role of private companies has grown. During my most recent fieldwork periods, in 2017 and 2019, the emergence of the quince as a profitable industry seemed to have shaped the **racialization** of the ritual. As the quince industry currently operates via the internet, I did a search for Cuban quince photography studios when writing this article. In the studios I encountered (see Pérez Hernández; Calás; Mahe), both the (male) photographers and the girls featured in the photos were white. The prices were significantly higher than I witnessed during my earlier fieldwork periods. For example, one photographer advertised quince packets starting at 120 CUC (of equal value to the US dollar) and ranging up to 850 CUC (Mahe); a sizeable sum when a state-employed Cuban's average monthly salary is currently about US$39 (ONEI 2020). While it is likely that there are cheaper studios and also Afro-Cuban businesses, it seems that the increasing professionalization and commercialization of quince parties is accompanied by its whitening in terms of both the participants and the ritual actors (see Härkönen 2017 on weddings). The quince appears to be returning to its roots as a white, elitist ritual, as Cuba transforms from a socialist island into a more capitalist society marked by intersectional inequalities.

racialization
the process of ascribing a racial identity and associated traits to a group. These characteristics are often defined by a dominant group with the aim of discriminating against and excluding the subordinate group.

Figure 13.5. A quinceañera at a luxurious quince party in Havana. Heidi Härkönen.

CONCLUSION

The quinceañera celebration is a girl's coming-of-age ritual that is popular across the Americas. In Havana, the ritual foregrounds the girl's sexual attractiveness. As a women's ritual, the quince celebrates a girl's entry into sexual adulthood and highlights her mother's role in bringing up such a beautiful young woman. While the ritual portrays the girl as an object of heterosexual male desire, it simultaneously grants women ritual and erotic agency, which they enjoy.

As a coming-of-age ritual, the quinceañera does not precipitate a change of status in the same way as an initiation ritual; girls become women whether or not they celebrate their quince. However, the ritual still plays a part in highlighting, reproducing, and marking gender as a socially central category in Cuba by emphasizing an image of girls as ultra-feminine, physically attractive, heterosexual agents: thus emphasizing the stark contrast between males and females in Cuba's complementary gender dynamics.

Life-cycle rituals are connected to larger social worlds through understandings of kinship, gender, and sexuality. I suggest that the centrality of a girls' coming-of-age ritual in Cuba is best understood in the context of my Habanero friends' Afro-Caribbean kin relations that emphasized women's position as mothers. Rituals are also shaped by and reflect historical changes over time. While the quince is rooted in Cuba's Spanish colonial legacy and high-class practices—ill-fitted for socialist egalitarianism—its resurgence during the 1990s connects it with the more general ritual revival in Cuban society. However, the contemporary quince rituals also reflect the island's recent political and economic turn toward a more capitalist society. The quince has increasingly become a professional, private, lucrative industry and thus a site for displaying the growing racialized and gendered inequalities on the island.

REVIEW QUESTIONS

1. How do you see gender, racial, and class ideologies reproduced through a ritual like the quince?

2. Why might girls and/or mothers want to participate in the quince?

3. What life-cycle rituals do you encounter in your own context and what kinds of gendered, racialized, or class-related aspects do they display?

KEY TERMS

coming-of-age ritual: rituals that mark a transition from youth to adulthood.

consensual union: a couple that cohabitates without being legally married.

erotic agency: the ability to act and gain pleasure and even a position of power due to being considered erotically attractive.

initiation ritual: a ritual that incorporates a person into a certain group or community.

life course: the lifetime of an individual person from birth to death.

life-cycle ritual: a ritual that marks or performs life-course transitions such as birth, marriage, and death.

monetization: when money enters areas of a society where it has previously played a minor role.

prerevolutionary: the time before the Cuban revolution in 1959.

quince: the festivities that mark a girl's fifteenth birthday, including the party, the photoshoot, and other possible events.

quinceañera: a girl celebrating her fifteenth birthday; can also refer to the festivities or to the party connected with a girl's fifteenth birthday.

racialization: the process of ascribing a racial identity and associated traits to a group. These characteristics are often defined by a dominant group with the aim of discriminating against and excluding the subordinate group.

relational: surrounded by relationships, differing from an individualist emphasis on personal autonomy.

reflexivity: critically examining one's own assumptions, motivations, power, conceptualizations, and practices in the research process.

remittances: money or goods sent by migrants back to family and friends in their home country.

RESOURCES FOR FURTHER EXPLORATION

- Anonymous. Estudio Fotográfico Mahe C website. https://fotosde15cuba.com/precios-de-servicio-de-fotografia-en-cuba-la-habana/. Accessed July 1, 2019.

- Calás, Iván. Photography Eikon Habana website. https://eikon habana.com/. Accessed July 1, 2019.

- CGTN America: https://www.youtube.com/watch?v=9oGEbE GtnkM.

- Pérez Hernández, Izuky. Izuky Photography website. http://www.izukyphotography.com/fotografo-de-quinceaneras-en-cuba/#. Accessed July 1, 2019.

ACKNOWLEDGMENTS

I want to thank the Academy of Finland (grants 294662 and 297 957) and the funders of my doctoral research: the Finnish Cultural Foundation, the Emil Aaltonen Foundation, the Ella and Georg Ehrnrooth Foundation, the Ryoichi Sasakawa Young Leaders Fellowship Fund, Finnish Academy of Science and Letters Eino Jutikkala Fund, The Oskar Öflund Foundation and the Finnish Concordia Fund. Most importantly, many thanks to my Cuban friends: *muchísimas gracias por su ayuda y amistad.*

BIBLIOGRAPHY

Alvarez, Julia. 2007. *Once Upon a Quinceañera: Coming of Age in the USA.* New York: Plume.

Andaya, Elise. 2014. *Conceiving Cuba: Reproduction, Women, and the State in the Post-Soviet Era.* New Brunswick, NJ: Rutgers University Press.

Anonymous. n.d. Estudio Fotográfico Mahe C (website). https://fotosde15cuba.com/precios-de-servicio-de-fotografia-en-cuba-la-habana/. Accessed July 1, 2019.

Barraud, Cécile, Daniel de Coppet, André Iteanu, and Raymond Jamous. 1994. *Of Relations and the Dead: Four Societies Viewed from the Angle of Their Exchanges.* Oxford: Berg.

Calás, Iván. Photography Eikon Habana (website). https://eikonhabana.com/. Accessed July 1, 2019.

Catasus Cervera, Sonia I., and Barbara N. Gantt. 1996. "The Sociodemographic and Reproductive Characteristics of Cuban Women." *Latin American Perspectives* 23, no. 1: 87–98.

Cerwonka, Allaine, and Liisa H. Malkki. 2007. *Improvising Theory: Process and Temporality in Ethnographic Fieldwork.* Chicago: University of Chicago Press.

Crenshaw, Kimberle. 1989. "Demarginalizing the Intersection of Race and Sex: A Black, Feminist Critique of Antidiscrimination Doctrine, Feminist Theory and Antiracist Politics." *University of Chicago Legal Forum* 1989, no. 1: 139–167.

Davalos, Karen Mary. 2003. La Quinceañera: Making Gender and Ethnic Identities. In *Perspectives on Las Américas: A Reader in Culture, History, and Representation,* edited by M. C. Gutmann, F. M. Rodríguez, L. Stephen, and P. Zavella, 299–316. Oxford: Blackwell.

de la Fuente, Alejandro. 2001. *A Nation for All: Race, Inequality and Politics in Twentieth Century Cuba.* Chapel Hill: University of North Carolina Press.

Eckstein, Susan Eva. 1994. *Back from the Future: Cuba under Castro.* Princeton, NJ: Princeton University Press.

———. 2004. Dollarization and its Discontents: Remittances and the Remaking of Cuba in the Post-Soviet Era. *Comparative Politics* 36, no. 3: 313–330.

Fariñas Acosta, Lisandra. 2018. Embarazo Adolescente, un Desafío para la Educación Integral de la Sexualidad. *Granma,* September 7, 2018. http://www.granma.cu/cuba/2018-09-07/embarazo-adolescente-un-desafio-para-la-educacion-integral-de-la-sexualidad-07-09-2018-13-09-56. Accessed October 2, 2019.

Fernandez, Nadine. 1999. "Back to the Future? Women, Race and Tourism in Cuba." In *Sun, Sex and Gold: Tourism and Sex Work in the Caribbean,* edited by K. Kempadoo, 81–89. New York: Rowman & Littlefield.

Gould, Jeremy, and Katja Uusihakala, eds. 2016. *Tutkija Peilin Edessä: Refleksiivisyys ja Etnografinen Tieto* Researcher in front of a mirror: Reflexivity and ethnographic knowledge]. Helsinki: Gaudeamus.

Hamilton, Carrie. 2012. *Sexual Revolutions in Cuba: Passion, Politics and Memory.* Chapel Hill: University of North Carolina Press.

Hansing, Katrin, and Bert Hoffmann 2019. "Cuba's New Social Structure: Assessing the Re-Stratification of Cuban Society 60 Years after Revolution." *GIGA Working Paper* 315, February 2019. Hamburg: GIGA.

Härkönen, Heidi. 2005. Quince Primaveras: Tyttöjen 15-vuotisjuhlat ja matrifokaalisuus Kuubassa [Quince Primaveras: Girls' Fifteenth Year Birthday Celebration and Matrifocality in Cuba]. Master's thesis, University of Helsinki.

———. 2011. "Girls' 15-Year Birthday Celebration as Cuban Women's Space Outside of the Revolutionary State." *ASA Online Journal: Association of Social Anthropologists of the UK and Commonwealth* 1, no. 44: 1–41. http://www.theasa.org/publications/asaonline.shtml.

———. 2014. *"To Not Die Alone": Kinship, Love and Life Cycle in Contemporary Havana, Cuba.* Helsinki: Unigrafia.

———. 2016a. *Kinship, Love, and Life Cycle in Contemporary Havana, Cuba: To Not Die Alone.* New York: Palgrave Macmillan.

———. 2016b. Intiimin etnografia: seksuaalisuus, sukupuolittunut väkivalta ja perhesuhteet Kuubassa [Intimate ethnography: Sexuality, gendered violence and family relations in Cuba]. In *Tutkija peilin edessä: refleksiivisyys ja etnografinen tieto* [Researcher in front of a mirror: Reflexivity and ethnographic knowledge], edited by J. Gould and K. Uusihakala, 165–192. Helsinki: Gaudeamus.

———. 2017. Havana's New Wedding Planners. *Cuba Counterpoints.* https://cubacounterpoints.com/.

La Fontaine, Jean S. 1985. *Initiation: Ritual Drama and Secret Knowledge across the World*. London: Pelican.

Lundgren, Silje. 2011. "Heterosexual Havana: Ideals and Hierarchies of Gender and Sexuality in Contemporary Cuba." PhD diss., Uppsala University.

Martinez, Hope. 2013. "From Social Good to Commodity, Reproducing Economic Inequalities." *Anthropology News* 54:11–37.

Martinez-Alier, Verena. 1974. *Marriage, Class and Colour in 19th Century Cuba: A Study of Racial Attitudes and Sexual Values in a Slave Society*. Cambridge: Cambridge University Press.

Napolitano, Valentina. 1997. Becoming a Mujercita: Rituals, Fiestas and Religious Discourses. *Journal of the Royal Anthropological Institute* 3, no. 2: 279–296.

ONEI 2020. Salario medio en cifras Cuba 2019. Oficina Nacional de Estadísticas e Información, Republica de Cuba.

http://www.onei.gob.cu/sites/default/files/salario_medio_2019_completa.pdf. Accessed July 1, 2021.

Pérez Hernández, Izuky. Izuky Photography (website).

http://www.izukyphotography.com/fotografo-de-quinceaneras-en-cuba/#. Accessed July 1, 2019.

Pertierra, Anna. 2015. "Cuban Girls and Visual Media: Bodies and Practices of (Still-) Socialist Consumerism." *Continuum: Journal of Media & Cultural Studies* 29, no. 2: 194–204.

Richards, Audrey. [1956] 1982. *Chisungu: A Girl's Initiation Ceremony among the Bemba of Northern Rhodesia*. London: Tavistock.

Safa, Helen. 2005. "The Matrifocal Family and Patriarchal Ideology in Cuba and the Caribbean." *Journal of Latin American Anthropology* 10, no. 2: 314–338.

Turner, Victor W. 1969. *The Ritual Process: Structure and Anti-Structure*. Chicago: Aldine.

Uriarte-Gaston, Miren. 2004. "Social Policy Responses to Cuba's Economic Crisis of the 1990s." *Cuban Studies* 35:105–136.

Van Gennep, Arnold. [1909] 1960. *The Rites of Passage*. Translated by Monika B. Vizedom and Gabrielle L. Caffee. Chicago: University of Chicago Press.

Wardlow, Holly. 2006. *Wayward Women: Sexuality and Agency in a New Guinea Society*. Berkeley: University of California Press.

14

Jamaican Realities of Masculinities and Sexualities

"How Far Have We Come since Michel Foucault?"

Natasha Kay Mortley and Keino T. Senior

LEARNING OBJECTIVES

- Explain the link between masculinities, sexualities, and the gendered relations of power.

- Situate masculinity studies within feminist scholarship.

- Describe Jamaican realities around manhood and sexualities.

In this chapter, the authors apply a gendered perspective to analyze views of masculinity among men from various socioeconomic groups in Jamaica. Using Michel Foucault's ideas of sexuality, they explain how the act of sexual intercourse is seen as more than the act itself but an essential part of one's identity. For Jamaican males, their sexualities are closely tied to their masculinities and what it means to be a Jamaican man. In this context, sexualities are both shaped by and influence power dynamics, not only between men and women but also among various groups of men.

INTRODUCTION

Masculinities scholarship within the Caribbean, and Jamaica specifically, has traditionally centered on family life (Chevannes 2001; Senior 2015), education (Miller 1991; Figueroa 1997), sexual violence, and violent crime (Mortley 2017). Discourse and understanding of male sexuality have been integral to the concept of and research on masculinities; in many ways, the concern with masculinities in the Caribbean has been fueled by the prevalence of sexual violence and the ineffectiveness of strategies to deal with it (Reddock 2004). Our chapter examines Jamaican masculinities and sexualities and seeks both a comprehensive understanding of as well as a move beyond the stereotypical Jamaican male sexuality with aggressive masculinities and issues of violence. This chapter is based on research we conducted in 2016 and 2017. Both studies were qualitative, using interviews and focus group studies with groups of men across various communities in Jamaica. The participants were urban and rural males of different ages and different socioeconomic and educational backgrounds. During the course of our research, we explored various identities, diverse expressions of manhood, power dynamics within the private and public spheres, and how these shaped sexualities. We explored how manhood and sexualities and power dynamics play out within gender relations and ask the question: to what extent is male sexuality constructed as a result of various gendered relations of power? Further, by examining Foucault's thesis on sexuality and its relevance to contemporary realities, we explored perceptions of male sexuality, how male sexualities manifest in various spaces, and the extent to which these perceptions and manifestations are contoured first by gendered power dynamics, as well as broader systems of power within society.

We begin with an overview of the Jamaican sociopolitical landscape, then we discuss how sexualities are situated within masculinities as well as Caribbean feminist scholarship. The key terms **masculinities** and **sexualities** have already been defined in the introductory chapter of this book, but we want to emphasize that both notions are embedded in historical, political, and sociocultural conditions of a particular society. In the 1990s scholarship shifted from the term "masculinity" (singular) toward the concept of "masculinities" (Connell 2005), which acknowledges that there are many forms of masculinity and that gender stratification also exists among men, not just between men and women. This shift in scholarship and discourse to acknowledging multiple "masculinities" recognizes that there are men who may or may not aspire to or fulfill local expectations of masculine performance (Connell 2016). Likewise, as it relates to the notion of sexuality, Weeks (1995) contends that sexuality is not given but is rather a product of negotiation, struggle, and human agency. He believes that sexuality only exists through its social forms and social organizations. In keeping with this conceptualization, we are of the view, like Kempadoo (2009), that for sexuality to be a viable springboard for research, its complexities need to be acknowledged, especially as it relates in this instance to Jamaican men's varied realities. For this reason, and in the same vein that we speak of "masculinities," we use the term "sexualities" in this paper, reflecting its complexity, diversity, and negotiated nature.

POSITIONALITY: MASCULINITIES AND SEXUALITIES RESEARCH AS PART OF OUR FEMINIST AGENDA

Feminism is not a singular or static notion, and the feminist movement and accompanying feminist research have evolved and expanded to explore wide-ranging issues that both directly and indirectly impact women's lives. Caribbean feminists today have generally adopted the **Gender and Development (GAD) approach** and contend that gender is both central and relevant to all social relations, institutions, and processes. They argue further that gender relations are characterized by patterns of domination, inequality, and oppression and that gender relations are the product of sociocultural and historic conditions. This GAD approach, which we apply to both our research and scholarship, has succeeded in improving understanding of gender and identifying new developmental challenges that require urgent attention from a gender perspective. In order for feminist scholarship to be truly feminist it cannot remain confined inside the walls of academia. It must be directed to influencing change as it relates to economic, political, and social developmental issues of the region and be integrated into related policies and programs designed to improve the lives of men and women for the betterment of Caribbean communities.

Gender and Development (GAD) approach originated in the 1980s and has been adopted by feminists who place gender at the center of development processes. It focuses on how social roles, reproductive roles, and economic roles are linked to gender inequalities of masculinity and femininity (Mortley 2017).

Masculinities research emerged out of feminist and gender studies in the Caribbean, and as Reddock (2004) reminds us, while some men took the opportunity to simply push back against the women's movement, for others it signaled a time for reflection on manifestations of manhood and masculinity in the Caribbean. Mohammed (2004) argues further that not only did masculinities studies come out of the feminist movement, but constructions of masculinity are interdependent with constructions of femininity. In keeping with this view posited by Mohammed, we believe that our feminist agenda should not only be concerned with femininities but should also seek to deconstruct masculinities and how these coalesce with and impact women's lives. Our positionality is that of feminist academics and scholars working within a gendered space. Natasha is a St. Lucian woman who has been residing and working in Jamaica for the past fifteen years, and Keino is a Jamaican man. We both teach and mentor young men and women within the Institute of Gender and Development Studies, and thus our concern is with how masculinities interact with femininities. When studying male sexualities, we seek to engage Jamaican males in order to better understand power relations not only among men but also between men and women. We understand that male sexualities exist within a gender system, which comprises relations between women and men, and men and men. Not only is masculinity part of this gender system, but positive masculinities contribute to better gender systems. As stated in the introductory chapter of this text, rather than focusing on defining masculinity as an object, we want to focus on the processes and relationships through which men and women conduct gendered lives. We agree with Barriteau (2019), who contends that the ongoing narrative on relations between men and women should seek to understand and not blame.

THE JAMAICAN CONTEXT

Jamaica is the largest of the English-speaking Caribbean islands and the third-largest island in the Caribbean. The country is divided into fourteen parishes, and Kingston, the capital, is located on the southeast coast. Jamaica's population was approximately 2.7 million at the end of 2018 (STATIN 2019). The vast majority of Jamaicans are of African descent (92.1 percent as of the 2011 census). The 2011 census also revealed that the majority of Jamaican males are single or have never been married (over 50 percent), while the second-largest group was married men. While relationship status of males within the Lesbian Gay Bisexual and Transgender (LGBT) community was not captured in the census, a survey conducted in 2016 among 316 persons from the LGBT community revealed that for males, 45 percent indicated that they were not in a relationship, 33 percent had a visiting partner and 15 percent lived with a partner (McFee and Galbraith 2016).

Jamaica is a patriarchal country where, along with the family, the state is historically and contemporaneously the most crucial purveyor of patriarchy. According to Thame and Thakur (2014) patriarchy of the Jamaican state is most concerned with domination by a specific group of men—that is, middle-class, heterosexual men—over society. They go on to state that "from its inception, the postcolonial state was captured by the Jamaican middle class and brown male, and control over it was later extended to the black middle-class male. In Jamaica, brown and black are used to distinguish between light skin and dark skin persons of African descent. Middle-class masculinity imposed itself as the legitimate power base within the state through symbolic manipulation and violence when it deemed necessary" (Thame and Thakur 2014, 12). This is still prevalent today in Jamaica, as we will discuss later in this chapter.

In 2011 the Jamaican government approved the National Policy for Gender Equality (NPGE). The policy sets a vision for gender equality and equity across all aspects of public and private life. Such policies recognize the unequal socioeconomic status of men and women, which are influenced by notions of masculinity and femininity that sustain patriarchy. Despite a long-standing tradition of activism in Jamaica and the establishment of strong policy frameworks, discussions around human rights and social justice remain controversial because of the lack of political will and a failure to actually implement a mechanism of protection for all. The extent to which policies have overcome or reduced inequalities and injustices in Jamaica thus remains questionable. In order to effectively overcome challenges, policies must be grounded in the specific sociocultural realities of gender in the countries where they are pursued. Studies such as ours are thus critical to providing authentic and contextualized knowledge that can inform planning, policies, and practices.

JAMAICAN MALE SEXUALITIES IN POPULAR CULTURE AND SCHOLARSHIP

Attitudes around sexuality in Jamaica are historically rooted in Victorian ideologies. Suzanne Lafont's 2001 study is one of the few that examine the colonial history of attitudes toward sexuality as they were expressed in Jamaica. She traces the development of Jamaica's sexual mores to slavery and British imposed Christianity. This Eurocentric view of sexuality forced an ideology of social respectability upon slaves and the belief that they were immoral and licentious individuals whose sexual appetites had to be tamed. Lafont's study tackled controversial issues such as attitudes toward female prostitution and male homosexuality in Jamaica, arguing that sexual intolerance in Jamaica is manifested in homophobia and public condemnation of heterosexual sodomy (such as oral sex). This sexual intolerance, she argues, stems from the slave era, which was characterized by a complex dialectic between colonial elites and Afro-Jamaicans. Historically, respectability and rectitude evolved as an Afro-Jamaican response to the slave experience.

McFee and Galbraith (2016) also contend that homophobia today is a legacy of the plantation system and reinforced by Jamaica's strong Christian faith. Homophobic sentiment persists as a source of national pride while also functioning to distance Afro-Jamaicans from their colonial past (Lafont 2001). The sentiment has been popularized through music and the arts. Scholars have noted that the sexual themes in Jamaican reggae for instance, often reflect homophobic views and identify the genre as a contributor to homophobia (Cooper 1994; Hope 2006; Sharpe and Pinto 2006). The literature has identified certain homophobic slurs such as "batty bwoy" or "chi chi man" and encouragement of violent acts that include murdering and burning gay men. There is no denying that the narrative has been overly negative.

On one hand, Jamaican culture is saturated with sexuality. Jamaican music, dance, and media feature implicit and explicit references to sexual behavior and practices. On the other hand, acceptable sexualities are narrowly defined, and Jamaicans themselves seem intolerant of sexual expressions that fall outside a strictly constructed paradigm of heteronormative activity. Brown middle-class males, who have the highest social status, manifest their masculinity through heterosexuality, respectability, and reproductive sexual activity. The popular dancehall genre of music in Jamaica, which has been one of the main outlets for expressing sexuality, has been characterized as policing the borders of Jamaican masculinity, encouraging heterosexuality and polygamy while discouraging cunnilingus, anal sex, and homosexuality (Sharpe and Pinto 2006).

In this area of scholarship, there has historically been a dearth of studies on Caribbean sexualities. While family dynamics including household and parenting dynamics in the Caribbean and Jamaica (Clarke 1957; Smith 1962) have long received attention from scholars, issues of sexualities (and male sexualities, specifically) have been understudied. Part of the forbidden nature of the subject according to Sharpe and Pinto (2006) had to do with a fear of reproducing the negative stereotyping of Black hypersexuality that emerged from a history of slavery and colonialism.

Recent work on gender roles and Caribbean masculinities has explored issues around sexuality (Chevannes 2001; Lewis 2003; Reddock 2004), and recent scholarship on sexuality has explored a broader range of sexualities (de Moya and Garcia 1996; Kimmel 1996; de Albuquerque 1998; Chin 1999; Phillips 1999; Mohammed 2004). The Spanish and French Caribbean countries have done prominent studies of male sexualities (Chanel 1994; Cabezas 1999). Gray et al. (2015) explored sexuality among fathers of newborns in Jamaica, where they assess sexual behaviors such as intercourse, as well as other facets of sexuality such as sexual desire and sexual satisfaction. They also explore relationship dynamics (e.g., relationship quality and availability of alternative partners) seen as important elements in contextualizing men's sexuality. Mark Figueroa is currently engaged in an in-depth examination of what sexuality means and how it manifests along a continuum. He contends that there is a need to extend the discussion in a way that considers the full range of what he refers to as the dimensions of human sexuality, thereby giving due regard to the complexity of the phenomenon. This work is important for Jamaica in terms of extending the discussion and analyses of male sexualities beyond the heterosexual mold.

Our work therefore emerges out of this context of burgeoning scholarship and public policy work around sexualities, as well as the need to engage men and give them a space to speak and reflect on their manhood and sexualities. We believe that this can help facilitate healthier relationships, foster better attitudes, and reduce gender-based violence within our communities. Our work aims to give men a space where they feel comfortable to unpack and perhaps unlearn all of those things that have been harmful and damaging to themselves, their families, and others. Our chapter, first and foremost, brings a more comprehensive understanding of masculinities and sexualities but also calls for a more nuanced understanding of Jamaican male realities. Our research goes beyond simple binaries, and we view sexuality on a continuum that recognizes and reflects the different modalities of manhood and masculinities.

FOUCAULT AND THE CONTEXT OF SEXUALITY AND POWER

Michel Foucault was a French historian and philosopher whose academic work came to prominence during the 1960s. We draw on Foucault's *History of Sexuality*, first published in 1976, in our analysis. His book's central argument is that sexuality is closely associated with structures of power in modern society. His work delves into an examination of sexual repression, sexual discourse, and societal power in the context of sexuality. For Foucault (1978) sexuality is not an obscure domain seeking to discover human beings, rather it is constructed historically, where there is an interrelationship between knowledge, power, body, and pleasure. Foucault describes this in his repression hypothesis, which is based on the widely held belief that during the Victorian era sex and sexuality were deliberately and systematically suppressed by unchallenged mechanisms of power within the state. As discussed earlier, the same applied in Jamaica during the slave era, where the planter class, as a matter of economic necessity and influenced by Victorian ideals, used power and force toward this suppression. This legacy continued during the colonial and postcolonial periods in Jamaica, where the elite class used various state machineries of power toward the same end. Foucault's writing on the repressive hypothesis raises some important questions still relevant today. These included whether power in society is really expressed mainly through repression and secondly whether our contemporary discourse on sexualities is a break with this history of repression or a part of that same history.

By the nineteenth century there was a shift from repression to an exploration of the "truth" of sexuality through confession and scientific inquiry. Part of this shift had to do with political necessity where the "truth" about sexuality had to be unearthed in order to deal with other ills plaguing society at the time. Knowledge of and discourse on sexualities thus remained under state influence, control, and power to the extent that the state exercised power over the construction of sexuality. The same can be said for Jamaica where a growing body of research and scholarship on toxic masculinities and sexualities responded to the need to address social ills such as gender-based violence, alcohol, drug abuse, the spread and impact of HIV/AIDS, and other sexually transmitted infections (Barker and Ricardo 2005). These same issues contribute to male sexualities being situated within gendered relations of power.

The Jamaican situation on male sexualities and power remains much the same as Foucault described it but with more nuance. Jamaican popular culture has never been repressed or silent. The dancehall space, as our respondents reminded us, has always been a space of free expressions of sexuality. The men that we interviewed spoke on the extent to which dancehall culture has been a main agent through which socialization on manhood and male sexualities has taken place in Jamaica. However, this freedom of expression has been related to only certain masculinities and sexualities. While the state has never really been able to police dancehall music and the dancehall space, dancehall culture has had its own internal mechanisms for policing the boundaries of male sexualities. Male sexualities are viewed as part of the everyday reality of being a Jamaican man—heterosexual, with the power to initiate and dictate the terms of sex.

Foucault explores how the idea of sexuality operates and is maintained within a system of power. He describes sexuality as not being a stubborn drive but a "transfer point for relations of power: between men and women" (Foucault 1978, 105). Ramirez (2004) agrees that masculinity is a multidimensional construct where power and sexuality interact in the construction of masculine identities. This means that while men collectively have power, as individuals that power is not experienced in the same way. Though not addressed by Foucault, when it comes to sexualities the Jamaican realities show us that power and the dynamics of power among men as a group can be analyzed through what Foucault terms "power relations." In our findings some men are powerless compared to other men and thus evaluate themselves differently. Thus, in order to understand how men express masculinities and sexualities, it is necessary to analyze broader inequalities and power dynamics within society. The differential access of men to power also entails hypothesizing in the existence of multiple masculinities, in which the margins of the representations of sexuality and gender identities are constantly being erased and redrawn (Ramirez 2004).

Our focus group discussions with males within the inner city reflected this association between power dynamics among males and their sexualities. The young men spoke about male police officers who had intimate sexual relations with the women who were also involved with them. "Police sleep with women here, these are our women, to find out more about our dealings in the community," said one male inner-city Kingston resident in his twenties. Our respondents believed that male officers who had positions of power and authority used sex to wield further power over the males and as a form of crime control within the communities. Our respondents thus spoke of feelings of powerlessness because of these sexual relations exercised by other men who represented "the system" and measured their sexual prowess against that of the policemen. This is reminiscent of Beckles (2004) who locates the early construction of Afro-Caribbean masculinity in the competitive and exploitative relationship between European and African males during slavery. He argues that the masculinity of Black slaves was constructed through its interaction with hegemonic structures of white masculinity, where white male power was based on control of property, including Black women.

Our respondents also spoke about the firearm as a symbol of Jamaican masculinities and sexualities. Carrying a firearm is commonplace and desirable among Jamaica men because they believe it gives them greater status. Carrying a firearm was also linked to sexualities because it was believed that women in Jamaica were attracted to men who carried firearms and that a man with a firearm could use it to get more women. "Having a gun, a licensed firearm is a way of displaying power. If you have one you are now elevated to a different level," said one professional male in his thirties. The firearm thus represented that link between power and sexualities in the Jamaican space.

SEX AND VIOLENCE

Though Foucault seldom delved into the concepts of sex and violence, when he did, he made reference to power and violence, adding that both are connected. For Foucault violence can be a drastic change or resistant to change, depending on historical and political agendas. He adds that violence can be harsh in an attempt to control individuals and their bodies. In Jamaica, men's sexualities are generally characterized as incorporating sex and violence. Kempadoo points to "stabbing in dancehall songs," whereby "the penis becomes a metaphorical dagger, stabbing pleasure into and out of the woman" (Cooper 2004, 13). Among Jamaican men, sexuality is perceived as being a site of pleasure for men and danger for women. As Kempadoo (2009) concludes, sexuality is powerful and violent and frequently acts as an economic resource, sustains polygamy, multiple partnerships, and polyamory, and is mediated by constructions of racism and ethnicity.

Hope (2006) indicates that men express their sexuality in dancehall culture within the confines of patriarchal, heterosexist, and elitist restrictions. Pieces of music played in dancehall reduce women to mere body parts, whereas men are celebrated for being promiscuous and aggressive. One of our interviewees, a Jamaican male academic in his forties, indicated that "men would be branded if they do not show aggressive masculinity, even without any proof of being man to avoid being branded as a homosexual." This is supported by Hope's (2006) argument that men who are unable to attain these attributes of masculinity are stereotyped as being gay. The Caribbean man still grapples with issues of emasculation he copes with through the medium of violence meted out especially on loved ones and in particular in the form of sexual violence (Marshall and Hallam 1993). During discussions in one of our mixed focus groups, participants indicated that

> males [are] always physically beating up the females and the females I guess most of them typically never physically fight back and so other females growing up sort of learned that as a behavior; and there is a thing though that a few females say dem [them] no want a man weh [who is] soft. So that's something to think about cause even though they are assertive they don't want a man they can bully. They tell you, if I feel like I can railroad you it's not going to work out; the typical Jamaican man is seen as bold and confident and aggressive so it is supposed to be one of many challenges. (Anonymous, focus group discussion by author)

The above illustrates that some men feel pressured to demonstrate violent sexuality, first by other men who will brand them as gay if they don't and secondly by women who will deem them "soft" if they don't.

One respondent lamented that homosexuality in Jamaica is characterized by "a special type of violence, where the batty man dem beat up and kill each other." In reference to cases of homosexuals being murdered in Jamaica, some respondents who agreed with the above statement were of the view that they were killed by their male partners who were driven by personal shame and rage brought on by pressures from having to cope with a homophobic sociocultural environment.

SEX AS PLEASURE AND SEX WITH MULTIPLE PARTNERS

Our findings corroborate Foucault's (1978) explanation that sexuality for men incorporates pleasure, and for our respondents such pleasure meant having multiple sexual partners. Our respondents were of the view that Jamaican males at an early age are pressured into engaging in sexual intercourse. In fact, a boy child is taught that he should have power over his female partner and should have several children to demonstrate his masculinity. Embedded in this, too, is an unwritten sexual and reproductive health law that every young Jamaican male must grapple with: "that he must have a steady girlfriend which makes him a man . . . and engaging in bareback sex—sex without a condom—is fine." (Anonymous, Focus group discussion by author). Furthermore, respondents believed that early sexual intercourse for males was influenced by lessons instilled in them as early as five years old. Males are taught from childhood that they are superior to women and should prove their manhood by engaging in sexual intercourse with multiple sexual partners. One respondent stated, "From man a youngster we are told to have plenty girlfriend," and a second respondent claimed, "the earlier the better:" (Anonymous, focus group discussion by author). These findings support Chevannes and Brown (1998), which concluded that men are expected to demonstrate sexual prowess and have serial or concurrent sexual partners and have several children. Also, our respondents measured their manhood by the number of children they are willing to bring into the world and also the number of women that they have those children with, to provide for their family, and also to ensure that their children are raised in such a way that they will become citizens who will contribute to society.

While our respondents believed this to be the way that young men are generally socialized, some made it clear that they did not subscribe to this behavior and that their personal experiences did not reflect this. One respondent explained: "I came from the ghetto where I saw that kind of behavior, with my father, my grandfather, my uncle . . . but now I don't live my life like that, and I don't want that for my son. Everything mi see mi father do, I try to do the complete opposite" (Anonymous, focus group discussion by author). This, we believe, indicates that not all Jamaican men subscribe to or perform the same masculinities. There are men who will publicly speak out against promiscuity among Jamaican males.

When respondents were asked whether young men generally have multiple sexual partners, one respondent answered, "It is the norm for men to have more than one sex partner, you can have many sex partners." In the inner city, young men believed that the ideal was seven women to one man: "Yes miss seven is de ideal, but due to economic hardships now it may be reduced to three women per man," said one inner-city resident in his twenties. Among men of middle to upper socioeconomic status, there was a general perception, even among women from other islands, that the Jamaican male is more promiscuous than men from other islands. This is reinforced through the popular culture, for example, in the dancehall. The lyrics of songs are usually laced with tunes explicitly suggesting that a man must have more than one woman, as this will help to identify him as a real man. This is similar to what Foucault refers to as the psychiatrization of perverse pleasure. This is referred to as the sexual instinct that "is biologically and physically distinct afflictions for which treatments could be sought" (Foucault 1978, 104). For example, one respondent stated that "sex is everything . . . if you don't have sex, you are a clown or other men will hate you." Another respondent stated that "sex is pleasurable, it is how you lose your oil and show a woman you rule." Yet another respondent stated that "when you have sex, you feel like a super king and you show a woman who is in charge . . . it makes you feel like a man." While another stated that "I have to prove that I am a girl's man . . . more woman the sweeter the sex is."

Respondents believed that these sexual acts were not only very pleasurable but also symbolized what makes one a man and forms his masculinity. This for respondents demonstrates strength and the "ability to stick to one's code of honor." However, a different view of masculinity surfaced during our group discussions. One respondent believed that "to be a man is not only to portray a masculine nature, homosexual men have strong[er] trait of masculinities than some heterosexual males." While this was not the shared view of most respondents, they all agreed that masculinity linked to sexuality was a part of their culture and history, which informs them about what is ideal for them as males. Our findings thus revealed that male sexualities with multiple partners represented both pleasure within relationships with women, as well as power vis-à-vis other men.

SEXUALITY AND GENDER RELATIONS

Jamaican men are socialized about sexualities along gender lines, which are rooted in a deeply entrenched gender system. The popular saying "loose the bull and tie the heifer" symbolizes this gender stereotype related to sexuality where boys are socialized differently than girls. All of the male participants irrespective of background subscribed to this view. According to Barriteau (2003) the material system is how the power dynamics between men and women are maintained and accepted socially, which affects how they gain access to material resources. While the nonmaterial system is how the ideological effects of said gender relations impact how women access material resources, status, and power. These paradigms reflect a clear interdependent relationship between ideology and resources of a social system, on the one hand, and sex stratification and status based on differential access to material and nonmaterial rewards on the other. This impacts the power construction of sexualities, directly or indirectly, in Foucault's (1978) discourse on sexuality and power specifically.

This power is manifested in the ways men are socialized to be protectors of their family, providers, and by extension have control over bodies, including women's (and other men's) bodies. Lessons that are instilled from an early age usually translate into sexuality and power in adulthood. Foucault describes sexuality as not being a stubborn drive but a "transfer point for relations of power: between men and women" (Foucault 1978, 103). On the other hand, one aspect of power for Foucault is conceived as performing a negative function, particularly in relation to sex. Jamaican men's realities corroborate Foucault's **hysterization** of women's bodies. He explains the hysterization of women's bodies as belonging to men in three relevant ways: medically/socially in the sense that the woman's body had the potential to produce many children, secondly in a family setting the woman had to play a substantial/main role, and thirdly the female had to be mother to the children that she produced as a matter of biological-moral responsibility (Foucault 1978). Some respondents in the study believed that women were expected to play the role of good mothers, as that was a part of their biology. One male respondent in his forties from rural Jamaica stated that "women are to stay home and take care of the family that is what they were born to do." These findings support Foucault's socialization of procreative behavior phenomena. For Foucault, this means treating the body or bodies of couples as somewhat belonging to the state and promoting social responsibility in the form of birth control practices. Not all respondents agreed with this, however. Our respondents in their twenties to late thirties believed that gender roles in Jamaica had changed and that women were no longer expected to be seen in this way. University-educated males particularly stressed this view.

While respondents thought it was wrong to force women to have sex with them, they also stated that they did not expect women to refuse sex with them. One respondent stated clearly that "women [should] not to hold off on a guy when him want sex from her . . . I don't mean he is to rape her, but she must just go along with having sex with him" (Anonymous, focus group discussions by author). This is in keeping with Foucault's belief that sex and sexuality were closely linked to unchallenged power mechanisms of male domination. This also plays out in some spaces in Jamaica as it relates to suppressing homosexuality in response to power mechanisms of male domination.

Our respondents believed that the state supports and reinforces many of the messages related to male sexuality. One respondent stated that "men's roles and what they do sexually is not only taught in the family, but government and society teach and reward us about what we are to do from a sexuality stance." This is in keeping with Foucault's suggestion that sexuality is used as a device of power within broader systems of power within society. The personages that Foucault mentioned as growing out of psychiatry are broad generalizations, some resonating and others a tad questionable, especially in a Jamaican context. Foucault speaks of everything as being about power and power being everywhere; but in a Jamaican context there is not much power in the margins, as heterosexuality is the dominant power construct. One respondent postulated that "sexual freedom is important because you get to express how you feel and what is it that you find pleasurable sexually . . . I think I have about 45 percent sexual freedom as a heterosexual man, but if me was homosexual I wouldn't have that freedom." Yet another respondent echoed similar sentiments that "as a straight male [heterosexual male] I have power and sexual freedom but only to do straight stuff [heterosexual sexual activities]."

TOWARD A CONCLUSION WITHOUT END

Foucault's writings have been instrumental in creating the atmosphere of intrigue and interest around sex and sexuality and related dynamics of power. Foucault argued that while repression and prohibition of sex prior to the nineteenth century may have been real, discourses around sex were always present, albeit in diverse ways. In Jamaica, while popular culture always spoke about male sexualities, there has been some repression by confining it within certain gendered norms and expectations. It is only in recent years that scholarship and discourse have begun to push beyond those boundaries in exploring different male sexualities. Likewise, men today are more open in voicing alternative views on masculinities and sexualities, as seen through our research.

Foucault expands the development and impact of power from the limited sovereign aspects to more phenomenological application, through "population" synergistic with the spread of social relations. Power, Foucault argues, is not simply concerned with domination by law, but it is also exercised through the social and physical body. This may have been a controversial and considerable shift in thought, and it is the deployment of sexuality, Foucault writes, that was crucial to this modification. Sexuality can be seen as an axis or transfer point of relations of power and one with great agency "useful for the greatest number of maneuvers and capable of serving as a point of support, as a linchpin, for the most varied strategies" (Foucault 1978, 103). Foucault's explanation of sexuality makes the act of sexual intercourse into not only the act itself but an essential part of one's being or identity. For Jamaican males, their sexualities are closely tied to their masculinities and their everyday realities of what it means to be a Jamaican man. Further, sexualities are both shaped by and influence power dynamics, not only between men and women but also among various groups of men.

Foucault's explanation that sexuality is in every facet of human social existence is useful. However, in the application of Foucault's thesis to the Jamaican context, it is important to understand the context of his writing, his own race and citizenship (a white French man), and the political, economic, and social biases of his society toward colonized countries like Jamaica. The use of his thesis as a point of reference to Jamaican realities impacts the ways we consciously or unconsciously experience, understand, and explain sexualities. It also provides a reference point for the deconstruction of and reflection on the sexualities of Jamaican males. In our research it helped us to think more fully about constructions of male sexualities and to explore various ways and spaces within which power manifests and contours issues around male sexualities. In this way his work remains relevant today.

RESOURCES FOR FURTHER EXPLORATION

- Anderson, P. 2017. "The Impact of Masculinity Ideologies and Conjugal Involvement on Sexual Risk-Taking among Young

Jamaican Males." *American Journal of Men's Health* 16, no. 1: 50–66. http://doi.org/10.3149/jmh.1601.49.

- Kempadoo, K. 2003. "Sexuality in the Caribbean: Theory and Research (with an Emphasis on the Anglophone Caribbean)." *Social and Economic Studies* 52, no. 3: 59–88. http://www.jstor.org/stable/27865341. Accessed July 12, 2021.

- Levtov, R., and Telson, L. 2021. "Man-Box: Males and Masculinity in Jamaica." Inter American Development Bank (IDB), Gender and Diversity Division. March 2021. https://publications.iadb.org/publications/english/document/Man-Box-Men-and-Masculinity-in-Jamaica.pdf.

REVIEW QUESTIONS

1. What is your understanding of Jamaican masculinities and sexualities?

2. What is the relationship between sexualities and gendered power relations in Jamaica? Can you use an intersectional analysis to think about them?

3. Discuss the ways in which Foucault's sexuality thesis is or isn't relevant to realities of Jamaican males today?

KEY TERMS

Gender and Development (GAD) approach: originated in the 1980s and has been adopted by feminists who place gender at the center of development processes. It focuses on how social roles, reproductive roles, and economic roles are linked to gender inequalities of masculinity and femininity (Mortley 2017).

BIBLIOGRAPHY

Armstrong, P. B. 2005. "Phenomenology." *Johns Hopkins Guide to Literary Theory and Criticism*. 2nd ed. Edited by Michael Groden, Martin Kreiswirth, and Imre Szeman. Baltimore, MD: Johns Hopkins University Press. https://litguide.press.jhu.edu.

Barker, Gary, and Dean Peacock. 2014. "Working with Men and Boys to Prevent Gender-Based Violence: Principles, Lessons Learned, and Ways Forward." *Men and Masculinities* 17, no. 5: 578–599.

Barriteau, Eudine. 2003. *Confronting Power, Theorizing Gender: Interdisciplinary Perspectives in the Caribbean*. Kingston: UWI Press.

———. 2019. "What Love Has to Do with It? Sexuality, Intimacy and Power in Contemporary Caribbean Gender Relations." *Caribbean Review of Gender Studies* 13:297–330.

Beasley, C. 2010. The Elephant in the Room: Heterosexuality in Critical Gender/Sexuality Studies. *NORA: Nordic Journal of Women's Studies* 18, no. 3: 204–209.

Beauvoir, Simone de. 1989. *The Second Sex*. New York: Vintage.

Beckles, Hilary with Verene A. Shepherd. 2004. *Liberties Lost: The Indigenous Caribbean and Slave Systems*. Cambridge: Cambridge University Press.

Blank, H. 2012. *Straight: The Surprisingly Short History of Heterosexuality*. Boston: Beacon.

Bliss, S. 1987. "Revisioning Masculinity: A Report on the Growing Men's Movement." *In Context: Celebrating Our Journeys as Women and Men*, Spring 1987, 21.

Butler, Judith. 1993. "Subjects of Sex/Gender/Desire" in *The Cultural Studies Reader* edited by Simon During, 340–353. London: Routledge.

Chambers, C., and Barry Chevannes. 1991. *Report on Six Focus Group Discussions: Report for the Project on Sexual Decision-making among Men and Women in Jamaica*. Kingston: AIDSTECH.

Chevannes, Barry. 1998. *Rastafari and other African-Caribbean Worldviews*. London: Macmillan.

———. 1999. *What You Sow and What We Reap: Problems in the Cultivation of Male Identity in Jamaica*. Kingston: Grace Kennedy Foundation.

———. 2001. *Learning to Be a Man: Culture, Socialization and Gender Identity in Five Caribbean Communities*. Kingston: University of the West Indies Press.

Clarke E. 1957. *My Mother Who Fathered Me: A Study of the Family in Three Selected Communities in Jamaica*. London: George Allen and Unwin.

Code, Lorraine. 1995. *What Can She Know? Feminist Theory and the Construction of Knowledge*. Ithaca, NY: Cornell University Press.

Collins, Patricia Hill. 2000. *Black Feminist Thought: Knowledge, Consciousness, and the Politics of Empowerment*. New York: Routledge.

———. 2005. *Black Sexual Politics African Americans, Gender, and the New Racism*. New York: Routledge. http://www.library.yorku.ca/e/resolver/id/2440805.

Connell, Raewyn. 2005. *Masculinities*. Cambridge, UK: Polity.

———. 2016. "The Social Organization of Masculinity. In *Exploring Masculinities: Identity, Inequality, Continuity, and Change*, edited by C. J. Pascoe and T. Bridges, 136–144. New York: Oxford University Press.

Connell, Raewyn, and James W. Messerschmidt. 2005. "Hegemonic Masculinity: Rethinking the Concept." *Gender & Society* 19, no. 6: 829–859.

Cooper, Carolyn. 2004. *Sound Clash: Jamaican Dancehall Culture at Large*. New York: Palgrave Macmillan.

Creswell, John. 2013. *Qualitative Inquiry & Research Design: Choosing Among the Five Approaches*. Thousand Oaks, CA: SAGE.

Crotty, M. 1998. *The Foundations of Social Research: Meaning and Perspective in the Research Process*. Los Angeles: SAGE.

Dean, James Joseph. 2016. *Straights: Heterosexuality in Post-closeted Culture*. New York: NYU Press. https://doi.org/10.18574/nyu/9780814762752.001.0001.

Hope, Donna. 2006. *Inna Di Dancehall*. Kingston: UWI.

———. 2010. *Man Vibes: Masculinities in the Jamaican Dancehall*. Kingston: Ian Randle.

Figueroa, Mark. n.d. "Towards a Framework for a Dialogue on the Dimensions of Human Sexuality: Beyond a Uni-Dimensional Notion of Orientation." (Unpublished manuscript).

Foucault, Michel. 1978. *The History of Sexuality*. 1st ed. New York: Pantheon.

———. 1979. *Discipline and Punish the Birth of the Prison*. New York: Vintage.

Gray, P. B. 2015. Sexuality among Men with Newborns in Jamaica. *BMC Pregnancy Childbirth* 15, no. 44 (2015). https://www.ncbi.nlm.nih.gov/pmc/articles/PMC4337314/pdf/12884_2015_Article_475.pdf.

Grow, Anne. 2018. "The Meaning of Sexuality: A Critique of Foucault's History of Sexuality Volume 1." Master's thesis, Brigham Young University. https://scholarsarchive.byu.edu/etd/6744.

James, C. E., and Davis, A. 2019. "Jamaican Males Readings of Masculinities and the Relationship to Violence." *Caribbean Review of Gender Studies: A Journal of Caribbean Perspectives of Gender and Feminism* 8, 79–112.

Katz, J. 2014. "Working with Men and Boys to Prevent Gender-Based Violence: Principles, Lessons Learned and Ways Forward." *Men and Masculinities* 17, no. 5: 578–599.

Kempadoo, Kamala. 2009. "Caribbean Sexuality: Mapping the Field." *Caribbean Review of Gender Studies* 3.

Kimmel, Michael. 1994. "Masculinity as Homophobia: Fear, Shame, and Silence in the Construction of Gender Identity." In *Theorizing Masculinities*, edited by Harry Brod and Michael Kaufman, 119–141. Thousand Oaks, CA: SAGE.

Levy, Horace. 2012. "A Community Approach to Community and Youth Violence in Jamaica." Keynote address presented at *Being Proactive Forum*, York Centre for Education & Community, York University, Toronto.

Lafont, Suzanne. 2001. "Very Straight Sex: The Development of Sexual More's in Jamaica." *Journal of Colonialism and Colonial History* 2, no. 3. http://muse.jhu.edu/journals/journal_of_colonialism_and_colonial_history/v002/2.3lafont.html.

Lewis, Linden. 2003a. "Caribbean Masculinity: Unpacking the Narrative." In *The Culture of Gender and Sexuality in the Caribbean.*, 94–125. Gainesville: University Press of Florida.

———, ed. 2003b. *The Culture of Gender and Sexuality in the Caribbean*. Gainesville: University Press of Florida.

Marshall, Annecka, and Julian Hallam. 1993. "Layer of Difference: The Significance of a Self-reflexive Research Practice for a Feminist Epistemological Project." In *Making Connections: Women's Studies, Women's Movements, Women's Lives*, 64–65. Warwick, UK: Warwick University Press.

McFee, R., and E. Galbraith. 2016. "The Developmental Cost of Homophobia: The Case of Jamaica." *Washington Blade*, January. http://www.washingtonblade.com/content/files/2016/01/The-Developmental-Cost-of-Homophobia-The-Case-of-Jamaica_2016-1.pdf.

Messerschmidt, James W. 2000. *Nine Lives: Adolescent Masculinities, the Body, and Violence*. Boulder, CO: Westview.

Mohammed, Patricia. 2004. "Unmasking Masculinity and Deconstructing Patriarchy: Problems and Possibilities within Feminist Epistemology." In *Interrogating Caribbean Masculinities: Theoretical and Empirical Analyses*, edited by Rhoda Reddock, 38–67. Kingston: University of the West Indies Press.

Mortley, Natasha Kay. 2017. *Contemporary Caribbean Masculinities: A Pilot Study of Males, Community and Crime in Jamaica*. Report prepared for the UNESCO National Commission in Jamaica.

Oksala, Johanna. 2012. *Foucault, Politics, and Violence*. Evanston, IL: Northwestern University Press.

Peacock, D., and G. Barker. 2014. "Working with Men and Boys to Prevent Gender-Based Violence: Principles, Lessons Learned and Ways Forward." *Men and Masculinities* 17, no. 5: 578–599.

Ramirez, R. L. 2004. "Interrogating Caribbean Masculinities: An Introduction." In *Interrogating Caribbean Masculinities: Theoretical and Empirical Analyses*, edited by Rhoda Reddock. Kingston, Jamaica: University of the West Indies Press, 1–3.

Reddock, Rhoda, ed. 2004. *Interrogating Caribbean Masculinities: Theoretical and Empirical Analyses*. Kingston: University of the West Indies Press.

Senior, Keino. 2015. "Gender Ideologies in Caribbean Drama Text." *Jonkonnu Arts Journal* 2 no. 1: 12–18.

Sharpe, J., and S. Pinto. 2006. "The Sweetest Taboo: Studies of Caribbean Sexualities." *Journal of Women in Culture and Society* 32, no. 1: 247–272.

Smith, M. G. 1962. *West Indian Family Structure*. Seattle: University of Washington Press.

STATIN. The Statistical Institute of Jamaica. https://statinja.gov.jm.

Thame, Maziki, and Dhanaraj Thakur. 2014. "The Patriarchal State and the Development of Gender Policy in Jamaica." In *Politics, Power and Gender Justice in the Anglophone Caribbean: Women's Understandings of Politics, Experiences of Political Contestation and the Possibilities for Gender Transformation*. IDRC Research Report 106430-001. Ottawa, ON: International Development Research Centre.

Totten, Mark. 2003. "Girlfriend Abuse as a Form of Masculinity Construction among Violent, Marginal Male Youth." *Men and Masculinities* 6, no. 1: 70–92.

Weeks, Jeffrey. 1995. *Sexuality*. London and New York: Routledge.

Yeng, S. 2010. "Foucault's Critique of the Science of Sexuality: The Function of Science within Bio-power." *Journal of French and Francophone Philosophy* 18, no. 1: 9–26.

Part V

The Global North
(North America and Europe)

CIA Maps.

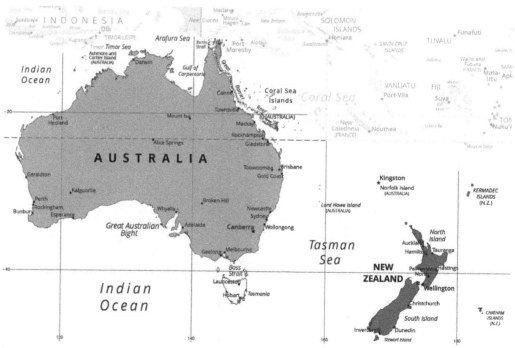

CIA Maps.

15

The Global North

Introducing the Region

Lara Braff and Katie Nelson

What is the **Global North**? The Global North does not refer to a geographic region in any traditional sense but rather to the relative power and wealth of countries in distinct parts of the world (figure 15.1). The chapters in this section explore the construction and complexity of gender within the Global North: particularly, the United States, Canada, and Belgium. To do so, we first consider how the Global North and South divide came to exist in the popular imagination. However, we should note that although the Global North is on the whole powerful and wealthy, it is not monolithic. Societies within it are internally stratified and diverse such that not everyone in the Global North is rich and powerful.

Attempts to categorize the world order have been based more on politics and economics than geography. These include East and West;

Global North
does not refer to a geographic region in any traditional sense but rather to the relative power and wealth of countries in distinct parts of the world. The Global North encompasses the rich and powerful regions such as North America, Europe, and Australia.

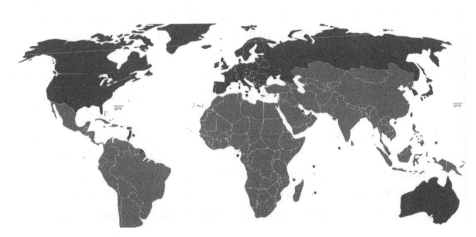

Figure 15.1. The Global North (in blue) includes many countries in the Northern Hemisphere and also some, such as Australia and New Zealand, that are located in the Southern Hemisphere. The Global South (in red) includes many countries in the southern hemisphere and some in the northern hemisphere. Kingj123/Public Domain.

289

developed and developing nations; and the First, Second, and Third Worlds. For example, if East/West were geographic entities, then all nations west of the Prime Meridian (i.e., the United States, Canada, and Latin America nations) would be grouped together, while all nations to the east (i.e., countries of Europe, Africa, and Asia) would be grouped together. But this is not the case. Rather, the "West" is meant to refer to countries—particularly European nations and the United States—that benefited from the exploits of colonialism, achieving a higher quality of life and more power than the East. Similarly, the terminology of "developed" and "developing" nations indexes a power differential along with the ethnocentric assumption that all countries follow a singular idealized trajectory. Anthropologists and social theorists have critiqued this notion, insisting that societies change over time, proceeding along varied developmental paths.

The First, Second, and Third World terminology developed in the mid-twentieth century during the Cold War to categorize nations based on their participation in the conflict between the democratic United States (and its allies) and the Communist Soviet Union (and its allies). The First World was said to include economically developed, high-income, politically stable capitalist nations. The Second World comprised Communist nations that despite stable incomes and decent social conditions were viewed by the First World as economically and politically unstable due to their totalitarian governments. The Third World referred to previously colonized nations (nonaligned) that both the United States and the Soviet Union were trying to incorporate into their respective political-economic orders. Third World leaders have critiqued this schema, asserting that they were not just pawns in the US-Soviet conflict; rather, they were actively engaged in improving their own social conditions, creating stable national identities, and participating in the global community (e.g., in the 1960s, some Third World countries joined the United Nations for the first time).

In the late twentieth century, the Global North and South terminology replaced previous descriptors of the global order. It was generally agreed that the Global North would include the United States, Canada, England, nations of the European Union, as well as Singapore, Japan, South Korea, and even some countries in the southern hemisphere: Australia, and New Zealand. The Global South, on the other hand, would include formerly colonized countries in Africa and Latin America, as well as the Middle East, Brazil, India, and parts of Asia. Many of these countries are still marked by the social, cultural, and economic repercussions of colonialism, even after achieving national independence. The Global South remains home to the majority of the world's population, but that population is relatively young and resource-poor, living in economically dependent nations.

Like prior attempts to characterize nations, the Global North/South distinction simplifies the world order, ignoring internal variation within both the North and South, while negating commonalities that exist between these large and diverse entities. Further, there are outliers that muddy the attempt to specify a clear North/South divide. For example, where do China, Russia, and Saudi Arabia fit? In terms of their economies and power, they resemble the North, but their political and social organization can also resemble the South. All global terminology systems discussed here are historically situated, politicized attempts to organize nations into a straightforward world order that is, in fact, quite complicated and increasingly interconnected.

THE WORLD ECONOMY

A rapidly globalized economy has highlighted the imagined divide between the North and South. According to Wallerstein's **world systems theory**, a global capitalist system separates countries into the core (the North), semiperiphery, and periphery (the South) based primarily on their economic participation (Wallerstein 1974). His theory is largely influenced by Karl Marx, who saw the economy as the foundation of society that determined all cultural phenomena. According to Marx, under capitalism, societies are composed of the bourgeoisie (the owners who control the means of production, e.g., the factories) and the workers (who labor and produce goods in exchange for wages). The owner's motive to maximize profit is achieved by exploiting the workers, who are paid less than what their labor is worth and who grow alienated from themselves, other people, and their labor. Despite the ideological attempts of the owners to obscure exploitation, Marx believed that the workers would eventually realize the systemic injustices of capitalism, rise up, and replace it with Communism.

For Wallerstein, similar actors and structural inequalities operate within the global capitalist system. The core nations of the Global North act like the owners, controlling multinational corporations that extract raw material and exploit labor from peripheral nations of the Global South. The core nations thereby amass profit that benefits them, hardening the divide between the haves and have-nots. Thus, core nations remain wealthy, politically stable, and culturally dominant, while peripheral nations remain economically dependent, politically unstable, and at the mercy of cultural trends. The semiperipheral nations are said to be in transition from the periphery to the core (see figure 15.2).

Like all binaries, the division of the world into core and periphery, North and South, is overly simplistic and assumes these are fundamentally

world systems theory Developed by Emmanuel Wallerstein to describe a global capitalist system that separates countries into the core (the North), semiperiphery, and periphery (the South) based primarily on their economic participation.

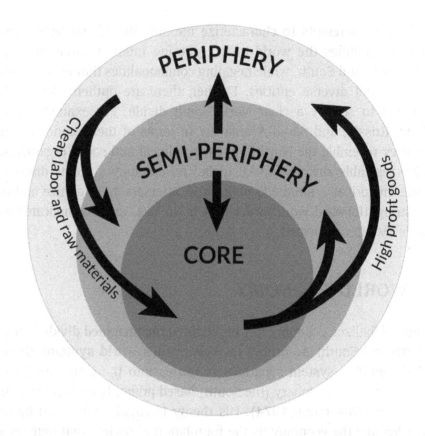

Figure 15.2. The world systems theory explains global inequality by emphasizing the extraction of natural resources (and low-skilled, labor-intensive goods) from countries in the periphery and semiperiphery and the exportation of (high-capital and high-skilled) finished goods from the core. Katie Nelson.

glocalization

a combination of the words "globalization" and "localization." Refers to ways that a cultural product is developed by one culture and adopted by the local culture to accommodate local needs and preferences.

globalization

the worldwide intensification of social and economic interactions and interdependence between disparate parts of the world.

different and unequal entities. Yet, we are not a world indelibly marked as wealthy or poor, producers or consumers, powerful or powerless. For many anthropologists, the world order is far more complex and interrelated. They consider, for example, the process of **glocalization**, whereby people around the world alter globalized goods, ideas, and practices to fit their own lived experiences. This is not the passive, wholesale adoption of Global Northern lifeways but the active adaptation of them into culturally relevant forms. Similarly, **globalization** does not just flow from the North to the South. From food to clothes to music and media, people in the Global North also consume and adapt the cultural products of the Global South.

Arjun Appadurai addresses this complexity by describing several global "scapes": social and cultural flows that move around the world in multiple directions, affecting nations and people in diverse ways. As he puts it, the "new global cultural economy has to be seen as a complex, overlapping, disjunctive order" (Appadurai 1996, 32). This order comprises five "scapes":

- ethnoscape (the movement of people)
- financescape (the movement of money)

- technoscape (the movement of technologies)

- mediascapes (the movement of media)

- ideoscapes (the movement of ideas)

These globalscapes are interlinked. Take, for example, cell phones: as objects, they are part of the technoscape that people use to access the mediascape through which they engage with the ideoscape. This idea of globalscapes helps us see the dynamic nature of people, things, and ideas that interact to defy any simplistic static division of North and South.

ENGENDERING THE GLOBAL NORTH

While globalization is an interactive process, the Global North has unde-niably played a leading role in it. The economic, political, and cultural **hegemony** of the Global North, hardened by colonialism, has affected many aspects of social life elsewhere, including gender. As anthropologists and gender scholars argue, there is nothing natural or universal about the North's binary gender system (male/female). There are other options: anthropological studies have described nonbinary gender systems with varied levels of gender inequality. For example, the Two-Spirit category among some Native American societies is a third gender category, one that recognizes that an individual's gender identity may not be the same as their **cisgender** embodiment. Two-Spirit individuals possess both male and female qualities that uniquely position them to interact with the supernatural realm. This is not considered to be a transgressive category but rather a transcendent one.

In the Global North, however, there exists a dominant portrayal of gender as a strict binary: male or female, whereby male is privileged over female. This was not always the case: the archaeological record and observations of modern hunting and gathering groups (used as a model for early human societies that were likewise small-scale, family-based, and fairly egalitarian) reveal societies with gender roles but less gender stratification. Such societies cannot afford to exclude half the population— the women—from the daily work of subsistence and survival. Indeed, women, in both ancient and modern hunting and gathering groups, make an essential contribution that complements men's activities. For example, these women supply the majority of the group's daily calories through the arduous labor of gathering wild plants and digging up tubers. It was only recently in human history, about ten thousand years ago with the advent of agriculture and permanent settlements, that a strict division

hegemony
the dominance of one group over another supported by legitimating norms and ideas that normalize dominance. Using collective consent rather than force, dominant social groups maintain power and social inequalities are naturalized.

cisgender
refers to people whose gender identity corresponds to their sex at birth.

of labor emerged that served to lower women's status. Men began to dominate the public sphere, relegating women to the (devalued) private domestic sphere. We see this gender hierarchy perpetuated within several domains, including philosophy, Christianity, and science.

Early Greek philosophers like Aristotle (384–322 BCE) and Galen (130–210 AD) were convinced of men's innate dominance over women. As Aristotle (1905, 34) writes: "The male is by nature superior, and the female inferior; and the one rules and the other is ruled; this principle, of necessity, extends to all mankind." This statement asserts a *universal* inequality between the sexes that justifies women's subservience to men. The Bible, and texts from other Abrahamic religions, convey similar ideas, as reflected by this famous quote from the Book of Genesis (2: 7):

> And the Lord God constructed the rib which He had taken from the earth-creature into a woman and brought her to the earth-man. And the earth-man said, this time is bone of my bone and flesh of my flesh. She shall be called wo-man, for from man was she taken.

Throughout the Middle Ages (fourth to fourteenth century), many stories in the Bible were read as reinforcing male superiority. Men were often portrayed as prominent actors, with women making secondary contributions. As people saw the church as a prominent source of authority, they further internalized this gender ideology.

It is not until the Enlightenment (1650–1800), or the so-called Age of Reason, that new sources of authority emerge as people use scientific principles to challenge biblical accounts of the world. Through firsthand investigations of nature and society, people were no longer dependent on religious authority to answer their questions; they could now seek answers via their own empirical observations and rationality. Yet, there was nothing truly "objective" about these scientific inquiries. With respect to gender, a **misogynous** view of women still influenced the questions and answers of (predominantly male) scientists.

misogynous/misogyny refers to the contempt or hatred for women, often expressed as prejudice or discrimination.

Take, for example, the question of whether men are more intelligent than women. In the eighteenth century, "scientific" illustrations of male and female bodies grossly exaggerated their proportions, showing males with extremely large heads and females with small heads but large hips (see figure 15.3) that conveyed their alleged inferior intellect and their fundamental child-bearing function (Biewen 2018).

Later, in the nineteenth century, the gender question was addressed through the then-popular pseudoscience of phrenology: the examination of skull features that allegedly reveal mental qualities and character. Such

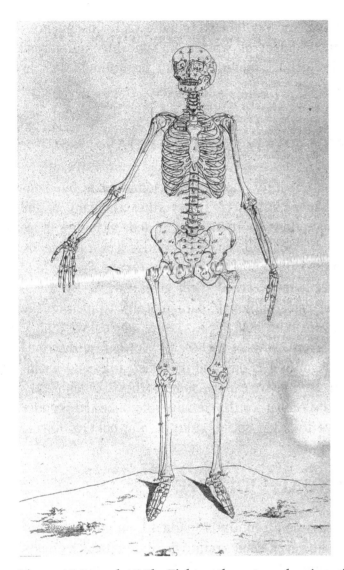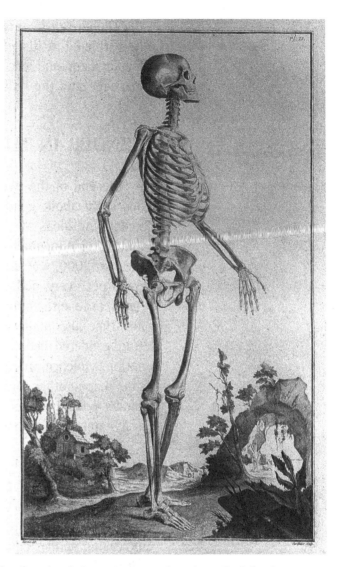

Figure 15.3a and 15.3b. Eighteenth-century drawing of a female skeleton annotated and studied for its deviation from the male skeleton. Women were depicted with much smaller skulls than men. Wellcome Trust/ CC 4.0 International license.

analyses pointed to women's "low foreheads" as proof that they lacked the necessary cognitive abilities for participation in intellectual pursuits (Staum 2003, 64). We now explain differences in male and female skull size as due to sexual dimorphism: since male bodies are (on average) slightly larger than female bodies, their skulls must be proportionate to the rest of their bodies. Further, there is no proven correlation between skull size and brain function: skull size does not correlate with intellectual capacity (Gould 1981). Nevertheless, the attempt to scientifically prove men's worth, like the attempt to theologically prove women's secondary status, served to affirm a strict binary gender hierarchy. In many parts of the Global North, this hierarchy has had profound social consequences: it justified the disenfranchisement of women in civic life and formal employment and excluded gender minorities from institutions such as marriage and the military.

GENDER IN THE GLOBAL NORTH TODAY

By the end of the twentieth century, most of the claims made by pseudoscience about gender had been corrected. Nevertheless, many of the underlying ideas and assumptions it produced persisted, including those that justified inequality for women and gender minorities. For instance, by the year 2000, women in the United States on average earned seventy-one cents per every dollar that a man earned (Graf et al. 2019). By 2020, that rate rose to eighty-five cents, although, paradoxically, women for the first time also made up more than half the workforce (Omeokwe 2020). Transgendered people in many parts of the Global North face discrimination, violence, anemic legal protections and obstacles accessing health care, among other concerns. While we explore some of these contemporary gender-related issues in the Global North, we also recognize that gender is dynamic and responsive to larger social, cultural, and political forces.

GENDER AND SEXUAL VIOLENCE

The Global North in the twentieth century is marked by a gradual arc of increasing gender equity; however, some countries, and particular groups within these countries, continue to experience high rates of gender-based violence. In the United States, Canada, and Australia, for example, ethnic minorities and Indigenous women tend to experience the highest rates of such violence. The concept of **intersectionality** allows us to understand the compounding factors of oppression (such as poverty, racism, sexism, social neglect, among others) that contribute to gender violence within some communities in the Global North. For instance, in the United States, murder is the third top cause of death for American Indian women, which is more than twice the rate than for white women (Heron 2018). In Canada, Indigenous women are sixteen times more likely than white women to be murdered or go missing (National Inquiry into Missing and Murdered Indigenous Women and Girls 2019). And in Australia, aboriginal women are thirty-two times more likely to be hospitalized as a result of domestic violence and ten times more likely to die from a violent assault than non-Indigenous women (Australian Institute of Health and Welfare 2018).

intersectionality refers to the interconnected nature of social categories such as race, class, and gender that creates overlapping systems of discrimination or disadvantage. The goal of an intersectional analysis is to understand how racism, sexism, and homophobia (for example) interact together to impact our identities and how we live in our society.

Figure 15.4. Gender-based violence is increasingly taken seriously by governments in the Global North. Here US President Barack Obama signs the Violence Against Women Reauthorization Act of 2013, which reauthorized several grant programs to target violence against women and strengthen trafficking victims' protections. Chuck Kenedy/ CC BY 3.0 license.

Sexual violence continues to plague the Global North, despite some progress overall. These issues received increased attention in the late 2010s. Most notably, the #MeToo movement gained international traction when a series of actresses and celebrities came forward accusing Harvey Weinstein, a US film producer, of rape and sexual assault. The Twitter hashtag #MeToo exploded after actress Alyssa Milano used it in a tweet

Figure 15.5. Social movements such as the #MeToo movement are raising awareness of the prevalence of sexual assault in the Global North. Sundry Photography/Shutterstock.

to highlight her connection to other survivors of sexual assault. Hundreds of thousands of women joined in by disclosing that they, too, had been sexually assaulted or abused. The movement was later criticized for ignoring the origin of the phrase, which was coined by activist Tarana Burke in 2006. Many claimed that Burke's work to bring awareness to the frequency of sexual assault had been overlooked because as an African American woman her voice was not heard or respected as much as white women's or celebrities' voices.

In the United States the #MeToo movement is credited with helping center sexual assault within the national narrative. Nevertheless, US society, like other societies, still struggles with how to talk about and address this problem. Further, awareness of sexual assault within other gendered populations (such as the transgender community) receives even less attention.

TRANSGENDER AND GENDER NONCONFORMING IDENTITIES

Similar to the increasing awareness and sensitivity to sexual assault, societal awareness of the lived experiences of transgender and gender-diverse people has improved in recent years. Transgendered people are those whose biological sex at birth is inconsistent with their gender identity. In addition, some Northern societies are increasingly recognizing people who do not identify as male or female, or whose gender identity is fluid. Languages are adapting to these changes by including new pronouns, verbs, and nouns. For instance, some English-speaking populations are using "they/them" or "xe/xem" instead of "he/she." In Spanish, words ending with "a" are usually considered feminine, and those ending with "o" are usually considered masculine. However, some Spanish-speaking populations are now using the gender-neutral "x" in place of "a" or "o" at the end of words, as in "Latinx."

Gender-diverse people are increasingly visible in popular television programs and movies, and some countries have established policies to protect their rights. For instance, in 2014, the Danish parliament passed legislation that allows legal gender recognition for transgender people based solely on their self-determined identity (Transgender Europe 2014). In 2016, a similar law was passed in Norway. However, many countries in Europe do not have such policies or protections, or they require a psychiatric or medical diagnosis for a legal gender change (Transgender Europe 2016). This is compounded by societal stigma and lack of public understanding, which results in widespread discrimination and marginalization of transgender people. For instance, in the United States, 29 percent of transgender people surveyed live in poverty, and 30 percent had been homeless at some point in their lives (according to a 2015 survey conducted by National Center for Transgender Equality). Their unemployment rate was 15 percent—three times the national average (National Center for Transgender Equality 2016). Transgender people are also more likely to avoid seeking medical care because they experience discrimination, disrespect, and even harassment in health-care settings.

In addition, transgender and gender nonconforming people have faced discrimination in bathroom use, particularly in the United States. For instance, 16 American states have considered legislation that would restrict access to multiuser bathrooms (and other sex-segregated facilities) on the basis of one's sex assigned at birth (Kralik 2019). Although most of these efforts failed or were withdrawn, the issue still remains highly contentious. As anthropologist Robert Myers stated, "Americans match deep convictions about males and females with binary spaces to perform those necessary biological functions. . . . the bathroom is the central space where beliefs and anxieties about gender, the body, identity, privacy and safety collide. It is a culture war waged over symbolic spaces reinforcing constructions of how we see ourselves privately and publicly" (Myers 2018). While bathrooms remain politically charged gendered spaces, people are becoming aware of gender diversity in ways that are starting to rattle their prior convictions. Many colleges and universities, and a variety of public and private institutions, are designating gender-neutral bathrooms that are available for anyone to use, regardless of their gender identity or expression.

Figures 15.6 and 15.7. Bathroom sign. Figure 15.6 is an example of binary gendered bathrooms. Increasingly, institutions in the Global North are providing more inclusive spaces for people to relieve themselves, regardless of their gender-identity (figure 15.7). Daveynin CC-BY; Cassiohabib/Shutterstock.

PATRIARCHY

patriarchy
a dynamic system of power and inequality that privileges men and boys over women and girls in social interactions and institutions. Patriarchy describes a society with a male-dominated political and authority structure and an ideology that privileges males over females in domestic and public spheres.

The problems of restrictions on transgender people's bathroom use, sexual assault, and sexual violence are tied to a lingering system of **patriarchy** that remains deeply embedded in societies in the Global North. Patriarchy has long been a central structural element of many societies and is characterized by a set of culturally specific symbols, behaviors, and ideas that are male dominated, male identified, and male-centric. This structure normalizes a worldview of binary gender, gender stereotypes, and the limitation of gender roles, among other things. Patriarchy reaches deep into the fabric of societies, which makes its existence difficult to see but profoundly influential. For instance, in the Global North, patriarchy influences inflexible notions of what it means to be "feminine" and "masculine." These notions are seen in the expectations for cisgender men to serve in the military and for women to be more responsible for domestic work. They are also seen in the paucity of men employed in care services, such as nursing and childcare, and a low number of women in manual labor-intensive work like construction or in political leadership positions.

Consider another example. You may have heard a popular riddle that goes something like this: "A father and son have a car accident and are both badly hurt. They are both taken to separate hospitals. When the boy is taken in for an operation, the surgeon says, 'I cannot do the surgery because this is my son.' How is this possible?" The trick (spoiler alert!) is that the surgeon is, of course, the boy's mother. This riddle is perplexing to many people who have been socialized to associate being a surgeon with being a man. The possibility that a woman (or mother) might be the surgeon seems so unlikely that we unconsciously do not even consider it. These types of associations are embedded within a patriarchal order that influences how people in the Global North see the world and their place in it.

Another manifestation of patriarchy can be seen in hypermasculine gender expressions, sometimes referred to as **toxic masculinity.** In the Global North, this form of masculinity tends to be characterized by qualities such as a competitive nature, physical strength, emotional suppression, rejection of femininity, risk taking, and violence. In January 2019 the American Psychological Association released a set of new guidelines for psychologists who work with males. The guidelines suggested that being enculturated into a traditional masculine ideology does harm not only to women and people with nonconforming gender identities but also to boys and men. The guidelines highlighted the impact of toxic masculinity on boys and men, which includes poor mental and physical health outcomes (American Psychological Association 2018). For example, toxic masculinity deems anger as the only appropriate emotion men can express, which can

toxic masculinity
tends to be characterized by qualities such as a competitive nature, physical strength, emotional suppression, rejection of femininity, risk taking, and violence.

lead to the distancing of men from others, resulting in difficulty developing and sustaining close relationships. Further, since toxic masculinity dictates that men should be strong and independent, some men feel they cannot seek help from others for their mental or physical issues.

Despite the influence of patriarchy, many of these gendered characteristics have been changing in recent years. More men and women are entering into nontraditional gender employment, and more women are taking on leadership roles. Men are increasingly active in childrearing, and some are even opting to stay home and raise children while their spouse works outside the home. Gender, and the influence of patriarchy, is in flux in the Global North.

CONCLUSION

Just as the Global North/South divide was developed to give order to an increasingly complex interrelated world system, the male/female divide, as rendered in the Global North, was developed to make sense of different yet interrelated sexed bodies. These bodies came to be understood in binary and hierarchical terms: one was either male or female, with male privileged over female. While in other places, males, females, and other genders had been understood in distinctive ways, the value-laden gender hierarchy of the Global North was disseminated widely due to the region's social, economic, and political power. To denaturalize these value-laden divisions—North/South, male/female—we must see them for what they are: social-historical constructs that are tied to power and carry real consequences for the lives of men, women, and sexual minority communities. And yet gender is dynamic: as we have discussed, gender roles are in flux, women are asserting their rights, members of sexual minority groups are being heard, and masculine ideals are being challenged.

The chapters in Part V: The Global North present anthropological research that showcases some of the gendered experiences of men and women from different places in the social hierarchy in highly unequal and stratified regions. Chapter 16 examines mothers in upper-middle-class households in a large northeast city. In online forums these women compete to perform "proper" motherhood. Their online performances serve as practice for how they will interact with their peers as ideal mothers in real life. Male sex workers are the focus of chapter 17. Here we see how gendered stereotypes of sex workers blind legislators and social service agencies to the violence and vulnerability of young men in the sex trade. In this case, an intersectional approach reveals the subordination and structural violence these men experience. Chapters 18 and 19 explore the gendered lives of migrants living in the Global North. Muslim women in Belgium respond to discrimination and reclaim their agency and resist marginalization. Chapter 19 shows how undocumented migrants from Mexico struggle to redefine their roles as fathers when children are left behind in the home village or parents are deported to Mexico leaving children behind in the United States. In these transnational families, fathers must negotiate different norms and expectations of parenthood on both sides of the border. Finally, the profile at the end of this introduction highlights the work of Kathleen Steinhauer, who fought for the rights and recognition of Indigenous women in Canada.

KEY TERMS

cisgender: refers to people whose gender identity corresponds to their sex at birth.

Global North: does not refer to a geographic region in any traditional sense but rather to the relative power and wealth of countries in distinct parts of the world. The Global North encompasses the rich and powerful regions such as North America, Europe, and Australia.

globalization: the worldwide intensification of social and economic interactions and interdependence between disparate parts of the world.

glocalization: a combination of the words "globalization" and "localization." Refers to ways that a cultural product is developed by one culture and adopted by the local culture to accommodate local needs and preferences.

hegemony: the dominance of one group over another supported by legitimating norms and ideas that normalize dominance. Using collective consent rather than force, dominant social groups maintain power and social inequalities are naturalized.

intersectionality: refers to the interconnected nature of social categories such as race, class, and gender that creates overlapping systems of discrimination or disadvantage. The goal of an intersectional analysis is to understand how racism, sexism, and homophobia (for example) interact together to impact our identities and how we live in our society.

misogynous/misogyny: refers to the contempt or hatred for women, often expressed as prejudice or discrimination.

patriarchy: a dynamic system of power and inequality that privileges men and boys over women and girls in social interactions and institutions. Patriarchy describes a society with a male-dominated political and authority structure and an ideology that privileges males over females in domestic and public spheres.

toxic masculinity: tends to be characterized by qualities such as a competitive nature, physical strength, emotional suppression, rejection of femininity, risk taking, and violence.

world systems theory: Developed by Emmanuel Wallerstein to describe a global capitalist system that separates countries into the core (the North), semiperiphery, and periphery (the South) based primarily on their economic participation.

BIBLIOGRAPHY

American Psychological Association. 2018. *APA Guidelines for Psychological Practice with Boys and Men.* Washington, DC: American Psychological Association.

Appadurai, Arjun. 1996. *Modernity at Large: Cultural Dimensions of Globalization.* Minneapolis: University of Minnesota Press.

Aristotle. 1905. *Aristotle's Politics.* Oxford: Clarendon.

Australian Institute of Health and Welfare. 2018. *Family, Domestic and Sexual Violence in Australia, 2018.* Canberra: Australian Institute of Health and Welfare.

Biewen, John. "Skeleton War." MEN. Scene on Radio, August 8, 2018. http://www.sceneonradio.org/tag/season-3.

Gould, Stephen Jay. 1981. *The Mismeasure of Man.* New York: W.W. Norton.

Graf, Nikki, Anna Brown, and Eileen Patten. 2019. "The Narrowing, but Persistent, Gender Gap in Pay." *Fact Tank.* Washington, DC: Pew Research Center.

Heron, Melonie. 2018. Deaths: Leading Causes for 2016. *National Vital Statistics Reports* 67, no. 6. Hyattsville, MD: National Center for Health Statistics.

Kralik, Joellen. 2019. "'Bathroom Bill' Legislative Tracking." Washington, DC: National Conference of State Legislatures.

Myers, Robert. 2018. "That Most Dangerous, Sacred American Space, the Bathroom." 10, no. 1 *Anthropology Now.*

National Inquiry into Missing and Murdered Indigenous Women and Girls. 2019. *Reclaiming Power and Place: The Final Report of the National Inquiry into Missing and Murdered Indigenous Women and Girls, Volume 1a.* National Inquiry, Canadian Government.

National Center for Transgender Equality. 2016. *The Report of the 2015 U.S. Transgender Survey.* Washington, DC: National Center for Transgender Equality.

Omeokwe, Amara. 2020. "Women Overtake Men as Majority of U.S. Workforce." *Washington Post.* January 10, 2020.

Staum, Martin. 2003. *Labeling People: French Scholars on Society, Race and Empire, 1815–1848*. Montreal: McGill-Queen's University Press.

Transgender Europe. 2014. "Denmark Goes Argentina!" June 11, 2014. https://tgeu.org/denmark-goes-argentina/.

Transgender Europe. 2016. "34 Countries in Europe Make this Nightmare a Reality." February 23, 2015. https://tgeu.org/nightmare/.

Wallerstein, Immanuel. 1974. *The Modern World-System: Capitalist Agriculture and the Origins of the European World-Economy in the Sixteenth Century*. Studies in Social Discontinuity. New York: Academic Press.

PROFILE: INDIAN RIGHTS FOR INDIAN WOMEN: KATHLEEN STEINHAUER, AN INDIGENOUS ACTIVIST IN CANADA

Sarah L. Quick

Kathleen Steinhauer (1932–2012) was a woman who bridged many worlds, many identities. She identified as First Nations and as Métis; while some assumed she was white. When I knew her she never wore pants, always skirts or dresses; and when she danced her traditional-style jigging in outdoor competitions, she would often wear a signature hat—daintily bobbing in time with the fiddle while her feet executed the steps with precision. She was also an activist but one who worked behind the scenes, collaborating with her more vocal friends on First Nations policy in Canada. It is important to note that after 1985 and Canada's constitutional reforms, three umbrella groups were recognized as "Aboriginal" or Indigenous—Inuit, First Nations, and Métis. Those who had previously been recognized as Indians via treaty and the Indian Act are now known as First Nations. Métis has complex and contested meanings. It may refer to an affiliation with the Métis Nation that has a specific cultural history stemming from the Red River region of Manitoba or to a broader understanding of individuals and groups with mixed European and Indigenous ancestry. In Kathleen's case, she is Cree (First Nations) and white through her parents, but she also identified with the Métis Nation culturally speaking.

Kathleen initially grew up on Saddle Lake reserve, a Cree First Nations reserve in eastern Alberta, Canada. She then attended a Protes-

See: Kathleen Steinhauer Red River Jigging at the John Arcand Fiddle Fest in Saskatchewan, Canada, https://youtu.be/qqlNZAVhJ9A.

tant residential school, the Edmonton Indian Residential School, from age five to eight. Here she and the other children regularly received corporal punishment, especially if they spoke Cree (see Steinhauer and Carlson 2013 for more details). A more positive story from her residential school years was when Kathleen recalled in an interview I conducted with her how she and other girls would secretly dance in the basement through a warning system they developed: one girl would watch and listen near the door, another at the landing to the upstairs, and another at the top of the stairs down to the basement. These girls were not completely passive in how they survived the residential school system. Once her mother realized that the school was mistreating Kathleen and her sisters, she began to homeschool them. Other First Nations and Métis children did not have this luxury, but she had some leeway, since her mother was white and adamant about the conditions there (Steinhauer and Carlson 2013, 16).

Kathleen continued her schooling by training as a nurse. After she had been a nurse for a number of years, she married her second husband in 1965. With this marriage, she lost her treaty rights because her husband was a "non-status Indian." She, along with many other First Nations women (over five thousand), were involuntarily "enfranchised" once they married someone who was not registered as an official member of an "Indian band" (Leddy 2016). Canada's enfranchisement policies promoted assimilation and Canadian citizenship. For example, before 1960, "enfranchised Indians" could vote in federal elections while those who retained their "Indian status" could not (Leslie 2016). In reality, these enfranchisement policies meant disenfranchisement or a loss of Indigenous rights. Those who were "enfranchised" were not allowed to live on the reserve, inherit reserve property, vote in reserve matters, or have access to health or education benefits recognized by treaty (Goyette 2013, xxxiii).

These enfranchisement policies also affected women differently than men. When men married women who were non-Indigenous or "non-status," their wives then gained access to these Indigenous rights. As Kathleen would remind me, her own white mother had gained access to these rights upon marrying her father, while she was denied them for marrying someone legally "non-status." The ideology behind these policies was that since women were the dependents, once they married someone non-Indigenous, they no longer needed to depend on the benefits granted by treaty to Indigenous people.

In protest of Canada's unequal treatment of Indigenous women, Kathleen joined forces in the late 1960s with other women activists from Saddle Lake living in Edmonton—Nellie Carlson, who had also been at the same residential school as Kathleen—Jenny Margetts, as well as more well-known activists from the east, Mary Two-Axe Early, Jeannette Corbiere Lavell, and Sandra Lovelace Nicholas. They eventually formed what became the national Indian Rights for Indian Women organization, which sought to overturn the inherently sexist and colonial ideology running through Canada's policies toward women. They met with politicians, protested at rallies, wrote letters to newspapers, and became legal experts through their many court battles with the Canadian state. They also suffered backlash from the government, the press, from groups like the National Indian Brotherhood (what became the Assembly of First Nations), and even from relatives in their families.

After years protesting their unfair loss of rights, these women finally saw some justice in 1985 when Canada amended these exclusionary policies with what is called Bill C-31. This bill reinstated women and their children's membership. However, for Kathleen, the struggle did not end here because Canada's Indian Affairs reinstated her to her first husband's band. It was not until 1999, thirty-nine years after she had lost her rights and after years of working with lawyers and another court case that Kathleen was reinstated to the Saddle Lake Cree Nation to which she belonged at birth (Steinhauer and Carlson 2013, 100–108).

As one of her granddaughters, Jessie Loyer, recalled in reflecting on Kathleen's legacy, "Activism was always at the heart of what she did. . . . She cared so strongly about justice that she worked tirelessly." Kathleen died in March of 2012, and Jessie thought that she would have appreciated the Idle No More movement that arose later that year in protest of the federal government's disregard for the environment and Indigenous sovereignty. It saddened Jessie that she could not speak to her grandmother directly about Idle No More nor take her to its rallies. Idle No More was founded by women, and while Kathleen was not a part of its emergence, she and the other activist women in the 1960s, 1970s, and 1980s laid the groundwork for these twenty-first-century Indigenous activists.

RESOURCES FOR FURTHER EXPLORATION

- Glenn, Evelyn Nakano. 2015. "Settler Colonialism as Structure: A Framework for Comparative Studies of U.S. Race and Gender Formation." *Sociology of Race and Ethnicity* 1, no. 1: 54–74.

- Canadian Encyclopedia online. http://www.thecanadianencyclopedia.ca.

- "Disinherited Love: Matrimony and the Indian Act." 2018. Permanent exhibit at the Royal Alberta Museum, Edmonton, Alberta.

ACKNOWLEDGMENTS

I would like to thank Kathleen Steinhauer's family, especially her daughter Celina Loyer and her granddaughter Jessie Loyer.

BIBLIOGRAPHY

Carlson, Nellie, and Kathleen Steinhauer. 2013. *Disinherited Generations: Our Struggle to Reclaim Treaty Rights for First Nations Women and their Descendants*. Edmonton: University of Alberta Press.

Goyette, Linda. 2013. "Introduction." In *Disinherited Generations: Our Struggle to Reclaim Treaty Rights for First Nations Women and their Descendants*, edited by Nellie Carlson and Kathleen Steinhauer, xxi–xliv. Edmonton: University of Alberta Press.

Leddy, Lianne C. 2016. "Indigenous Women and the Franchise." *The Canadian Encyclopedia*. https://www.thecanadianencyclopedia.ca/en/article/indigenous-women-and-the-franchise. Accessed July 27, 2019.

Leslie, John F. 2016. "Indigenous Suffrage." *The Canadian Encyclopedia*. https://thecanadianencyclopedia.ca/en/article/indigenous-suffrage. Accessed November 6, 2019.

16

Mothers Acting up Online

Susan W. Tratner

LEARNING OBJECTIVES

- Identify and analyze gender and parental social roles.

- Distinguish between backstage and front-stage behaviors and impression management using Goffman's dramaturgical method.

- Interpret the rise of the Mommy Wars as a result of both technological change and unachieved feminist goals.

In this chapter, the author explores the competitive nature of the fishbowl culture in upper-middle-class communities in the northeastern United States and the ways that online forums mediate idealized parenting performances. The author addresses how these sites are used to help mothers with "impression management," allowing women to practice their performances and improve the impressions they will provide for their real-life audiences in the future.

This chapter discusses research done with upper-middle-class cisgender heterosexual mothers in New York City who participate in the anonymous online discussion boards UrbanBaby.com (UB) and YouBeMom.com (YBM). In the age of "intensive parenting," the social status of these mothers is inexorably tied to their parenting. Many in this social arena believe that if a mother is unwilling to give up (almost) everything in her previous life, then she should not have children. There are few who achieve this ideal, but many feel pressure to present this image to the world. This creates a tension between the **social role** of mother and the private reality of wanting to complain and have another identity. A social role is the expected behavior of a person who holds a known status. These boards are where female posters can drop the "perfect" façade and be their more "authentic" selves. These online spaces allow them to express insecurity when they should appear confident, to be rude when they are expected to be polite, and to be clueless when they are looked to for answers. In other words, these boards allow them to be more authentically human. On YBM and UB, it is possible to see some of the social tensions around the role of mother not changing as much as the role of a female employee. This leads to heated debates regarding parenting choices in paid employment versus maternal-only childcare that is part of the "Mommy Wars."

social role
the expected behaviors of a person who holds a known status.

DESCRIPTION OF BOARDS

There are many websites with discussion boards devoted to the topics of pregnancy and childhood. Patricia Drentea and Jennifer Moren-Cross (2005) found these parenting boards to be places of both emotional and instrumental support that create and maintain social capital. The 2011 book *Motherhood Online*, edited by Michelle Moravec, discusses websites where mothers can get support regarding their personal lives. BabyCenter.com is currently the largest and most popular parenting site, serving over forty-five million users (babycenter.com/about). It has usernames and images that identify every post with a user. Those users are expected to be warm and supportive, giving virtual hugs "(((((((HUGS)))))))" when someone is having trouble.

UB and YBM do not provide this gender-specific comfort and loving support. They are believed to be populated by mean and nasty women. Even asking about how to change one's eating patterns to more healthy ones can lead to a poster being told: "You sound fat." John Suler coined the phrase "online disinhibition effect" for how people behave online in ways that might be hurtful to others, while they would not in real life (IRL). People act this way because of anonymity, invisibility (those being attacked cannot be seen), solipsistic introjection (lack of face-to-face cues), dissociative imagination (online is not "real life"), minimization of status and authority, individual differences, and predispositions and shifts among intrapsychic constellations (individuals showing a "true self" that they would typically hide) (Suler 2004). It happens to both genders but is more shocking to the viewer when the verbally abusive posters are female, never mind mothers.

Susan and John Maloney founded urbanbaby.com in August 1999. The site provided articles and information to expectant and new parents across the country. The most popular feature was the message board because it was an anonymous place for parents to speak without negative repercussions IRL. CNET bought the site in 2006 (Benkoil 2013) and is run by CBS. UB was ranked the 63,435th most popular website in global internet engagement in 2008 but fell to 314,048th in 2019 (Alexa.com 2019). This popularity came with notoriety as well. Jen Chung (2004) of Gawker.com said that it is a "must read if you're about to have a kid in the five bouroughs [*sic*]." Journalist Emily Nussbaum (2006) called UB "the collective id" of some groups of New York City mothers and a "snake pit." The site is famous not only for the snark but also as an anonymous and free resource on parenting in the New York area.

UB's design is currently a relatively straightforward discussion board.

In 2008, UB changed its format to what you see in figure 16.1. Anyone can read the content, but commenting requires a username and password. The "Search Box" is not functional since a second reorganization in 2012. The "Most Popular" posts, listed on the right, are the ones

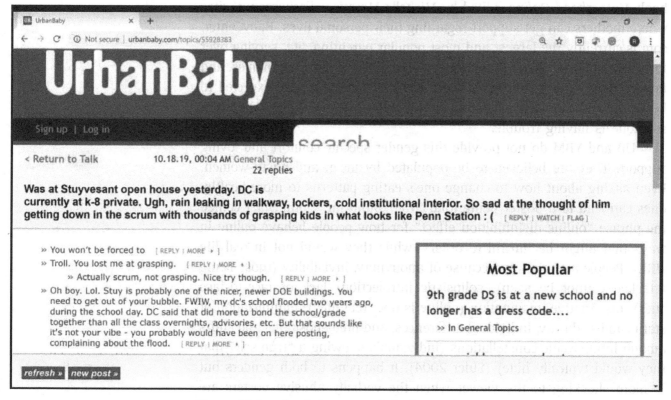

Figure 16.1. urbanbaby.com website homepage.

that get the most responses. The gray links underneath the black posts allow a user to reply to a post, click on "watch" to create a personalized list, and "more" for the time stamp and ability to "flag" a post. Flagging is an effort to get CBS.com moderators to delete inappropriate (offensive or spam) posts.

The 2008 changes upset many longtime UB users, claiming the site was slower and less agile. Several New York–based news outlets reported users' anger; in fact, the *New York Times* titled their article "Don't Mess with Mom's Chat" (Kaufman 2008). The negative fallout indicated how popular the site was in New York City and how UB members are politically and socially well connected. Mondeep Puri and an anonymous other former UB user founded a new website called YouBeMom.com. It has been called "the 4chan for mothers" (O'Conner 2014). The user demographic is similar and overlapping, and some move fluidly from one to the other, as verbatim questions appear within minutes of each other.

On YBM, only the first 180 characters are visible, and a user must click to see the remainder. It became possible to "delete" posts in mid-June 2017, a feature that posters have been using as a hedge against embarrassment. If three other users hit "dislike," a comment will be "hidden" from view but not deleted. The "hide—like—dislike—reply" buttons are visible when a user clicks on a post. There is a "most liked" category and "most discussed" on the top navigation bar as well as a search box.

GEOGRAPHIC SETTING—VIRTUAL OR NEW YORK CITY?

The research setting is a **virtual community**. It is a social network of people interacting using technology to pursue shared interests and goals that cross boundaries of geography, time, and politics (Rheingold 1993). The issue with saying UB and YBM are exclusively virtual communities is that it ignores the geographic grounding to the participants and their knowledge bases. These boards are used to communicate about parenting in a geographic location—the stores, schools, playgrounds, activities, etc.—that community members access regularly. Therefore, these virtual communities have a tie to the locations where their participants live. Posters are not looking for someone to tell them that they are insane to spend up to $50K a year for kindergarten. Instead, they want to know about the admissions process for a particular school. The geographic base of knowledge is small, and some people are only interested in getting recommendations close to their own homes.

virtual community
a social network of people interacting using technology to pursue shared interests and goals that cross boundaries of geography, time, and politics.

"WHO ARE THESE WOMEN?"

It is virtually impossible to know the exact demographics of the users of these sites because their personal data are not collected. In various articles about the users of these sites, community members are described as rich and mean women with too much time on their hands. Nolan (2012) says the site is "home to some of the most self-loathing, wealthy, haughty, and miserable parents in all of America." I have a sense of demographics based on personal experience from 2009 to 2012 and official research between 2012 and 2019. YBM and UB populations skew heavily female, parents, geographically in the boroughs (counties) of Manhattan and gentrified Brooklyn with a significant subset of former Manhattanites and residents of the greater Tri-State Area commutable to New York City (meaning southern New York State, northern New Jersey, and much of Connecticut). They also are significantly wealthier than the median income (over $71,897 in 2018; see datausa.com) college-educated, Democratic political leanings, and white/Caucasian. There are indications of different lengths of tenure on each of the sites, longer on YBM and shorter on UB. One of my interviews was with a woman who said she was a former resident of Manhattan who moved to New Jersey, had two children, and stayed at home with them. She had initially gone to the site (as many informants reported) to find out about New York City's competitive preschool application process. Although her children were in middle school by the time we talked, she enjoyed the ability to speak her mind and engage in "the drama" from the safety of her own home. In fact, she may enjoy it too much as she said she was "addicted" and had to ask her husband to block the website from their router most of the time in order to have a strict limit on her usage.

MOTHERHOOD AND IMPRESSION MANAGEMENT

Most people can recognize that a job interview is a performance. Job seekers research the organization, get business attire ready in advance, prepare answers to potentially tricky questions, and ensure that they show their best selves at the interview. Parenting has increasingly become a performance as well. Since Sharon Hays reported the rise of "intensive parenting" in 1998, pregnancy, birth, childhood, and parenthood have become part of a carefully executed show requiring parental (read: maternal) supervision. Aspects of this have been true for centuries. The competitive nature of the culture in upscale parts of the northeastern United States shows how UB or YBM can become an invaluable lifeline.

One of the primary reasons posters ask questions about UB and YBM is to poll others "like me." They may ask, "What would you think if—" followed by a variety of parenting (or nonparenting) questions to shield themselves from judgment IRL. The anonymity allows people to give and get advice without harm to an individual's reputation as a "good mother."

The boards demonstrate the dramaturgical method, developed by Erving Goffman (1959) in *The Presentation of Self in Everyday Life*. He suggested that humans interact differently depending on the time, place, and audience present to view that "performance" or action. It indicates that people are actors playing (social) roles during their daily lives. The status that a person has is the part in the play, while the role is the script. The script informs the person of the appropriate words and movements for the part they are playing at this moment. Individuals can present themselves and create an impression in the minds of others (**impression management**) by changing status and role depending on social interaction. For example, most people present a different "self" to an in-law than to a spouse in terms of behaviors and expressions.

Goffman says that daily interactions in which people know there is an audience for his/her status and role are called **front-stage** behaviors. People are aware that they are performing in the front stage. There is a set of observers for whom a performance is being put on and a series of behaviors that social actors are expected to demonstrate. The performance has a goal of infallibility as "errors and mistakes are often corrected before the performance takes place, while telltale signs that errors have been made and corrected are themselves concealed" (Goffman 1978, 52). Those errors are discussed and fixed in **backstage areas** with compatriots who want to help you perfect your performance.

There are several signs to indicate that someone is in a backstage region or engaging in backstage behavior. First, they are among people for whom status does not depend on a positive review, or where one can "let down [their] hair." Goffman quotes feminist writer Simone de Beauvoir who stated the following:

> With other women, a woman is behind the scenes; she is polishing her equipment, but not in battle; she is getting her costume together, preparing her make-up, laying out her tactics; she is lingering in a dressing-gown and slippers in the wings before making her entrance on the stage; she likes this warm, easy, relaxed atmosphere . . . for some women this warm and frivolous intimacy is dearer than the serious pomp and relations with men. (Goffman 1959, 113, ellipses in original)

impression management
the manner in which individuals present themselves and create a perception in the mind of others by changing status and roles depending on social interaction.

front stage
a social or physical space where people are aware that they are performing a role for observers and a series of behaviors that social actors are expected to demonstrate.

backstage
a social or physical space where people get help putting together a performance. Others help them perfect their portrayal of a particular role that they will demonstrate at another time or place.

This sort of informality and willingness to challenge authority is what Goffman called "backstage language," which might be taken as disrespectful for people and places considered "front stage." Posters on UB and YBM use atypical "female" language, including profanity or aggressive, opinionated speech patterns, further indicating that this is a backstage area.

Rebecca Tardy (2000) provided a Goffmanesque analysis of a playgroup of mothers in a college town. Tardy discusses the social pressure put on mothers to prove they are "good" moms. If they meet this standard, they should be able to protect their children from getting sick, which is impossible. She suggests that these mothers have two front stages. The first is in front of the "regular" world of mixed genders and representations of themselves as successful stay-at-home mothers. The next is the playgroup, which on the surface appears to be backstage because they can get information about being a mother, discuss their parenting issues, and talk about the messy biology of motherhood. However, Tardy found that in this backstage, the women were playing the role of a devoted mother. Tandy found that only in the activities associated with "Mom's Night Out," where the children were not present, could the women drop the role of mother and engage in less "good mom" impression management.

Drew Ross analyzed the benefits of using anonymous people as backstage resources to achieve goals. He researched an online community of people trying to pass a difficult test to become a London taxi driver. The average applicant spent two to four years studying over three hundred routes on twenty-five thousand streets as well as over twenty thousand landmarks within a six-mile radius of Charing Cross (TheKnowledgeTaxi). As studying for this test is an isolated and competitive situation, a website was created by test takers and those who have passed the test to assist others. People would post questions before or after they went out to learn one of the routes. Ross's discussion of expertise pooling shows how these boards are learning networks based on active participation and communication between those who know and those who do not. Both future cabbies and these mothers need a space where more experienced learners mentor those less experienced ones by answering questions.

FEMINISM ON DISPLAY

Gender and **gender roles** (see introduction) in the United States support the idea that women are viewed primarily as caregivers and that their contribution to the household is valued less than that of males. The idea of these discussion boards being a place for women to communicate about

gender
the set of culturally and historically invented beliefs and expectations about gender that one learns and performs (e.g., masculine, feminine). Gender is an "identity" one can choose in some societies, but there is pressure in all societies to conform to expected gender roles and identities.

gender roles
the tasks and activities that a specific culture assigns to a gender.

the problems and to assist each other, harkens back to First Wave feminism. **Feminism** is the idea that there should be economic, social, and political equality between people regardless of sex or gender. Feminist critique in anthropology was defined by Henrietta Moore (1988) as the analysis of gender and how gender is a structuring principle in society. Carol Hanisch (1969) stated that "the personal is political." The "political" was not referring to elected office but a way to show that women do not have unique problems in society. Women who experience disrespect and discrimination have a set of challenges that can be addressed politically. **First-wave feminism** focused on earning the right to vote and other legal protections, while **second-wave feminism** looked at discrimination and equality with the slogan "the personal is political." The idea behind this slogan is that if all housewives (typically white, middle-class, and heterosexual) discussed their personal issues they would become conscious of their common oppression. **Third-wave feminism** was to address the class and racial biases of the preceding two movements. In theory, YBM and UB could function as such consciousness-raising environments. There are elements of this where women get help in determining how to manage a tough workplace, "I just reached out to a former boss. Only been here a week and I hate it. How do I phrase it?" Yet when women admit to taking time to themselves, they are flamed (criticized) for maternal neglect. "My child just drew a picture of me sitting on my computer YBMing" resulted in a huge backlash. The pressures of the expectations of female behavior are demonstrated in the various ways that educated and wealthy women bicker and defend their choices. In theory, these backstage spaces should provide a greater awareness of the common problems of a single gender. Instead, there is anger and criticism. The division of women into warring factions rather than as a united whole has been a significant failing of the feminist movement. Nussbaum (2006) said, "If you read UrbanBaby, it's hard not to be unsettled by the same conclusion that hit Friedan when she surveyed the mothers of America: that what seem like women's private struggles can be seen as an expression of their shared experience."

feminism
the idea that there should be economic, social, and political equality between people regardless of sex or gender.

first-wave feminism
from the late nineteenth through the early twentieth century, focusing on earning the right to vote and emancipation of women from fathers and husbands.

second-wave feminism
focused on gender-based discrimination in the 1960s–1980s

third-wave feminism
brought up the idea that feminism and gender-based needs and oppressions differ based on class, race/ethnicity, nationality, and religion.

MOMMY WARS

Mommy Wars refers to the idea that choices that women make in their roles as mothers line them up on opposing sides of a battlefield. It starts with the decisions around birth, to have an unmedicated childbirth, an epidural (a shot in the spine to stop the pain) or a cesarean section, continues with circumcising male babies or leaving them "intact," to co-sleep or put a baby in a separate crib. Breastfeeding or formula feeding, letting

Mommy Wars
the idea that choices that women make in their roles as mothers line them up on opposing sides of a battlefield.

a six-month-old baby "learn to sleep" by "crying it out" or if a child is rocked to sleep until he or she learns how to "go to sleep" is worthy of arguments with strangers. Daycare for socialization or a private nanny is not only a status signifier but can be seen as setting a child up for a lifetime of success or failure, depending on the individual's opinion. One of the most hotly debated topics is that of a mother's employment status. A woman's different decision in this arena is taken as a personal affront on another woman's choice. Here it is important to note that it is not a question of a woman working or not impacting women or the feminist movement as a whole. Instead, it is a questioning of the other woman's individual choice as being "wrong" or "right" in a grander scheme.

Historically, two people would meet face to face and talk behind the back of the individual. They were engaging in "gossip" while criticizing another person known to them. It was considered a shameful thing for the other person to know that the busybodies had discussed him or her. With the internet, these conversations are not only more public, but also people are more ready to directly confront another person about the choices that they are making with their children. An example arose in October 2019 when a mother was talking about how "outrageous" she thought it was that her children expected her to provide regular childcare to her grandchildren, calling her daughter-in-law "entitled." After being flamed (criticized) on one thread in YBM, she started another where she was told, "Don't tell us. Tell them." But that is a harder thing to do, particularly with criticism of another woman's lifestyle.

The Mommy Wars are about a social system that pits women against each other rather than focusing on raising their children to be productive adults. As Steiner said, "Motherhood in America is fraught with defensiveness, infighting, ignorance, and judgment about what's best for kids, family, and women—a true catfight among women" (2007, x). A 2013 Quester poll stated that 64 percent of mothers believed the Mommy Wars exist, but only 29 percent of them have experienced it. This statistic implies that the Mommy Wars are about stereotypes of different styles of mothering, rather than the reality of mothering. Women appear to only engage in the sort of competitive discussions or direct attacks in situations where the "other" is not personally known to them. It is difficult to criticize one's sister-in-law to her face for her parenting choices. It is far easier to do it to a close friend one has little to no contact with by saying, "She's so lazy. My brother works so hard, and she just sits at home." But even more comfortable is to post comments on UB or YBM where no one can defend this friend (they can only support a stereotype of her). More importantly, no one can trace this criticism back to either her or you.

The Stay at Home/Work Out of the Home [SAH/WOH] debate is almost a daily "Most Discussed/Popular" on UB and YBM. Some posters go online to the boards to argue their side of an issue they have in real life, but others may be genuinely looking to understand the "opposing" points of view better. Many posters believe these choices indicate what sort of a mother you are—kind or cruel, selfish or selfless. The decision for a mother to stay at home with her child(ren) includes her desires, her spouse, as well as gender roles and economics. Many women on the boards suggest that their posttax salaries were not significantly higher than that of the nanny. According to Gold (2018), nannies earned $17.63 per hour for an average of fifty hours a week totaling just over $45,000 per annum. This is the take-home salary of a pediatric nurse (Ward 2017). While in college, women are not as strongly encouraged as men to think about the economic impact of their career choices. Also, they are encouraged implicitly or tacitly toward the more "feminine" careers of teaching, social work, or human resources. These are often believed to be more suited to a woman's interests in relationships and interactions with people or a desire to help. They also pay significantly less than being a professor, psychologist, or accountant. Even if a husband and wife are both on career tracks to be corporate lawyers, the woman's role as a "litigator" takes a back seat to that of "mother" and often not by choice. Johnston and Swanson's 2006 research indicates that many mothers must plan their work around their duties as a mother.

Many of these culturally defined choices restrict how mothers can behave in the workplace, much more so than in the case of men. Men are fathers if they have a child, but women are only mothers if they meet specific social standards. Men are rarely judged negatively for their interactions with their children. If they provide financial support for their children, they are considered acceptable fathers, but the reverse is not always true for mothers. Women who work for a salary twelve hours a day may be derided on the boards as "auntie mommy," implying that they are only partially in their children's lives. Conversely, fathers can travel to another city for work from Monday through Friday and still be "good fathers" because they are "providing."

The dynamic of the man earning more than the woman is expected. The economic provision to the family is believed to be biologically male work while child-rearing or home-making is female work. As Enobong Hanna Branch (2016) points out, these dichotomies are not as strong in the African American culture, which is a further indication that members of these boards are culturally Caucasian. In truth, there are no male or female childrearing tasks (other than breastfeeding); there are only tasks around the house and money that needs to be earned.

There is a sizable portion of the UB/YBM population who believe that women are uniquely and biologically destined to be caregivers. These posters not only talk about their own choices as being "natural" and "normal" but also denigrate those women who do not make the same ones. When asking a woman why she chose to go part time, she said "because I want to raise my own children." This is coded language implying that those mothers who work are no longer the ones raising their kids. Instead, the "mother" role has been transferred to the (often) nonwhite and less educated nanny. This attitude is reflected in the core belief that women are born nurturers and the current cultural obsession of protecting children to the point at which they become "snowflakes." To call a person a "snowflake" means that they are sheltered and coddled (or they might "melt" easily). To maintain protection of these precious children, a parent (read: mother) is necessary, as a paid help is often not as careful or nurturing.

second shift

the time parents spent on household and child-rearing tasks after the paid work has ended.

One of the things that drives many women to quit good jobs and that many posters discuss is that they are expected to take care of the **second shift**. Hochschild and Machung's (1989), "second shift" refers to the time spent on household and childrearing tasks that mothers feel constitutes unacknowledged work. It is the time spent on these domestic chores that her social status of "mother" depends on. The second shift of work is unrecognized by the first paid job, as employers do not allow for flexibility regarding family demands on their employees. This means that as long as the idea of "caregiver" remained female, women feel this second shift as being their responsibility. When discussing a poster's decision to move from a work-at-home job to work in an office, another said, "It's not as easy as outsourcing and forgetting about it [childcare]. It's still a lot of work to manage plus a commute and a full-time new job" (UB 2019, errors in original). This reflects a difference in expected "responsibility" for the children. This feeling of responsibility leads to a great deal of mental labor, which M. Blazoned (2014) labeled the "default parent." This is a gender-neutral term for what most Americans would say is the "mom." If a woman on YBM or UB tries to complain that her husband "has no idea when our son has to go to his therapies" or "out of town and husband didn't send our daughter with a packed lunch for her trip. So the teacher called me" instead of receiving support for a common issue, she is often chastised. Typical responses might be, "Well, you married him" a reaction reflective of a patriarchal tone that continues to assign women the primary responsibility for family care, according to economist Nancy Folbre (2012). She suggests that one of the keys to an equal society is to define "family care as a challenging and important achievement for everyone rather than a sacred obligation for women alone."

Women on UB and YBM have the education and means to reject that these stereotypical social roles of mothers are for women only, but they are deeply internalized. If these women accept the social norms of men as financially supporting the family, they are criticized by those on the opposite side, namely those who work. If a woman laments that she cannot afford to buy something, she is told: "Well then get a job." The most virulent arguments happen when a divorce is on the horizon, and the SAH spouse is told that she has to support herself. The soon-to-be-divorced poster will argue that she and her husband made the decision together, so he should continue to support her and the children financially. The argument against her is that once she became "dependent on a man" that she was running the risk of this happening. One of the advantages of these boards is that your "backstage helpers" can provide clear and actionable advice before women are ready to tell people in real life. This can include the need to collect financial documents, set up a separate bank account, and obtain the names of good local divorce attorneys.

These rigid roles are reflected in discussions of an SAH dad or those husbands who are unemployed. Some posters say that the family decided that the mother's career was more lucrative, so the father stayed home. This works for them, but their posts are often tinged with defensiveness and guilt, likely representing their experiences going against the cultural norm. The husbands who are out of work often claim that the nanny needs to continue her work because he cannot both care for the children and look for a new job. The reverse is not true because SAH mothers report that they are able to get interviews and are hired before they get a nanny to replace their household labor. The SAH fathers who achieve the female ideal are still not given the same respect expected by the SAH mothers. They are described as "beta" men, meaning that they were SAH because they were not strong enough to dominate with the alphas in the workplace.

DISCUSSION

While YBM and UB can help mothers present better offline impressions, they can also be harsh and accusatory, criticizing these women's perceived internalized lack of respect for their roles in a family, employment, and society as a whole. As such, the Mommy Wars and the conversations around them provide a critical window into American feminism that has

participant observation
A research methodology used in cultural anthropology. It consists of a type of observation in which the anthropologist observes while participating in the same activities in which her informants are engaged.

not yet been addressed. Online disinhibition explains the angry backstage behaviors but not the particular virulence that arises when discussing topics that surround the Mommy Wars. Based on the **participant observation** research, it is possibly due to three potentially interrelated reasons. First, the required changes in social roles have not occurred. Although girls have been taught that they "can be anything," this related only to the workplace. If they choose to be mothers, that social status of all-encompassing love and protector of children with a father as a provider has not changed. Second is the internet. Online disinhibition and the increased contact through discussion boards (such as UB and YBM), social media (Facebook and Instagram), and the proliferation of online information sources have brought people the means of expressing opinions to people with different points of view. Parents (indeed everyone) can find an echo chamber that reinforces their particular worldview, which leads to hardened opinions and stronger adverse reactions to "the other." Third, there remains a good deal of internal misogyny that is revealed in these anonymous backstage spaces. Women attack each other's choices, not only to bolster their own decisions but because there is seemingly no choice a woman can make that is the correct one. Both working outside the home and staying at home with children are "wrong" choices that either hurt the family, the children, or all women. Conversely, fathers can get social support for working hard or finding work/life balance, and they only experience social backlash if they engage in the female task of SAH parenting. This is the paradox of so-called choice feminism being accepted before basic respect for women was achieved. Instead of every choice being a feminist one to be celebrated, none of the options are respected.

REVIEW QUESTIONS

1. What social roles do you play in a typical day?

2. What is your "backstage" and who helps you with your "impression management"?

3. What was your thought process in deciding on your major (or prospective major)? Did gender play a role? Did future career earnings? Why or why not?

4. Why have gender roles in the workplace changed more readily than those of mother and father?

5. The author puts forth several possible reasons for the Mommy Wars. Which is most convincing to you? Why?

RESOURCES FOR FURTHER EXPLORATION

- Ammari, T., S. Schoenebeck, and D. M. Romero. 2018. "Pseudonymous Parents: Comparing Parenting Roles and Identities on the Mommit and Daddit subreddits." In *Proceedings of the 2018 CHI Conference on Human Factors in Computing Systems* (April): 1–13.

- Collett, J. L. 2005. "What Kind of Mother am I? Impression Management and the Social Construction of Motherhood. *Symbolic Interaction* 28, no. 3: 327–347.

- Marshall, Debra. "Erving Goffman's Dramaturgy." YouTube. https://www.youtube.com/watch?v=VpTSG6YtaeY.

- Scarborough, W. J., R. Sin, and B. Risman. 2019. "Attitudes and the Stalled Gender Revolution: Egalitarianism, Traditionalism, and Ambivalence from 1977 through 2016." *Gender & Society* 33, no. 2: 173–200.

KEY TERMS

backstage: a social or physical space where people get help putting together a performance. Others help them perfect their portrayal of a particular role that they will demonstrate at another time or place.

feminism: the idea that there should be economic, social, and political equality between people regardless of sex or gender.

first-wave feminism: from the late nineteenth through the early twentieth century, focusing on earning the right to vote and emancipation of women from fathers and husbands.

front stage: a social or physical space where people are aware that they are performing a role for observers and a series of behaviors that social actors are expected to demonstrate.

gender: the set of culturally and historically invented beliefs and expectations about gender that one learns and performs (e.g., masculine, feminine). Gender is an "identity" one can choose in some societies, but there is pressure in all societies to conform to expected gender roles and identities.

gender roles: the tasks and activities that a specific culture assigns to a gender.

impression management: the manner in which individuals present themselves and create a perception in the mind of others by changing status and roles depending on social interaction.

Mommy Wars: the idea that choices that women make in their roles as mothers line them up on opposing sides of a battlefield.

participant observation: A research methodology used in cultural anthropology. It consists of a type of observation in which the anthropologist observes while participating in the same activities in which her informants are engaged.

second-wave feminism: focused on gender-based discrimination in the 1960s–1980s

second shift: the time parents spent on household and child-rearing tasks after the paid work has ended.

social role: the expected behaviors of a person who holds a known status.

third-wave feminism: brought up the idea that feminism and gender-based needs and oppressions differ based on class, race/ethnicity, nationality, and religion.

virtual community: a social network of people interacting using technology to pursue shared interests and goals that cross boundaries of geography, time, and politics.

ACKNOWLEDGMENTS

I would like to acknowledge the academic support of Roger Sanjek, Julie Gedro, Cynthia Ward, and Ruth Goldberg and the personal support of my parents (Alan and Irene Warshauer), my husband (Matthew Tratner), children (Ian and Miles) as well as friends and family. I would like to dedicate this work to my mother, a trailblazing woman in the legal profession who found her own way as a wife and mother, and my father, a feminist in word and deed.

BIBLIOGRAPHY

Alexa. http://www.alexa.com/siteinfo/urbanbaby.com. Accessed August 6, 2019.

Babycenter. https://www.babycenter.com/about. Accessed August 6, 2019.

Barriteau, Eudene, ed. 2003. *Confronting Power, Theorizing Gender: Interdisciplinary Perspectives in the Caribbean.* Kingston: University of West Indies Press.

Becker, Mary E. 1986. "Barriers Facing Women in the Wage-Labor Market and the Need for Additional Remedies: A Reply to Fischel and Lazear." *University of Chicago Law Review* 53: 934.

Beneria, Lourdes. 1981. "Conceptualizing the Labor Force: The Underestimation of Women's Economic Activities." *Journal of Development Studies* 17, no. 3: 10–28.

Benkoil, Dorian. 2013. "Tumblr CEO David Karp's Wild Ride from 14-Year-Old Intern to Multimillionaire." *Mediashift* (website), http://mediashift. org/2013/05/tumblr-ceo-david-karps-wild-ride-from-14-year-old-intern-to-multimillionaire/. Accessed August 6, 2019.

Blazoned, M. 2014. "The Default Parent." The Huffington Post. https://www. huffpost.com/entry/the-default-parent_b_6031128. Accessed August 6, 2019.

Branch, Enobong Hanna. 2016."Racializing Family Ideals: Breadwinning, Domesticity and the Negotiation of Insecurity." In *Beyond the Cubicle: Job Insecurity, Intimacy, and the Flexible Self*, edited by J. Allison Pugh. Oxford: Oxford University Press, 2016.

Brown, Tamara Mose. *Raising Brooklyn: Nannies, Childcare, and Caribbeans Creating Community*. New York: New York University Press.

Chung, Jen. 2004. "NYC to Parents: Watch Your Baby!" *Gothamist* (website). https://gothamist.com/2004/08/30/nyc_to_parents_watch_your_baby.php. Accessed August 6, 2019.

Coleman, Gabriella. 2014. *Hacker, Hoaxer, Whistleblower, Spy: The Many Faces of Anonymous*. New York: Verso.

Coleman, E. Gabriella. 2012. "Am I Anonymous?" *Limn* 1, no. 2. https://limn. it/articles/am-i-anonymous/. Accessed August 9, 2019.

Datausa. 2019. New York Profile. https://datausa.io/profile/geo/new-york-northern-new-jersey-long-island-ny-nj-pa-metro-area. Accessed August 9, 2019.

De Beauvoir, Simone. 2012. *The Second Sex*. New York: Vintage.

Drentea, Patricia, and Jennifer L. Moren-Cross. 2005. "Social Capital and Social Support on the Web: The Case of an Internet Mother Site." *Sociology of Health & Illness* 27, no. 7: 920–943.

Folbre, Nancy. 2012. "Patriarchal Norms Still Shape Family Care." *New York Times* Economix (blog). http://economix.blogs.nytimes.com/2012/09/17/women-should-take-care-of-home-and-family/?_r=0. Accessed August 9, 2019.

Gold, Tammy. 2018. "What Is the Average Nanny Salary in NYC: Survey Results." The Huffington Post. https://www.huffpost.com/entry/what-is-the-average-nanny-salary-in-nyc-survey-results_b_5a561ed8e4b0baa6abf162e4. Accessed August 9, 2019.

Goffman, Erving. 1959. *The Presentation of Self in Everyday Life*. London: Harmondsworth.

Crow, Barbara A., ed. 2000. *Radical Feminism: A Documentary Reader*. New York: New York University Press.

Hays, Sharon. 1998. *The Cultural Contradictions of Motherhood*. New Haven, CT: Yale University Press.

Hochschild, Arlie, and Anne Machung. *The Second Shift: Working Families and the Revolution at Home*. New York: Penguin, 2012.

Johnston, Deirdre D., and Debra H. Swanson. 2006. "Constructing the 'Good Mother': The Experience of Mothering Ideologies by Work Status." *Sex Roles* 54, no. 7–8: 509–519.

Kaufmann, Joanne. 2008. "Urban Baby's Lesson: Don't Mess with Mom's Chat." *New York Times*, May 19, 2008, https://www.nytimes.com/2008/05/19/business/19baby.html.

Knowledge Taxi. https://www.theknowledgetaxi.co.uk/. Accessed August 7, 2019.

Moore, Henrietta L. 1988. *Feminism and Anthropology*. Minneapolis: University of Minnesota Press.

Moravec, Michelle, ed. 2011. *Motherhood Online*. Cambridge: Cambridge Scholars.

Nolan, Hamilton. 2012. "Rich Person or Troll? The Perpetual UrbanBaby Riddle." *Gawker* (website). https://gawker.com/5889700/rich-person-or-troll-the-perpetual-urbanbaby-riddle. Accessed July 15, 2019.

Nussbaum, Emily. 2006. "Mothers Anonymous." *New York Magazine*. http://nymag.com/news/features/17668/. Accessed August 7, 2019.

New York County. Information. https://www.ny.gov/counties/new-york#.

O'Conner, Brendan. 2014. "YouBeMom: The Anything-Goes Parenting Cult That's Basically 4chan for Mothers." https://www.dailydot.com/unclick/youbemom-4chan-for-moms/. Accessed August 7, 2019.

Pinch, Trevor. 2010. "The Invisible Technologies of Goffman's Sociology from the Merry-Go-Round to the Internet." *Technology and Culture* 51, no. 2: 409–424.

Portes, Alejandro. 1998. "Social Capital: Its Origins and Applications in Modern Sociology." *Annual Review of Sociology* 24: 1–24. http://www.jstor.org/stable/223472. Accessed August 7, 2019.

Reference for Business. 2019. iVillage Inc. Company Profile. https://www.referenceforbusiness.com/history2/69/iVillage-Inc.html. Accessed August 6, 2019.

Quester. "Do Mommy Wars Exist?" August 29, 2013. https://www.quester.com/do-mommy-wars-exist/.

QuickFacts, New York City. https://archive.org/details/perma_cc_D6K2-CW2B. Accessed May 19, 2014.

Rheingold, Howard. 2000. *The Virtual Community: Homesteading on the Electronic Frontier*. Cambridge, MA: MIT Press.

Rosaldo, Michelle Z. 1980. "The Use and Abuse of Anthropology: Reflections on Feminism and Cross-cultural Understanding." *Signs: Journal of Women in Culture and Society* 5.3: 389–417.

Sannicolas, Nikki. 1997. "Erving Goffman, Dramaturgy, and Online Relationships." *Cibersociology*. https://www.cybersociology.com/files/1_2_sannicolas.html. Accessed July 16, 2021

Schoenebeck, Sarita Yardi. 2013. "The Secret Life of Online Moms: Anonymity and Disinhibition on YouBeMom.com." *Seventh International AAAI Conference on Weblogs and Social Media*.

Steinberg, Ronnie J. 1990. "Social Construction of Skill: Gender, Power, and Comparable Worth." *Work and Occupations* 17, no. 4: 449–82. doi:10.1177/0730888490017004004.

Steiner, Leslie Morgan. 2007. *Mommy Wars: Stay-at-Home and Career Moms Face Off on Their Choices, Their Lives, Their Families*. New York: Random House.

Suler, John. 2004. "The Online Disinhibition Effect." *Cyberpsychology & Behavior* 7, no. 3: 321–326.

Tardy, Rebecca W. 2000. " 'But I Am a Good Mom': The Social Construction of Motherhood through Health-Care Conversations." *Journal of Contemporary Ethnography* 29, no. 4: 433–473.

Urbanbaby. http://www.urbanbaby.com/topics/55921444. Accessed August 7, 2019.

US Census Quick Facts, https://www.census.gov/quickfacts/fact/table/newyork citynewyork,NY/RHI425216#viewtop. Accessed August 6, 2019.

Ward, Marguerite. 2017. "In Demand Entry Level Jobs Every College Student Should Consider." *CNBC.com*. https://www.cnbc.com/2017/04/26/5-in-demand-entry-level-jobs-every-college-student-should-consider.html. Accessed August 9, 2019.

17

Male Sex Work in Canada
Intersections of Gender and Sexuality

Nathan Dawthorne

LEARNING OBJECTIVES

- Define and describe the diversity of sex work and sex workers.

- Summarize the gendered nature of sex work law and policy in Canada.

- Articulate how the experiences of male sex workers over the lifespan are shaped by gender and sexuality.

In this chapter, the author explores the experiences of male sex workers in a midsized Canadian city. He critiques the legal and political perspectives that portray prostitution as exploitative, regardless of what sex workers say or feel, (re)producing gendered stereotypes of masculinity and femininity and naturalizing a certain type of heterosexual behavior. This, the author argues, overlooks how intersectionality shapes autonomy and vulnerability. Through their stories, the author addresses the structural violence that these men experience.

INTRODUCTION

For every hundred girls peddling their wares on street corners, there are a hundred unobtrusive male prostitutes, of all ages, offering their services to both heterosexual and homosexual clients. Students, university graduates—some married, some with other jobs—they are almost invisible, and the police hardly know of their existence. (Taylor 1991, 97)

Labor involving "sexual, sensual, and erotic energies and parts of the body" (Truong 1990 as cited in Kempadoo 2001, 38) has been interwoven into the fabric of many societies throughout world history. Nevertheless, sex work and the people involved remain misunderstood, marginalized, and devalued. Between 2014 to 2017, I conducted ethnographic research with forty-three male sex workers in London, Ontario, Canada. Through semistructured interviews they shared their life stories while also giving insight into the sex industry in the region. These stories help inform this text. All names are pseudonyms, and descriptors of occupation, activity, or behavior are self-identified labels. London is a midsized city located two hundred kilometers (125 miles) from Toronto and Detroit along the Quebec City–Windsor transportation corridor. With a metropolitan population of close to a half million people, it is the eleventh most populous municipality in Canada (Statistics Canada 2016). I chose London for study in part because it has served as a historic epicenter of female-centered research and advocacy in Canada since the 1970s and 1980s. This reinforced and created **structural violence** (Nathanson and Young 2006) with fewer (if any) equivalent services for men, and is linked to the lack of previous research on male sex work.

structural violence
the systematic ways in which social structures harm or disadvantage individuals and thus create and maintain social inequalities.

Due to the mostly underground nature, contentious legal status, and stigmatization of the sex industry, defining its actual size and scale is problematic. In Canada, like much of the world, policymakers and service providers use statistics from incompatible and biased samples of limited size and inconsistent scope, privileging gender as the essential factor involved in sexual transactions. Declaring that women selling sex to men is the primary form of sex work ignores a spectrum of gendered and sexualized interactions, situational and cultural contexts, historical variability, and the complex socioeconomic conditions that produce sexual relations and desire. This practice and belief, however, does not explain why men (and those of other genders) who sell sex are most often overlooked (Dennis 2008).

WHAT IS SEX WORK?

Generally defined, sex work encompasses activities related to the exchange of intimate services for payment. What counts as intimate (or sexual) and what counts as payment varies from person to person, over time, in law, and by society and other structural conditions (Gozdiak 2016). Sex work occurs in a variety of settings and includes a multitude of behaviors, including escorting, massage, prostitution, erotic dance and stripping, pornographic performances, professional domination (sadomasochism), fetish work, internet cam shows, and phone chatlines (van der Meulen, Durisin, and Love 2013). Informal sexual encounters in exchange for small cash gifts, a meal out or a bar tab, or a place to sleep, as well as relationships that prioritize the economic security of the other partner (sugar relationships), press at the edges of what may be classified as commercial sex (Mitchell 2015).

Sex work and prostitution as terms convey specific cultural histories that are not universal. The Latin root of the term *prostitute* signifies "to dishonor" or "expose someone to shame and rebuke" (Buschi 2014, 726). This resonates with *prostitut*ion as a social category, used to ostracize and stigmatize; to deny *women* the same rights as average citizens (Pheterson 1989). Resisting this and other discourses that delineated sex workers as diseased, deviant, criminal, or disturbed, American activist Carol Leigh conceived the term "sex work," redefining prostitution as a type of labor (Bell 1994; Bindman 1997; O'Connell Davidson 1998; Parent and Bruckert 2013; Pateman 1988; Tong 1998). While Marxism depicts *all* labor as exploitation in capitalist systems, this paradigm helped illustrate that regardless of how they feel about their jobs, people sell sex for the same reason everyone else works: to make money. Meanwhile, some feminists define prostitution as violence against women (symptomatic of patriarchal oppression), which for them means that selling sex could never be "work" (Dennis 2008).

To complicate matters further, some individuals do not define their actions as sex work due to the type of activities involved. This is the sentiment shared by Mike, a gay, twenty-eight-year-old professional companion for men: "I'm not technically a sex worker. I'm more of a companion with benefits technically. The only reason is because it's not always about the sex" (Mike, interview by author, July 3, 2015). Since there is a hierarchy among sex workers, some people do not want to be lumped together with other people selling sex (Simon 2018). Phil, a forty-three-year-old gay escort for men emphasizes his professional identity: "I'm not a junkie and I'm not a thief and I take my work seriously" (Phil, interview by author, July 20, 2016). Some people, like exotic dancers who do not actually "sell sex" as part of their primary job, do not consider themselves sex workers. Bashir, a twenty-one-year-old straight stripper and former model speaks about one of the two times he escorted: "Because I was at my prime and not completely broke, I got to choose. She looked hot, and she looked clean. I just don't go after random girls . . . [she paid me] $1,500 for a . . . private dance" (Bashir, interview by author, March 11, 2016). There are also those who do not consider what they did or what they do as sex work due to the frequency of interactions or a change in their relationship with a client. This could include someone who sold sex once out of desperation; someone who does not receive money but receives payment in another form; someone dating a rich man who pays for everything; or those dating former clients.

Despite its political purpose, the term *sex work* can be problematic because it highlights the taboo part of the job, the sexual act, which is not always a requirement. As workers engage in **emotional labor**, sometimes there is no physical contact of any kind as they provide companionship, a shoulder to cry on, or paid friendship. Some clients and workers develop long-lasting friendships or relationships, countering stereotypes of exploitation, objectification, and depersonalization. Of course, like other jobs, there are negative aspects of the work and undesirable people a worker must deal with. Depending on a sex worker's level of financial freedom and ability to choose which clients they will work with, the enjoyment experienced in some sexual encounters can become integral to their nonwork sex lives (Walby 2012). For Phil, attractive clients were a fringe benefit: "Sometimes I'll get a guy who actually turns me on . . . I should be paying him for this, I think, but I can't tell him that. Your personal life crosses into work" (Phil, interview by author, July 20, 2016). When a sex worker does find a client attractive or engages in nonsexual activities such as mutual nonsexual massage, caressing, kissing, cuddling, and hugging, they further complicate the personal and professional, sex and work.

emotional labor
the process of managing one's own feelings in order to manage the feelings of others, as described by Hochschild (1983). For example, workers are expected to regulate their emotions during interactions with customers, coworkers, and superiors.

OVERVIEW OF SEX WORK LAWS IN CANADA

The government doesn't care about us. If you're not a woman and you don't have problems then we don't really care.

—Dylan, twenty-three, flexible identity, escort for men and women (interview by author, October 10, 2014).

All forms of sex work have been subject to the changing whims of local, provincial, or federal police forces and lawmakers regardless of time period. The Indian Act of 1879 criminalized Indigenous women engaging in prostitution and barred others from providing these women housing. From about the 1890s to the 1970s prostitutes were depicted as subversives (vagrants), and any woman who was "found in a public place" without a chaperone and did not give "a good account of herself" was deemed arrestable under the Criminal Code (Martin 2002). For the most part, there was a narrow range of acceptable gendered behaviors, and for women "even minor deviance [could] be seen as a substantial challenge to the authority of the family" (Chambers 2007, 58). Under this patriarchal paradigm, prostitution was particularly threatening in that it defied gendered notions of the respectability of monogamous procreative relations where sexuality was consigned to the privacy of the bedroom of married heterosexual couples. Women and children of "good standing" needed to be protected from such public debauchery (Hubbard and Sanders 2003). No law was needed for men who sold sex to men because they fell under laws that criminalized same-sex sexual activity until 1969.

In the early 1970s, the institutionalization of women's status and rights in the government structures of the Canadian nation-state helped to prioritize the needs of women-as-a-group (Stetson and Mazur 1995). During this period, feminist activism generally focused on issues of equal wages, affordable childcare, food, and housing, as well as access to reproductive health services (McKenna 2019). By the mid-1980s, feminists of color and lesbian feminists had been advocating against the "the dominance of white 'Western,' 'north' or 'First World' assumptions about what it means to be a feminist and what women need to be liberated where race, class and other intersecting positionalities were de-emphasized" (Bunjun 2010, 116; see Bumiller 2008; Heron 2007; Srivastava 2005). During the same period, further debate and fracture occurred over "the effects of commercial sexuality on the representation and treatment of all women" (McKenna 2019). Here stories of (male) violence against (female) sex workers were appropriated and whitewashed to illustrate the vulnerability of women and subsequently taken up in political discourse and policy.

In political response to public pressure to "do something" about the problem of street prostitution and violence against women, Parliament set up committees on pornography and prostitution (Fraser 1985) and on sexual offenses against children and youths (Badgley 1984). Fraser identified prostitution as symptomatic of women's inequality and recommended partial decriminalization and strategies to reduce social and financial inequities. Badgley labeled young prostitutes as victims of abusive homes but favored criminal law strategies that would "help" fallen women and girls. In both cases no attempt was made to acknowledge or explain why men and boys (or others outside of the binary) sell sex. In the end, all aspects of street prostitution were criminalized and the "systematic murder of poor, racialized, and disproportionately Indigenous, street-based sex workers" was ignored for decades (McKenna 2019).

Between 2007 and 2013, both the province of Ontario Superior Court and the Supreme Court of Canada declared that the criminalization of prostitution had, in fact, violated the constitutional rights of sex workers by creating unsafe work conditions. In cases of violent or abusive clients, workers could not go to the police, hire security, or work in groups for fear of criminal punishment (Pivot Legal Society 2013). While sex worker rights organizations advocated for complete decriminalization, some radical-leaning feminist organizations such as the London Abused Women Centre had extensive political and public influence (Dawthorne 2018). They dominated media coverage declaring that prostitution reinforces gender inequalities "allowing men . . . paid access to female bodies, thereby demeaning and degrading the human dignity of all women and girls" (Department of Justice 2014).

For those outside of the gender binary, their erasure in antiprostitution arguments is a continuance of systems of **cisnormativity**. Under the frame of exploitation, sex work is reduced to penetrative (penile-vaginal) sexual intercourse, relegating heterosexual behavior to one assumed form, while heteronormative monogamous families and relationships are deemed universal (Dawthorne 2018). Here men are positioned as always sexually interested in women, and an ideology of **hegemonic masculinity** is reinforced, where "men are not supposed to be the objects of lust" or pursued as they are socially constructed as dominant, in-control, and virile (De Cecco 1991; Phoenix and Oerton 2005; Satz 1995).

Combined with the pressure to belong to an international system of antitrafficking states (with Canada ratifying the **Palermo protocols** in 2002), prostitution laws were harmonized into the Protection of Communities and Exploited Persons Act (PCEPA) by 2014. Instead of targeting sex workers themselves through arrest, the law focused on "ending demand," arresting and fining male clients, reeducating them in **John schools,** and criminalizing the means to advertise sexual services (Hua and Nigorizawa 2010). Reflecting this change, police started labeling all incidents of men buying sex from women as sex trafficking, making it seem as if Canada was in a growing crisis.

MEN WHO SELL SEX

If I was a girl, it would be the biggest deal in the world. They'd be worried about my wellbeing and me getting hurt . . . there's no such thing as a Jane school.

—Matt, twenty-three, heterosexual, "whore-for-women" (interview by author, May 24, 2016).

Men who sell sex in London are not copies of each other nor do they share any sort of collective activist identity or sense of community. They are a diverse group: at the time of interviews these men were between the ages of eighteen and fifty-one. Approximately 40 percent (n=18)

cisnormativity
the assumption that privileges cisgender as the norm (that is, gender identity that corresponds to a person's sex at birth).

hegemonic masculinity
a concept developed by Connell (1995) arguing that there are certain traits, behaviors, and discourses associated with masculinity that are valued and rewarded by dominant social groups and that the performance of hegemonic masculinity helps to legitimize power and inequality.

Palermo protocols
a group of three international treaties adopted by the United Nations to supplement the 2000 Convention against Transnational Organized Crime Exploitation. One of these protocols described the crime of human trafficking as "the exploitation of the prostitution of others or other forms of sexual exploitation" (United Nations 2004, iii).

John schools
forced rehabilitation program for men arrested for solicitation that teaches the negative consequences of prostitution on communities, families, and women (Nathanson and Young 2001).

entered the sex trade between fourteen and eighteen (μ=19.78) years of age. While a quarter (n=11) of the men grew up in lower-income families, more than half (n=27) reported coming from the middle class; seven men never completed high school, yet almost thirteen had completed or attended university.

Seventy-five percent (n=33) identified as white Canadian/Caucasian. One man identified as Southwest Asian, another as Cree/Indigenous, one Black/Rwandan, and another Arabic/Muslim from the Horn of Africa. The remainder identified as mixed ancestries of some variation: white, Black, or from an Indigenous community. Although some white men were racialized in their own way (i.e., working-class emotionless heteromasculinity), men of color discussed being fetishized. For nineteen-year-old Blake this extended to "acting black," using street slang and acting aggressively, or requests for slave and master roleplay. Those few who had immigrated to Canada when they were children described having to deal with the heteromasculine norms and expectations of their parents' home cultures. As 75 percent of the men identified as gay, queer, flexible, bisexual, **Two-Spirit**, or **nonlabel**, this was also common regardless of racial or ethnic background.

REASONS WHY MEN SELL SEX

Often, experiences fit with normative ideas of causation and the preconceived notions of outsiders. These types of connections illustrate attributional biases, considering the fluidity and complexity of people's lives and identities. Not all people with negative life experiences partake in the sex industry, and the industry is not solely composed of people with troubled pasts. While the internet facilitated about half of the men's ability to sell sex, a third were introduced to the sex industry by male or female friends already in it; others had a friend or sibling who served as their broker. Regardless of the method of entry, earning money is the main motive for most when it comes to selling sex.

When faced with unfulfilled needs and impeded financial goals, sex work is one of the few options available for some (Smith and Grov 2011; Vanwesenbeeck 2012). Younger men who leave home for whatever reason can obtain earnings in sex work that they could not get anywhere else. In Canada, rental housing costs alone are higher than a full-time minimum-wage worker makes in any province (Macdonald 2019). Those who receive disability support payments typically only receive half this amount and those on unemployment even less. For postsecondary stu-

Two-Spirit
an English-language term meant to represent a diverse pan-Indigenous umbrella of gender, sex and sexuality variance, and subsequent ceremonial and social roles; often misunderstood as a term solely for individuals who are both male and female.

nonlabel sexuality
a nonidentity; can include people who are uncertain about their sexuality, are sexually fluid, or are resistant to the norms of identity labels.

dents in Ontario, campus grants and government student loans also place people in precarious positions. Compared to other jobs, working in the sex industry can mean more pay and fewer hours; the flexibility in working hours provides the freedom to attend to other commitments such as schoolwork. Furthermore, having a criminal background (over a quarter [n=12] of the men did disclose that they had some sort of criminal record), lack of qualifications, or the seasonality of work restrict the job options available.

The lower emotional, social, or cognitive requirements of particular sex work encounters, as well as flexibility and fewer hours also make sex work appealing for those who struggle with or are not accommodated by traditional employment due to substance use disorders, physical health, mental illness, lack of well-being, or mindset (Dawthorne 2018). Jobs in retail and fast-food restaurants (and manual labor) were found to be oppressive or demoralizing; coworkers, employers, and customers were said to be abusive; and the paycheck and hours were exploitative. Matt illustrates the point:

> I have a lot of mental barriers, it makes it difficult for me to do certain types of work . . . not a lot of people are understanding of my different abilities, so it can really become stressful at times and I don't always perform the best . . . they make you feel like children . . . I thought making a sandwich would be a lot less mentally stressful than having to put my dick into something that could potentially disease me, you know? But no, no, it was—it was way harder on my head. I—physically it was easier, it wasn't a lot of back motion, it was more just standing there all day working with the hands, but mentally, like, when someone's sitting there watching you make their food, it freaks you out, you know? (Matt, interview by author, May 24, 2016)

Given the discourses that men have available to them about their own sexual agency, the discourse of men's sexual pleasure in sex work is fairly common (Dawthorne 2018; McLean 2013; Vanwesenbeek 2012). Some men like Doug, twenty-five, who is **sexually fluid** and escorts for men and women, expressed that sexual pleasure and curiosity were motivators to sell sex, with the breaking of taboos adding to the excitement:

> It was mainly the pleasure of it, but it also was the rush—the adrenaline rush. I even have had sex outside with people. Just

fluid sexuality
romantic and sexual attraction can change over time, situation, and context.

when you're done, your heart's beating and wow, you feel more alive. Sometimes you do things that you only see in a movie . . . I was thinking to myself, oh I heard that in a movie once. Now I'm actually doing it. It's like wow, I never thought I'd be here and now I'm doing this. (Doug, interview by author, July 20, 2016)

Money becomes eroticized, and a worker may derive a sense of value from being admired and feeling desirable (Kort 2017). For a male stripper like Bashir, (hyper)heteromasculinity is vital: in other words, staying in prime physical shape and knowing how to talk to and please women. Moving beyond stripping, these men are often offered large sums of money for "private dances." Instead of being framed as pursued, the ability to choose a client that he finds desirable and his penetrative act (and climax) serve as the ultimate expression of heteromasculinity (Dawthorne 2018; Montemurro and McClure 2005).

Some like Dylan identified sex work is a part of a significant downward spiral in his life, where he was indeed exploited due to his vulnerabilities and drive to purchase drugs:

My uncle had molested me when I was twelve. And then a year later he did it to me again . . . my mom stopped like paying attention to me and really giving any care to me. Yeah. So, when I was twelve I attempted suicide twice. She kind of just put up a wall and said, "You're not mine." When I was about fourteen she told me that she wished I was adopted and that she'd rather not breathe my air anymore; when I was sixteen she drove me downtown, said that I was going to a meeting for school, and then left. And I was not allowed back in the house after that. (Dylan, interview by author, October 10, 2014)

On the streets, Dylan dropped out of school and was quickly introduced to drugs, partying, and drinking and would wake up in the morning not knowing where he was:

[The clients] were like doing what they wanted to me, and I really wasn't okay with it, but I was out there selling . . . so taking advantage of me . . . because they know I'm young, they know that I'm vulnerable, they know that I'm gullible, and they're still willing to give me a load of cash so that they can satisfy themselves. (Dylan, interview by author, October 10, 2014)

GROWING UP

I grew up the same way any other person would.

—Bill, twenty-eight, straight, escort
for women (interview by author, June 24, 2014)

I don't know where to start because it's like a huge chain of reaction—
like a huge chain of things that happened.

—Ted, twenty-one, gay, escort-for-men
(interview by author, January 22, 2016).

I feel depressed about my past a lot. It actually really bothers me. It
haunts me . . . I actually had a very troubled childhood.

—Grant, twenty-one, gay, sex worker for men
(interview by author, September 14, 2016).

We understand the sex industry better when we approach it as highly
intersectional, fluid, and subjective, rather than treating people and their
experiences as fixed and homogenous (Mitchell 2015). Intersectional
analysis moves beyond the essentialist notion that all members of a
population are equally and automatically subordinate (or privileged) just
because they occupy a particular social position (Berger and Guidroz
2009; Bowleg 2012; Rolin 2006). Just like everyone else, "a sex worker's
work life, personal life, family life, spiritual life, upbringing, and class
background all interrelate and shape one another" (Handkivsky 2007;
Mitchell 2015, 127). Despite this, we know very little about how family
functions in the lives of male sex workers.

This story of a sex worker's upbringing illustrates perceived degrees
of **agency**. Regardless of class background, these echoed institutionalized
(middle-class) notions of how children and parents should act and what
children should be allowed or expected to do (Lachman and Weaver 1998).
Those from working-class or otherwise less privileged backgrounds like
Howie spoke of their hardships and how they adapted to or pushed against
interpersonal stressors and structural violence. Howie, twenty-five, sells sex
to older women that his brother sets him up with to pay for his addiction
and repay his debts, including putting his girlfriend through university.
His childhood fits with the mainstream images of the neighborhood he
grew up in: one of the largest low-income housing complexes in the
city of London (London Community Chaplaincy, 2017). This community
consists of row housing built in the 1970s during a period of increased
public housing spending by the federal government and is one of Lon-

agency
the capacity of a person
to act independently and
make their own choices.

don's seven rent-geared-to-income complexes administered by the city. The average income, as of 2015, is approximately CDN$15,000 a year, compared to the adjacent suburban community with an average income of about CDN$110,000 a year. This highlights an inner-city and suburb divide (Smuck 2015). The majority of these inner-city residents face the challenges of living in poverty daily. Many are single parents, working poor, and some are immigrants. Struggles with mental health, substance use, or abuse are common, and lack of food, crime, and financial insecurity are the norm. Howie tells his story:

> All my uncles and my dad we were . . . in and out of jail doing dope their whole lives, so. It was inevitable, it's just in the family . . . I found out my uncle was selling [hard drugs]. I was getting it dirt cheap, bringing it to school . . . one thing led to another, got kicked out of school, and. . . . When I was fifteen my dad got me and my brother our own place where he would pay the rent, but we had to cover groceries . . . [we started] robbing houses for food. My other cousin lived with us. (Howe, interview by author, July 9, 2014)

While those like Matt, with a lower-class background, felt the issues of his youth would be mediated if he had access to the perceived opportunities and choices available to the middle class:

> I think that if I had money, I wouldn't have been motivated to take [this] path. If I would have had more opportunities. If we weren't—wouldn't have been ghetto. If we would have had a house and a car. If I would have gone, like, in sports when I was a kid and been in clubs and made friends, you know, go on vacations and, you know, like that's what normal kids do. They go on spring break with their parents, or they join like the soccer team and every Wednesday, mom has to take you and watch you not score a goal for an hour. You know, that's what kids do. That's what you see in the movies and media all the time, I never had that. I grew up, you know, playing, hanging out by myself, walking around the gulley, getting myself into trouble, you know, drinking and stuff like that. Like when I was a kid, I didn't have a lot of opportunities or options. I feel like if my family was loaded, that I would have never been that desperate for money; I would have never had to go on welfare at fifteen years old, you know? I wouldn't have sold sex. (Matt, interview by author, May 24, 2016)

The culture of the Canadian middle class is consistent with ideals of being able to make choices, pave our own paths, and voice our ideas and opinions. For individuals from this background, these norms are often taken for granted, and they had little to say about their pasts. They tend to live in a relatively certain world where their basic needs are met; food and shelter are rarely an issue. Some of these expectations include fulfilling employment, educational opportunities, the supports of family, and recreational pleasures, while clean water, abundant food options, and ample lodging are taken for granted regardless of age (Kohn 1969; Miller, Cho and Bracey 2005).

COMING OUT

Regardless of upbringing, mental illness, sexual abuse, substance use disorders, and coming to terms with one's sexuality permeated all backgrounds. While London tries to maintain an image that equates certain local industries like the biosciences and education with cosmopolitanism and tolerance (Bradford 2010), other dominant sectors such as finance, manufacturing, and military-industrial have been associated with **heteronormative**, masculinized, and sometimes homophobic work cultures and environments (Lewis et al. 2015; McDowell et al. 2007). Located within a socially conservative regional Bible Belt, London does act as a magnet for younger, rurally situated LGBT people moving from homophobic environments (Bruce and Harper 2011). Despite this, there is a small LGBT public presence and lack of LGBT-oriented services, so the city serves as a transition to larger cities like Toronto where these supports exist (Lewis et al. 2015).

heteronormativity inspired by French philosopher Michel Foucault, this term refers to how social institutions and policies reinforce the assumption that heterosexuality is normal and natural, that gender and sex are binary, and reproductive monogamous sex is moral.

Selling sex (and hiring a sex worker) is not unknown among men who have sex with men, and male sex workers have an established (while contentious) place in gay history and culture (Scott, MacPhail, and Minichiello 2014; Koken et al. 2005). One turning point in the life of the nonheterosexual, however, is the coming-out story, which is an essential theme in the narratives of gay and queer men. Coming out is about reclaiming an authentic self in response to discrimination, concealment, and living a double life. With the knowledge that society treats homosexuality a certain way, "being gay" means learning to cope with stigmatization, having the courage to disclose one's orientation in fear of retribution, and learning to feel good about oneself (Schneider 1997).

Coming out can be uneventful for some like Phil where "nobody was particularly surprised" (Phil, interview by author, July 20, 2016); others suffered from varying degrees of rejection (Padilla et al. 2010). Particularly traumatic were the reactions of extremely conservative and religious families. In the United States and Canada, LGBT youth can be kicked out due to parental disapproval of their sexual orientation or run away from homophobic abuse (Durso and Gates 2012). This is David's experience. At the time of our interview, he was twenty-three years old, couch surfing with his boyfriend Ted, and trying to pay for his substance use and supplement his Ontario Works income through panhandling and sex work:

> My family life was . . . really . . . unstable because my parents, my step-mom and my dad were Jehovah's Witnesses . . . if you are gay you are basically hated [by] the Jehovah's Witnesses. You are, like, shunned. Like none wants to talk to you. I've known since grade three that I was gay. I just didn't like come-out or like know what my feelings were . . . until I was like seventeen or eighteen. So when I came out they [said] there is the door and you can leave. I was like ok I'm surprised you are doing this to your own son but whatever . . . there's still some days where [I feel like] my brain is trapped in a cage because of . . . my upbringing and my parents . . . I still want to talk to them but they don't want anything to do with me. (David, interview by author, July 21, 2014)

survival sex work
the practice of people who are extremely disadvantaged trading sex for basic necessities; usually denotes those who would not otherwise choose to work in the sex industry if they could.

Youth like David disproportionately make up 25 to 40 percent of Canada's 40,000 to 150,000 homeless youth (Abramovich and Shelton 2017; Keohane 2016). Such youth report resorting to living on the streets, couch surfing, or turning to **survival sex work**. In addition to discrimination, isolation, and depression, hostile family reactions to sexual orientation significantly influence teen mental health (Ryan et al. 2009; Steinberg and Duncan 2002); for example, 10 to 40 percent of all LGBT people will attempt suicide once in their lifetimes (Marshal et al. 2011). Child services may intervene if alerted to school truancy after a youth has been kicked out of the home; however, there is often a lack of family welfare accountability in secondary schools. Many of the men I interviewed experienced inappropriate foster placements, homophobic group homes, rejection and discrimination at shelters, and a disproportionate lack of accommodations (Dame 2004; Dawthorne 2018). In this context, sex work is one of the few options left (Cianciotto and Cahill 2003).

SEXUAL ABUSE

Regarding gay identity development and experience, there is evidence that gay males are at increased risk for sexual abuse as children, or at least they are more likely to report and recognize abuse (Brady 2008; Dawthorne 2018). Before the age of sixteen, one in six men (irrespective of adult sexuality) has been sexually abused (Gartner 2011). The men who sell sex (at any age) in my study reported similarly, and their stories of survival and victimization predominate their recollections of childhood. Due to shame and the prevailing view (and subsequent institutionalization) that sexual assault is a women's issue, men rarely speak up (Millard 2016). Men and boys are socialized to experience sexual assault differently, through a form of masculinity that does not allow for victimization, leading to denial and psychological repression (Bera 1995; Bogin 2006; Gartner 1999). These men were never given the space to recover and are further traumatized by a culture of silence, lack of supportive resources, and the shame and humiliation they felt from friends and family. Men like Blake told me how, after telling family members of the abuse at the hands of an older relative, their mother's boyfriends and siblings, they were neglected, ridiculed, and otherwise emotionally abused. It is this betrayal that dominates recollections and feelings of trauma (see Clancy 2009; Summit 1983).

SUBSTANCE USE DISORDERS

Studies of substance use show correlations between adverse childhood experiences and earlier risk of substance use disorder (Mate 2009). Almost half of the men interviewed had experience using drugs before the age of eighteen, including nearly three-fourths of those who were sexually abused. Regardless of age, other men were introduced to drugs on the streets or from family, and for others, opioid use began after a doctor prescribed it to treat a medical condition. Dylan describes his use of a plethora of substances to self-medicate his mental illness and the trauma of childhood sexual abuse by an uncle:

> I think it was an emotional downfall. And I definitely do think it was boredom. I mean when you're on the streets what is there to do besides sex and drugs and sleeping with god knows who? And I think it also too was like just a longing for something. I have figured out in the last like couple of months that I look like, on the inside, I've been really longing for my mother. And I think just like, oh, I could have crack, and it won't leave me behind. You know, it's kind of like I replaced my mother with the drugs because it gave me that same feeling. You know? When I had it around it felt really good and I felt really happy. (Dylan, interview by author, October 10, 2014)

Overall, substance use can offer a way of coping with stress, pain, and other issues deemed outside of one's control, such as grief and loss (Pickard 2017). With a lack of places to turn, the substance and the act of using become a substitute for the relationships men like Dylan do not have and for needs they cannot meet. The combination of hegemonic masculinity and substance use discourages men from help-seeking behaviors, especially for problems considered nonnormative (e.g., sexual abuse) or personally controllable (e.g., mental illness). This creates a vulnerability that encourages the use of numbing and comforting substances as an escape (Addis and Mahalik 2003; Lye and Biblarz 1993).

There does appear to be a connection between selling sex and substance use disorders (Minichiello et al. 2003; de Graaf et al. 1995; Pleak and Meyer-Bahlburg 1990) as more than a quarter of the men I interviewed identified substance use as part of their motivation for selling sex. Tim, twenty-nine, who sells sex to women, confirms this: "[Its] pretty much what kept me in. . . . Because if I didn't have sex with someone to make the money then I'd be feeling like shit. You know, I'd just kind of wait it out. Like I'd feel like more shit if I don't have the external source of endorphins that I'm used to" (Tim, interview by author, July 21, 2014).

HEGEMONIC MASCULINITY

Regardless of background, sexuality, or the gender of one's clients, most men evaluate the benefits of sex work against the risks. Violating hegemonic masculinity by engaging in a "gender-inappropriate" form of work, a man sells sex at the risk of being shamed by peers, family, and the broader community. Simultaneously, hegemonic masculinity allowed men to shield themselves from shame. Jimmy, twenty-five and straight-identifying, has "prostituted" for men and women. He distances himself from female sex workers and feminized tropes of victimization and vulnerability: "I did this to myself. I'm not a victim. [Clients] didn't approach me. They didn't know what I needed the money for. They didn't take advantage of me. I had no one to answer to. I lived by myself, I was doing whatever I wanted to do. It was easy" (Jimmy, interview by author February 9, 2015).

To "do what a man has got to do" to survive meant taking risks, being adventurous, and remaining resilient, with no help from anyone (including the government). Some also spoke of panhandling, selling drugs, breaking and entering, and stealing to survive in this manner. Emphasizing hypersexuality or sexual voraciousness, discussing attractive clients, and seeking out the taboo pleasures of sex with many different clients reinforced a man's masculinity, shielding him from shame. This was another strategy to position oneself as in control. The act of making money to support himself, his spouse, and/or children allowed a sex worker to reify his masculinized role as breadwinner and generous provider (McDowell 2014).

For some like Doug, the ability to purchase luxury goods or make more money than people in other jobs symbolized personal empowerment:

> I had everything I wanted. Went from wearing some ripped up jeans to like designer stuff like Makaveli and Banana Republic. I was wearing like Prada and Versace, Sean John and everything. I was loaded. I had real diamond earrings. [After I had a client], I'd go down and get my hair done, get piercings, contacts and everything all that. Live life. I kept buying like headphones, scarves and what not. (Doug, interview by author, July 20, 2016)

Lastly, workers took pride in their professional expertise and altruism. Maintaining a sense of professionalism with "disfigured" or otherwise undesirable clients was framed as self-sacrifice. Stuart, thirty-three, sells sex, is a model, and acts in pornographic films: he took pride in creating a safe environment that empowered emotional and sexual positivity, thereby giving his work some social value (Kumar, Scott, and Minichiello 2017). "You're out there providing a service . . . everyone needs loving too. It's all about faking. You're in it . . . to make money. They're in it to get off or the companionship. It's more, 'I want you to come home and cook dinner with me and watch a movie,' and its rarely sex" (Stuart, interview by author, December 15, 2015).

STIGMA

Masculinity can be a valuable tool to understand the experiences of some men but to appeal to masculinity that constructs men as strong and powerful is deceptively simplistic and seriously flawed. Not only does it perpetuate a fantasy that "victims" do not have agency, resilience, or show evidence of resistance, it assumes that those who do have power have not suffered. Stigma is a situation "when a person possesses (or is believed to possess) some attribute or characteristic that conveys a social identity that is devalued in a particular social context" (Crocker, Major, and Steele 1998). Nonheterosexual men discussed issues of homophobia ranging from being bullied, rejected by family, or being victims of hate crime. The intersection of other aspects of their lives along with the stigma of sex work intensifies feelings of shame and experiences of discrimination.

The perception or anticipation that people are not or will not be accepting has negative consequences on personal well-being (Allison 1998). Vulnerability can lead to feelings of uncertainty and anxiety, impairing self-esteem, and social functioning (Crocker, Major, and Steele 1998). Many men like Link, a twenty-four-year-old online escort for men, live double lives to protect themselves, concealing their involvement with the industry in order not to be judged or penalized (echoing those who have to hide their sexuality). "I am afraid to tell [my boyfriend] because I mean . . . I don't tell anybody just to save face. I don't like the lying and I hate lying about myself and about things that you know I feel I should be able to express" (Link, interview by author, November 14, 2014). Other men were reluctant to socialize or start new relationships due to similar fears of rejection. While many men do have strained relationships with family, those who do not were worried about causing them emotional pain. Others wish to avoid moralizing, ridicule, and removal of any form of parental financial support.

The knowledge that an individual has been involved in the sex industry has and can be used to discriminate against them in other work environments. For those who use sex work to supplement their income or are involved due to a desperate situation, the economic need to sell sex means that losing any other job would be devastating. Teachers, bankers, police officers, restaurant workers, and real estate employees are public examples of people who have been fired from their jobs because of their current or former involvement in sex work (Carey 2018; Dickson 2013; McLean 2011; Petro 2012; Schladebeck 2017). Rick, a thirty-four-year-old who describes himself as **gay for pay**, describes this need for discretion:

> Anonymity is [important] because like I do have a day job and family and stuff here that know nothing about what I do . . . I don't think I'd get fired over this because that's illegal, but I do think my boss is the type of person that would really look hard for another excuse to fire me . . . I work retail for a boss who is heavily religious . . . If he were to know that I'm like turning tricks, yeah that would be the end of it. (Rick, interview by author, July 7, 2014)

This secrecy is one factor in why myths regarding the number of men in the industry continue.

Some sex workers compared their desire for upward social mobility with their current quality of life. The loss of a middle-class lifestyle, inability

gay for pay
individuals who identify as heterosexual but engage in homosexual behaviors and acts, for money, material goods, or other forms of security (e.g., housing)

to get ahead, or the precarity of their finances brought about feelings of shame. Though there are structural reasons for economic struggle, those from middle-class backgrounds internalized their failures as personal deficits, while those of lower-class upbringings felt they were set up to fail. The sector of the industry, the sexual practices, the types of clients seen, how much is earned, as well as their level of agency: these are all part of a moral hierarchy of more or less acceptable behavior.

Those men dealing with substance use disorders were shamed by peers and the public and some tried to cover up needle marks or otherwise remain discreet; to counter internalized shame some men engaged in downward comparison, separating themselves from being associated with "junkies." Some nonsubstance users also separated themselves from "crack-whores." The intersection of sex work and substance use served as a way for some like Steven, a bisexual thirty-eight-year-old man who cruises the downtown area as a "street ho," to position himself as better off than other street workers. "You might think the odd woman that's a junkie on the street with all picks and sores all over her face probably will suck their crack dealer's dick for more drugs, but when you're ho-ing . . . you're walking up to nice people's houses, and nice cars . . . it's not for your next piece of rock" (Steven, interview by author, July 13, 2015).

Male sex workers can be victims of sexual violence as adults (just like everyone else). The trauma of being raped by a female client is exacerbated by stereotypical paradigms that frame men as perpetrators and women as victims; that rape involves penetration, and for men, all sex is welcome (Smith 2012). Matt gave an account of being raped by a female client as an adult and the traumatization and shame he feels. "They say men can't be raped by women. Which is bullshit, like, it's happened to me, I know it can happen. I experienced it" (Matt, interview with author, May 24, 2016). The stereotype of female sexual victimization by men reinforces ideas that feminize and stigmatize victims and that female-perpetrated abuse is rare or nonexistent (Mendel 1995); it prioritizes interventions for women and excludes male victims (Stemple and Meyer 2014). Matt continues, "Rape doesn't have to mean just being penetrated . . . they're doing things to you that you don't want. . . . When we were done fucking I went to get up, she said, 'You're just going to lay there and when we're done, we're done, and if you don't like it, good fucking luck, try getting up,' and she was like three times my size" (Matt, interview with author, May 24, 2016). His account challenges the assumption that male victims experience less harm and women are disproportionately affected by sexual violence (Scarce 1997). It also undermines the stereotype that men are physically and emotionally stronger than women (Koss et al. 2007). Matt continues, "I couldn't do nothing man. So I started crying laying there. Like it hurt so bad. She gave me the money and I was like—I just took it and I, like, looked down—I don't know, but like that broke me man. I didn't feel tough. I didn't feel like a hotshot. I didn't feel cool, I didn't feel like what I was doing was worth it anymore at that point" (Matt, interview with author, May 24, 2016). Here is where the stigma of selling sex and rape intersect: "At that moment, like, I wanted to quit so bad. If I didn't need the money, that would have made me quit, but I was still hurting; so . . . I was scared. Traumatized. I feel like everyone I was with was using me. Like, you know, I wasn't there because anybody cared. At that point I was a whore" (Matt, interview with author, May 24, 2016). Though his heterosexuality is not questioned here, Matt's understanding of what happened to him is framed by cultural ideas of heteromasculinity. He no longer felt in control or powerful; he felt the shame of being emasculated and powerless to do anything about it. He also felt that because he had consented initially, no one would take him seriously if he reported it. The concerns of ridicule are echoed when a man's rapist is a man; institutionalized homophobia, or in the case of a heterosexual victim, internalized homophobia adds to rape stigma; the loss of control and helplessness can exacerbate the trauma.

Despite some men feeling shame for engaging in sex work (especially with undesirable clients), the idea of using social services or receiving any form of social assistance that would reduce the need to or frequency of sex was seen as more shameful. They framed the people who used them with visceral discourses of filth, degradation, and extreme poverty (Halnon 2013). Those who had previous interactions with these services or refused to use them engaged in defensive othering, asserting that they are better than others in some manner. Claiming social benefits conveyed a devalued identity and admission of failure; it also meant increased precarity. Unfortunately, without visibility, these men also fail to challenge the status quo (Koken, Bimbi, and Parsons 2015).

THE MEN LEFT BEHIND

Regardless of age or sexuality, men require safe, nonjudgmental, and accessible services for substance use and mental illness as well as for other vulnerabilities. Also needed: improved accountability through justice, educational, and social support systems to help those youth who have been sexually abused, lack emotional or financial support from family, or have been kicked out because of their sexuality (Dawthorne 2018). Generalizations and competitive statistics—taking a snapshot of reality that ignores the bigger picture, has created hierarchies that inform our decisions on who is important and who is disposable. For many of my informants, I was often the only person they had ever talked to about their sex work experiences. Social policies and laws that pathologize and exclude with the mindset that (only) women are vulnerable, that the sex industry employs only women, and that the industry is inherently harmful, have reinforced hegemonic masculinity and ignored the ways women are implicated (Dawthorne 2018; Whitlock 2018). The existence of male sex workers disrupts gendered binaries of choice and constraint, illustrating that sex work can be freely chosen but also that men are not always in control of their own lives.

REVIEW QUESTIONS

1. Define sex work and identify the factors that should be considered when claims are made about sex work.

2. Why is framing sex work as the exploitation of women by men inaccurate and harmful?

3. In what ways are male sex workers stigmatized? How do ideas of masculinity factor in?

4. What issues does this chapter raise about feminism?

KEY TERMS

agency: the capacity of a person to act independently and make their own choices.

cisnormativity: the assumption that privileges cisgender as the norm (that is, gender identity that corresponds to a person's sex at birth).

emotional labor: the process of managing one's own feelings in order to manage the feelings of others, as described by Hochschild (1983). For example, workers are expected to regulate their emotions during interactions with customers, coworkers, and superiors.

fluid sexuality: romantic and sexual attraction can change over time, situation, and context.

gay for pay: individuals who identify as heterosexual but engage in homosexual behaviors and acts, for money, material goods, or other forms of security (e.g., housing)

hegemonic masculinity: a concept developed by Connell (1995) arguing that there are certain traits, behaviors, and discourses associated with masculinity that are valued and rewarded by dominant social groups and that the performance of hegemonic masculinity helps to legitimize power and inequality.

heteronormativity: inspired by French philosopher Michel Foucault, this term refers to how social institutions and policies reinforce the assumption that heterosexuality is normal and natural, that gender and sex are binary, and reproductive monogamous sex is moral.

John schools: forced rehabilitation program for men arrested for solicitation that teaches the negative consequences of prostitution on communities, families, and women (Nathanson and Young 2001).

nonlabel sexuality: a nonidentity; can include people who are uncertain about their sexuality, are sexually fluid, or are resistant to the norms of identity labels.

Palermo protocols: a group of three international treaties adopted by the United Nations to supplement the 2000 Convention against Transnational Organized Crime Exploitation. One of these protocols described the crime of human trafficking as "the exploitation of the prostitution of others or other forms of sexual exploitation" (United Nations 2004, iii).

structural violence: the systematic ways in which social structures harm or disadvantage individuals and thus create and maintain social inequalities.

survival sex work: the practice of people who are extremely disadvantaged trading sex for basic necessities; usually denotes those who would not otherwise choose to work in the sex industry if they could.

Two-Spirit: an English-language term meant to represent a diverse pan-Indigenous umbrella of gender, sex and sexuality variance, and subsequent ceremonial and social roles; often misunderstood as a term solely for individuals who are both male and female.

RESOURCES FOR FURTHER EXPLORATION

- Aggleton, Peter, and Richard Parker, eds. 2015. *Men Who Sell Sex: Global Perspectives.* London: Routledge.

- Dennis, Jeffery. 2008. "Women Are Victims, Men Make Choices: The Invisibility of Men and Boys in the Global Sex Trade." *Gender Issues* 25: 11–25.

- Minichiello, Victor, and John Scott, eds. 2014. *Male Sex Work and Society*. New York: Harrington Park.

- Shoden, Clarisa, and Samantha Majic, eds. 2014. *Negotiating Sex Work: Unintended Consequences of Policy and Activism.* Minneapolis: University of Minnesota Press.

- Walby, Kevin. 2012. *Touching Encounters: Sex, Work, and Male-for-Male Internet Escorting.* Chicago: University of Chicago Press.

ACKNOWLEDGMENTS

This research was partially funded by an Ontario Graduate Scholarship.

BIBLIOGRAPHY

Abramovich, Alex, and Jama Shelton. 2017. *Where Am I Going to Go? Intersectional Approaches to Ending LGBTQ2S Youth Homelessness in Canada & the U.S.* Toronto: Canadian Observatory on Homelessness.

Addis, Michael, and James Mahalik. 2003. "Men, Masculinity, and the Contexts of Help Seeking." *American Psychologist* 58, no. 1: 5–14.

Allison, Kevin. 1998. "Stress and Oppressed Social Category Membership." In *Prejudice: The Target's Perspective,* edited by Janet Swim and Charles Stangor, 145–70. San Diego: Academic Press.

Badgley, Robin. 1984. *Sexual Offences against Children: Report of the Committee on Sexual Offences against Children and Youths.* Ottawa: Minister of Supply and Services Canada.

Bell, Shannon. 1994. *Reading, Writing and Rewriting the Prostitute Body.* Indianapolis: Indiana University Press.

Benoit, Cecilia, Michaela Smith, Mikael Jansson, Samantha Magnus, Jackson Flagg, and Renay Maurice. 2018. "Sex Work and Three Dimensions of Self-Esteem: Self-worth, Authenticity and Self-efficacy." *Culture, Health, and Sexuality* 20, no. 1: 1–15.

Bera, Walter. 1995. "Betrayal: Clergy Sexual Abuse and Male Survivors." In *Breach of Trust: Sexual Exploitations by Health Care Professionals and Clergy,* edited by John Gonsiorek, 91–111. Newbury Park, CA: SAGE.

Berger, Michele, and Kathleen Guidroz. 2009. "Introduction." In *The Intersectional Approach: Transforming the Academy through Race, Class, and Gender,* edited by Michele Berger and Kathleen Guidroz, 1–25. Chapel Hill: University of North Carolina Press.

Bettio, Francesca, Marina Della Giusta, and Maria Laura Di Tommaso. 2017. "Sex Work and Trafficking: Moving beyond the Dichotomies." *Feminist Economics* 23, no. 3: 1–22.

Bindman, Jo. 1997. "Redefining Prostitution as Sex Work on the International Agenda." *Anti-Slavery International*. http://www.walnet.org/csis/papers/redefining.html. Accessed July 11, 2017.

Blevins, Kristie, and Thomas Holt. 2009. "Examining the Virtual Subculture of Johns." *Journal of Contemporary Ethnography* 38, no. 5: 619–648.

Blume, Lawrence. 2002. *Stigma and Social Control*. Vienna: Institute for Advanced Studies.

Bogin, Gina. 2006. "Out of the Darkness: Male Adolescents and the Experience of Sexual Victimization." *School Social Work Journal* 30, no. 2: 1–21.

Bowleg, Lisa. 2012. "The Problem with the Phrase Women and Minorities: Intersectionality—an Important Theoretical Framework for Public Health." *American Journal of Public Health* 102, no. 7: 1267–1273.

Boyd, Susan. 1997. *Challenging the Public / Private Divide: Feminism, Law and Public Policy*. Toronto: University of Toronto Press.

Brady, Stephen. 2008. "The Impact of Sexual Abuse on Sexual Identity Formation in Gay Men." *Journal of Child Sexual Abuse.*17, no. 3–4: 359–376.

Bumiller, Kristin. 2008. *In an Abusive State: How Neoliberalism Appropriated the Feminist Movement against Sexual Violence*. Durham, NC: Duke University Press.

Bunjun, Benita. 2010. "Feminist Organizations and Intersectionality: Contesting Hegemonic Feminism." *Atlantis* 34, no. 2: 115–126.

Buschi, Eva. 2014. "Sex Work and Violence: Focusing on Managers in the Indoor Sex Industry." *Sexualities.* 17, no. 5–6: 724–741.

Carey, Corinne. 2004. *No Second Chance: People with Criminal Records Denied Access to Public Housing*. New York: Human Rights Watch. https://www.hrw.org/report/2004/11/17/no-second-chance/people-criminal-records-denied-access-public-housing. Accessed November 3, 2017.

Castle, Tammy, and Jenifer Lee. 2008. "Ordering Sex in Cyberspace: A Content Analysis of Escort Website." *International Journal of Cultural Studies* 11, no. 1: 107–121.

Chambers, Lori. 2007. *Misconceptions: Unmarried Motherhood and the Ontario Children of Unmarried Parents Act, 1921–1969*. Toronto: Osgood Society for Canadian Legal History.

Cianciotto, Jason, and Sean Cahill. 2003. *Education policy: Issues affecting lesbian, gay, bi-sexual, and transgender youth*. New York: The National Gay and Lesbian Task Force Policy Institute.

Clancy, Susan. 2009. *The Trauma Myth*. New York: Basic Books.

Connell, Raewyn and James Messerschmidt. 2005. "Hegemonic Masculinity: Rethinking the Concept." *Gender and Society.* 19, no. 6: 829–859.

Cossman, Brenda. 2002. "Family Feuds: Neo-liberal and Neo-conservative Visions of the Reprivatization Project." In *Privatization, Law and the Challenge to Feminism*, edited by Brenda Cossman and Judy Fudge, 128–169. Toronto: University of Toronto Press.

Crocker, Jennifer, Brenda Major, and Claude Steele. 1998. "Social Stigma." In *The Handbook of Social Psychology*, edited by Daniel Gilbert, Susan Fiske, and Gardner Lindzey, 504–553. New York: McGraw-Hill.

Dame, Linda. 2004. "Live Through This: The Experiences of Queer Youth in Care in Manitoba." *Canadian Online Journal of Queer Studies in Education* 1, no. 1: 1–28.

Dawthorne, Nathan. 2018. *Intelligible Variability: Narratives of Male Sex Work in London Ontario Canada.* PhD diss., University of Western Ontario.

De Cecco, John. 1991. "Introduction: Investigating Hustlers." In *Understanding the Male Hustler*, edited by Sam Steward, 29–52. Binghamton, NY: Harrington Park.

de Graaf, Ron, Ine Vanwesenbeeck, Gertjan van Zessen, Cees Straver, and Jan Visser. 1995. "Alcohol and Drug Use in Heterosexual and Homosexual Prostitution, and Its Relation to Protection Behaviour." *AIDS Care* 7: 35–47.

Dickson, E. J. 2013. "Fired for Doing Porn: The New Employment Discrimination." *Salon,* June 13, 2018. https://www.salon.com/2013/09/30/fired_for_doing_porn_the_new_employment_discrimination/.

Dennis, Jeffery. 2008. "Women are Victims, Men Make Choices: The Invisibility of Men and Boys in the Global Sex Trade." *Gender Issues* 25:11–25.

Department of Justice Canada. 2014. *Technical Paper: Bill C-36, Protection of Communities and Exploited Persons Act.* https://www.justice.gc.ca/eng/rp-pr/other-autre/protect/p1.html#sec2. Accessed June 25, 2019.

Dorais, Michel. 2005. *Rent Boys: The World of Male Sex Workers.* Translated by Peter Feldstein. Montreal: McGill-Queen's Press.

DuBois, Ellen. 1978. "The Nineteenth Century Woman Suffrage Movement and the Analysis of Women's Oppression." In *Capitalist Patriarchy and the Case for Socialist Feminism,* edited by Zillah Einstein. New York: Monthly Review.

Durso, Laura, and Gary Gates. 2012. *Serving Our Youth: Findings from a National Survey of Service Providers Working with Lesbian, Gay, Bisexual and Transgender Youth Who Are Homeless or at Risk of Becoming Homeless.* Los Angeles: Williams Institute with True Colors Fund and The Palette Fund.

Epstein, Charlotte. 2008. *The Power of Words in International Relations: Birth of an Anti-Whaling Discourse.* Cambridge, MA: MIT Press.

Ezzell, Matthew. 2009. "'Barbie Dolls' on the Pitch: Identity Work, Defensive Othering, and Inequality in Women's Rugby." *Social Problems* 56, no. 1: 111–31.

Ezzy, Douglas. 2017. *Narrating Unemployment.* Abingdon, UK: Taylor and Francis.

Fanon, Frantz. 2007. *The Wretched of the Earth.* New York: Grove Atlantic.

Findlay, Tammy. 2015. *Femocratic Administration: Gender, Governance, and Democracy in Ontario.* Toronto: University of Toronto Press.

Fraser, Paul. 1985. "Pornography and Prostitution in Canada." In *Report of the Special Committee on Pornography and Prostitution.* Ottawa: Minister of Supply and Services Canada.

Fudge, Judy, and Brenda Cossman. 2002. "Introduction: Privatization, Law and the Challenge to Feminism." In *Privatization, Law and the Challenge to Feminism,* edited by Brenda Cossman and Judy Fudge, 3–40. Toronto: University of Toronto Press.

Gartner, Richard. 1999. *Betrayed as Boys: Psychodynamic Treatment of Sexually Abused Men.* New York: Guilford.

Gartner, Richard. 2011. "Talking about Sexually Abused Boys, and the Men They Become." *Psychology Today*. January 30. https://www.psychologytoday.com/blog/psychoanalysis-30/201101/talking-about-sexually-abused-boys-and-the-men-they-become. Accessed October 11, 2017.

Goffman, Erving. 1963. *Stigma: Notes on the Management of Spoiled Identity*. New York: Simon and Schuster.

Gozdiak, Elzbieta. 2016. "Human Trafficking in a Time of Crisis." *Anthropology News* 57, no. 11–12: 28–9.

Galtung, Johan. 1969. "Violence, Peace and Peace Research." *Journal of Peace Research* 6, no. 3: 167–191.

Halnon, Karen. 2013. *The Consumption of Inequality: Weapons of Mass Distraction*. London: Palgrave-Macmillan.

Hankivsky, Olena. 2007. "Gender Mainstreaming in the Canadian Context." In *Critical Policy Studies*, edited by Michael Orsini and Miriam Smith. Vancouver: UBC Press, 111–136.

Heider, Fritz. 1958. *The Psychology of Interpersonal Relations*. New York: Wiley.

Heron, Barbara. 2007. *Desire for Development: Whiteness, Gender, and the Helping Imperative*. Waterloo: Wilfrid Laurier University Press.

Hochschild, Arlie. 1983. *The Managed Heart: Commercialisation of Human Feeling*. London: UCL Press.

Hua, Julietta, and Holly Nigorizawa. 2010. "US Sex Trafficking, Women's Human Rights and the Politics of Representation." *International Feminist Journal of Politics* 12, no. 3–4: 401–423.

Hubbard, Phil, and Teela Sanders. 2003. "Making Space for Sex Work: Female Street Prostitution and the Production of Urban Space." *International Journal of Urban and Regional Research* 27, no. 1: 75–89.

Karam, Maisie. 2016. "Trafficking in Persons in Canada, 2014." *Juristat*. Ottawa: Statistics Canada. http://www.statcan.gc.ca/pub/85-002-x/2016001/article/14641-eng.htm#c1. Accessed January 17, 2017.

Kempadoo, Kamala. 2001. "Women of Color and the Global Sex Trade: Transnational Feminist Perspectives. *Meridian* 1, no. 2: 28–51.

Keohane, Ilyana. 2016. "Making LGBTQ2S Shelter Spaces Safe, Inclusive and Affirming." *Homeless Hub*. http://homelesshub.ca/blog/making-lgbtq2s-shelter-spaces-safe-inclusive-and-affirming. Accessed June 22, 2018.

Kille, Julie. 2015. *Communications in Sex Work: A Content Analysis of Online Sex Work Advertisements among Men, Women and Transgender People in Vancouver*. Master's thesis, University of British Columbia.

Kohn, Melvin. 1969. *Class and Conformity: A Study in Values*. Chicago: University of Chicago Press.

Koken, Juline, David Bimbi, and Jeffrey Parsons. 2015. "Positive Marginality and Stigma Resistance among Gay and Bisexual Male Escorts in the USA." In *Men Who Sell Sex: Global Perspectives*, edited by Peter Aggleton and Richard Parker, 188–201. London: Routledge.

Koken, Juline, David Bimbi, Jeffrey Parsons, and Perry Halkitis. 2005. "The Experience of Stigma in the Lives of Male Internet Escorts." *Journal of Psychology and Human Sexuality* 16: 13–32.

Kort, Joe. 2017. "The New Buy-Sexual? Straight Men Who Are Gay for Pay." Huffington Post (website). https://www.huffingtonpost.com/entry/the-new-buy-sexual-straight-men-who-are-gay-for-pay_us_5977d929e4b01cf1c4bb7424. Accessed November 19, 2017.

Koss, Mary, Antonia Abbey, Rebecca Campbell, Sarah Cook, Jeanette Norris, Maria Testa, Sarah Ullman, Carolyn West, and Jacquelyn White. 2007. "Revising the SES: A Collaborative Process to Improve Assessment of Sexual Aggression and Victimization." *Psychology of Women Quarterly* 3, no. 4: 357–370.

Kumar, Navin, John Scott, and Victor Minichiello. 2017. "Masculinity and the Occupational Experience of Independent Escorts Who Seek Male Clients." *Social Sciences.* 6, no. 58: 1–14.

Lachman, Margie, and Suzanne Weaver. 1998. "The Sense of Control as a Moderator of Social Class Differences in Health and Well-Being." *Journal of Personality and Social Psychology* 74, no. 3: 763–73.

Lakoff, George, and Mark Johnson. 1980. *Metaphors We Live By.* Chicago: University of Chicago Press.

Lewis, Nathan, Greta Bauer, Todd Coleman, Soraya Blot, Daniel Pugh, Meredith Fraser, and Leanna Powell. 2015. "Community Cleavages: Gay and Bisexual Men's Perceptions of Gay and Mainstream Community Acceptance in the Post-AIDS, Post-Rights Era." *Journal of Homosexuality* 62, no. 9: 1201–1227.

London Community Chaplaincy. 2017. *Home.* http://www.londoncommunitychaplaincy.com. Accessed September 25, 2017.

Lye, Diane, and Timothy Biblarz. 1993. "The Effects of Attitudes Toward Family Life and Gender Roles on Marital Satisfaction." *Journal of Family Issues* 14, no. 2: 157–188.

Macdonald, David. 2019. *Unaccommodating Rental Housing Wage in Canada.* Ottawa: Canadian Centre for Policy Alternatives

Marcus, Anthony, and Edward Snajdr. 2013. "Anti-anti-trafficking? Toward Critical Ethnographies of Human Trafficking." *Dialectical Anthropology* 37: 191–194.

Marshal, Michael, Laura Dietz, Mark Friedman, Ron Stall, Helen Smith, James McGinley, Brian Thoma, Pamela Murray, Anthony D'Augelli, and David Brent. 2011. "Suicidality and Depression Disparities between Sexual Minority and Heterosexual Youth: A Meta-analytic Review." *Journal of Adolescent Health* 49, no. 2: 115–123.

Martin, Dianne. 2002. "Both Pitied and Scorned: Child Prostitution in an Era of Privatization." In *Privatization, Law and the Challenge to Feminism*, edited by Brenda Cossman and Judy Fudge, 355–402. Toronto: University of Toronto Press.

Mate, Gabor. 2009. *In the Realm of Hungry Ghosts: Close Encounters with Addiction.* Toronto: Vintage Canada.

McDowell, Linda. 2014. "The Sexual Contract, Youth, Masculinity and the Uncertain Promise of Waged Work in Austerity Britain." *Australian Feminist Studies* 79: 31–49.

McKenna, Emma. 2019. *The Labour Feminism Takes: Tracing Intersectional Politics in 1980s Canadian Feminist Periodicals.* PhD diss., McMaster Ontario.

McLean, Andrew. 2013. *An Evolving Trade? Male Sex Work and the Internet.* PhD diss., RMIT University.

Mendel, Matthew. 1995. "The Male Survivor: The Impact of Sexual Abuse." Thousand Oaks, CA: SAGE.

Millard, Alex. 2016. "The Stories of Male Sexual Assault Survivors Need to Be Heard." *The Establishment* (blog). https://theestablishment.co/male-survivors-of-sexual-assault-speak-out-bdfe9820d0ef. Accessed October 22, 2017.

Miller, Peggy, Grace Cho, and Jeana Bracey. 2005. "Working-Class Children's Experience through the Prism of Personal Storytelling." *Human Development* 48, no. 3: 115–135.

Minichiello, Victor, Rodrigo Marino, A. Khan, and Jan Browne. 2003. "Alcohol and Drug Use in Australian Male Sex Workers: Its Relationship to the Safety Outcome of the Sex Encounter." *AIDS Care* 15: 549–562.

Mitchell, Gregory. 2015. *Tourist Attractions: Performing Race and Masculinity in Brazil's Sexual Economy.* Chicago: University of Chicago Press.

Montemurro, Beth, and Bridget McClure. 2005. "Changing Gender Norms for Alcohol Consumption: Social Drinking and Lowered Inhibitions at Bachelorette Parties." *Sex Roles* 52, no. 5–6: 279–288.

Nathanson, Paul, and Katherine Young. 2001. *Spreading Misandry: The Teaching of Contempt for Men in Popular Culture.* Montréal and Kingston: McGill-Queen's University Press.

Nathanson, Paul, and Katherine Young. 2006. *Legalizing Misandry: From Public Shame to Systemic Discrimination against Men.* Montréal and Kingston: McGill-Queen's University Press.

O'Connell Davidson, Julia. 1998. *Prostitution, Power, and Freedom.* Ann Arbor: University of Michigan Press.

Oerton, Sarah, and Joanna Phoenix. 2001. "Sex/Bodywork: Discourses and Practices." *Sexualities* 4, no. 4: 387–412.

Padilla, Mark. 2007. *Caribbean Pleasure Industry: Tourism, Sexuality, and AIDS in the Dominican Republic.* Chicago: University of Chicago Press.

Parent, Colette, and Chris Bruckert. 2013. "The Current Debate on Sex Work." In *Sex Work: Rethinking the Job, Respecting the Workers*, edited by Colette Parent, Chris Bruckert, Patrice Corriveau, Maria Nengeh Mensah, and Louise Toupin, 9–30. Vancouver: UBC Press.

Pateman, Carole. 1988. *The Sexual Contract.* Stanford, CA: Stanford University Press.

Petro, Melissa. 2012. "Life After Sex Work." *Daily Beast.* https://www.thedailybeast.com/life-after-sex-work. Accessed June 13, 2018.

Pheterson, Gail. 1989. *A Vindication of the Rights of Whores.* Seattle: Seal.

Phoenix, Jo, and Sarah Oerton. 2005. *Illicit and Illegal Sex: Regulation and Social Control.* Portland, OR: Willan.

Pickard, Hanna. 2017. "Responsibility without Blame for Addiction." *Neuroethics* 10, no. 1: 169–180.

Pivot Legal Society. 2013. *Canada v. Bedford—the Decision in 750 Words.* http://www.pivotlegal.org/canada_v_bedford_a_synopsis_of_the_supreme_court_of_canada_ruling. Accessed July 20, 2016.

Pleak, Richard, and Heino Meyer-Bahlburg. 1990. "Sexual Behaviour and AIDS Knowledge of Young Male Prostitutes in Manhattan." *Journal of Sex Research* 27, no. 4: 557–587.

Razack, Sherene. 1993. "Exploring the Omissions and Silence in Law around Race." In *Investigating Gender Bias: Law, Courts and the Legal Profession*, edited by Joan Brockman and Dorothy Chunn, 37–48. Toronto: Thompson Educational.

Robertson, James. 1988. *Sexual Offences against Children: The Badgley Report*. Ottawa: Library of Parliament, Research Branch.

Rolin, Kristina. 2006. "The Bias Paradox in Feminist Standpoint Epistemology." *Episteme: A Journal of Social Epistemology* 3, no. 1–2: 125–136.

Roots, Katrin, and Ann De Shalit. 2016. "Evidence that Evidence Doesn't Matter: The Case of Human Trafficking in Canada." *Atlantis* 37, no. 21: 65–80.

Rotenberg, Christine. 2016. "Prostitution Offences in Canada: Statistical Trends." *Juristat* 85-002-X. Ottawa: Statistics Canada. http://www.statcan.gc.ca/pub/85-002-x/2016001/article/14670-eng.htm#r17. Accessed January 19, 2007.

Ryan, Paul. 2016. "#Follow: Exploring the Role of Social Media in the Online Construction of Male Sex Worker Lives in Dublin, Ireland." *Gender, Place, and Culture* 23, no. 12: 1713–1724.

Satz, Debra. 1995. "Markets in Women's Sexual Labour." *Ethics* 106, no. 1: 63–85.

Scarce, Michael. 1997. *The Spectacle of Male Rape, Male on Male Rape: The Hidden Toll of Stigma and Shame*. New York: Insight.

Schladebeck, Jessica. 2017. "Texas Teacher Fired for Working as Porn Actress More than 16 Years Ago." *New York Daily News*. http://www.nydailynews.com/news/national/texas-teacher-fired-working-porn-actress-16-years-article-1.2961568. Accessed June 13, 2018.

Schneider, Margaret. 1997. *Pride and Prejudice: Working with Lesbian, Gay, and Bisexual Youth*. Toronto: Central Toronto Youth Services.

Scott, John, Catherine MacPhail, and Victor Minichiello. 2015. "Telecommunication Impacts on the Structure and Organisation of the Male Sex Industry." In *(Sub)Urban Sexscapes: Geographies and Regulation of the Sex Industry*, edited by Paul Maginn and Christine Steinmetz, 81–100. London: Routledge.

Sharma, Nandita. 2005. "Anti-trafficking Rhetoric and the Making of a Global Apartheid. *NWSA Journal* 17, no. 3: 88–111.

Simon, Caty. 2018. "What Constitutes as Sex Work?" In *Hopes and Fears* (blog). http://www.hopesandfears.com/hopes/now/question/216863-what-constitutes-sex-work. Accessed May 10, 2018.

Smith, Brenda. 2012. "Uncomfortable Places, Close Spaces: Female Correctional Workers' Sexual Interactions with Men and Boys in Custody." *UCLA Law Review* 59, no. 6: 1690–1745.

Smith, Michael, and Christian Grov. 2011. *In the Company of Men: Inside the Lives of Male Prostitutes*. Santa Barbara, CA: Praeger.

Smuck, Tim. 2015. *Sharing the Lived Experience of Public Housing: A Critical Discourse Analysis and Perspectives from Residents of Public Housing in London Ontario*. MPA Major Research Papers 143. http://ir.lib.uwo.ca/cgi/viewcontent.cgi?article=1142&context=lgp-mrps.

Srivastava, Sarita. 2005. " 'You're Calling Me a Racist?' The Moral and Emotional Regulation of Antiracism and Feminism." *Signs: Journal of Women in Culture and Society* 31, no. 1: 34.

Stardust, Zahra. 2015. "Critical Femininities, Fluid Sexualities, and Queer Temporalities: Erotic Performers on Objectification, Femmephobia, and Oppression." In *Queer Sex Work*, edited by Mary Laing, Katy Pilcher, and Nicola Smith, 67–78. London: Routledge.

Statistics Canada. 2016. Census Profile Ontario. *2016 Census*.

Steinberg, Laurence, and Paula Duncan. 2002. "Work Group IV: Increasing the Capacity of Parents, Families, and Adults Living with Adolescents to Improve Adolescent Health Outcomes." *Journal of Adolescent Health* 31, no. 6: 261–263.

Stemple, Lara, and Ilan Meyer. 2014. "The Sexual Victimization of Men in America: New Data Challenge Old Assumptions." *American Journal of Public Health* 104, no. 6: 19–26.

Stetson, Dorothy, and Amy Mazur. 1995. "Introduction." In *Comparative State Feminism,* edited by Dorothy Stetson and Amy Mazur. Thousand Oaks, CA: SAGE.

Summit, Roland. 1983. "The Child Sexual Abuse Accommodation Syndrome." *Child Abuse and Neglect* 7: 177–193.

Taylor, Allegra. 1991. *Prostitution: What's Love Got to Do with It?* London: Macdonald-Optima.

Tong, Rosemarie. 1998. *Feminist Thought: A Comprehensive Introduction.* 2nd ed. Boulder, CO: Westview.

Truong, Than-Dam. 1990. *Sex, Money and Morality: The Political Economy of Prostitution and Tourism in South East Asia.* London: Zed.

United Nations. 2004. *United Nations Convention against Transnational Organized Crime and the Protocols Thereto.* New York: United Nations.

US Department of State. 2013. "Tier Placement." *Trafficking in Persons Report.* http://www.state.gov/j/tip/rls/tiprpt/2013/210548.htm.

van der Meulen, Emily, Elya Durisin, and Victoria Love. 2013. *Selling Sex: Experience, Advocacy, and Research on Sex Work in Canada.* Vancouver: UBC Press.

Vanwesenbeeck, Ine. 2012. "Prostitution Push and Pull: Male and Female Perspectives. "*Journal of Sex Research* 50, no. 1: 11–16.

Walby, Kevin. 2012. *Touching Encounters: Sex, Work, and Male-for-Male Internet Escorting.* Chicago: University of Chicago Press.

Warner, Michael. 1993. *Fear of a Queer Planet: Queer Politics and Social Theory.* Minneapolis: University of Minnesota Press.

Whitlock, Kay. 2018. "Threshold: #MeToo, with Justice Complications—Part 1." *Beacon Broadside.* http://www.beaconbroadside.com/broadside/2018/01/threshold-metoo-with-justice-complications-part-1.html. Accessed July 26, 2018.

Winnicott, Donald. 1960. "Ego Distortion in Terms of True and False Self." *The Maturational Process and the Facilitating Environment: Studies in the Theory of Emotional Development*, 140–57. New York: International Universities Press.

18

Intersectionality and Muslim Women in Belgium

Elsa Mescoli

LEARNING OBJECTIVES

- Define the key concept of intersectionality, including the multiple notions that this approach mobilizes.

- Analyze the processes of discrimination and subordination Muslim women face by highlighting the effect of intersecting identity factors.

- Identify the strategies used by Muslim women to counter discrimination.

In this chapter, the author applies an intersectional lens to discuss the impact of Islamophobia on Muslim women in Belgium. By exploring the stories of some of these women, the author highlights the ways they negotiate their multiple identities to resist marginalization and discrimination, and thus reaffirm their role as active agents in their lives and in Belgium society. (Note: the names of research participants in this chapter are pseudonyms.)

This chapter addresses the intersectional discrimination affecting Muslim women or those perceived as such. Muslim women constitute a diverse group and are often the target of multiple forms of discrimination and subordination. As members of minority groups in Western society, and as migrants or people with a foreign background in most cases, they face difficulties in finding their place in a society that despite its multiculturalism still places obstacles in the path to the fulfillment of their desired professional and social status. The discrimination of Muslims operates in numerous domains, and it targets their religious and racialized belonging. In particular, laws and policies that limit the wearing of religious and cultural symbols and clothing result in the exclusion from employment of those Muslim women who decide to visibly express their religious or cultural belonging. The aim of this chapter is to analyze these facts through recalling concrete life experiences of women and through approaching the discrimination that they live with an intersectional lens. This approach highlights how the combination of different identity markers operates within processes of discrimination. It also stresses the fact that Muslim women are active agents with a set of strategies to confront the difficulties that they encounter. Through a variety of actions ranging from individual resilience to collective resistance, Muslim women manage to capitalize their multiple belongings that are objects of discrimination and to struggle against marginalization, thus reaffirming their role as active players not only in their life experiences but also in the society in which they live.

The chapter begins by introducing the research topic and analytical tools then presents and discusses contextual elements and experiences of a sample of Muslim women. The research is based on both a literature review and extended ethnographic fieldwork conducted with Muslim women and men, as well as with organizations dealing with discrimination issues from 2015 to 2018 in Belgium. Fieldwork included semistructured interviews with key social actors, as well as participant observation of antidiscrimination initiatives (seminars, meetings, sensitization activities, women's "safe spaces" for discussion, etc.). Through fieldwork, I collected life histories and experiences of Muslim women with different sociocultural and economic profiles. Most were born in Belgium but had a migrant family background with their parents coming, in most cases, from Morocco but also from Turkey or from other Arab countries such as Tunisia or Algeria.

INTERSECTIONALITY AND MUSLIM WOMEN

As already discussed in the introduction of this book, **intersectionality** is both a complex concept and an approach originally used to study issues of discrimination and subordination affecting women's life experiences. The concept of intersectionality describes a process of discrimination and subordination that operates at the intersection of race, class, gender, sex, ethnicity, nationality, ability, age, and any other identity markers and that shapes complex social inequalities (Crenshaw 1991; Collins 2015). As an

intersectionality
refers to the interconnected nature of social categories such as race, class, and gender that create overlapping systems of discrimination or disadvantage. The goal of an intersectional analysis is to understand how racism, sexism, and homophobia (for example) interact together to impact our identities and how we live in our society.

analytical approach, intersectionality emerged in a US context to unpack the categories of "women" and "Blacks" in order to study the intersection of different social divisions in women's life experiences (Yuval-Davis 2006), and intersectionality denounces the tendency to naturalize these divisions (hooks 1981). Intersectionality is an approach attentive to power relations and social inequalities; it is an analytical strategy that provides new perspectives on social phenomena, thus becoming not only a field of study but also a critical praxis (practical-oriented research work) that informs social justice projects (Collins 2015).

This approach constitutes an alternative feminist tool that counters the **hegemonic discourse** about women in Western contexts (Anthias 2002, 279). This means that it provides different views and different claims about gender inequalities than those commonly found in Western mainstream feminist discourse. In fact, the latter, despite its wide adoption, is not necessarily adapted to address particular forms of discrimination experienced by women from minority cultural backgrounds, since it does not take into account elements affecting them in their specific and complex contexts. In particular, the Western feminist approach based on the denunciation of patriarchy and men's domination is reductive and does not function in every cultural context (Mohanty 1984). Besides shedding light on different and/or additional factors that contribute to gender inequalities, the intersectional approach gives feminist social actors, who are originally excluded from the development of this hegemonic discourse, the possibility to propose new forms of understanding and thus fight against intersectional gendered-based discrimination. With regard to Muslim feminists in particular, the intersectional approach enables them to counter those discourses spread within the Western feminist hegemonic narratives that see Islamic feminism as an "oxymoron," since this religious tradition is seen as inhibiting the possibility of women's emancipation. In general, a process of politicization of women's voices addresses the overall system of domination affecting women beyond the private sphere and helps elaborate new forms of empowerment and social reconstruction (Crenshaw 1991). The socially imposed identity is reversed and becomes an anchor of subjectivity: women adopt a positive discourse of self-identification and actively position themselves within the lived political context.

Applying an intersectional lens to the study of the discourses about Muslim women in Europe means, first, to highlight the specific forms of discrimination that they undergo and, second, to describe the particular ways adopted to fight them. Muslim women in the West are often depicted as either dangerous or oppressed others (Mirza 2013, 7), and this occurs through a process of **racialization** that essentializes (religious gendered) identity. It is a process of "race-making" and "othering" connected to

hegemonic discourse
a discourse that promotes the dominance of one group over another supported by legitimating norms and ideas that normalize dominance. Using collective consent rather than force, dominant social groups maintain power, and social inequalities are naturalized.

racialization
the process of ascribing a racial identity and associated traits to a group. These characteristics are often defined by a dominant group with the aim of discriminating against and excluding the subordinate group.

racism, a particularly virulent form of construction of cultural boundaries through discourse and practices aimed at subordinating, excluding, and exploiting racialized individuals on the basis of an assigned origin (Anthias 2016) and skin color (Torrekens and Adam 2015). In Belgium, this process operates in the context of a secularized and Christian-origin state of white European majority, where Muslim people embody the "cultural other," (i.e., individuals seen as nonwhite and with religious beliefs based in foreign contexts and origins). This process of othering may concretely shape in different forms and engage a variety of discriminating discourses and practices, depending on the specific origins associated with Muslim people such as North African, sub-Saharan, or European descent. Keeping Muslim people outside this majority is a means of perpetuating state sovereignty over its subjects (Fadil 2016), constraining any possible challenge to it. A process of racialization is at the heart of anti-Muslim discrimination and also has a profoundly gendered dimension (Fadil et al. 2014, 226; Bracke 2007; Mescoli 2016, 2019). In fact, discourses on the extent of women's emancipation are used as "boundary marker[s] of Western civilization" and they aim at depicting Islam as "women-unfriendly" (Fadil et al. 2014, 226). Therefore, Western feminist discourse about Muslim women mainly comprises rescue narratives and politics (Abu-Lughod 2002). As highlighted by Fadil et al., "The question of women's oppression, neutrality, or the need for an 'enlightened' or 'modern' Islam" (2014, 242) generates "a sense of discomfort over the headscarf" conceived of as "a sign of a return to tradition or a rejection of Western norms and values" (2014, 226). Antiveiling sentiments (and policies) emerge as parts of anti-immigrant prejudice (Saroglou et al. 2009) and significantly affect Muslim women's everyday experiences.

Scholars show that these processes generally occur within discursive contexts that are not neutral and, through discriminatory legislation and negative media representation of Muslims, contribute to the emergence of Islamophobic and racist acts (Ameli et al. 2012, 2). **Islamophobia** is a form of "racialized governmentality" composed of "a series of interventions and classifications that affect the well-being of populations designated as Muslim" (Sayyid 2014, 19). In parallel, Islamophobia results in culturalist discourses and acts that target Muslims' alleged "unsuitable cultural and religious background as the reason for economic exclusion and marginalisation" (Zemni 2011, 29). Different Belgian actors (scholars, associations and NGOs, state institutions) use or critically address the term of Islamophobia and thus produce knowledge from diverse perspectives. Some also question the appropriateness and efficacy of the notion of Islamophobia, since the etymology of the word—recalling a fear and an irrational rejection—would not appropriately describe the processes of

Islamophobia
fear of, and prejudice against the Islamic faith and Muslims in general

discrimination at stake (Dassetto 2009), making the term counterproductive (Maréchal et al. 2016). Islamophobia is then "a contested concept, both in and outside of academia, which also accounts for the reluctance in its adoption" (Fadil et al. 2014, 251). Despite divergent perspectives on Islamophobia, there is agreement on the spread of discourses that target the presence of immigrants as generating or worsening economic, social, and political problems of a society, thus putting social integration at risk (Martiniello, 1996) and on the fact that in recent years "it is Islam which is more and more often put in the dock" (Martiniello 1995, 80; also see Allievi 2005).

MUSLIM WOMEN IN BELGIUM: BETWEEN UNDERGONE DISCRIMINATION AND EXERTED AGENCY

Belgium is among those territories where Muslims are represented mainly as immigrants (Sayyid 2014, 64–65). The number of Muslims in the country is determined through estimations, since there is no registration of religious or philosophical affiliations (Husson 2015). Estimates range from 250,000 to 400,000 (Torrekens 2005, 56) and up to more than 600,000 Muslim people including converted persons (Hertogen 2008).

In Belgium, the principle of neutrality stipulates that the state does not intervene in the nomination of religious officials and that it ensures equal treatment to the officially recognized religions (Catholicism, Protestantism, Judaism, Anglicanism, Islam, and Orthodox liturgy). The process of recognition of Islam as official religion in Belgium has led to the creation of an official representative body (the Executive of Muslims in Belgium, EMB) to function as the main interlocutor between the "Muslim community" and the state. However, these assumptions and the existence of this organization do not prevent the shaping of an institutional context that affects Muslims and Muslim women in particular. Indeed, despite alerts about the increase of racist discourse and action against Muslims EMB has made no overt opposition, shifting from neutrality to a widespread laïcité (meant as public and institutional secularism), the state creates forms of structural discrimination in the public sphere and contributes to their emergence in the private one. This process mainly operates with regard to veiling. The face veil ban was created by the law of June 1, 2011, with almost unanimous approval and supported by arguments depicting the wearing of face veils as an extreme form of women's cultural oppression. This and other regulations based on the principle of neutrality have consequences for Muslim women who wear headscarves. For example, women are usually forbidden to wear headscarves in educational institutions and when working in the public sector. This taken together with recent international decisions provides a sort of institutional legitimization to those employers who restrict the wearing of headscarves in the private sector. For instance, in 2017 the Court of Justice of the European Union allowed employers in the private sector to adopt internal regulations that prohibit wearing visible signs of political, philosophical, or religious convictions (Court of Justice of the European Union Cases). In Brussels, the ban was lifted in July 2019 from high schools, thus leading to an improved situation concerning the access to higher education for Muslim women wearing headscarves. This is not the case in other regions of the country such as Flanders and Wallonia, where bans existing in schools are lifted only in the case of successful lawsuits. This complex situation depends on the fact that in the Belgian federal state, regions are in charge of competences related to education.

Several civil society and antidiscrimination bodies denounce the increased occurrences of religious discrimination, as well as the over-representation of Muslims, and Muslim women in particular, in these incidents. Figures and facts are provided by international associations such as Amnesty International but also and mainly by the Interfederal Centre for Equal Opportunity (Unia), that is the institutional body in charge of combating discrimination, and by associations such as the Collective against Islamophobia in Belgium (CCIB). The restrictions on wearing the Islamic headscarf influence the educational and professional choices women make, and act as levers for auto-exclusion (Ben Mohamed 2004) from some professional routes. In fact, women frequently evaluate their employment opportunities based on the constraints that they will face as Muslim women, especially if they wear headscarves. The discrimination targeting Muslim women's religious belonging intersects with other processes of subordination. First, there is the process of **ethno-stratification** of the job market (Okkerse and Termotte 2004; Tratsaert 2004; Martens and Ouali 2005). This notion describes a socioeconomic process leading to the concentration of workers of certain nationalities or origins in some employment sectors and jobs (Adam 2007, 225–226). People with foreign origins are overrepresented in the most precarious and poorly paid employment sectors, where working times are irregular and tasks are arduous. By contrast, they are underrepresented in public services and cultural institutions, among other sectors (Unia 2017). In parallel, unemployment rates and durations are higher among people of foreign origins than for Belgian people without foreign origin, also because youth, in particular, face difficulties finding and keeping a job

ethno-stratification

In the workplace, this notion describes the socioeconomic process leading to a concentration of workers of certain nationalities or origins in particular sectors and jobs.

(Adam 2007, 226–229). Discrimination (also operating in the domain of education) plays a role in the shaping of these structural constraints. Second, in Belgium as in other European countries, wage and employment gender gaps are persistent and amplified when comparing individuals with non-EU citizenship with Belgians, as highlighted by the research of the Institution for the Equality of Women and Men (Institute 2015, 44). This results in keeping women in a dependent status (EWL 2014, 18), and in orienting them toward limited professional choices. Consequently, the ongoing process of domestication of women, meaning their relegation to the domestic sphere, in terms of household and childcare (Rogers 2005, 18), is reinforced and extended to the work domain, where it results in a gendered stratification of jobs. This means more precisely that women are more often associated and oriented to jobs within the domains of care and education, for example, than toward the broader job market and its possibilities. Muslim women report that employment agencies may contribute to this process when they directly or indirectly orient Muslim women toward jobs that are supposed to be "adapted" to their needs. Many women recount having been asked to apply for housekeeping jobs, despite the fact that this was not necessarily their first aspiration and did not correspond to their professional or educational profile. Moreover, discrimination operates during job interviews with potential employers, where the latter ask women questions aimed at assessing their private experience of faith as Muslims, thus measuring their level of "Muslim-ness" (Mescoli 2016, 2019; Toğuşlu 2015). The aim would be to evaluate whether the interviewed women's values and practices would be compatible or not to with those of the concerned firm or company. Unlike non-Muslim women, Muslim women have to face questions about their domestic intimacy rooted in the employer's stereotypical visions of gender relationships within Muslim families. Imane, a Belgian-born woman, converted to Islam and married to a Muslim man, recounted to me discriminatory experiences that she underwent when she was looking for a job. Having a Belgian name, she was not discriminated against in the first selection phase, which often happens to women whose names are associated with a foreign origin. However, when she arrived at the interview wearing a headscarf, employers were often surprised. Moreover, this generated unexpected questions, such as, "Does your husband beat you?" Employers posed other questions concerning individual behaviors that were not related to the job requirements and tasks, such as, "Do you shake hands with men? Do you pray five times a day?" Indeed, answers to these types of questions seem to take priority over assessing the Muslim women's professional skills, and it can be particularly intense with women wearing headscarves. The consequence, as was the case for this woman, is often to reorient one's professional ambitions (even if it is not necessarily always connected with dissatisfaction, as we will see later).

Muslim women wearing headscarves also suffer from discrimination when they try to access goods or services. For example, social workers and legal advisors of the Interfederal Centre for Equal Opportunities have recorded several cases of women whom dentists refuse to treat unless they take off their headscarves and of women who were not served in some shops without being given an explicit reason. In discussion with me during interviews, some Muslim women also reported other episodes of discrimination such as when bus drivers did not stop when they were the only ones waiting at the bus stop, or when they were asked to take off their headscarves when entering the polling station to vote. Moreover, physical aggressions targeting Muslim women are not rare (Unia 2015; CCIB 2015) Furthermore, women face verbal abuse, both face to face and through the media: cyberhate speech appears through different Internet channels, such as email chains, comments on social networks or to online newspapers articles, etc. (see Centre 2009, 14–15). Attacking Muslim women also seeks to blame Islam for gender-oriented violence. Brems et al. report that several women experienced an increase in aggressive reactions starting after the previously mentioned face veil ban and from the debate generated by its mediatization: "The negative image of Islam in general and of the face veil in particular that is projected in the media seems to give people permission to react in an aggressive manner. . . . Moreover, it appears that many people now refer to the ban in their interventions vis-à-vis women who wear the face veil, acting as a kind of vigilante police" (Brems et al. 2014, 106). The authors report the "refusal of treatment of a veiled woman by hospital staff, refusal of vendors at a curio market to sell their goods to a veiled woman, and refusal by a school director to let a mother pick up her child from school when wearing her face veil" (106). Paradoxically, while in some cases some women abandoned the face veil or limited its use without changing their other habits, many others finally stop going out by themselves, since without the veil they no longer felt free to move or safe from the male gaze.

The multiple dimensions of discrimination toward Muslim women also include the fear of reinforcing stereotypical representations. In fact, some women who have suffered from domestic violence or from socio-cultural pressure on gender roles by members of their family, may decide not to complain about the constraints that they live within in order "not to feed to the stigma" concerning gender relationships between Muslim women and men. As Imane explains, Muslim women often "do not want to talk about conflicts. . . . Maybe they were beaten, maybe they had a nice marriage . . . but if it was bad and violent, they don't talk about it" (Imane, interview by author). The representation of Muslim women as either dangerous (allegedly connected to acts of terrorism directly or through their children or husband) or oppressed is hardly challenged in the media because of the absence of Muslim women in this domain, apart from cases where their religiosity is addressed. This is also connected to the fact that, in general, press and other media products are mainly produced by men in Belgium, as in other European countries, and that minority groups and people associated with Islam do not have the same access to public expression. In fact, the recognition of the active role of Muslim women in the social and political sphere is not systematic. Many Muslims affirm that their statements are often discredited through their religious affiliation as alleged prior interest in their claims and reasoning. While interviewing a Muslim woman working as a lawyer and scholar, she told me that for her and other Muslim women occupying similar roles in the society "it is difficult to be considered a valid intellectual, we are never detached from this belonging" (Nour, interview by author). This discrimination is perceived as a reiterated subtle form of microaggression (Solorzano 1998).

Reactions to discrimination are multiple, and the narratives that women shape are equally based on the intersection of diverse belongings. Muslim women shape a feminist discourse in which they promote women's rights. Such discourse is also connected with a religious meaning, and it is for this reason that activists and scholars speak of specific forms of **Islamic Feminism** (see, for example, Hamidi 2015). Femininity is described as multifaceted life experience that includes religiosity without affecting the right of being active agents within society. Thus, Islamic feminists argue for guaranteeing freedom of religion. The actions implemented toward this aim by a variety of social actors including, but not limited to, those who associate with Islamic feminism, function in different ways. First, they promote a description of Muslim women's life histories as diverse in order to highlight their autonomy and counter the idea that they are victims of patriarchal and misogynist cultural and religious principles. As a consequence, the decision to wear (any form of) headscarf is the result of "plenty of reasons and individual strategies. . . . There is a multitude of histories, a multitude of experiences, and we have to listen to this diversity," as explained by Sarah (interview by author), a woman employed as a social worker and local politician. In her opinion, as for many other Muslim women with whom I spoke, wearing a headscarf also has personal meanings. The different existing forms of headscarves and their use testify to the complex rationales that underlie the active choice of wearing one among these head coverings (see, for example, Tarlo 2010). However, all forms of headscarf do not receive the same appraisal

Islamic feminism
A feminist movement that seeks freedom of religion on the basis of a multifaceted definition of femininity that recognizes both religiosity and women's agency within society.

in the social and professional environment of women. Another woman, Nabila, working in a local association, recalled her experience of having been asked to wear a "more alternative and fashionable" form of veil than the traditional hijab that she used (Nabila, interview by author).

Additionally, several Muslim women can opt not to wear any form of headscarf. This choice can be driven by structural constraints, for example, if women are asked to remove their headscarf or in case they decide by themselves to do it to avoid discrimination in the professional domain. However, this choice may also be determined by the fact that some Muslim women do not consider the headscarf as a relevant element needed to shape and affirm their religious identity or because they do not find it necessary to make this identity visible. Both veiling and unveiling are bodily practices (Fadil 2011) adopted to shape Muslim women as autonomous subjects that embody and perform diverse "ideals of womanhood and of the moral system" and responding to different codes of modesty (Abu-Lughod, 1987: 160). Individual stories can also be publicly narrated, for example during sensitization activities such as intercultural initiatives, or through websites or blogs. During my ethnographic studies I had the occasion to meet Nadia, a young Muslim woman who was among the founders of a blog where everyday life stories are narrated by Muslim women living in Brussels. The aim of this and other similar initiatives is to deconstruct racialized gendered stereotypes that essentialize the religious component of Muslim women's identity. Sarah narrated to me how important it was to show that Muslim women are engaged in a variety of initiatives: "I study at a music academy . . . I follow piano courses, I sing, I am in a theatre company and I think that when you see on the stage a person wearing a headscarf, this can also deconstruct prejudices . . . this puts questions." (Sarah, interview by author) This woman also contradicts prejudices targeting the religious or racialized belonging of Muslim women by asserting her professional skills, as shown in the following statement:

> When I was looking for a [sic] work, they told me: "how would you act tomorrow if in a help care interview you have in front of you a woman, a young girl, that wants an abortion . . . you with your headscarf, with your beliefs . . . how would you react?". I always had the same answer: "I am here to listen to the person, I am here to give her space to speak about whatever problem she encounters, I am not here to judge her, I am not here to decide in her place, I am not there to direct her . . . I am here to help her, and if her choice is abortion, I will orient

her toward those services that could accomodate her." (Sarah, interview by author).

By this statement, this woman highlights the professional attitude that she takes when facing the requests in her job as a social worker, showing that this attitude is independent of her religious belonging. Similarly, Dounia, another woman working in an association that promotes gender rights, among other activities, stated:

> Sometimes people do not imagine an Arab woman, Muslim or not, that is also professionally ambitious, that is interested in having a career . . . there are plenty of young women that are very engaged, they wear headscarves, they do not wear headscarves, some of them declare to be Muslim, others we do not know" (Dounia, interview by author).

Other ways of reacting to discrimination consist of detecting and denouncing racist and Islamophobic acts. Besides relying on the general antidiscrimination law of May 10, 2007, Muslim women and other social actors supporting their actions, such as the Collective against Islamophobia in Belgium, point to the need for developing specific forms of reporting that could enable women to describe the intersectional character of the discrimination they face. Specific forms of reporting would better account for the extent of the intersectional discrimination affecting Muslim women, as well as for the multiple criteria used to detect it, so to "have voices that speak about this, in order to objectify the phenomenon and make it possible to do advocacy . . . and to put the issue of Muslim woman on the European agenda," in the words of a Muslim woman working as an advocacy officer in an NGO dealing with issues of racism (Loubna, interview by author). For Karim, a man engaged in fighting against Islamophobia, reporting includes "listing the factual, the observable and the measurable" so to "categorise and structure [victims'] ideas." (Karim, interview by author). Legal fights against the undermining of Muslim women's rights help women in their personal lives and are also effective in addressing the structural discrimination present in public institutions. An example is when a legal action results in the removal of the restriction to wearing headscarves from higher education institutions. Successful case laws and strategic court litigations foster the creation of specific "legal arsenals and coherent juridical arguments," as stated by a lawyer expert in court cases related to the discrimination of Muslim women wearing headscarves (Safia, interview by author). Another example is the 2015 Actiris (the

Brussels public employment service) case, concerning three women who were forbidden to wear headscarves in this service. Its positive outcome marked an important point in combating the discrimination of Muslim women since from that moment on the case could be used to support "lobbying, . . . advocacy, awareness raising, training," and it reiterates the right to work as a "source of autonomy and subsistence," recalled one activist Muslim man (Selma, interview by the author) and many of my research participants.

Other forms of combating the intersectional discrimination of Muslim women consist of various individual and contextual strategies that women use to deal with a professional and life context that is constraining. Some strategies may help women "adjust" to this context, a sort of resilience adopted to keep feeling comfortable with their bodies and with the space they cross and inhabit. Some women recount that they have finally been obliged to give up a professional career since wearing a headscarf was not allowed on the job. They then reoriented themselves professionally to other jobs, and they found reasons and motivations to engage with these new careers. This is the case for example of Louna, a woman that found her passion and vocation in teaching Islamic religion, notwithstanding the fact that this did not correspond to her original professional project. Other adjustments may include the choice of not wearing a headscarf while working, or of finding other types of head covering that are accepted at work. Other women also put in place acts of resistance supported by a sharp awareness of their rights—acquired through experience and study— and by the will of having their rights respected in spite of the difficulties that this implies. For example, Yasmine, a young woman providing for the needs of her two children, insisted on (and finally obtained) her right to wear a headscarf at work, and she did so by leaning on the fact that the social service agency who found her the job did not put restrictions on the wearing of religious symbols. In many cases, resisting social constraints and exercising individual strategies led women to share their expertise with other women. These efforts result in some women forming associations to support (financially, psychologically, and through legal advice) Muslim women victims of discrimination, and some others aimed at coaching and empowering women not to be discouraged by the difficulties they face. These were the choices some of my research partici- pants made, particularly those who were determined to capitalize on their experience of discrimination and to promote actions aimed at reducing the possibility that other women face similar difficulties. Since employers were not willing to hire her, nor even test her professional skills, because she was "visibly" showing her Muslim religion by wearing a headscarf, Imane finally opted to create her own business. One service her firm provided was supporting other Muslim women in their job search, including preparing appropriate ways of answering discriminatory and stereotypical questions that employers might ask during job interviews. The aim of this, and other similar efforts (in the words of the initiators), is to remind Muslim women that they do have valuable skills despite potential employers' attempts to dismiss them. Other possible actions are boycotting shops that do not allow employees to wear the headscarf, going to exams with witnesses able to record if discrimination takes place, among others. They also consist of more generalized actions of mediation (i.e., attempting first to find a negotiated solution among parties before or instead of resorting to legal procedure). A woman active in an antiracist association stated: "It is more through negotiation that we try to put forward the rights of the parties . . . we try to remind people that the law allows freedom of religion for everyone . . . and later [come] the sanctions, we first remind of the principle that is in this case that of the freedom of religion" (Lina, interview by author). Negotiation is aimed at promoting the adoption of inclusive policies that benefit Muslim women and potentially other individuals (e.g., when they help put in place more flexible regulations that comply with a variety of individual needs). Some examples of companies or institutions that implement an "inclusive neutrality" exist in Belgium. For instance, the public social welfare center in Louvain recently adopted an internal regulation allowing Muslim employees to wear headscarves if they desired to. Other organizations create more general "diversity plans" aimed at providing victims of discrimination with appropriate support, as well as to promote diversity within public services or businesses. However, the introduction of an "ethnic" or "diversity" quota that can be included in such policies is strongly criticized by several actors that point out the risks of using a tool that may contribute to the perpetuation of a process of racialization aimed at marginalizing people with migrant backgrounds.

CONCLUDING REMARKS

The feminist project of adopting an intersectional approach to the study of women's subordination and, in particular, of the life experiences of Muslim women, is based on the consideration of women's multilayered identities operating at "the interplay of different locations relating to gender, ethnicity, race and class (amongst others)" (Anthias 2002, 275). As any other individuals, Muslim women are associated with a set of categories that link to gender (they are women), religious belonging (they are Muslim), cultural or ethnic belonging (they may have foreign origins and they are racialized), socioeconomic and professional status (they are students, workers, unemployed, etc.), and personal status (they are wives, mothers, daughters, etc.). This composite positioning, on the one hand, has to be considered when analyzing the specific and complex forms of discrimination and subordination that Muslim women may undergo and that affect their life experience at the intersection of these categories. Yet this positioning has a political scope that allows women to formulate claims related to each of their identity markers and at their intersection, for example regarding equal access to education, jobs, and social resources. Women's life histories and narratives of belonging are then forms of social action that operate in a context where institutions attempt to regulate and control the political subjectivities of the members of minority groups. The aim is to contribute to "a process of maintaining and sustaining a cultural and political hegemony within the nation" that responds to a moral "anxiety over the potential loss of hegemony in defining the contours of the nation state" (Fadil 2014, 251; also refer to Appadurai 2006 and Povinelli 1998). Operating in such a context means to challenge and transform hegemonic discourses of race, gender, and religion (Mirza 2002, 6), thus exerting **agency** (the capacity of action within a given sociopolitical structural context that may constrain individual and collective responses) (see Ahearn 2001, among others). Going beyond the dichotomy between subordination and resistance and "mak[ing] sense" of their religious life experiences (Bilge 2010, 22; Mahmood 2005), contemporary Muslim women enact agency through embodying the intersectional categories of belonging that they are assigned to or that they claim. Their action consists of defining specific forms of feminisms that are anchored in their identities, including their religion, and that are situated in the European context, thus contributing to the constitution of a European intra-Islamic field and its integration into global/worldwide (Muslim) space (Djelloul and Maréchal 2014). By doing this, they assert the need for an institutional recognition of their legitimate inclusion in the sociopolitical and cultural context where they live: that means fulfilling their rights, just as any other citizens, and ensuring the possibility of exerting them.

agency

the capacity of a person to act independently and make their own choices within the constraints of the social structure; these can conform to or resist cultural expectations.

REVIEW QUESTIONS

1. Describe how intersectionality operates with regard to the discrimination and subordination of Muslim women, by:

   a. defining the key notions that you use; and

   b. bringing a concrete example in form of life history (not necessarily among those studied in the chapter);

2. What does the notion of "agency" mean and how can it be applied to describe the strategies put in place by Muslim women to counter discrimination and subordination (provide with a concrete example)?

KEY TERMS

agency: the capacity of a person to act independently and make their own choices within the constraints of the social structure; these can conform to or resist cultural expectations.

ethno-stratification: In the workplace, this notion describes the socioeconomic process leading to a concentration of workers of certain nationalities or origins in particular sectors and jobs.

hegemonic discourse: a discourse that promotes the dominance of one group over another supported by legitimating norms and ideas that normalize dominance. Using collective consent rather than force, dominant social groups maintain power, and social inequalities are naturalized.

intersectionality: refers to the interconnected nature of social categories such as race, class, and gender that create overlapping systems of discrimination or disadvantage. The goal of an intersectional analysis is to understand how racism, sexism, and homophobia (for example) interact together to impact our identities and how we live in our society.

Islamic feminism: A feminist movement that seeks freedom of religion on the basis of a multifaceted definition of femininity that recognizes both religiosity and women's agency within society.

Islamophobia: fear of, and prejudice against the Islamic faith and Muslims in general

racialization: the process of ascribing a racial identity and associated traits to a group. These characteristics are often defined by a dominant group with the aim of discriminating against and excluding the subordinate group.

RESOURCES FOR FURTHER EXPLORATION

The ethnographic material used in this chapter has been collected within the framework of the following research programs, whose publications are of help to deepen some of the topics as well as further contextual elements addressed in this chapter:

- *Forgotten Women: The Impact of Islamophobia on Muslim Women*, ENAR—European Network Against Racism (2015–2016), see: https://www.enar-eu.org/Forgotten-Women-the-impact-of-Islamophobia-on-Muslim-women;

- *Countering Islamophobia through the Development of Best Practice in the Use of Counter-Narratives in EU Member States*, EC-DG Justice (Coordination: University of Leeds, UK, 2017–2018), see: https://cik.leeds.ac.uk/.

ACKNOWLEDGMENTS

The author thanks all the Muslim women who have shared their life experiences for this chapter.

BIBLIOGRAPHY

Abu-Lughod, Lila. 2002. "Do Muslim Women Really Need Saving? Anthropological Reflections on Cultural Relativism and Its Others." *American Anthropologist* 104, no. 3: 783–790.

Abu-Lughod, Lila. 1987. "Modest Women, Subversive Poems: The Politics of Love in an Egyptian Bedouin Society." *British Journal of Middle Eastern Studies* 13, no. 2: 159–168.

Adam, Ilke. 2007. "Les immigrés et leurs descendants sur le marché de l'emploi. Qu'en savons-nous en Belgique francophone (1989–2004)?" In *Immigration et intégration en Belgique francophone. État des savoirs*, edited by Marco Martiniello, Andrea Rea, and Felice Dassetto, 223–235. Brussels: Bruylant.

Ahearn, Laura M. 2001. "Language and Agency." *Annual Review of Anthropology* 30, no. 1: 109–137.

Allievi, Stefano. 2005. "How the Immigrant Has Become Muslim." *Revue européenne des migrations internationales* 21, no. 2: 135–163.

Ameli, Saied R., Merali, Arzu M., and Shahasemi, E. 2012. *France and the Hated Society: Muslim Experiences*. Wembley, UK: Islamic Human Rights Commission.

Anthias, Floya. 2002. "Beyond Feminism and Multiculturalism: Locating Difference and the Politics of Location." *Women's Studies International Forum* 25, no. 3: 275–286.

———. 2016. "Interconnecting Boundaries of Identity and Belonging and Hierarchy-Making within Transnational Mobility Studies: Framing Inequalities." *Current Sociology* 64, no. 2: 172–190.

Appadurai, Arjun. 2006. *Fear of Small Numbers: An Essay on the Geography of Anger*. Durham, NC: Duke University Press.

Barriteau, Eudine. 1993. *Confronting Power, Theorizing Gender: Interdisciplinary Perspectives in the Caribbean*. Kingston: University of West Indies Press.

Ben Mohammed, Nadia. 2004. "Les femmes musulmanes voilées d'origine maro-caine sur le marché de l'emploi." In *Féminité, islamité, minorité: question à propos du hijâb*, edited by Fabienne Brion, 49–62. Louvain-la-Neuve: Academia Bruylant.

Bilge, Sirma. 2010. "Beyond Subordination vs. Resistance: An Intersectional Approach to the Agency of Veiled Muslim Women." *Journal of Intercultural Studies* 31, no. 1: 9–28.

Bracke, Sarah. 2007. "Feminisme en islam: Intersecties." In *Vrouw(on)vriendelijk? Islam feministisch bejejen*, edited by Inge Arteel, Heidy M. Müller, Machteld De Metsenaere, and Sarah Bossaert, 13–38. Brussels: VUB.

Brems, Eva, Yaiza Janssens, Kim Lecoyer, Saïla Ouald Chaib, Victoria Vandersteen, and Jogchum Vrielink. 2014. "The Belgian 'Burqa Ban' Confronted with Insider Realities." In *The Experience of Face Veil Wearers in Europe and the Law*, edited by Eva Brems, 77–114. Cambridge: Cambridge University Press.

Centre pour l'égalité des chances et la lutte contre le racisme (Centre). 2009. *Delete cyberhate racisme et discrimination sur internet octobre*. Brussels: Centre pour l'égalité des chances et la lutte contre le racisme.

Centre Interfédéral pour l'égalité des chances (Unia). 2017. Travail et Concerta-tion sociale, Marché du travail et origine, Monitoring socio-économique SPF emploi. Brussels: Unia.

Centre Interfédéral pour l'égalité des chances (Unia). 2015. *Le travail du centre exprimé en chiffres pour l'année 2014*. Brussels: Unia.

Collectif Contre l'Islamophobie en Belgique (CCIB). 2015. *Droits des femmes et dimension sexiste de l'islamophobie: factsheet*. Brussels: CCIB.

Court of Justice of the European Union Cases. C-157/15 Achbita and C-188/15 Bougnaoui. https://curia.europa.eu/jcms/upload/docs/application/pdf/2017-03/cp170030en.pdf. Accessed on June 20, 2019.

Collins, Patricia H. 2015. "Intersectionality's Definitional Dilemmas." *Annual Review of Sociology* 41: 1–20.

Crenshaw, Kimberlé. 1991. "Mapping the Margins: Intersectionality, Identity Politics, and Violence against Women of Color." *Stanford Law Review* 43: 1241–1299.

Dassetto, Felice. 2009. *Interculturalité en clair. Question en marge des « Assises de l'Interculturalité »* (Unpublished manuscript). https://www.uclouvain.be/cps/ucl/doc/espo/documents/Interculturalisme.pdf. Accessed April 17, 2017.

Djelloul, Ghaliya, and Brigitte Maréchal. 2014. "Muslims in Western Europe in the Late Twentieth Century. Emergence and Transformations in 'Muslim' Revindications and Collective Mobilization Efforts." In *Routledge Handbook of Islam in the West*, edited by Tottoli Roberto, 85–105. New York: Routledge.

European Women Lobby (EWL). 2015. *1995–2015: From Words to Action. Assessment of the Implementation of the Beijing Platform for Action, 20 years after Its Adoption*. Brussels: EWL.

Fadil, N. 2016. " 'Are We All Secular/ized Yet?': Reflections on David Goldberg's 'Are We All Post-racial Yet?.' " *Ethnic and Racial Studies* 39, no. 13: 2261–2268.

———. 2014. "Asserting State Sovereignty. The Face Veil Ban in Belgium." In *The Experiences of Face Veil Wearers in Europe and the Law*, edited by Eva Brems, 251–262. Cambridge: Cambridge University Press.

———. 2011. "Not-/Unveiling as an Ethical Practice." *Feminist Review* 98, no. 1: 83–109.

Fadil, Nadia, Farid El-Asri, and Sarah Bracke. 2014. "Chapter 5 Belgium." In *The Oxford Handbook of European Islam*, edited by Joceline Cesari, 222–262. Oxford: Oxford University Press.

Hamidi, Malika. 2015. "Féministes musulmanes dans le contexte postcolonial de l'Europe francophone." *Histoire, monde et cultures religieuses* 4: 63–78.

Hertogen, Jan. 2008. "In België wonen 628.751 moslims." *Indymedia* 12. http://www.indymedia.be/index.html%3Fq=node%252F29363.html. Accessed June 24, 2019.

hooks, bell. 1981. *Ain't I a Woman: Black Women and Feminism*. Boston: South End.

Husson, Jean-François. 2015. "Belgium." In Vol. 7, *Yearbook of Muslims in Europe*, edited by Oliver Scharbrodt, Samin Akgönül, Ahmed Alibašić, Jørgen S. Nielsen, Magnus Vytautas, and Egdūnas Račius, 87–113. Leiden, The Netherlands: Brill.

Institute for the Equality of Women and Men (Institute). 2015. *L'écart salarial entre les femmes et les hommes en Belgique*. Brussels: Institute.

Mahmood, Saba. 2005. *Politics of Piety. The Islamic Revival and the Feminist Subject*. Princeton, NJ: Princeton University Press.

Maréchal Brigitte, Bocquet Célestine, and Dassetto Felice. 2016. "Islamophobia in Belgium. A Constructed but Effective Phantasm?" *Journal of Muslim in Europe* 5, no. 2: 224–250.

Martens, Albert, and Ouali Nouria. 2005. *Discriminations des étrangers et des personnes d'origine étrangère sur le marché du travail de la Région de Bruxelles-Capitale*. Rapport de synthèse. Brussels: Université Libre de Bruxelles—Katholieke Universiteit Leuven/ORBEM.

Martiniello, Marco. 1995. "Dinamica e pluralismo culturali nell'area di Bruxelles." In *Pluralismo culturale in Europa*, edited by René Gallissot, and Anna Rivera, 73–91. Bari: Edizioni Dedalo.

Martiniello, Marco. 1996. "La question nationale belge à l'épreuve de l'immigration." In *Belgique, la force de la désunion*, edited by Alain Dieckoff, 85–104. Brussels: Complexe.

Mescoli, E. 2019. Countering Islamophobia in Belgium. In *Countering Islamophobia in Europe*, edited by Ian Law, Amina Easat-Daas, Arzu Merali, and Salman Sayyid, 253–287. Cham: Palgrave Macmillan.

Mescoli, Elsa. 2016. *Forgotten Women: The Impact of Islamophobia on Muslim Women in Belgium*. Brussels: ENAR.

Mirza, Heidi S. 2013. " 'A Second Skin': Embodied Intersectionality, Transnationalism and Narratives of Identity and Belonging among Muslim Women in Britain." *Women's Studies International Forum* 36: 5–15.

Mohanty, Chandra T. 1984. "Under Western Eyes: Feminist Scholarship and Colonial Discourses." *Boundary* 2: 333–358.

Okkerse, Liesbet, and Anja Termotte. 2004. *Étude statistique n°111. Singularité des étrangers sur le marché de l'emploi. A propos des travailleurs allochtones en Belgique*. Brussels: Institut National de Statistique.

Povinelli, Elizabeth A. 1998. "The State of Shame: Australian Multiculturalism and the Crisis of Indigenous Citizenship." *Critical Inquiry* 24, no. 2: 575–610.

Saroglou, Vassilis, Bahija Lamkaddem, Matthieu Van Pachterbeke, and Coralie Buxant. 2009. "Host Society's Dislike of the Islamic Veil: The Role of Subtle Prejudice, Values, and Religion." *International Journal of Intercultural Relations* 33, no. 5: 419–428.

Sayyid, Salman. 2014. "A Measure of Islamophobia." *Islamophobia Studies Journal* 2, no. 1: 10–25.

Solorzano, Daniel G. 1998. "Critical Race Theory, Race and Gender Microaggressions, and the Experience of Chicana and Chicano Scholars." *International Journal of Qualitative Studies in Education* 11, no. 1: 121–136.

Tarlo, Emma. 2010. *Visibly Muslim: Fashion, Politics, Faith.* Oxford: Berg.

Toğuşlu, Erkan. 2015. *Everyday Life Practices of Muslims in Europe.* Leuven: Leuven University Press.

Torrekens, Corinne. 2005. "Le pluralisme religieux en Belgique." *Diversité Canadienne* 4, no. 3: 56–58.

Torrekens, Corinne, and Adam Ilke. 2015. *Belgo-Marocains, Belgo-Turcs, (auto) portrait de nos concitoyens.* Brussels: King Baudouin Foundation.

Tratsaert, Katrien. 2004. "Analyse de la position des étrangers sur le marché du travail. Zoek de Gelijkenissen, vind de verschillen." In *Minorités ethniques en Belgique: Migration et marché du travail*, edited by Pierre Desmarez, Peter Van de Hallen, Nouria Ouali, Véronique De Graef, and Katrien Tratsaert, 35–70. Ghent: Academia Press.

Yuval-Davis, Nira. 2006. "Intersectionality and Feminist Politics." *European Journal of Women's Studies* 13, no. 3: 193–209.

Zemni, Sami. 2011. "The Shaping of Islam and Islamophobia in Belgium." *Race & Class* 53, no. 1: 28–44.

19

Fatherhood and Family Relations in Transnational Migration from Mezcala, Mexico

Elizabeth Pérez Márquez

LEARNING OBJECTIVES

- Analyze diverse practices and meanings of fatherhood.

- Identify the key elements in the construction of fatherhood and conjugality among young Indigenous Mexican migrants.

- Discuss how transnationalism affects Indigenous peoples' lives and how their undocumented condition makes them vulnerable in the United States.

In this chapter, the author explores the experiences of fatherhood among migrant men in the United States and Mexico and demonstrates how they disrupt common models of fatherhood. Through case studies, the author addresses the ways in which these men negotiate roles and create strategies to be present, have authority, and support their relationships with their spouses and children, even in their absence. The author concludes that their migration experiences profoundly shape their practices and identities as fathers.

INTRODUCTION

In some Latin American societies, especially Mexico, fatherhood marks a change of status as men become parents. Through access to economic and symbolic resources as fathers, men consolidate themselves as "complete men," as long as they comply with family obligations such as providing financial support and using the authority that comes from being male and a parent in a patriarchal environment. However, the experience of fatherhood is not universal but rather informed by socially and culturally specific practices. For example, some scholars suggest that peasant parents from central Mexico are more involved in raising their children than urban parents in Mexico City because "there are a multiplicity of cultural practices and patterns in which paternity is based on the divergence of experiences" (Gutmann 1996, 57). Moreover, according to Luis Bonino, "fatherhood will be diverse as long as the social sector, class, age, and religion are different" (Bonino 2003, 172). Furthermore, fatherhood in the context of transnational migration creates, on the one hand, vulnerable conditions for men, but on the other may also provide financial benefits to support their families in Mexico.

My research disrupts universal models of fatherhood by demonstrating its complexity. I focus on the diverse meanings and practices of fatherhood among Indigenous Coca men from Mezcala, Jalisco, Mexico, who migrated to the United States. The meanings and practices of family for these men are based on Indigenous community experiences. They negotiate and create strategies to be present, have authority, and support their relationships with their spouses and children. In other words, they become parents, not only because they biologically produced children but because they are recognized by their community as upholding their parenting roles even in their physical absence. However, these parenting experiences are shaped by their various migration experiences, which, in turn, transforms their identity as fathers in various ways.

As you read in the introduction of this book, culture is constructed through a myriad of complex social processes. Similarly, gendered identities such as "father" are also social constructions, which for these men are shaped by history, community composition, and the migratory experience. To begin this chapter, I will examine the impact of transnational migration on the concepts of fatherhood and conjugality and their roles in migrant men's lives.

BACKGROUND

In 2011 I began to study the fatherhood practices of young migrant men (aged eighteen to twenty-six) from the Indigenous Coca community of Mezcala, Jalisco, Mexico, and what these practices reveal about their relationships with their spouses and children. The Coca Indigenous community of Mezcala, Mexico, is located on the north shore of Lake Chapala, Jalisco. It is a town of fishermen, peasants, merchants, and (recently) skilled tradesmen who work in housing construction and electronics assembly. The town is struggling with the Mexican state for recognition of its Indigenous autonomy and ancestral practices. Its Indigenous identity is based on community, religious, and family organization linked to the land and lake territories. For more information on this community see Castillero 2005, Bastos 2012, and Ochoa 2006.

The men I studied migrated to the United States looking for better living conditions. Some were deported to Mexico under President Obama's Secure Communities program (2008–2017). My research examines how this policy affected the migrants and their family life. Other men in my study (with and without documents) returned voluntarily to Mexico to attend to family issues at home. In this chapter I explore the interconnected realities of "being a father" and "being a husband" in the context of this transnational migration. Through interviews and ethnographic observations in Mezcala, Mexico, and Los Angeles and Sanger in California, I identify the tensions and the strategies these men develop as they parent from a distance. I also suggest that fatherhood is constructed through conceptions and practices of gender, conjugality, and migratory experiences. These men had more education and specialized skills that allowed them to obtain employment in the United States in construction, assembling electronics, and food packaging, which eased their lives as migrants compared to their predecessors who were farmers, fishermen, or **bracero migrants**. In the three cases I present in this chapter, the young men use their skills to survive in California in a context where harassment and discrimination are ever increasing. All three men lacked the proper documents to work in the United States, which greatly complicated their lives and affected fatherhood practices and relations with their spouses and children. In all of these cases, the names of the interviewees were changed in order to protect their identities.

TRANSNATIONALISM AND FATHERHOOD

To understand the importance of fatherhood to these men, it is important to contextualize their transnational movements and the complexity of their practices of fatherhood at a distance. Scholars have argued that transnationalism indicates a weakening of nation-states, and simultaneously, the strengthening of the contemporary global economy contributing to the formation and continuity of global financial and political institutions. For Jürgen Habermas, the weakening of the state was expressed by the

Bracero program
a temporary worker program operating from 1942 to 1964 to address the labor shortages in the 1940s caused by World War II. The original objective of the Bracero program was to employ a large, temporary labor force to harvest fruits and vegetables for US consumption.

crisis of capitalism and the system of national institutions: that is, the states no longer had the power to regulate the domestic market or the authority to make policy decisions. Rather, these powers were exercised by other institutions such as the World Bank (WB) or the International Monetary Fund (IMF), which produced what Habermas called the "postnational" era (Habermas 1998). Global institutions such as the World Trade Organization (WTO), IMF, and WB imposed their policies and agendas in many Latin American countries, resulting in conditions of inequality, poverty, and socioeconomic exclusion within their population. With transnationalism, large corporations moved operations around the world searching for countries with, for example, lax environmental regulations that would allow the use of toxic chemicals in the production of fabrics, clothing, and electronics. Corporations also searched for locations with cheap labor and few labor rights, compounding job insecurity and social inequality in these countries.

Scholars (Ong 1999; Kearney 1995) have analyzed the detrimental impacts of transnationalism on the economies and societies in peripheral areas of the globe. These global processes have contributed to the motivations of the people to move between countries producing a visible moment called the "age of migration" (Castles and Miller 2004). These migrations, particularly for undocumented laborers, have been shaped by class, gender, and ethnicity (Alarcón 1999; Alba 1999; Arroyo 1989; Bustamante 1975, 1997; Cornelius 1990; Delgado and Márquez 2007). The men participating in my research from the Coca community are among those undocumented migrants whose lives and movements have been deeply affected by the transnationalization of capital. These individuals are trying to reconfigure their lives, their community, and their gender identity and fatherhood as well. From this perspective, Malkin (1999) suggests that migration must be examined from the construction of gender to differentiate the participation of men and women within the transnational migration circuit because "we run the risk not only of granting priority to the 'political' over the 'domestic' but not to reinforce duality" (Malkin 1999, 475). Furthermore, migration affects "family dynamics," which allows us to understand social cohesion, elements of solidarity, and reciprocity but also tension, conflict, and violence in the private sphere of families (Boehm 2008, 21).

Fatherhood in Latin America has emerged as a central topic in scholarship starting in the 2000s. Fuller's *Paternities in Latin America* (2000), for example, positioned fatherhood at the center of analysis examining cases from different countries such as Mexico, Peru, Argentina, and Chile. Each case shows diverse practices in the context of the global economy, which generates unequal relations based on gender, ethnicity, and migration.

Recognizing Mexico as a multicultural country, Bonino (2003) proposes models of fatherhood based on different types of cultures, religions, and societies. Likewise, Alatorre argues that fatherhood is "an interpretation of the subject that places him in relation to sons and daughters and includes a series of practices and meanings, which are not universal or homogeneous, and therefore we will have to observe these men in their particular contexts without losing sight of their ethnic, relational, social, origins etc." (Alatorre and Luna 2000, 244). Building on this literature, I recognize fatherhood as a shifting identity that includes the idea of being a "good father" and a "good spouse." It is a social and cultural identity that is built on the relations with spouses and children, whether co-located or living at a distance.

MEZCALA, A VILLAGE OF TRANSNATIONAL INDIGENOUS MIGRANTS

Mezcala is an Indigenous enclave that represents one of the last riverside towns in Jalisco that still preserves their religious practices and identity. Anchored in the territory, they have a long history of struggles to defend their Indigenous Coca autonomy (Bastos 2010; Martínez and Alonso 2009). Although the Cocas no longer speak Nahuatl (their native language), they express their ethnic identity through their strong community organization structure, family, and community ties. In Mezcala, agriculture has been a fundamental part of the local and regional economy. It is a community of farmers and fishermen, which in recent years has changed as access to education has led to other jobs such as in the electronics industry and the building trades. Since the mid-1980s the maquiladoras near Mezcala have created jobs for local residents. Although they offer only minimum wage jobs, workers found these positions attractive as they provided better working and living conditions. Despite these factory jobs, Mezcala is still a poor Indigenous community, not fully benefiting from the global economies nor the Mexican state.

For most of the twentieth century, Mezcala residents have been migrating to the United States, starting with the Bracero program (1942–1964). Due to a labor shortage in the 1940s caused by World War II, the original objective of the Bracero program was to employ a large, temporary labor force to harvest fruits and vegetables for US consumption. Since then, migration from Mezcala (and other parts of Mexico) to the United States has continued virtually unabated. Mezcala has become a transnational community, with the Indigenous Cocas living in both Mexico and in the

United States. California is home to a large population of migrants from Mezcala, particularly in the cities of Los Angeles and Sanger. In California, migrants have formed associations and groups that organize community gatherings to share and continue the traditions practiced in their community of origin. For example, Club Mezcala Inc., located in South Central Los Angeles, has been an active hometown association since 2006 with 120 engaged members. The club organizes fundraising events to support the community in Jalisco such as the construction of a community library and other projects. In the city of Sanger, groups of dancers practice for months prior to the December 12 celebration for the Virgin of Guadalupe. In both cities, Mezcala celebrations include dances, music, and special costumes. Migrants also have a soccer team that competes locally and participates in the annual soccer tournament in California (Perez-Marquez 2015).

In the city of Los Angeles, the Cocas reside in the central and southern parts of the city, in neighborhoods that are poor and considered by many to be dangerous. Some arrived between 1963 and 1987 escaping domestic violence, conditions of poverty, and marginalization in Mezcala. Those in Sanger arrived during the last stages of the Bracero program in the 1960s and remained in this city. Others arrived during the 1980s driven by the economic crises in Mexico at the time. There they worked in the harvesting of citrus and other fruits. Sanger is a city of fourteen thousand inhabitants located about fifteen miles east of Fresno, in the Central Valley of California. There the Cocas live in neighborhoods around the periphery of the city, where housing conditions are more precarious and pesticides part of the air they breathe.

The three young migrant fathers I discuss below all arrived in California without documents between 1996 and 2007. They all had support networks in both cities to help pay the costs of migration and settling in their new homes. The Mexican origin population in these cities includes both documented and undocumented people, although the young Indigenous undocumented people who continue the migratory flow from Mezcala are among the most vulnerable in terms of deportation.

The implementation of the Obama administration's Secure Communities immigration program marked a change in the historic rhythms and cycles of migration from Mezcala. The program implemented a new level of collaboration between federal and state government agencies, local police forces, and the US Immigration and Customs Enforcement Agency (ICE). Through this program, security forces identified foreigners who were detained, had previous arrest histories, or were deemed threats to the security of US citizens and were deported to their country of origin. The efficiency of this program was reflected in the number of people deported to their countries of origin. Under the Obama administration, the United States deported more than three million people, the greatest number in US history (Nowrasteh 2019). One of the cases presented in this study was affected by this policy, and my final analysis includes the impact the Obama administration policies had on the Coca community.

YOUNG MIGRANT PARENTS: BEING FATHERS AND HUSBANDS

In this context of deportation and mass return of Mexicans to Mexico, some young fathers from Mezcala who migrated in the late 1980s and during the early 2000s did not have residence documents in the United States and faced great challenges exercising their fatherhood because of their status. Being undocumented forced them to live in the shadows as they constantly were afraid of being deported. Being undocumented also prohibited them from traveling back and forth across the US border to spend time with their family, forcing them to stay as long as possible in the US and making their stay semipermanent. For these men, all of these experiences generate feelings of guilt, frustration, and remorse regarding their fatherhood because of their absence during the birth of their children or because of the prolonged absence in general. However, from their point of view, they try to remain closely connected to their children and seek to protect their families while they are absent from Mexico by sending **remittances** and maintaining constant communication. They consider it their responsibility to maintain the family economically.

A common theme among migrant Cocas fathers who had small children was that they sought to maintain the position of authority they had before migrating. They were "vocal and opinionated" and actively participated in the care of their children, albeit from a distance. Compared to their fathers or grandfathers, they considered themselves to be much less detached and more active fathers.

According to their wives, the migrant fathers changed after returning from the United States. This change was sometimes "for the better" and sometimes not. The wives noted that they became more demanding in terms of caring for their children and improving the conditions of family life. They exercised their presence as fathers by seeking authority, which sometimes involved using some type of violence, as the migrant fathers sought to regain the position they had before migrating. Sometimes they did not succeed, and the couple decided to separate. Javier's case shows this dynamic.

remittances
money sent from migrants to their families residing in the country of origin.

JAVIER: THE FRUSTRATION AND GUILT

Javier is a thirty-year-old man. His father is a peasant; his mother a housewife. He is the third born among his thirteen brothers and sisters. He finished high school in Mezcala and then worked for a few years in Guadalajara as a merchant in the largest market in the city and in construction work at El Salto, a municipality near Mezcala. He married Paty in 2003, and less than a year later his first son Rafael was born, followed by his son Ramiro the next year. He lived with his family in the city of Guadalajara, the capital of the state of Jalisco.

In 2006, Javier and his wife separated, and they agreed to each take custody of one child. Javier took custody of Rafael, the eldest, and his wife took Ramiro, the youngest. With Rafael, Javier went back to live in his mother's house in Mezcala. Due to a lack of employment options and the stress of the divorce, Javier decided to go to the United States to find work, leaving Rafael in the care of Javier's mother. Javier crossed the northern border of Mexico en route to the United States without documents or formal migratory authorization. His brothers, who lived in California helped him pay for the costs of a person (coyote) who helped him cross the border near Nogales, Sonora. The person(s) that provide such services are known as Coyotes; this nickname is usually associated with the animal's behavior when trying to avoid detection by those who are under his surveillance. Crossing modern state borders without the proper documentation requires a coyote who should have a topographical knowledge and high level of cunning.

This area of Mexico is very dangerous and also closely monitored by organized criminals and the US border patrol, but it was the only viable option he had to get to Los Angeles. It took him several days to arrive, and he walked a few days in the desert. Then one of the coyotes picked him up in Arizona, hid him in the trunk of a car, and drove him to California.

Javier arrived in the city of Compton, south of Los Angeles, thanks to the financial help of his two brothers who already lived here. His brother Rodrigo worked as a supervisor at a fast-food packing house and got Javier a job at the company. Javier then began to work in the maintenance of the food-packing machines. Javier distributed his income between his living expenses (rent, food, gasoline) and sending money to his mother. His remittances varied between $100 and $150 a month, which were meant to cover the expenses of his son Rafael in Mezcala. At the age of eight years old, Rafael should have been in the fourth grade; however, after failing the second grade twice, he remained in the second grade. According to Javier's mother, Rafael had a hard time learning and had behavioral problems (he gets distracted), but Javier's mother thinks he is sick with sadness for not having his father or mother nearby. For Javier, he felt that leaving Rafael in the care of his grandmother was the only option he had after the divorce. In his words.

> I know that the child has many doubts, why did I leave him with his grandmother instead of his mother? Why was I not there when he was little? Why did I leave others in charge? I am getting prepared and will return when the time is right. God will put the moment and the precise words in my mouth. I personally have a lot of guilt for having left him, which is why he does poorly in school. He needs his parents, at minimum his mom, but his mom is now his grandmother. I ask the Lord to enlighten me and let me be together with my son when I return to Mezcala. We will have better living conditions and I will be able to care for him. (Javier, interview by author, August 15, 2012)

Javier expresses his concerns about the neglect of his son because, according to him, every time he sees Rafael in photographs he doesn't seem well cared for, with old clothes and tattered shoes.

> I'm angry that he lives like this, all dirty, disheveled and broken. I am sure, he spends all day in the street . . . It would be better if I cared for him because his mother never visits him in Mezcala. I know that she gave up her rights to him, but she should at least visit him from time to time. (Javier, interview by author, August 15, 2012)

When talking with Javier about the long-distance relationship he has with his children, he stated, "I am prepared for the questions. I am prepared to answer all their doubts. Why his mother rejected him, why we divorced and why I left him with his grandmother. The main reason I want to return to Mexico is that I want Rafa to feel loved and appreciated at least by me, I am his father; in fact, that is why I want to go back to Mezcala." In 2013, after living and working in California for seven years, Javier returned voluntarily to Mezcala. He lives permanently in Mezcala and started a new family, and his son Rafael continues to live with his grandparents.

Javier's experience provides insight into a number of factors that influence fatherhood for these men. First, the vulnerable conditions of being an undocumented immigrant living in California restricted his ability to return more frequently to Mexico to visit his family. This negatively affected his connection and relationship with his son. Second, his identity as a responsible father was disrupted because his mother was caring for his son, and his son was not doing well. In other words, for Javier being a good father required him to be present in his son's life, to guide him, and participate in his everyday life activities to ensure his well-being. Not being able to do these things negatively affected Javier's self-identity as a good father, which was further compounded by constraints on his masculinity as an undocumented migrant.

RAUL: VOLUNTARY RETURN AND THE NEGOTIATION OF HIS CONJUGALITY

In another case, the migrant father's absence and disconnection from his children became the very source of the loss of his parental position. After a long absence, he did not recognize himself as a father despite being the one responsible for supporting the family financially. Raul is a thirty-year-old man who was born in Mezcala. After high school, he left to work for a construction company for a year and a half in a neighboring town. This work allowed him to travel and get to know different parts of Mexico as the company did projects in Cancún, León, Guanajuato, Guadalajara, and Mexico City. When he was nineteen, he met Lilia with whom he then had two children in the next two years: Rosalia and Carlitos. In 2008, when Raul was twenty-one, he went to Los Angeles where four of his brothers live. He did not have a way to get to the United States legally, so his brothers helped him pay for all the costs of crossing the border, which involved hiring a coyote. When Raul arrived, he started working in a tire factory and then later for a fast-food packing house where two of his brothers worked. He stayed in Los Angeles from 2008 until 2010, when he decided to return to Mexico to meet his son Carlitos, who was already a year old.

After his two-year stay in the United States, Raul thought that his experience had changed his perspective on being a man in several ways: "There you are a man and a woman, because there you have to work outside of the house and also wash your clothes, iron and cook. There is no distinction between being male or female" (Raul, interview by author, May 13, 2011).

Raul lived with his brothers in a garage that served as an apartment. This allowed him to save up to buy a van, which was one of the goals of the trip to the United States, in addition to sending money to Lilia to pay for the household expenses back home. While Raul was in the United States, Lilia lived with his parents. In their home, he felt confident that his wife and children would not lack food or necessities; however, he also thought it was important for Lilia to have some money for emergencies, birthday parties, and for medicines if his children got sick.

> I sent money to Lilia every time I could, every fifteen days or every month I would send her a little money so she could buy the baby's milk or buy gasoline to take them to the hospital if they got sick. I also sent her money to have a big birthday party for Rosalia and buy her a princess dress or whatever she wants. I wanted her to buy her a dress and send me pictures. (Raúl, interview by author, May 13, 2011)

Raul returned to Mezcala voluntarily in 2010 because he was not present at the births of either of his two children and felt estranged from his family. Although Raul did not have any work options in Mexico, he decided to stay there permanently. Raul's experience as an undocumented migrant allowed him to understand and negotiate his identity as a husband and economic responsibility as a father. He reflected that in the United States undocumented migrants, both men and women, have similar working and everyday life experiences. He understood that men and women must work hard to obtain their goals in life. Through the lens of gender, he reflected on his role as a father, his position as man, and his ability to support his family.

PEPE: DEPORTATION AND FAMILY SEPARATION

Pepe was born in Mezcala in 1980, the youngest in a family of seven brothers and sisters. His parents immigrated to the United States in 1988, and although they had already had previous experiences of temporary migration, they secured permanent US residency during the Simpson-Rodino Amnesty or IRCA of 1986. His father had begun migrating in 1975, going back and forth between Mezcala and California. Then his mother began to take the eldest children to the United States. They applied for permits for temporary and then permanent stays through the IRCA Amnesty, which allowed them to stay indefinitely. However Pepe did not have the same fate because his mother did not request identity documents within the required period to process the paperwork, and as a result he became undocumented.

Pepe grew up in the United States, and because he was the youngest of all his brothers, he had more financial resources, which allowed him to finish high school. After high school he worked picking fruit in Sanger. Later he worked in a jam factory in the city of Fresno, California, shortly before he was deported in 2012. At the age of twenty, Pepe married a woman of Mexican origin born in Fresno whom he met in high school. They have four sons aged eight, seven, five, and two years old.

Regarding his relationship with his children, he reflects:

> I am very close to them, I am the one who gave them break-
> fast, and I took them to school. I was the one who took care
> of them when Ana, my wife, worked many hours . . . I have
> been very careful with my children because my parents took
> care of me because I'm the youngest of my brothers and sisters
> and I know how important it is to have your mom and dad
> close to you. That is why I try to take care of my children as
> much as I can, to tell them how to do things and all that, but
> now that I am away, they have even told me they are skinny.
> (Pepe, interview by author, February 20, 2012)

This dynamic changed when in 2012 the police took him to a jail in Fresno for driving without a driver's license, and later he was deported. He arrived in the city of Mexicali, where he stayed for one year hoping to find a way to return. He finally decided to go to Mezcala and to the house of his only sister. When I interviewed him in Mezcala, he had been here for six months and could not find a job, nor could he return to his family in Fresno. His mother sent him some money every two weeks, money that he shared with his sister Martha in Mezcala and used to buy phone cards to talk to his wife in Fresno and find out about his legal migration situation in the courts. When I spoke with his mother Fernanda in Sanger, she told me that Pepe's children "are very sad because he was the one who looked after them. Pepe was the one who took care of them, took them to school, made them dinner." Fernanda showed us photographs of the children and explained that the children have lost weight due to the absence of their father. Pepe feels frustrated and guilty for not being more careful when he was detained on the road.

That event marked his and his family's life. While at times he feels proud of being a loving father and very close to his children, at other times he feels that he has not done enough to be able to return to them, though he had tried once to cross the border without documents. In June of 2015 I learned that Pepe had decided to cross the northern border of

Tijuana-San Diego with the identification documents of one of his brothers. Now he lives in Fresno but not with his wife and children because his wife decided she wanted a divorce. He lives alone in an apartment and works harvesting oranges at the factory where much of his family works. He sees his children every weekend and occasionally picks them up from school to take them to lunch and spend time with them.

In Pepe's case, three points are clear. First, migration from Mezcala is so complex even within the same families, his brothers were able to obtain the proper documents to reside in the United States, but Pepe remained undocumented. Second, his commitment as a father was unmatched in relation to other cases, but his deportation to Mexico challenged his dedication to his children. Furthermore, it showed the vulnerability of the children due to their father's undocumented condition. Finally, it shows Pepe's willingness to return to the United States to be with his children despite the permanent threat of being deported due to harsher migratory laws.

CONCLUSION

The cases presented in this study demonstrate how young fathers who face migration to the United States today realize that fatherhood is a relationship that needs one's physical presence and requires constant affection, care, and attention to children and spouses. The idea of fatherhood intersects with conjugality in the context of transnational migration and entails: (a) being an economic provider, for example, through remittances but also (b) demonstrating paternal affective presence and care and (c) negotiating marital readjustment, that is, the relationship with their wives. Above all, the experience of migrating marked a significant change in the way they constructed their identity as fathers, as it made them aware of the importance of being close to their children, rather than just supporting them economically.

These issues emerge as constant concerns in these three cases of young fathers, the temporary separation of families generated tense dynamics with their spouses and children and in the cases of Javier and Pepe, their absence has been a real crisis for their children. For migrant parents, it is important to maintain a bond with their families; even at a distance, economic and emotional presence is a relevant issue in their lives.

Despite the distance and complexity of staying in hiding, young migrant parents sought family reunification insofar as it was possible. With the vicissitudes and complexity of fatherhood under physical separation, it is necessary to depend on other people to be present as a parent, for example, grandmothers and of course mothers who take the role of absent fathers. In that sense, the presence of wives or mothers of these men is fundamental to reconstruct the contents of fatherhood, which is based on physical presence and economic support.

Complex and adverse situations arise when people experience migratory vulnerability. Due to these factors, ideals of fatherhood are slowly changing for these men. Vulnerability is experienced daily. It involves uncertainty because one runs the risk of losing one's work, being separated from the place one is living, and being deported. These men live in a state of constant precarity, which causes them to reconsider their stay in the United States and maximize their resources for the well-being of their families in Mexico.

These experiences of vulnerability as undocumented Indigenous migrants were a recurrent theme during my interviews in their community of origin. Despite this vulnerable condition, these men felt they must continue being responsible fathers by being economic supporters of the family and caring for their children.

These constant concerns about deportation among the migrant fathers of Mezcala also affected their possibility of voluntary return until they had met their goals for migrating. This affected, above all, their children, since they were the ones who lived without their fathers. Migration to the United States results in multiple experiences and produces diverse situations where the identity of these Indigenous men is challenged through universal conceptions about how to be a father, the meaning of family, gender perceptions, and community.

In this way, the complexities in the lives of young migrant fathers are relevant in light of the actions of recent US government policies that separate families.

KEY TERMS

Bracero program: a temporary worker program operating from 1942 to 1964 to address the labor shortages in the 1940s caused by World War II. The original objective of the Bracero program was to employ a large, temporary labor force to harvest fruits and vegetables for US consumption.

remittances: money sent from migrants to their families residing in the country of origin.

RESOURCES FOR FURTHER EXPLORATION

- Doehner, Walter, dir. 2008. *Teo's Journey*. Astillero Films.

- Loza, Gustavo, dir. 2004. *To the Other Side*. Adicta Films.

- Parra, H., C. González, and M. Díaz. 2021. *(Trans)Fronteriza: cuando los cuidados interpelan las fronteras: estrategias por el sostenimiento de la vida de las personas migrantes ante las (in)movilidades en América Latina*. Fronteras: movilidades, identidades y comercios. Argentina: No. 6, Mayo, CLACSO. https://www.academia.edu/48982776/Bolet%C3%ADn_Trans_Fronteriza_N%C3%BAmero_06_Mayo_2021_GT_Fronteras_Movilidades_Identidades_y_Comercios_CLACSO

- Riggen, Patricia, dir. 2007. *Under the Same Moon*.

- Torre, E., and M. Rodríguez. 2019. Paternidades a distancia: Malestares de padres separados de sus hijas e hijos tras la deportación. *Estudios Fronterizos*, 20, e023. https://doi.org/10.21670/ref.1902023.

- Zalla, Christopher, dir. 2007. *Blood of My Blood*. Cinergy Pictures.

BIBLIOGRAPHY

Alatorre, J. and R. Luna. 2000. Significados y prácticas de la paternidad en la ciudad de México, in *Paternidades en América Latina*, edited by Norma Fúller. Perú: Pontificia Universidad Católica del Perú, 241–275.

Alba, F. "Política migratoria: Un corte de caja." *Nexos*, January 5, 2004. http://www.nexos.com.mx/?P=leerarticulo&Article=2102167.

Arroyo, J. 1989. *El Abandono Rural*. Guadalajara: Universidad De Guadalajara.

Bastos, S. 2010. *La Defensa de Mezcala. Historia y lucha de una Comunidad Indígena Coca*. (Unpublished manuscript.)

Boehm, D. 2008. '"Now I Am a Man and a Woman!': Gendered Moves and Migrations in a Transnational Mexican Community." *Latin American Perspectives* 3:16–30. http://www.jstor.org/stable/27648071.

Bonino, L. 2003. "Las nuevas paternidades." *Cuadernos de Trabajo Social* 16: 171–182.

Bustamente, J. 1975. Espaldas mojadas: Materia prima para la expansión del *capitalismo*, México: Cuadernos del CES, El Colegio de México.

———. 1997. *Cruzar la línea. La migración de México a Estados Unidos*. México: Fondo de Cultura Económica.

Castles, S., and J. Miller. 2004. *La era de la migración. Movimientos internacionales de población en el mundo moderno*. México: Fundación Colosio, Universidad Autónoma de Zacatecas, Miguel Ángel Porrúa, Secretaria de Gobernación, Instituto Nacional de Migración.

Cornelius, Wayne. 1990. Los migrantes de la crisis: El nuevo perfil de la migración de mano de obra mexicana a California en los años ochenta. In *Población y Trabajo en contextos regionales*, edited by Gail Mummert, 103–141. Zamora: El Colegio de Michoacán.

Delgado, R., and H. Márquez. 2007. El Sistema migratorio México-Estados Unidos: Dilemas de la integración regional, el desarrollo y la migración. In *Migración y desarrollo: Perspectivas desde el sur*, edited by S. Clastles and R. Delgado, 125–154. México: Colección Desarrollo y Migración.

Escobar, A., L. Lowell, Susan Martin. 2013. *Diálogo binacional sobre migrantes mexicanos en Estados Unidos y México. Reporte final*. México: CIESAS, Georgetown University.

Fuller, N., ed. 2000. *Paternidades en América Latina*. Peru: Pontificia Universidad Católica del Peru.

Gutmann, M. 1996. *The Meanings of Macho: Being a Man in Mexico City*. Berkeley: University of California Press.

Habermas, J. 1998. *Más allá del Estado nacional*. Mexico: Fondo de Cultura Económica.

Los Angeles Times. n.d. *Mapping L.A and Regions*. http://maps.latimes.com/neighborhoods/region/eastside/. Accessed June 20, 2019.

Marcus, G. 1995. "Ethnography in/of the World System: The Emergence of Multi-Sited Ethnography." *Annual Review of Anthropology* 24: 95–117.

Martinez, R., and J. Alonso. 2009. *Mezcala: una larga historia de resistencia*. Guadalajara; La Casa del Lago.

Malkin, V. 2009. "La reproducción de relaciones de género en la comunidad de migrantes mexicano en New Rochelle, Nueva York." In *Fronteras Fragmentadas*, edited by Gail Mummert, 339–351. 2nd ed. Zamora: El Colegio de Michoacán, CIDEM.

Mummert, G. 2005, June. "Transnational Parenting in Mexican Migrant Communities: Redefining Fatherhood, Motherhood and Caregiving." Paper presented at the Mexican International Family Strengths Conference, Cuernavaca, Morelos. http://imumi.org/attachments/article/118/Transnational_Motherhood.pdf.

Nowrasteh, Alex. 2019. Deportation Rates in Historical Perspective. *Cato at Liberty*. Washington DC: Cato Institute.

Ong, A. 1999. *Flexible Citizenship. The Cultural Logics of Transnationality*. Durham, NC: Duke University Press.

Pérez Márquez, C. 2015. *Ser padre y migrante: Cuatro generaciones de mezcalenses en California, 1942–2012*. PhD diss., Centro de Investigaciones y Estudios Superiores en Antropología Social (CIESAS), Guadalajara, Mexico.

United States Department of Homeland Security. "Secure Communities." http://www.ice.gov/secure_communities/. Accessed July 10, 2019.

Contributors

Lara Braff is an anthropology professor at Grossmont College, where she teaches cultural and biological anthropology courses and serves as a co-coordinator for the college's Zero Textbook Cost (ZTC) initiative. She is a coeditor of *Explorations: An Open Invitation to Biological Anthropology*, a free, open access textbook. She received her BA in anthropology and Spanish from the University of California at Berkeley and her MA and PhD in comparative human development from the University of Chicago, where she specialized in medical anthropology. Her research has focused on the cultural nuances and social disparities that shape family-making and assisted reproduction in Mexico City.

Silvia Carrasco, PhD, is professor of social anthropology in the Universitat Autònoma of Barcelona (UAB). Founder of the Centre of Research on Migrations, her research focuses on school experiences and trajectories of migrant, refugee and working-class students, education policy, and social inequality. She is currently working on two lines of research: early school leaving and social integration among working-class and second-generation students, as well as the penetration of neoliberal ideologies in education and their impact on coeducation from a feminist approach. A specialist in school ethnography, she has conducted fieldwork in Europe and the United States. Her teaching activities include research methods and anthropology applied to public policy.

Alba Castellsagué, PhD, is an educator and social anthropologist at the Universitat Autònoma of Barcelona (UAB). Her research focuses on gender, education, and development, particularly on the intersectional analysis of educational inequalities in Nepal. She has also collaborated on research about mobility and education in Spain and intersectionality and equality policies in Spanish higher education institutions.

Serena Cosgrove is an assistant professor of international studies at Seattle University. She is the director of the Latin American studies program and also coordinates Seattle University's Central America Initiative. She is the coauthor of *Surviving the Americas: Garifuna Persistence from Nicaragua to New York City* (2021) and author of *Leadership from the*

Margins: Women and Civil Society Organizations in Argentina, Chile, and El Salvador (2010), among other publications.

Nathan Dawthorne is a queer sociocultural anthropologist and advocate whose research background includes male sex work, sexuality and gender politics, and social determinants of health. He obtained his PhD in anthropology from the University of Western Ontario. Nathan is a caregiver advisor for research at the Centre for Addiction and Mental Health in Toronto (Canada) and former research associate with the Franz Boas Papers Project, an interdisciplinary collaboration reassessing and recontextualizing early American anthropology.

Dannah Dennis is a political and cultural anthropologist. She completed her PhD at the University of Virginia in 2017 and is currently a visiting assistant professor of anthropology at Bucknell University. In addition to her research on citizenship, she has published work on the politics of infrastructure in Kathmandu, Nepal's claim to Buddha's birthplace and its circulation on social media, the history of visual representation of Nepal's first Shah king, and the obligations of care and gift-giving in transnational families. You can find her on Twitter @dannahdennis.

Holly Dygert is a lecturer of anthropology at Tufts University. She received her BA in music performance from Hartwick College, and her MA and PhD in anthropology from Michigan State University. Her areas of expertise include gender and development, income transfer programs, Indigenous cultural politics, and community health initiatives. Her research has primarily focused on the experiences of Ñuu Savi (Mixtec) villagers living in the Mixteca Alta region of southern Mexico.

Nadine T. Fernandez is a cultural anthropologist and professor in the Social Science and Public Affairs Department at SUNY Empire State College. She has a BA in urban studies and history from the University of Pennsylvania, and a master's and PhD in cultural anthropology from the University of California, Berkeley. She has over twenty years of experience teaching traditional and nontraditional students in the classroom and online and is committed to creating and using Open Educational Resources (OERs). Her research examines race and gender relations in Cuba and Cuban migration to Europe. In 2015 she received the SUNY Chancellor's Award for Excellence in Scholarship and Creative Activities. Her publications include: *Revolutionizing Romance: Interracial Couples in Contemporary Cuba* (2010); an edited book (with Christian Groes) *Intimate Mobilities: Sexual Economies, Marriage and Migration* *in a Disparate World* (2018); and several book chapters and journal articles.

Ina Goel is the founder of award-winning digital platform, The Hijra Project. She has a BA in journalism and an MA in social work from the University of Delhi in India. She completed her MPhil in social medicine and community health from Jawaharlal Nehru University. Ina has worked with All India Radio and Al Jazeera English. She was a recipient of a German Academic Exchange Service (DAAD) scholarship at the department of epidemiology and international public health at Bielefeld University and the INLAKS scholarship at the department of gender and sexuality studies at University College London. Ina has also worked with FHI 360, UNICEF, the National AIDS Control Organization in India, the Indian Institute of Mass Communication, and the humanitarian organization Plan International. She is currently an HKPFS doctoral candidate at the Department of Anthropology, Chinese University of Hong Kong and a visiting fellow at Anthropos India Foundation.

Hemangini Gupta is a visiting assistant professor in gender, sexuality, and feminist studies at Middlebury College. She has a PhD in women's gender and sexuality studies from Emory University, and her writing has been published in *Feminist Review*, *Feminist Media Studies*, the *Journal of International Women's Studies*, and in the edited anthology *Gender: Love*. Prior to her PhD, she was a national print and TV journalist in India and currently curates public humanities exhibits to expand the reach of academic research.

Heidi Härkönen is a social and cultural anthropologist currently working as a postdoctoral researcher at the University of Helsinki. She earned her doctorate at the University of Helsinki in 2014 and has been a visiting researcher at the City University of New York, the University of Amsterdam, and the University of Cambridge. She has been conducting ethnographic research in Cuba since 2003 and is the author of *Kinship, Love and Life Cycle in Contemporary Havana, Cuba: To Not Die Alone* (2016). Her research interests include gender, kinship, body, personhood, care, love, life course, digitalization, politics, the state, socialism, and postsocialism.

Ashley Kistler is a professor of anthropology at Rollins College in Winter Park, Florida. She is an ethnographer and linguist who has conducted fieldwork in Maya communities in Mexico and Guatemala. Dr. Kistler's research focuses on globalization and contemporary Maya culture, collaborative ethnography, ethnohistory, and revitalization movements. Dr.

Kistler has authored numerous peer-reviewed articles, published in the *Journal of Latin American and Caribbean Anthropology*, *Anthropology and Humanism*, and *The Latin Americanist*, among other journals. She is the author of *Maya Market Women: Power and Tradition in San Juan Chamelco, Guatemala* (2014) and editor of, *Faces of Resistance: Maya Heroes, Power, and Identity* (2018). At Rollins, Dr. Kistler teaches courses on the Maya, Latin American studies, ethnographic theory and methods, and linguistic anthropology.

Lynn Kwiatkowski is a professor of cultural anthropology at Colorado State University. Her research interests include gender violence, medical anthropology, global health, critical studies of development, and hunger in Vietnam and the Philippines. Her current research focuses on gender violence and the social and cultural influences on such violence, its impacts on health and well-being, and the effects of global movements against violence toward women in local communities in northern Vietnam. She has also had a special focus on investigating marital sexual violence in these communities, analyzing its particular sociocultural influences and impacts and the cultural interpretations of this form of domestic violence. She is the author of *Struggling with Development: The Politics of Hunger and Gender in the Philippines* (1998), which is based on her research in Ifugao Province, the Philippines. Dr. Kwiatkowski has served as secretary and executive board member of the Association for Feminist Anthropology (AFA) (2011–2014).

Abha Lal completed her bachelor's degree in sociology and anthropology from Swarthmore College in 2018. She is working as a journalist at *The Record*, a Nepali digital media outlet, covering human rights, politics, and development.

Elizabeth Pérez Márquez holds a PhD in social anthropology from the Center for Research and Higher Education in Social Anthropology (CIESAS), Guadalajara, Mexico. Dr. Pérez Márquez is a professor at University of Guadalajara at Department of Cultural Management. Her work explores, from an interdisciplinary perspective, the diversity of fatherhood, contemporary Indigenous practices, and identities in transnational migration in Mexico and the United States.

Melanie A. Medeiros is an associate professor of anthropology at the State University of New York at Geneseo. Her research examines the experiences of cisgender Black women in the Americas, and Latinx im/migrant farmworkers in Western/Central New York. As a cisgender woman with US and Portuguese citizenship who identifies as a white person, Melanie is committed to using her multiple levels of privilege to address health inequity through both her research and teaching. She is the author of *Marriage, Divorce and Distress in Northeast Brazil: Black Women's Perspectives of Love, Respect and Kinship.*

Elsa Mescoli is an anthropologist affiliated with the Centre for Ethnic and Migration Studies (CEDEM) at the Faculty of Social Sciences of the University of Liege, where she is working as lecturer assistant and post-doctoral researcher. She obtained a joint doctorate in anthropology at the University of Milan-Bicocca, Italy, and political and social sciences at the University of Liege, Belgium. Her thesis focused on food as a means of defining subjectivity in the context of migration. Mescoli's present research interests include the discrimination of Muslims and public opinion on migrants, with a focus on asylum seekers, refugees, and undocumented migrants. The list of her publications and presentations is available at http://orbi.ulg.ac.be/simple-search?query=mescoli.

Natasha Kay Mortley has a bachelor's in sociology and MPhil in sociology of development from the University of the West Indies (UWI), Trinidad, and a PhD in migration and development studies from the UWI, Jamaica. Dr. Mortley is currently a lecturer at the Institute for Gender and Development Studies, Regional Coordinating Office, at the UWI, Jamaica. She has extensive experience in the field of development studies, and over the past fifteen years she has been dedicated to integrating a gender perspective to Caribbean social development and policy issues. She therefore considers herself a social developmentalist working in the area of gender and development studies, as well as an advocate for gender equality, social justice, and female empowerment. Her recent research work includes Caribbean masculinities. In 2017 Dr. Mortley conducted a study on "males, masculinities and crime in Jamaica," and in 2019 completed a "masculinities and positive fathering" study also for Jamaica.

Nolwazi Nadia Ncube is a Zimbabwean PhD student at the University of Cape Town (UCT) in the Department of Sociology. She is a Research Fellow for a research project funded by the South African National Research Foundation (NRF), *The Rand and the Reproductive Body: Markets for Reproduction in South Africa*, and its extension *Global Fertility Markets: New Reproduction and (Old) Stratifications*. In 2018, Nolwazi was awarded the Margaret McNamara Education Grant (MMEG) for her work with Save the Girl Movement promoting sanitary dignity for indigent girls in Zimbabwe. She is also a 2021 Summer Research Fellow for the Black

Girls Matter project at the African American Policy Forum (AAPF). Nol-wazi is passionate about theory of Africa produced by African scholars. She believes that African languages are a rich archive for social scientific theorization. Her main research interests are Black girlhoods, development, gender, sociology and southern Africa.

Katie Nelson is instructor of anthropology at Inver Hills Community College. Her research focuses on migration, identity, belonging, and citizenship(s) in human history and in the contemporary United States, Mexico, and Morocco. She received a BA in anthropology and Latin American studies from Macalester College, an MA in anthropology from the University of California, Santa Barbara, an MA in education and instructional technology from the University of Saint Thomas, and a PhD from CIESAS Occidente (Centro de Investigaciones y Estudios Superiores en Antropología Social Center for Research and Higher Education in Social Anthropology), based in Guadalajara, Mexico. She is Associate Editor for the *Teaching and Learning Anthropology Journal*. Her publications include *Explorations: An Open Invitation to Biological Anthropology*, an edited textbook with Shook, Braff and Aguilera (American Anthropological Association, 2019), *Doing Field Projects: Methods and Practice for Social and Anthropological Research*, with John Forrest (forthcoming) and several other book chapters and journal articles.

Sarah Quick is an associate professor of anthropology at Cottey College in Missouri, where she teaches cultural anthropology courses, qualitative research methods, interdisciplinary courses overlapping with environmental studies, and Cottey's first semester writing course. Dr. Quick is trained in sociocultural anthropology and ethnomusicology, and it was through her doctoral field research on Indigenous fiddle dance performance in Western Canada that she met Kathleen Steinhauer. Her research interests span from contemporary Indigenous music and dance performance to farm-oriented youth groups and food movements.

Keino T. Senior is the dean of the School of Arts Management and Humanities (SAMH) and the Gender Focal Point at the Edna Manley College of the Visual and Performing Arts (EMCVPA) in Jamaica. He is chairperson and coeditor of the *Jonkonnu Arts Journal*, and founder and chair of the Annual Gender and Development Lecture. Dr. Senior received his PhD (with high commendation) in gender and development studies from the University of the West Indies (UWI) in the area of masculinities, fatherhood, and abortion. His scholarly research and publications focus on masculinities, fatherhood, culture, the arts, men against violence, climate change and disaster risk management, sexual and reproductive health rights, and sexuality. He is currently engaged in a research project on masculinity and fathering and lectures in Caribbean sexualities at the Regional Office of the Institute for Gender and Development Studies at the University of the West Indies.

Susan W. Tratner earned a master's in Latin American studies and a doctorate in anthropology from the University of Florida. She has completed anthropological field research on gay men in San Jose, Costa Rica, investigated the impact of free trade zones on domestic servants in the Dominican Republic, and studied variations in business culture and corporate communication in Monterrey, Mexico. Professor Tratner worked as a market research ethnographer and moderator for Fortune 500 and start-up companies. Her research focus has been anonymous online communities since 2006. Prof. Tratner coedited the book *EFieldnotes: The Makings of Anthropology in the Digital World* (2015) with Roger Sanjek. Currently, she holds the rank of full professor at SUNY Empire State College in the Business, International Business, and Marketing Department.

Ana Marina Tzul Tzul is a medical doctor with a master's in public health. She is the head of the College of Health and Nursing at the Universidad Rafael Landívar's Quetzaltenango Campus in Guatemala.

Emily Wentzell is an associate professor of anthropology at the University of Iowa, where she also directs the school's international studies program. Her research focuses on the relationships between changing gender norms and emerging sexual health interventions targeted at men and draws on ideas from medical anthropology, gender/sexuality studies, and science and technology studies.

Index

Note: Page numbers in *italics* indicate illustrations.

abortion, 136, 364–65; sex-selective, 60; Trump policies on, 80

Afghanistan, 58

agency, 251, 335, 341, 368

AIDS, 180, 274

Aikman, Sheila, 128

Alatorre, J., 378

Albanian *Burrnesha*, 18–19

alcoholism. *See* substance use disorders

Amnesty International, 360

Anderson, Eric, 28

Appadurai, Arjun, 292–93

Arapesh people, 13–14

Aristotle, 294

asexuality, 8

Assam, 57, 58

Auick, Sarah L., 304–6

authoritarianism, 134, 137, 142, 144, 145, 240

backstage/front-stage behaviors, 313–14, 319, 320

Badgley, Robin, 330

Bangladesh, 56–58; domestic violence in, 62; gender equality in, 53; malnutrition in, 52

Barriteau, Eudine, 270, 279

Baruah, Swati Bidhan, 58

Batista, Fulgencio, 143, 239–41, 253

Beauvoir, Simone de, 313–14

Belgium, 358–68; in Cuba, 253; job discrimination and, 177; segregation and, 129; sexism and, 39–40, *40*. *See also* slave trade

Benedict, Ruth, 17–18

Bhandari, Bidhya Devi, 88

Bhutan, 57

biocultural approach, 17

biological determinism, 13–17, 21

bisexuality, 8, 332. *See also* LGBTQ persons

Blank Noise project, 69–71

Blazoned, M., 318

Boas, Franz, 35

Bohra communities, 60

Bonino, Luis, 375, 378

bracero program, 376–79

Braff, Lara, 289–302

brain drain, 245

Branch, Enobong Hanna, 317

Brazil, 170–85; demographics of, 173; domestic violence in, 180; ecotourism in, 174, 177; unemployment in, 177–80, 185

breastfeeding, 315, 317

Briggs, Laura, 80

Burrnesha ("sworn virgins"), 18–19

Cahn, Peter S., 212

Carey, David, 142

Caribbean, 235–47; colonialism in, 235–39; gender diversity in, 246–47; maps of, 133, 234; migration from, 244–45; tourism industry of, 242–44

Carlson, Nellie, 305–6

Carrasco, Silvia, 116–29

caste system, 55–56; definition of, 99; hijras in, 98–99, 101, 104, 108, 112; of Nepal, 56, 82, 85, 93; patriarchy and, 53

Castellsagué, Alba, 116–29

Castro, Fidel, 143–44, 241, 253

Chant, Sylvia, 172

chauvinism, exculpatory, 182

Cherokee, 44

Chettri, Diwakar, 86–87

children, 16; infanticide of, 60; malnutrition of, 52; nannies of, 245, 300, 317, 318; sexual abuse of, 334, 338–39. *See also* parenting

China, 291

Chung, Jen, 310

cisgender, 25, 136, 293

cisnormativity, 331

citizenship: by descent, 83, 84, 89–91; of India, 57–59, 90–92; *jus sanguinis/jus soli*, 80–81, 91; maternal, 190–92, 198–206; naturalized, 57–59, 83–84, 89–91; of Nepal, 79–94

class, 39; inequality of, 26–27; race and, 173–74, 238, 261–62, 270–71; sex work and, 335–37, 342–43. *See also* intersectionality

Coca Indigenous community, 375–76, 379

colonialism, 40–46, 141, 290; in Caribbean, 235–39, 253, 271, 272; globalization and, 44, 215; "patriarchal," 44

Columbus, Christopher, 40–41, 140, 235, 247

coming-of-age rituals, 252, 260, 262. See also *quinceañeras*

coming-out stories, 337–38

Confucianism, 73

Connell, Raewyn, 25–28, 171–72

consensual unions, 258. *See also* marriage

Cosgrove, Serena, 134–46, 150–54

COVID-19 crisis, 45–46

Crenshaw, Kimberlé, 39–40

critical race theory, 39–40

Cuba, 143–44, 183, 239–41; globalization pressures on, 253, 255; LGBTQ rights in, 246–47; migrants from, 245; *quinceañeras* in, 250–62; remittances to, 255; salaries in, 255–56, 261; teenage pregnancies in, 258–59; tourism in, 253, 255

cultural relativism, 5

Dahomey Kingdom, 42

Dalit caste, 55–56, 85, 98–99

Dawthorne, Nathan, 326–45

Dennis, Dannah, 79–94

Diamond, Jared, 40–41

division of labor: in Guatemala, 215–16; in Nepal, 120–21, 125–29; of plantation system, 237

divorce, 55, 93, 319

domestic violence, 60–62, 72–76, 180, 362–63. *See also* gender-based violence

domestic workers, 46, 119, 143; nannies as, 245, 300, 317, 318

Dominican Republic, 240, 244

Dore, Elizabeth, 241

dowry, 52–53, 61–62

Drentea, Patricia, 309

drugs. *See* substance use disorders

Drysdale Walsh, Shannon, 142

Dube, Joice, 23

Dygert, Holly, 190–206

Early, Mary Two-Axe, 306

educational opportunities: for Mixtecs, 195–96, 201; for Nepali women, 125–26

effeminacy, 13, 99–100, 108

El Salvador, 143, 151

emotional labor, 329

Equal Rights Amendment (ERA), 38

erectile dysfunction, 146, 156–65

ethnocentrism, 5, 18, 82, 290

ethno-stratification, 360

eunuchs, 102–3, 111

Fadil, Nadia, 358, 359

Faure, Aymeric, 245

Fausto-Sterling, Anne, 9, 21

Federation of Associations for Relatives of the Detained-Disappeared (FEDEFAM), 145

female genital mutilation/cutting (FGM/C), 60–61

femicide, 54, 151–54, 296, 330

"femininity," 25, 99–100, 108, 326, 363

feminism, 35–38; first-wave, 36, 38, 315; second-wave, 36, 38, 315; third-wave, 37–40, 315; fourth-wave, 37, 38, 59; definitions of, 36–37, 315; Islamic, 363; Latin American, 143–45; masculinities studies and, 269–70; parenting and, 314–15, 319–20; on prostitution, 328; on salaried jobs, 129; on sex workers, 328

Ferree, Myra Marx, 171, 177

Figueroa, Mark, 272–73

Fobre, Nancy, 318–19

Foucault, Michel, 268, 273–81, 337

Fraser, Paul, 330

Freedman, Estelle, 36–37

Freud, Sigmund, 12

Friedan, Betty, 315

front-stage/backstage behaviors, 313–14

Fuller, N., 377

Galbraith, E., 285

Galen, 294

Geddes Foundation, 24

gender, 21; citizenship and, 81; definitions of, 5, 7, 314; "geographies" of, 129; kinship and, 253; race and, 356–57; sexuality and, 7, 11, 279–80. See also intersectionality

Gender and Development (GAD) approach, 269

gender complementarity, 215

gender equality: Aristotle on, 294; in Bangladesh, 53; domestic violence and, 60–62; of Indigenous women, 198; Jamaica and, 271; in Nepal, 86–88; among Q'eqchi', 215–16

gender identities, 8–12, 314, 375; binary, 17, 21, 25, 295–96, 301; in Caribbean, 246–47; marianismo and, 135; in Nepal, 89, 93–94; nonbinary, 17–21, 101–4, 138, 145, 293, 332; nonconforming, 298–99; pronoun choice and, 103–4

gender ideologies, 9, 12–13, 35–36; in Bible, 294; Confucian, 73; globalization of, 73; history of, 12–13; of jobs, 177

gender reveal parties, 60

gender roles, 13–15, 314; "effeminacy" and, 13, 99–100, 108; "femininity" and, 25, 99–100, 108, 326; fluidity of, 175, 181, 298, 333; job-defined, 45–46; "manliness" and, 163, 276; marriage and, 175; Mexican migrant on, 383; parenting and, 317, 319; among Q'eqchi' people, 215–16; sexual preference and, 13; sexuality and, 272, 279–80

gender studies, 25

gender-based violence, 72–76, 180, 362–63; femicide and, 54, 151–54, 296, 330; in Global North, 296–98; Guatemalan Women's Group against, 150–54; in India, 54, 57, 60–62; in Jamaica, 273, 275–77; in Latin America, 139–43. See also sexual violence

Ghana, 42

Glasenberg, Ivan, 43

Global North, 41, 42, 289–302; definition of, 289; engendering of, 293–96; maps of, 287–89; sexual violence in, 296–98

Global South, 37, 41, 290–91

globalization, 35, 40–46, 215; Cuba and, 253, 255; definition of, 292; dis/advantages of, 45; of gender ideologies, 73; multilevel marketing and, 210–12, 216, 221–27; tourism and, 243–44

globalscapes, 292–93

glocalization, 292
Goel, Ina, 52–78, 98–113
Goffman, Erving, 313–14
Gold, Tammy, 317
Gramsci, Antonio, 26
Gregory, Christopher, 213
Guatemala, 210–27
Gupta, Hemangini, 69–71
Gutmann, Matthew, 28–29, 158, 375

Habermas, Jürgen, 374–87, 376–77
Haiti, 240, 241, 245–46
Hanisch, Carol, 315
Härkönen, Heidi, 250–62
Hautzinger, Sarah, 180
Hays, Sharon, 312
head scarfs, 55, 356, 358, 360–61, 363–66
hegemonic discourse, 357
hegemonic masculinity, 26–28, 172, 331, 340–41
hegemony, 26–27, 293
hermaphrodites, 6
heteronormativity, 28, 337; Brazilian men and, 170–85; in Jamaica, 272, 280; of *quinceañeras*, 257–58, 260, 262
heterosexuality, 7, 8, 27; cisgender, 25, 136, 293, 331
hijab. *See* head scarfs
hijras, 19, 20, 98–113; caste system and, 98–99, 101, 104, 108, 112; definitions of, 59, 98, 100; demographics of, 101; eunuchs and, 102–3, 111; as intersex, 19, 102, 111; kinship system of, 100, 102–13; livelihoods of, 101, 108–9; in *Mahabharata*, 110; *nayak*, 107; prestige economy system of, 100, 105–9, 111–12; *reet* ceremony of, 100, 103–4; as sex workers, 59, 101, 108–9; sexual reassignment surgeries for, 19, 108–11. *See also* third gender
Hinchy, Jessica, 103

Hindu nationalism, 58
HIV/AIDS, 180, 274
Hochschild, Arlie, 318
homophobia, 246, 271–72, 277, 280; hegemonic masculinity and, 27; intersectional approach to, 39; LGBTQ youth and, 337–38, 341–42
homosexuality, 7–8; decriminalization of, 102, 111, 330; gay/straight binary, 28; gender ideologies of, 13; in Jamaica, 271–72, 276–77, 280; in Mexico, 161; in Nepal, 93; in South Asia, 52; Two-Spirit people and, 18. *See also* LGBTQ persons
Honduras, 151
honor killings, 54. *See also* gender-based violence
Hopkins, Peter, 40
hormones, 7, 16
hormone therapy, 20, 108
human trafficking, 297, 331, 381
Hurston, Zora Neale, 36

immigration. *See* migration
impression management, 308, 312–20
India, 52–63; Caribbean migrants from, 239; caste system of, 53, 55–56; citizenship laws of, 57–59, 90–92; domestic violence in, 60–62; hijras of, 19, 20, 98–113; independence of, 53–54; sexual harassment in, 69–71, 99–100; sexual violence in, 57
Indigenous people, 17–18, 293, 332; of Canada, 304; of Caribbean, 235; of Latin America, 138, 140–41, 146, 159, 378–80; sex workers and, 329; sexual violence against, 296, 330; women's rights of, 304–6
infanticide, 60
initiation rituals, 252
intersectionality, 39–40, 121, 170–85; definitions of, 35, 136, 171, 296, 356; Freedman on, 37; Muslim women and, 355–68; of

quinceañeras, 253, 259–61; of sex industry, 335
intersex, 6–7, 19–20, 60–61; hijras as, 19, 102, 111
Inuit people, 304
Islamic feminism, 363
Islamophobia, 358–60, 365

Jamaica, 267–81
Japan, 36, 290
job opportunities for women, 116–29, 173
Johnston, Deirdre D., 317
joint-family household, 100

Kabeer, Naila, 129
Kashmir, 57
Kempadoo, Kamala, 268–69, 276
Khanal, Jhalanath, 90
kinship systems, 253; of hijras, 100, 102–13; of transgender persons, 61
Kistler, S. Ashley, 210–27
Koirala, G. P., 85
Kroeber, Alfred, 35
Kutenai people, 18
Kwiatkowski, Lynn, 72–76

ladinos, 142, 225
Lafont, Suzanne, 271
Lal, Abha, 79–94
Latin America, 134–46; authoritarianism in, 134, 137, 142, 144, 145; economic crisis of 2008 in, 138; LGBTQ rights in, 138–39; maps of, 133, 234; reproductive health in, 136
Lavell, Jeannette Corbiere, 306
Leigh, Carol, 328
Lemus, Giovana, 152–54
LGBTQ persons, 13, 105; coming-out stories of, 337–38; of Jamaica, 270, 277; in Latin America, 246–47; Queer Muslim Project and, 59; in South Asia, 59. *See also* homosexuality; trans identity

Liberia, 42
life-cycle rituals, 252, 258
Lorde, Audre, 37
Loyer, Jessie, 306

machi (Chile), 138
machismo, 134–35, 146; in Brazil, 170–71; definition of, 159; in Guatemala, 215–16; *marianismo* and, 135, 198–99; in Mexico, 28–29, 146, 156–65, 198. *See also* masculinity
Machung, Anne, 318
Madhesi people, 83–94
Malinowski, Bronislaw, 5, 35
Malkin, V., 377
Maloney, Susan, 310
Manusmriti (Laws of Manu), 55
Mapuche people, 138, 141
maquiladoras, 378
Margaret Mead, 13–14
Margetts, Jenny, 305–6
marianismo, 135, 198–99
marriage: of adolescents, 257–59; Brazilian norms of, 172, 175, 179–80; Caribbean norms of, 241, 246–47, 277–78; of children, 61, 205; companionate, 160, 163; consensual unions and, 258; divorce and, 55, 93, 319; gender roles and, 175, 179–80; infidelity in, 180–85, 278; kinship and, 253; *quinceañeras* and, 258; same-sex, 246–47; unemployment and, 179–80, 185
Marx, Karl, 291
masculinity, 172; in Brazil, 170–85; compensatory, 180–85, 278; definitions of, 25–26, 157; exculpatory chauvinism and, 182; fatherhood and, 374–87; Gutmann on, 28–29, 158; hegemonic, 26–28, 172, 331, 340–41; hyper, 334; Jamaican, 267–81; marginalized, 172, 179; Medeiros on, 25–29; in

masculinity *(continued)*
  Mexico, 28–29, 146, 156–65, 198;
  "normative," 28; theories of, 25–29,
  268–69, 339; thwarted, 172; toxic,
  300–301; types of, 28–29, 171–72;
  unemployment and, 179–80, 185;
  women's studies on, 25. *See also*
  machismo
masculinity studies, 25, 269–70
maternal altruism, 199, 202–3
matrifocal groups, 15–16
Mayan women, 210–27
Mayblin, Maya, 177–78
McFee, R., 285
Mead, Margaret, 36
Medeiros, Melanie A., 25–29, 170–85
Menjívar, Cecilia, 142
menstruation, 21–24, 63, 157
mestizos, 141–43, 194, 254
Métis people, 304–6
MeToo movement, 37, 297–98
Mexico, 28–29, 146, 156–65;
  antipoverty program in, 190–206;
  Indigenista project of, 194–97;
  maternal citizenship in, 190–92,
  198–206; migrant workers from,
  194, 200, 374–87; neoliberal
  policies of, 191
Middles of the World, The (film), 178
migration, 44; from Caribbean,
  244–45, 247; of Chinese workers,
  239; coyotes and, 297, 331, 381;
  feminization of, 45; of Latin
  American women, 145; of Mexican
  workers, 194, 200, 374–87; of
  Nepali workers, 123; Obama policies
  on, 376, 379–80; remittances from,
  245, 255, 380; of Sherpa families,
  119–20, 123; Trump policies on, 80
Milano, Alyssa, 297–98
milpa farming, 193–94, 200, 202
Mixtec women, 190–206
Mohammed, Patricia, 269
Mohanty, Chandra, 40
Mommy Wars, 315–20

Mongols, Nepalese, 56–57
Moore, Henrietta, 315
Moravec, Michelle, 309
Moren-Cross, Jennifer, 309
Mortley, Natasha Kay, 267–81
multiculturalism, 144, 355–56, 378
multilevel marketing corporation
  (MLMs), 210–12, 216, 221–27
Mundugumor people, 13–14
Muslim women, 355–68
muxes (Mexico), 138
Myers, Robert, 299
mysogyny, 294

Nanda, Serena, 104–5
nannies, 245, 300, 317, 318
Native Americans. *See* Indigenous
  people
naturalized citizens, 57–59, 83–84,
  89–91
Ncube, Nolwazi, 22–24
neoliberalism, 43, 137–38, 144, 191,
  377
Nepal, 82–85; caste system of, 56,
  82, 85, 93; citizenship requirements
  of, 79–94; civil war in, 83, 84;
  constitutions of, 80, 84–85, 88–90,
  93–94; domestic violence in,
  62; intersex children in, 60–61;
  malnutrition in, 52; Mongols of,
  56–57; Sherpa women of, 116–29;
  third gender in, 81, 89, 93–94
Network of Rural Women in Latin
  America and the Caribbean (Red
  LAC), 145
New Guinea, 13–14
Nicholas, Sandra Lovelace, 306
Nigeria, 42
nikah halala, 55
Nolan, Hamilton, 312
Nussbaum, Emily, 310, 315

Oaxaca, Mexico, 20
Obama, Barack, 80, 297, 376, 379–
  80

Pakistan, 58; domestic violence in, 62; independence of, 53–54; malnutrition in, 52

Panchayat system, 82, 83

Pankhurst, Emmeline, 36

parenting, 317, 319; feminism and, 314–15, 319–20; impression management of, 308, 312–20; "intensive," 308–9, 312; of LGBTQ youth, 337–38, 341–42; "second shift" of, 318; transnational migration and, 374–87

participant observation, 4–5, 320

Patheja, Jasmeen, 69–71

patriarchy, 27, 61–62, 300; in Caribbean, 241, 270–71; colonialism and, 44; Confucianism and, 73; in Global North, 300–301; "illegitimate" children and, 237–38; Indian caste system and, 53; masculinity and, 27–28; in Nepal, 83; normative masculinity and, 175; sex workers and, 330; "state," 81

patrilocal society, 61

Peña Nieto, Enrique, 191

Pérez Márquez, Elizabeth, 374–87

Peru, 144

Pinto, S., 272

pornography, 328, 330

prestige economy system, 100, 105–9, 111–12

prostitutes. *See* sex workers

Pueblo people, 18

Puerto Rico, 238, 239, 245–46

purdah (seclusion of women), 55

Puri, Mondeep, 311

Q'eqchi', 210–27

queer, 26, 28, 332. *See also* LGBTQ persons

Queer Muslim Project, 59

quinceañeras, 250–62; as colonial ritual, 254–56; parents' role in, 259–60, 262; photos of, 251, 254–59, 261; as sexual ritual, 254–56

race, 39, 56–57; class and, 173–74, 238, 261–62, 270–71; gender and, 356–57; sexuality and, 182–83, 185, 272; "whitening" policies of, 238. *See also* intersectionality

racialization, 261, 357–58

rape. *See* sexual violence

Reddy, Gayatri, 105

remittances from migrant workers, 245, 255, 380

reproductive health, 80, 124, 136

Rhodesia, 43

Rohingya refugees, 56

Ross, Drew, 314

Rowell, Thelma, 15–16

Russia, 43, 291

Saudi Arabia, 291

Senior, Keino T., 267–81

sex, 5–7; definitions of, 5, 12; gender and, 21; safer, 277; surgical assignment of, 6, 60–61

sex education, 258

sex workers, 326–45; backgrounds of, 334–36; definitions of, 326, 327, 331; drug use by, 333–34, 336, 338–40, 343; feminist views of, 328; "gay for pay," 342; hijras as, 59, 101, 108–9; motivations of, 332–34; stigmatization of, 327, 328, 341–44; types of, 328

sexual dimorphism, 16–17

sexual harassment, 69–71, 99–100, 297–98

sexual orientation, 7–8, 12–13, 27. *See also* LGBTQ persons

sexual reassignment surgeries, 19, 60–61, 108–11

sexual violence, 275–77; to children, 334, 338–39; in Global North, 296–98; male victims of, 334, 339, 343–44; substance use and, 339–40. *See also* gender-based violence

sexuality, 7–8, 268–69; definition of, 7; fluid, 333; Foucault on, 268,

sexuality *(continued)*
273–81; gender and, 7, 11, 279–80;
gender roles and, 272; nonlabel,
332; promiscuous, 277–78; race
and, 182–83, 185, 272; repressive
hypothesis of, 273–74; stereotypes
of, 326; Victorian, 271
Sharma, Kedar, 90
Sharpe, J., 272
Sherpa women, 116–29
slave trade, 41–42, 141, 236–37, 239
South Asia, 51–78. *See also specific
countries*
Sri Lanka, 52
St. Barthélemy, 239
Steiner, Leslie Morgan, 316
Steinhauer, Kathleen, 304–6
stigmatization, 337–38; of sex
workers, 327, 328, 341–44
structural violence, 327
subaltern, 56–57
substance use disorders, 180, 274;
sex workers with, 333–34, 336,
338–40, 343; treatment of, 344–45
Suler, John, 309
survival sex work, 336, 338
Swanson, Debra H., 317
Switzerland, 43–44

talaq (divorce), 55
Tamang, Seira, 81
Tanzania, 42
Tardy, Rebecca, 314
Taureg people, 44
Tchambuli people, 13–14
teenage pregnancies, 258–59
Telangana Hijra Intersex Trans Samiti,
59
Thakur, Dhanaraj, 270–71
Thame, Maziki, 270–71
Thapa, Manjushree, 90
third gender, 7, 52, 293; definitions
of, 101; hijras as, 19, 20, 58, 59,
98–113; in Nepal, 81, 89, 93–94;

transphobia and, 63. *See also*
LGBTQ persons
Tibet, 88, 90
Torres, Gabriela, 142
tourism, 45, 213; Brazilian, 174, 177;
Caribbean, 242–44; Cuban, 253,
255
trans identity, 7, 98–113, 298–99. *See
also* third gender
transnationalism, 376–80
transphobia, 63
Tratner, Susan W., 308–20
triple talaq (divorce), 55
Trump, Donald, 80
Two-Spirit people, 17–18, 293, 332
Tzul Tzul, Ana Marina, 134–46,
150–54

Uganda, 42
unemployment, 45, 146, 319; among
Belgium Muslims, 360–61; among
Brazilian men, 177–80, 185;
among sex workers, 332; among
transgender people, 299
"untouchables." *See* Dalit caste

value systems of Q'eqchi', 213, 215,
219–20, 224–27
van Gennep, Arnold, 252
veiling. *See* head scarfs
Vietnam, 72–76

Wade, Lisa, 171, 177
wage jobs for women, 116–29, 175
Wallerstein, Immanuel, 41, 291, 292
Wardlow, Holly, 251
Weeks, Jeffrey, 268
Wentzell, Emily, 156–65
Wesch, Michael, 5, 11, 43–44
Weston, Kath, 105
Wilson, Kalpana, 117
Wodaabe people, 14
Women against Sexual Violence and
State Repression, 57

women's rights, 36, 143–44;
educational opportunities and,
125–26, 195–96, 201; Indigenous
people and, 304–6; in Nepal, 82,
86–94, 120–21, 128–29

World Bank, 377; structural
adjustment policies of, 137–38;
Zambia and, 43

world systems theory, 41, 291,
292

Zambia, 43–44
Zapotecas, 20
Zedillo, Ernesto, 191
Zimbabwe, 21–24
Zuni Pueblo, 18